P. W. P.

Plot? What Plot?

Book II

Mavis Applewater

C-opyright 2003 © by Mavis Applewater

ISBN 0-9755739-1-8
First Printing 2004
Cover art and design by Anne M. Clarkson
Cover photographs by Joy Argento
Author Photo by A.J. Hoffman

Published by:
Dare 2 Dream Publishing
A Division of Limitless Corporation
Lexington, South Carolina 29073

Find us on the World Wide Web
http://www.limitlessd2d.net

Printed in the United States of America and the UK by

Lightning Source, Inc.

Acknowledgements

I would like to thank the members of YoMavis, my little egroup that started the Wednesday Afternoon Series; without all of you this would not have happened. My thanks also go to the Bards Village where I posted my very first PWP. I would also like to thank Lisa Raymond, Joanne Forbes-Murphy, Sam and Anne, Toni Zulig, Theresa Nezwicki, Heather Stewart, Chris Ewen, David Bryson, Shaun Kelly, David Crowder, Rae Haggerty. A very special thanks to Ma Kessler who gave birth to me and Ma Bardsley who accepted me as her daughter-in-law. A big thanks to Nana and Sunny for telling me to let my light shine no matter what anyone else said.

As always, this is for Heather.

P.W.P.
Plot? What Plot?
Book II

Bring on the Ice

The second in a series by Mavis Applewater

Table of Contents

Table of Contents
[Continued]

MATINEE

PART ONE

Rhea walked into the dark movie theatre with her popcorn and Pepsi held firmly in her hands. As usual, it was almost empty. The tiny cinema didn't do much business on weekday afternoons. They did their real business on the weekends. Friday through Sunday they would show more current titles. During the week, the small theatre would offer older titles. Normally there would be a few scattered people, most of them familiar faces - college students, retirees and, of course, *her* - the tall dark stranger.

Rhea took a seat and relaxed, scanning the darkness to see if she could find *her*. There she was, just a few rows back. Rhea liked coming to the small cinema. It specialized in older films. True, she could simply rent the videos or DVDs. But there was something about spending her time here, with the really good, old fashioned, artery-clogging popcorn and the classic films. Of course the tall ebony skinned woman had been an added incentive.

It was the middle of winter and there wasn't much to do in the small town. Since she was a hairdresser, Rhea had every Mondays off. She enjoyed stopping in and catching a movie every once in awhile. Then, about two months ago, she'd noticed the tall woman seated in the back.

Since then Rhea hadn't missed a Monday afternoon. Each time she hoped that she would see the woman again. Each time she wasn't disappointed. Slowly Rhea had moved closer to where the woman sat. The mysterious beauty had been doing the same. The only thing that Rhea regretted was that neither woman had worked up enough courage to speak to the other. At least, she hoped that the other woman felt the same.

The furthest they had progressed in their timid courtship was a shy polite smile every time one of them caught the other looking at them instead of the movie. Rhea settled in, looking over to find shy hazel eyes staring back at her. She smiled at the taller woman. Feeling a sense of warmth flowing through her, she turned her attention back to the screen. This week it was *The Magnificent Ambersons*.

Rhea watched the film, merrily noting that, as usual, the tall dark-skinned woman would get up periodically and leave the theatre. She would return later and take her seat. She would also disappear just prior to the end of the movie and not return. Today was no different. Rhea found herself looking around the plush lobby just as she always did. She could never find her. Rhea had come to the conclusion that the woman either worked at the cinema or had the smallest bladder on the face of the planet.

The following week Rhea found herself sloshing through a mini-blizzard trying to get to the cinema on time. It was silly and she knew it. But she had spent the entire week convincing herself that today would be the day she would finally talk to her mystery woman. She grimaced as she looked at her watch noting that the film would have already started. 'The African Queen' was one of her favorites. She had always wanted to see it on the big screen.

PART TWO

Rhea's heart sank as she noticed the cinema was suspiciously dark. Just as she was about to try the main door to see if it was open, it swung out and the familiar faces of the ticket girl, the concession worker, and the usher stepped out into the horrid weather.

"Sorry, Miss. We're going to shut down," the usher explained.

"It's okay," a sultry voice said from inside. "Let her in."

"Are you sure, Judy?" the young woman who usually sold her popcorn queried.

"Yeah," the tall woman reassured the girl as she held the door open, ushering Rhea inside the warm theatre.

"Do you want us to stay?" the young girl pleaded as her co-workers groaned in disgust.

"No," Judy added firmly. "You kids get going before the weather gets any worse."

Rhea watched as the young girl's face dropped. Rhea instantly understood the young girl's disappointment as she looked over at the tall woman whose hazel eyes and smooth features had dragged her out in a snowstorm. *'Oh yeah, kid. I know what you're thinking,'* Rhea thought in amusement as she took off her soaking wet cap. As she watched Judy locking the door behind the three teenagers, a sudden panic washed over her. *'I must look like a major idiot! I'm standing here dripping in the lobby, when she probably just wants to go home like any other sane person would do.'*

"Hi," Judy said just as Rhea was about to hyperventilate.

"Uh, Hi," she replied as she nervously ran her fingers through her wet short blonde hair.

They stood there in an awkward silence, each shifting nervously as they tried to come up with something to say. "Looks like you're closed for the day. I should get going," Rhea stammered nervously.

"Well, if you want to stay. . . ," Judy began in a nervous voice. "I was going to run the movie anyway. I wanted to see it," she explained.

"You're the projectionist?" Rhea inquired.

"Among other things." Judy flashed her a brilliant smile. "I'm Judy, by the way," she said as she offered her hand to Rhea.

"Rhea," the smaller blonde responded as she accepted Judy's hand. Realizing how wet her hand was, she pulled back in embarrassment. "Sorry," she apologized. "I'm wet," she added, wiping her hand on her parka. She blushed suddenly as she realized what she had just said. It was an innocent comment that was true on far too many levels. Judy simply smiled at her.

"Why don't you go inside the theatre," Judy suggested.

"Are you sure?" Rhea inquired quickly. "I'll understand if you want to get out of here."

"I'm sure," Judy replied warmly. Rhea felt a shiver from the look she was receiving from those intense eyes.

"Why don't you go find a seat and make yourself comfortable? I just need to get things set up. I'll bring us some snacks," Judy suggested.

"Won't the boss mind?" Rhea asked. Her heart raced at the thought of being alone with this woman.

"No, I'm looking forward to it," Judy smiled as she gave Rhea a little wink. "So what do you like?" Judy teased her. Rhea blinked in surprise as her mouth went suddenly dry. "For snacks," Judy continued, ". . . what would you like?"

"Anything," Rhea teased in return. She couldn't help but smile at the way this snowy afternoon was turning out.

"I'll hold you to that," Judy purred as she stepped slightly closer to Rhea.

Rhea could feel her body warming from their closeness. She shivered slightly as Judy stepped away. "Go on inside." Judy shrugged. "I'll be there just as soon as I can." Rhea wet her lips as she watched the gentle sway of hips as Judy walked away.

PART THREE

Rhea walked into the empty theatre and decided on a seat in the center. She removed her damp parka and shook out the snow. Then she removed her gloves, placing them on the seat next to her. She felt a twinge in the pit of her stomach as the lights were lowered. She took her seat and quickly ran her fingers through her hair as she prayed that she didn't have a case of hat hair.

She peeked up to the projectionist booth to see if she could see anything. All she could detect was shadows. She continued to primp herself as the movie began. She watched in delight as images of Katherine Hepburn in the sweltering African landscape began to fill the screen. As much as she wanted to see this movie again, she kept looking behind her in hopes that Judy was about to join her.

Finally, just as Kate was convincing Humphrey to take her with him, Judy sat down beside her. The taller woman was balancing a tray. "Here we go, hot chocolate to warm us up," Judy handed her a steaming cup. Rhea thanked her, biting back a sigh as their fingers brushed. She placed it in the cup holder on her seat. Judy did the same with hers as she handed Rhea a large tub of popcorn. She stored the tray away. "I love this scene," Judy said with a smile.

Rhea couldn't look at the screen; she could only focus on the beautiful woman seated next to her. "Cheers," Judy said brightly as she held up her cup and turned to her. Rhea reached for her own paper cup and clicked it against Judy's. They sipped their hot chocolate. It warmed her frozen body almost as much as Judy's smile had. "You . . . Uhm . . . have a little . . . ," Judy said softly as she motioned towards Rhea's face. Rhea reached up, hoping that it was the hot chocolate on her face. "Here," Judy halted her movements as she reached over, her thumb brushing away the damp liquid just above Rhea's lips. Rhea's eyes fluttered shut as Judy touched her.

"Thank you," Rhea managed to squeak out.

"You're welcome," Judy whispered softly as she moved closer. Rhea could feel her breath caressing her face. Their lips brushed in a shy gentle manner.

Rhea's heart pounded as her lips tingled from the touch. Judy pulled back slightly, looking at her with a nervous expression. "That was nice," Rhea said softly.

"Yeah." Judy smiled back as she sighed with relief.

They settled back in their seats and watched the movie as their thighs brushed together. Rhea settled the tub of popcorn on her lap. She smiled, knowing that Judy would have to reach across her to reach it. As she sipped her hot chocolate, Judy's arm brushed against her body. Rhea managed to hold back the moan as Judy grabbed a handful of popcorn.

They continued to watch the movie as they rested against one another's shoulders. Fingers brushed as they reached for popcorn. Rhea's breathing became erratic as their fingers strayed and brushed against an arm or thigh. Feeling bolder and definitely more passionate sitting so close to this woman that she had been fantasizing about, Rhea rested her hand on Judy's firm thigh. She felt the muscles tighten from her touch.

Her nipples hardened as Judy leaned closer to her. "I need to change the reel," Judy whispered softly.

"Oh," Rhea pouted in disappointment. "How do you know?" She inquired, suddenly.

"Watch the top right hand corner of the screen," Judy informed her. "When you see the white circle, it's a cue. I'll be right back." Judy kissed her quickly before gathering up some of their trash and making her way up the aisle.

Rhea sighed deeply as she watched her go. She tried to watch the movie but her thoughts kept straying to the beautiful woman who had just left her. Out of the corner of her eye she saw the white circle appear. She smiled, knowing that it meant the next reel had started and Judy would be returning.

PART FOUR

Judy returned and placed herself as close to Rhea as humanly possible. Their fingers brushed once again as they both reached into the tub of popcorn at the same time. Judy smiled as she held up a kernel of popcorn for Rhea to sample. Rhea leaned over and allowed Judy to feed it to her. She caught the tips of Judy's fingers and began to lick the salt and butter off of them. Judy moaned as Rhea licked her fingers clean.

Rhea smiled to herself, unable to believe she was acting so boldly. She in turn placed a kernel of popcorn against Judy's quivering lips. Judy's tongue snaked out and sucked the popcorn into her mouth. Rhea's excitement grew as she leaned over and captured Judy's lips with her own.

Unlike the first kiss, which had been shy and gentle, this kiss exploded passionately as their mouths parted. Tongues danced together, fighting for control. The tub of popcorn crashed to the floor as Rhea reached over and pulled Judy closer to her. She groaned in frustration as the armrest prevented their bodies from touching.

Judy's hands moved down her back, trying to bring them closer.   Unable to manage it, the brunette's touch shifted, smoothing a path to the swell of Rhea's breast. Rhea was fueled on by Judy's hand cupping her breast. The small blonde allowed her hands to begin their own exploration.

As Judy caressed her breast with one hand, the other began to unbutton her shirt. Rhea ran her own hands down Judy's back as she pulled the soft flannel shirt out of her pants. Rhea's shirt was opened and strong hands began to caress her abdomen. Her own hands slid up the back of Judy's shirt. Her fingers burned from the feel of Judy's exposed skin beneath them.

Their tongues continued to explore one another's mouths as each of them unclasped the other's bra. Eager finger began teasing hardened nipples. The kiss ended as they gasped for air. Never in her life had Rhea been kissed with such passion. She knew she couldn't stop now. She needed to feel all of this woman.

Her body arched as Judy began to tease her nipple with her tongue. She groaned as she wrapped her fingers in Judy's long curly hair, pressing her closer. Their bodies collided with the armrest once again.   Rhea chuckled as Judy growled in frustration. Once again Judy's mouth captured her nipple and began to suckle it.

Rhea felt as if she was going to explode as Judy teased her with her teeth and tongue. Her hips arched up, lifting her off the seat. Her jeans pressed into her center as Judy devoured her breast. Rhea's hips began to grind, increasing the friction. Unable to hold back any longer, she reached down and unbuttoned her jeans. Judy moaned against her skin as she lowered the zipper.

Rhea was gasping for air as she dipped her fingers into her own pants. She moaned weakly as she felt how wet her panties were. She slipped her finger past the elastic band of her underwear and down into her own wetness. As Judy suckled her harder, she began to stroke her throbbing clit.

She looked down and watched Judy feasting upon her as she touched herself. Hazel eyes twinkled up at her, encouraging her to continue. Slipping her hand from the warm confines of her passion, she held up her glistening fingers. Judy halted her movements, licking her lips eagerly as Rhea held her fingers up to her. Rhea smiled as Judy reached for them. Pulling away at the last moment, she heard Judy whimper. Rhea continued to smile as she painted her nipple with her wetness.

Judy began to lick and suck Rhea's breast as she clasped the blonde's hand. "You taste so good," Judy murmured as she guided Rhea's hand back to warmth of her own wetness. Rhea's head fell back as she once again began to touch herself. She whimpered as Judy pulled away. She could hear the sound of popcorn crunching as the tall woman stood before her.

Rhea looked up at Judy who was standing in front of her. Her breath caught as she watched Judy unbutton her shirt. "Don't stop," Judy requested as she left her shirt hanging open slightly, revealing her breasts. Rhea licked her lips with desire as she continued to touch herself. Judy shifted and maneuvered her large frame so she could kneel before Rhea.

Through hooded eyes, Rhea watched as Judy ran her hands along her trembling thighs. She reached up and began to lower Rhea's pants. Rhea continued to pleasure herself, raising her hips to allow Judy to pull her jeans down to her ankles. She parted her thighs as Judy began to kiss her way up her legs. "I want to see you," Judy explained as she began to lower Rhea's underwear.

Once her panties joined her pants around her ankles, Judy removed her hand from the warmth of her damp curls. Rhea watched in amazement as Judy brought her fingers to her lips. The sensation of Judy's tongue licking her fingers was tantalizing. As Judy teased her digits, Rhea reached out and slipped her free hand into Judy's shirt. She moaned as she ran her palm across Judy's already erect nipple.

She continued to tease Judy as the goddess before her released her hand and began to kiss her way down Rhea's body. She trembled as Judy's course hair caressed her exposed skin. Her hands moved so she could run her fingers through the long black curly hair. Her hips arched as she felt Judy's breath on her damp curls. Rhea shifted to move closer to the edge of her seat, opening herself up to her lover.

She trembled as Judy's tongue flicked across her throbbing clit. She could feel strong arms reaching beneath her. She watched as Judy lifted her hips, bringing her closer to her mouth. Judy's tongue explored her lips, tasting all that she had to offer. She felt her tongue pressing against her opening. Rhea's hips arched, eager to feel this woman inside of her. Judy plunged her tongue inside of her as Rhea thrust against her.

Judy continued to plunge in and out of her, driving Rhea closer to the edge as she thrust against her lover. They didn't notice that the film had stopped or the flickering of the blank screen. Judy's mouth continued to feast upon her wetness as she moved her attention to Rhea's swollen nub. She suckled it while teasing her with her teeth. Judy held her tightly as her body trembled. Rhea gasped and whimpered as Judy took her higher.

Rhea rocked against her lover as she screamed out her name. Her body convulsed as she collapsed against the hard seat. She trembled as she tried to focus on what had just happened. Once her breathing returned to normal, she looked down to see Judy looking up at her while resting her head on the blonde's stomach.

"I think we missed the movie," Rhea managed to squeak out.

"Hmm," Judy smiled up at her. "I have it on DVD back at my apartment if you really want to see it," Judy suggested before she kissed Rhea's stomach.

"How far away is your apartment?" Rhea inquired.

"Next door," Judy smiled playfully. "My uncle left me this place and the building when he died."

"Let's go," Rhea agreed.

"You really want to see the movie?" Judy asked.

"No," Rhea reassured her as she ran her fingers through Judy's long tresses. "I want to see more of you and, if we stay here, I think we'll both end up in traction."

"Let's go," Judy agreed.

The End

9

Mavis Applewater

THE REPAIRWOMAN

The Present

Sandy twisted the napkin on the restaurant table nervously as Meg, her dearest friend in the entire world, stared at her in bewilderment.   "Sandy, what's the problem?" Meg persisted. "Not that I mind going out to dinner with you, but you should have your refrigerator fixed. So why don't you just call Jenkins? You said they did a great job when your air conditioner broke down," the curly-haired brunette asked.

"Oh, they did," Sandy chuckled as she blushed.

"What is going on with you?" Meg pressed as Sandy sipped her wine and shrugged. "No, there's something you're not telling me."

Sandy ran her fingers through her short red hair as she tried to avoid her best friend's penetrating gaze. She released a deep sigh, knowing that she wouldn't be able to get away with a lie. "Promise me you won't tell anyone," Sandy demanded firmly.

"I promise," Meg promised warily.

"I'm serious, Meg; you can't tell a soul," Sandy pushed until Meg conceded. "It all started when I was standing in my kitchen waiting for the repairman."

A few months earlier

Sandy stood half naked in front of her refrigerator with the door open, praying that it would provide some much needed relief from the stifling heat. She was clad only in a pair of panties and a blue over-sized oxford shirt, which hung open revealing her firm body to the contents of her refrigerator. "When is that repairman going to get here?" The redhead grumbled as the sweat ran down her abdomen. It was just her luck that her air conditioning had died in the middle of a heat wave. "I wonder if it would help if I stuck my head in the freezer?" Sandy muttered helplessly.

The heat wave that was encompassing the East Coast was taking its toll on the petite woman. It wasn't bad when she was at work. One of the advantages of working at the small bank was that it was air-conditioned. The down side was that the eight hours a day she spent at her teller window were tedious. The rushes always came at the same time and the remainder of the day she and her fellow tellers were bored senseless. The others all had families and chatted endlessly about their children or grandchildren. Sandy was gay, and based on the number of small-minded comments she'd heard from some of her fellow employees, being out would only further alienate her colleagues. "Great! Now I'm hot, sweaty, and depressed," Sandy groaned as she closed the refrigerator. "This was not the summer I was hoping for."

Sandy pulled her shorts on and buttoned her shirt as she glanced at the clock hanging on the kitchen wall. "Okay, the guy on the telephone said that Max would be here around three and now it's almost five," Sandy grumbled. "These guys are worse than the cable company." Sandy understood that an air conditioner repairman must be overworked during the unexpected heat wave. Still she was miffed since she had to take a half-day off from work since she couldn't afford to pay double for a weekend call.

Just as she was about to pick up the telephone to call Jenkins

Appliances, the doorbell chimed. "Please be Max," she sighed in relief as she pictured a large sweaty workman whose first question was probably going to be *'Is is hot enough for you?'* She stood on her toes and peered through the peephole; her mouth dropped open at the sight she found waiting for her. In spite of the distorted image, she could see that the tall dark-haired woman was drop dead gorgeous.

The disgruntled repairwoman pushed back her sunglasses and looked at her watch while Sandy kept admiring her through the peephole. The tall woman pressed the doorbell once again, snapping Sandy out of her musings. She quickly threw open the door, startling the tall brunette on the other side. "Ms. Brooks?" The woman inquired as she looked at her work order.

"Yes?" Sandy noticed the name patch on the dark blue work shirt that read, *'Max'*.

"I'm from Jenkins Appliance; I'm here to fix your air-conditioner," the woman explained in a bored tone.

Sandy stood there for a moment, thoroughly mesmerized by the tall woman. "Can I see your work order?" She inquired once she forced herself to stop staring at the woman. The woman flashed her a brilliant smile as she handed her the paperwork. "What?" Sandy said with slight smile of her own as she examined the form before showing Max into her tiny apartment.

"You'd be surprised how many women don't ask," Max explained as she accepted her clipboard back and followed Sandy into the apartment. "I usually offer it to them anyway," she explained as she removed her sunglasses and stuffed them into the top pocket of her shirt. "I hope that maybe by doing that, the next time they let a stranger in their home, they'll think twice and ask."

"I promised my Dad when I moved out on my own that I would never let a workman in without checking their credentials first, even if I had requested them," Sandy explained. She was about to continue when she found herself staring into the most incredible hazel eyes she'd ever seen.

"Your father sounds like a very wise man," Max added with a smile. "So it says here you have two units and neither one is working."

Sandy shook her head in an effort to clear her thoughts of the lustful route they had descended. "Yes; here's one," she explained as she pointed to the window at the front of her living room, "and the other one's in the bedroom."

"How old are they?" Max inquired as she laid out a towel on the carpet and then placed her toolbox on top of it.

"I don't know. They came with the apartment," Sandy explained as Max knelt before the unit.

"So why didn't your landlord send for us?" Max inquired as she began to look at the large air conditioner.

"They were left behind by the previous tenant," Sandy continued. "I never tested them since I moved in last winter. When I first tried to turn them on, nothing happened. I tried to buy new ones but everyone's sold out."

"Well, let me have a look," Max said as she began her work. "Usually when they've been sitting for a long time they just need a cleaning and a shot of Freon."

"I hope so; my budget is stretched as it is," Sandy sighed as she caught herself gazing down at the muscles flexing in Max's arms.

"I'll see what I can do for you, Ms. Brooks," Max offered as she turned to Sandy with a captivating smile.

"Sandy," the red head squeaked out as her body tingled. "Call me Sandy," she added in a breathy tone as her palms began to sweat.

"Max," the woman added with a polite nod before turning back to her work.

Sandy continued to stand there peering at the woman's body as Max hummed, seemingly oblivious to Sandy's presence. "So what do you do?" Max inquired casually as Sandy snapped out of her lustful musing. *'What is wrong with me? I'm standing here ogling her like a frat boy at a strip club!'* she mentally admonished herself.

"I'm a teller at Sovereign," Sandy confessed as she took a shy step back from Max. "Would you like something to drink? Ice tea or lemonade?" She offered, feeling a need to distance herself from the attractive woman kneeling before her.

"Spring water?" Max inquired hopefully with another brilliant smile.

"Coming right up," Sandy volunteered as she thought that Max's smile could light up an entire city.

Sandy quickly retreated into her kitchen and buried her face in her hands. *'I'm losing it!'* her mind screamed as she took a cleansing breath and steadied herself. "Okay, it's not like you've never seen a beautiful woman before," she muttered as she tried to calm her breathing. She wiped her sweaty palms on her shorts and poured a tall glass of spring water for Max.

When Sandy stepped back into her living room, she found that Max had removed her shirt and was now clad in a revealing tank top. She considered pouring the water down her own body. Max's muscles rippled as she pulled her hair up into a ponytail. Sandy whimpered and the glass of water threatened to spill from her hand. She remained rooted firmly in place as Max stood and stretched out her body. Her breathing caught as Max turned and approached her. "Thanks," Max said softly as she took the glass of cool water from Sandy's trembling grasp. Sandy watched the beads of sweat trickling down Max's neck as she took a long swallow. "I'm finished with this one. I just need to let it run for a minute," Max explained before taking another long swallow of water. "Care to show me your bedroom?"

Sandy's dark brown eyes widened in surprise until her mind caught up with what was really happening. Once she realized that Max needed to get on with her work, she felt a slight pang of disappointment. "Gladly," Sandy responded with a slight blush. Max smirked down at her as she handed her the now empty glass. Their fingers brushed slightly and Sandy felt a jolt of electricity shoot through her body. "Hmm," she sighed softly before heading towards the bedroom to show Max the second broken air conditioner.

They stood in the tiny bedroom as Max quickly examined the unit. "This one looks in better shape than the one in the living room," Max noted absently as she turned her attention to Sandy who was still staring at her. "I think the unit in the living room will probably get you through the summer, but I'd suggest replacing it at the end of the season. You can usually get a good closeout deal around then. If I can get this one up and running, it should last you a couple of years."

Max gave her a curious glance. Sandy blushed, understanding the message in Max's amazing hazel eyes. It was one of those 'are you listening to me or are you just going to stare at my chest' questions? Sandy diverted her gaze in sudden embarrassment. "I'll just get my tools," Max said with a wry chuckle. Sandy stepped aside to allow her to pass as she prayed for the floor to just swallow her up. The lack of space in the small bedroom forced Max to brush against her.

Sandy's stomach clenched as she felt the heat emanating off the taller woman. Max's body remained touching her quivering form and Sandy looked up to find herself lost in an intense gaze. Max flashed her a crooked grin before finally moving away. The taller woman left a stunned and trembling Sandy standing in her bedroom trying to figure out what was happening. She looked down to see the empty glass still clutched in her hand. She decided to take it to the kitchen in an effort to keep from further embarrassing herself in front of the gorgeous repairwoman.

Sandy turned to make a quick exit from her bedroom before Max could return. Her timing was off and she plowed right into Max. She stumbled backward and Max quickly wrapped one arm around her waist to hold her upright, while she kept a tight grip on her toolbox with her free hand. "We really need to stop meeting like this," Max offered in a voice closely resembling a purr, as her arm remained firmly wrapped around Sandy's waist. Sandy's knees buckled slightly and she braced herself by pressing her hands against Max's broad shoulders.

"You are incorrigible," Sandy quipped.

"Absolutely," Max responded with a playful wink.

Sandy blinked in surprise as they continued to stand in the doorway of her bedroom. "I guess I should get back to work," Max sighed with regret as she finally released her grasp on Sandy's body.

"I'll get out of your way," Sandy offered as she fought to regain her composure.

"Pity," Max, sighed as she brushed past Sandy, their bodies touching lightly once again.

Sandy was trembling as she stumbled into her kitchen. Her mind was whirling as she placed the glass in the sink. *'Okay, I have a goddess in my bedroom who's flirting with me. So why am I hiding in the kitchen?   She was flirting, wasn't' she?'* Sandy emitted a deep groan as she realized how ridiculous she was behaving. She looked over at her refrigerator and seriously contemplated trying to fit her overheated body in the tiny freezer.

"I've finally snapped," she reasoned as she stepped out of the kitchen. She could hear Max humming in the bedroom. Sandy paused for a moment, briefly toying with the idea of going back to the bedroom so she could spend more time with Max. Once again she smacked herself on the forehead for being an idiot. "Ouch," she squeaked as she rubbed her throbbing temple. Sandy changed direction and headed into the living room.

The first thing Sandy noticed was that the temperature seemed much more tolerable. She wandered over to the window and felt the cool blast from the repaired air conditioner. The cool air felt good against the palm of her hand. Sheepishly she looked through the window to see if anyone could see in.   Then she looked around the living room to ensure that she was still alone. She licked her lips as she began to unbutton her oversized shirt. It was then that she realized she'd been parading around in front of Max without a bra on. Once again she mentally cursed herself before taking another shy look around to ensure her privacy.

She just needed a little relief. Between the stifling weather and Max, her body temperature was ready to boil over. Once her shirt was open she leaned over into the cool blast of air, allowing it to caress her skin. Her nipples became erect as the icy breeze teased them. Her aching clit throbbed in response as her eyes drifted shut. "Feels good, doesn't it?" A sultry voice whispered in her ear as a hand came to rest on her hip. Sandy's eyes snapped open and she jumped in surprise, quickly closing her shirt. Sandy's heart raced as Max leaned slightly into her body. Sandy was unable to respond as her breathing became erratic. "So is there a Mr. Brooks?" Max inquired in the same sultry tone, her breath tickling Sandy's ear.

"What do you think?" Sandy quipped with a smile as she leaned into the woman standing behind her.

"I think that you're a very beautiful woman," came the husky response as Max's soft lips brushed her ear. "That has made it very difficult for me to concentrate on my work."

Sandy inhaled sharply as Max's hands circled her waist and reopened her shirt. She released a needy whimper as Max guided her body back towards the cool air. Max reached up and drew the window shade down a little further to ensure their privacy. Sandy melted into the woman's touch as Max's thigh nudged her legs slightly apart, her hands drifting up Sandy's torso.

Sandy's hips swayed into Max's firm body as the brunette's hands cupped her breasts. She moaned as she felt Max's lips tease the nape of her neck while her hands gently massaged her breasts. Sandy shamelessly ground her backside into Max's body, grunting in discomfort when the tool belt pressed into her. She whimpered as Max's touch left her body. She heard the tool belt crash to the floor. Max's hands returned to her hips as she molded her body into Sandy's. "Better?" Max whispered in her ear before sucking her earlobe into her mouth.

"Yes," Sandy groaned in agreement as her arms reached behind her and grasped Max's hips.

Max teased her sensitive ears before her mouth drifted back down to Sandy's neck. The red head was once again grinding her body into the taller woman. She tilted her head slightly and offered more of her neck up to Max's mouth. She felt the repairwoman's hands drifting along her abdomen. Her skin burned from the brunette's touch. Sandy refused to question the quickness of their intimacy as Max's hands drifted lower. She reached up and cupped Max's face, drawing her into a lingering kiss as the brunette began to lower the zipper of Sandy's shorts.

Sandy wrapped her fingers in Max's silky hair as their tongues explored the warmth of each other's mouth. As the kiss continued to grow in intensity, Sandy felt her shorts sliding down her legs and pooling around her ankles. She moaned into Max's mouth as one of the repairwoman's hands slid back up her body and cupped one of her breasts. Max teased her nipple with long fingers as her other hand drifted down to the waistband of her panties.

Sandy's hips thrust backward, needing even more contact with this woman. She was gasping for air as the kiss ended and Max's hips began to thrust in rhythm with her own. She whimpered as Max's hand left her waist and traveled up her body. She released a needy cry as Max's talented fingers captured her other nipple. The cool air caressed her body as they rocked wildly against one another and Max teased her breasts.

Sandy was quickly drowning in this woman's touch as she reached out and braced herself against the window frame. Max's hands left her body and her knee parted her quivering thighs. Sandy stepped out of her shorts and kicked them aside as she leaned her upper body slightly forward. Her lips began to quiver as she heard Max's lower the zipper of her worn blue jeans. Her anticipation grew as she heard the sounds of Max lowering her own pants and then firmly clasping Sandy's hips.

Sandy leaned her backside into Max's touch as her panties were lowered down to her thighs. She was breathing heavily as the brunette's hands caressed her. Sandy could feel her desire growing as Max slowly ran her hands along her firm cheeks. Sandy's thighs were trembling and her mind and body were screaming for more. Afraid to speak, Sandy swayed her hips, responding to Max's touch. Thankfully she finally felt Max's strong hands coming to rest upon her swaying hips. "Yes," she hissed as she felt Max's wetness press into her body.

Their bodies fell into a slow sensual rhythm and the brunette's wet curls pressed against Sandy's trembling skin. She could hear Max moaning in pleasure as their rhythm steadily increased. Sandy gripped the window frame tighter as she felt one of Max's hands slip between her legs. "So wet," Max sighed deeply.

"Max, please," Sandy pleaded.

"What do you want?" Max asked, teasing her as she pressed her body into Sandy's and dipping her fingers into her wetness.

"Please," Sandy repeated as the brunette's fingers teased her clit.

"Tell me," Max requested in a quiet voice.

"Fuck me," Sandy demanded as she pushed her body into Max's touch.

She felt Max lowering her underwear further down her legs. She opened herself up further to Max's touch as two fingers pressed against her center. Sandy released a gasp as Max entered her. The brunette's long fingers filled her completely. "You feel so good," Max whispered as she began to slowly glide in and out of Sandy. The red head's body matched the rhythm of the brunette's hand. Sandy gripped the wall tighter as Max's fingers increased their pace.

"More," Sandy pleaded as she thrust into the brunette's touch.

Sandy's body arched as Max responded to her request by adding another finger inside of her passion. Sandy gave herself up as Max took her harder. Sweat poured down her body as her body bucked wildly. Max held her steady as she gave herself over to the feel of this woman's touch. "Sandy?" Max panted in her ear. "I need more of you."

"Yes," Sandy gasped in response. "I'm yours."

Sandy had no idea what Max wanted but she was willing to do whatever the woman requested. "I need to slow this down just a little," Max explained with a hard swallow. Sandy could only nod in response as she felt Max's touch slip from her body. Sandy's body ached with desire as she tried to control her breathing. She could hear Max moving around behind her, removing her clothing. She didn't need to see the brunette to know that's what she was doing.

Max's arm wrapped around her body and guided her up. She turned into Max's embrace and drank in the taller woman's naked body. She smiled as her eyes caressed each curve. "This is much better," Max said with a smile as she brushed Sandy's locks from her sweaty brow. "I needed to see you. To look into your eyes while I touch you."

"And will I touch you?" Sandy inquired as she ran the tips of her fingers along Max's broad shoulders.

"I hope so," Max said with another bright smile before she reclaimed Sandy's lips.

Once again Sandy found that she was lost in the taste of

Max's mouth as their hands began a sweet gentle exploration. Sandy's body melted into the taller woman as she felt herself being lowered down to the floor. They never broke the kiss as Sandy lay beneath her lover, allowing her hands to caress the other woman's smooth skin. She cupped Max's breasts and slowly began to tease her nipples. She felt her desire growing stronger as they hardened from her touch.

Sandy continued to caress Max as the kiss came to an end. The brunette's eyes were dark with desire as she removed Sandy's shirt. Sandy shifted in an effort to help Max remove the garment. Max's breast was so close to her lips that she couldn't resist the temptation. She sucked the brunette's nipple into the warmth of her mouth as she felt her shirt leave her body.

Max's body melted into her own as she continued to feast upon her breast. Max's thigh pressed against her center as they wrapped themselves around one another. She whimpered as Max pulled away. Her whimpers of protest quickly faded as Max kissed her once again. Sandy ran her hands down the taller woman's back. Her fingertips burned as she felt the brunette's skin respond to her touch.

Max's kisses grew more insistent as her hands wandered up and down Sandy's quivering body. Max began to kiss her way down Sandy's body as she lifted her larger frame slightly away from the trembling red head. Sandy gasped once again as Max suckled the pulse point on her neck. Max's silky hair tickled Sandy's body as the brunette slowly tasted her way down to the swell of her breasts.

The sight of this beautiful woman suckling her breasts mesmerized Sandy. Max suckled and teased each nipple slowly. Sandy could barely breath from the delightful torture. Her body arched as Max began to taste her way down her ribs. Max continued working even further down Sandy's body, dipping her tongue playfully into Sandy's navel. Then she leaned back and ran her fingers along the inside of Sandy's thighs. Max's fingers dipped and glided along her wetness as Sandy leaned up to watch.

Then Max slowly removed Sandy's panties and tossed them aside. They shared a knowing smile before Max began to kiss her way up Sandy's legs. Sandy draped her legs over Max's shoulders as the taller woman nestled herself between Sandy's thighs. Sandy moaned, as Max tasted her for the first time. The brunette's tongue slowly slid through Sandy's wetness as the red head's head fell back. Sandy's body arched when Max's tongue flickered across her clit.

The brunette held her steady as she suckled her clit. Sandy was clutching at the carpeting as Max's fingers entered her warm wet center. The brunette's mouth and fingers moved in unison as Sandy's body arched. Max continued to feast upon her as Sandy's body lifted up off the floor. The feel of Max's fingers plunging in and out of her while she suckled her clit quickly drove the small red head over the edge. Sandy screamed as the waves of ecstasy rushed through her.

She collapsed on the floor and before she had a chance to recover, Max's fingers once again drove her to frenzy while the brunette sat beside her and watched. Sandy reached up and pulled Max into a fiery kiss while she wrapped her legs around Max's waist. The brunette's fingers continued to plunge in and out of her as they rolled across the floor. Max was now lying beneath her as Sandy straddled her body. Sandy's hips thrust urgently against the brunette's touch.

Sandy's body arched and trembled as she exploded against her lover. Max held her steady as the climax ripped through her body. Sandy fought against the urge to simply collapse into Max's embrace. She needed to pleasure the brunette until neither of them was capable of speaking coherently. She captured Max in a lingering kiss, savoring the taste of her own passion on the other woman's lips.

She felt Max's fingers slip from her center as she deepened the kiss. Sandy's hand drifted between their sweat-covered bodies and cupped the brunette's mound. Max opened herself up to Sandy's touch as the red head dipped her fingers into her wetness. They continued to exchange kisses as Sandy entered her lover's center. While her small fingers plunged in and out of Max's desire she teased her clit with her thumb. She watched in amazement as the brunette's body began to tremble from her touch.

Sandy's body thrust in rhythm as she ground her clit against Max's firm abdomen. Max clasped Sandy's hips, guiding her to ride against her body. She trembled as the walls of her center gripped Sandy's fingers. The brunette screamed out in ecstasy and Sandy drove her own body quickly over the edge, joining her lover in bliss. They collapsed against one another and wrapped each other up in a tight embrace. "Max?" Sandy whispered against the brunette's skin as her body trembled from the aftershocks of pleasure and the cool air of the room. "Can we see how the air conditioner is working the bedroom?" She suggested playfully.

They quickly scrambled up and on shaky legs made their way into Sandy's bedroom. She smiled as the cool air embraced her naked body. "You do good work," Sandy praised her.

"You haven't seen anything yet," Max teased her with a leering glance.

"Not so fast," Sandy cautioned her as she pushed the taller woman onto the bed and knelt before her.

Sandy began to kiss her way up Max's endless legs and began to lick the inside of her thighs. The brunette draped her long legs over Sandy's shoulders as the red head began to taste her passion. Sandy moaned in pleasure as she drank in the brunette's wetness. She ran her tongue across her clit while Max muttered words of encouragement. Sandy parted her lover and pressed her tongue against her center. She held Max steady while she plunged her tongue in and out of her.

Max's body thrust urgently against her as she continued to pleasure her. Sandy's tongue slipped from the warmth and quickly resumed teasing her clit. She buried herself deeper in Max's passion as she suckled her clit in her mouth. Max's body arched and trembled as her cries of ecstasy filled the room. Sandy was still savoring the taste of the brunette's passion when Max collapsed onto the bed.

Max unwrapped her legs from Sandy's body. Sandy climbed up onto the bed and kissed the brunette gently. The strange sound of music came from the other room as Max bolted up. "That's my cell," she explained as she looked at her watch. "Oh no, I'm in trouble."

"Go answer it," Sandy instructed her.

Max bolted off the bed; Sandy giggled at the sight of the naked beauty stumbling out of the room. She shook her head in amusement as she got up and grabbed her robe from the closet. She put on the robe and strolled out to the living room, finding Max hurriedly getting dressed while she chatted on the telephone. "No, I'm just finishing up here," Max explained as she hopped around.

Sandy returned to the bedroom and gathered up the brunette's tools and brought them out to the living room. "No, Dad; I'm on my way to Mr. Farmer's place now," Max frantically explained as Sandy placed the toolbox on the floor. Max ended the call and released a heavy sigh.

"Dad?" Sandy asked in confusion.

Max began to gather up the rest of her belongings and clothing. "Ron Jenkins," Max explained as she put the last of her things together. "He's my Dad."

"So you . . . I'm assuming that it's Maxine," the brunette rolled her eyes at the comment. "Nice to meet you, Miss Jenkins," Sandy teased with a smile.

"The pleasure was all mine," Max reassured her before brushing her lips with a gentle kiss. "I'm sorry I have to go," Max added regretfully.

"I understand," Sandy responded with a heavy sigh of her own. "I need to pay you," she added as Max began to pick up her tools. Max flashed her a surprised look. "For the AC," Sandy explained.

"Right," Max responded with a light chuckle. "That would be hard to explain. It's going to be hard enough to explain the discrepancy in the hours." Sandy looked at her in confusion as Max quickly wrote up the invoice. "I'm certainly not going to charge you for . . . you know."

Sandy nodded in understanding as she accepted the invoice. She scanned it to find it to be much less than she expected.

"Can I use your restroom?" Max inquired. "I think I should get cleaned up before Old Man Farmer gets the wrong idea."

"Down the hall on the right," Sandy directed with a smile as she went to retrieve her checkbook.

When Max returned Sandy handed her the invoice and the check. The sudden awkwardness of the situation filled the room. "Well...," Sandy began uncertainly.

"Yeah, I . . . Uhm . . . ," Max stammered in response as she handed Sandy her copy of the invoice.

They both stood there for a moment until Max finally picked up her belongings. "Here's my card," Max said as she handed Sandy her business card. "If you need anything," Max stammered as she diverted her gaze. Sandy simply nodded before showing the repairwoman out.

Back to the present

"Now you know the whole sordid story," Sandy concluded as Meg stared at her with her mouth hanging open. "I did call another repair place about the refrigerator. They said they fixed it but it's not fixed. And Jenkins is the best place in town. But I can't call them; what if they send Max back out? And will you stop staring at me like that?"

"Sorry," Meg apologized before downing the contents of her cocktail. "I can't believe it."

"It's true," Sandy reassured her.

"Did you call her?" Meg pushed.

"No," Sandy admitted with a hint of regret.

"Why ever not?" Meg squeaked. "She gave you her number."

"What would I say?" Sandy tried to explain. "I had sex with a complete stranger. That's not something I do, although it was really good."

"Then call Jenkins and ask them not to send her out there," Meg suggested. "But if it was me I'd be more than willing to let Wonder Woman come over and . . ."

"I know," Sandy said harshly. "I'm a little embarrassed about the whole thing. And I don't want to suggest another repair person because that will make it look like Max didn't do a good job."

"Apparently she did," Meg teased.

"As a repairwoman," Sandy growled. "What can I do? Besides go to Sears and buy a new refrigerator?"

"You have two choices," Meg explained. "Take another chance on a different repairman or call Jenkins and hope they don't send Max."

A few days later Sandy was answering her front door cursing Meg. "Good afternoon, Miss Brooks," Max greeted her shyly as she stepped into Sandy's apartment. "I understand you're having problems with your refrigerator." Sandy nodded as she started to show Max the way to the kitchen. "Its okay; I remember," Max said awkwardly.

"Of course," Sandy grumbled in a similarly awkward tone.

Max made her way into the kitchen while Sandy curled up on the sofa, wondering if she should at least try and have a conversation with the other woman. "I don't freaking believe it!" Max shouted from the kitchen. Sandy jumped to her feet and ran into the kitchen. She found a very irate looking repairwoman glaring at her. "You called someone else?" She accused the frightened teller. "Not calling me after what happened is one thing, but to call another shop really hurts."

"My God, you're serious," Sandy responded in amazement. "Look, I'm sorry. I felt a little awkward calling your Dad's shop after we slept together."

"Fine," Max responded with a heavy sigh. "Can I ask you something else?"

"I wanted to call you," Sandy blurted out in frustration. "But I was embarrassed. I don't normally sleep with people I've just met."

"Neither do I," Max confessed. "That's why I was hoping that you would call so we could get to know one another outside the bedroom. But that isn't what I was going to ask."

"Oh?" Sandy responded with a mixture of surprise and hopefulness.

"I was going to ask if you believe in new appliances?" Max teased.

"Believe in? Yes. Afford? No," Sandy quipped in response. "Can you fix it?"

"I honestly don't know," Max answered sincerely. "It might be toast. Not to mention the hatchet job whoever you hired did on the poor old thing. I'll see what I can do. If not, my Dad has a couple of display models that are about to be replaced. I can work out a deal that won't break you. We can talk about it over dinner tonight."

"Dinner?" Sandy asked as she approached Max.

"Well, you don't have anything to cook," Max teased her with a cocky grin.

"Okay," Sandy agreed.

"Okay?" Max inquired shyly.

"Yes. I'll have dinner with you tonight," Sandy agreed as her heart skipped a beat.

"Good. Now get out of here; I have a lot of work to do," Max chastised her as she shooed Sandy out of the kitchen.

"Are you taking me somewhere nice?" Sandy teased.

"We'll see," Max grumbled playfully.

"Yes, we will," Sandy said to herself as she smiled.

The End

RAIN'S JOURNEY

The Western Territories 1849

Rain looked across the trail as the sun burned down, baking her skin. It was one of those hot sticky days when even the twilight wouldn't bring relief to the sweat-soaked woman or her trusty horse. She removed her hat and wiped her sweaty brow with the worn sleeve of her shirt. The scratchy material of the ragged shirt grated against her fair skin. She adjusted the long blonde braid that was hanging down her back, lifting it in an effort to cool the back of her neck. She had contemplated cutting her long locks on several occasions since she already endured odd looks and sneers from the folks she encountered on her travels. A woman dressed in masculine attire and traveling alone led to all sorts of unpleasant assumptions. Having no desire to add more grist to the mill, Rain left her long unruly hair in place.

She looked back up at the blazing sun and hoped that the night would bring some relief. "Not much longer," she commented aloud, noting how low the fiery orb stood in the late afternoon sky. No one but her horse was around to hear her words. Together they had survived another day in her dismal existence. "What do you say, boy? Another night camping out at the Widow Jenkins place?"

Her horse snorted in response and she patted the tired animal softly. The appaloosa had been her sole companion for almost two summers now. She had saved him from being destroyed by an uncaring owner who couldn't see the horse's worth until she offered to take him off of the man's hands for him. Of course she hadn't had the means to buy the animal, so under the cover of darkness, she liberated the beast.

"Maybe it's about time I named you," she pondered as she continued along her path. But if she named him then it would be as if he belonged to her. She didn't want to own anything or to have anything owning her. She couldn't do that. They were both free. He was simply horse or boy and she was Rain; Rain because of the fierce rainstorm she'd survived the night she was cast out of her parents' home. She was no longer Abigail Smoothers. Abigail died that night and had been reborn as Rain.

The unnamed horse seemed to know his way to the Jenkins farm. "Ah, the Widow Jenkins," she said with a pleasant smile. "Now that is a tall drink of water." Her smile grew brighter as the image of the dark-haired beauty filled her senses. The familiar warm sensation that filled her was the reason the young blonde found herself drifting from one dusty township to the next.

She tried to convince herself that she was returning to Mrs. Jenkins' small farm night after night simply because the woman had made it clear that she was welcome to camp there. Rain was quite accustomed to being driven off from most folk's homesteads.

For over three years, she'd been drifting the countryside clad in men's clothing. It was what she could steal and they were more suited for her travels. She was constantly forced to leave places because the *decent* folk she encountered didn't want someone of her kind lingering around.

Stafford had been no different. That was until the night she set up her camp just outside of the widow's fence line. She could see the small house from where she'd set up for the night and became fearful that she wouldn't get to sleep when she spotted the tall dark-haired beauty standing out on her front porch. She was a vision of beauty bathed in the light of the summer moon. Rain's stomach clenched with desire and she found herself watching the woman until she retreated into her home.

Rain had kept her meager belongings close at hand, fully expecting Henry, the woman's hired hand, to appear at any moment to send her on her way. The request for her to vacate the premises never came. Instead, when the morning sun and the sounds of birds chirping woke her, she noticed that the fence gate was slightly open. Just beyond the gate lay a pot of coffee, a basket of freshly baked biscuits, and a clean blanket.

Rain looked around to see whom the items belonged to. Finding no one else she realized that they'd been left for her. The friendly gesture touched Rain's heart and melted a thin layer of ice from it. After she had eaten, she silently replaced the items on the front porch when she was certain that no one could observe her actions. On top of the neatly folded blanket, she placed a bunch of wildflowers that she'd picked in the field just outside of Mrs. Jenkins property.

The normally hardhearted blonde felt silly leaving flowers for her hostess; sillier yet that she'd taken the time to pick flowers that matched the tall woman's amazingly blue eyes. She had seen the Widow Jenkins up close earlier that day when she was riding through town and couldn't help becoming mesmerized by the woman's eyes. Perhaps that's why she had chosen her small ranch to camp outside of? She shrugged off the silly romantic notions as she climbed up on her horse and made her departure.

The following evening Rain had returned to Mrs. Jenkins farm. She'd convinced herself that she was simply returning since it was a safe place to set up camp for the night. It wasn't at all possible that she fancied the tall attractive woman who'd shown her the only act of kindness she'd received in far too many years.

She couldn't have stopped the smile that emerged on her face when she returned to the same spot to discover the gate open and a basket of food and a fresh blanket waiting for her. That night she feasted upon the Widow Jenkins' fine cooking and then wrapped up in a clean blanket. As she snuggled into the warmth of the blanket, she inhaled the scent of jasmine and vanilla and wondered if the Widow Jenkins smelled that way as well.

Now it had been over a fortnight and Rain found that she was once again returning to the same place she camped every evening, silently accepting the meals, fresh blanket, and the invitation to camp within the confines of Mrs. Jenkins' fence. From her camp she could see the light coming from the house; on occasion Henry or his employer would be outside but no one disturbed her solitude.

Rain found it odd when she kept hoping that the Widow Jenkins would approach her. Of course she understood that her desire to spend time with the attractive woman was based solely on her baser desires. They were the same feelings that had started her on her desolate journey.

Still it didn't prevent her mind from picturing the young widow in the throes of passion while she pleasured herself. "When was the last time I had a little fun?" She asked her nameless steed. "Flagstaff, wasn't it?" The horse merely snickered in response. "I think it was that redheaded dancer, or at least she said she was a dancer. She sure was pretty." She smirked as the memory of her last experience of true passion replayed in her mind.

A frightened scream broke her from her thoughts. She halted her steed's steady gait and searched the empty field. Another scream pierced the silence. Rain's heart raced, knowing it was the sound of a woman and it was coming from Mrs. Jenkins' farm.

Rain spurred her horse into a full gallop, exhausting the poor tired animal that was only slightly bettered cared for than herself. Rain's heart was pounding when she came upon the now familiar fence line. The Widow Jenkins was wrapped up in a fierce struggle with a scruffy man. Rain recognized the rogue instantly as Brett Thornsby. Brett was the local bully who fancied himself as something of a ladies' man. Rain had correctly deduced that the only time he spent with a lady was paid for.

As he attempted to maul the struggling woman, Rain realized that Brett had another tactic with the ladies. A man like him made the young blonde sick to her stomach. Her horse neatly jumped the fence, and as his hooves touched the ground, Rain jumped off. The grace of their motion surprised both the woman and her steed.

As she struggled with Brett, Mrs. Jenkins was proving that she was not the shrinking violet that most women Rain encountered pretended to be. The raven-haired beauty was pummeling the unruly cad senseless as Rain made her descent. As Rain neared the battling duo, the blonde harbored sincere doubts that Mrs. Jenkins required her assistance.

Still the petite blonde possessed an urgent desire to beat the bully senseless as well. She hated bullies and everything the callous cowards stood for. Her father had been a bully. He and all the pious folks back in Twin Corners were nothing but a group of ignorant bullies that had made her who she was today.

Just as Mrs. Jenkins landed a powerful blow directly into Brett's midsection, Rain spun the despicable creature around and delivered a powerful blow of her own. She hit him squarely in his ugly face.

"Nice shot," Mrs. Jenkins complimented her.

"Bitches," the stunned man spat out as he lunged for the both of them.

"Oh no," Rain grumbled as she ducked away from the large man.

"I'm going to kick your sorry ass," Mrs. Jenkins screamed as she yanked him away from Rain. The blonde smiled at her bravado.

Soon she was jumping in to rescue the brunette. Together they unleashed a melee of punches and kicks against their larger opponent. Finally Rain landed a powerful blow in the man's face; the sickening sound of bones crunching as blood oozed from his nose confirmed that she had hit what she'd aimed for. Thankfully Brett finally collapsed onto the ground in a heap.

Henry had just returned in a cart and was rushing towards them as Mrs. Jenkins smoothed out her dress. "Well, your dinner is ruined," Mrs. Jenkins commented dryly. Rain just stared back in surprise after noticing the ruined basket lying on the ground.

Rain was still staring as Henry's large form reached them. The widow was a tall woman, close to six feet, and Henry stood a good shoulder above her and had a chest the size of a small wagon. "Henry, you missed all the fun," Mrs. Jenkins merrily quipped. "Would you mind hogtying this pig and hauling his sorry ass down to the jail?"

"Well, it is my job to dispose of the garbage," Henry drew out slowly.

Rain's emerald eyes widened even further at Mrs. Jenkins' colorful language. During the fight itself the respectable widow had strung together some words that would have made a hardened foot soldier blush. At the time Rain had been too involved with the heated battle to notice. Now she was shocked right down to her blonde roots.

Henry snatched Brett's limp body up by the back of his shirt collar and began to drag him towards the house. Mrs. Jenkins wrapped her arm in Rain's and urged her to follow him. "Do I want to know what happened?" Henry inquired.

"I'll tell you in the morning." Mrs. Jenkins sighed. "Just tell the sheriff that he tried to take advantage of me. It's late so why don't you stay in town for the night? Take some money from the jar and have yourself a good time."

Henry simply nodded in response as Rain allowed the brunette to lead her towards the small well kept home. The blonde looked over her shoulder to find the horse following close behind. "Now I need to fix you some dinner," Mrs. Jenkins offered thoughtfully to Rain.

The blonde turned to the woman in surprise, her arm tingling from the intimate contact. "I couldn't . . . ," she began to protest.

"I insist," Mrs. Jenkins asserted firmly. "I need to thank you for your extreme heroism."

"Excuse me?" Rain said in confusion. She looked over at Henry who was still dragging Brett across the ground. She was quite certain that Henry could have easily carried the man, yet he seemed happier to be dragging him. Rain was pleased with the idea as well.

"Are you doubting your bravery?" Mrs. Jenkins inquired as she began to gently caress Rain's arm. The blonde wanted to sink into the sensations Mrs. Jenkins' touch was sending through her body.

"I am," Rain finally managed to choke out. "I think you had the situation quite well in hand." Henry snorted in agreement.

"Ssh, Henry," Mrs. Jenkins scolded him. "No, you're my heroine and I must properly thank you."

A rash of goose bumps erupted on Rain's skin as the timber of Mrs. Jenkins tone dropped to sensual level. If Henry noticed he didn't show it. "No disrespect, Mrs. Jenkins, but I was about ready to sell tickets and place a wager on your impending victory." Mrs. Jenkins released a hearty laugh.

"Since you know my name perhaps you will share yours, my beautiful savior?" Mrs. Jenkins implored her as she released her arm to step up onto the porch.

"Rain," the blonde replied as she blushed from the compliment.

"Rain?" Mrs. Jenkins responded with a doubtful look.

"It's what I call myself," Rain boldly responded as her body craved to feel the woman's touch once again.

"Rain it is then," Mrs. Jenkins concluded with a flourish. "And what is his name?" She pointed towards her horse.

"Doesn't have one," Rain responded with a shrug.

"Shame on you," Mrs. Jenkins scolded her. "Well, put your fine stallion in the barn. Henry will show you the stall that would be appropriate and then please join me inside the house. I don't pay attention to such matters."

"Mrs. Jenkins . . . ," Rain began to protest once again, wishing only to escape back to the safety of the open road. There she could indulge her body in what she was certain Mrs. Jenkins would never offer her.

"Shirley," the attractive woman cut her off.

"Shirley?" Rain uttered in surprise.

"Problem?" Mrs. Jenkins shot back.

"No, it's lovely," Rain lied, thinking that the name did not suit the vision of beauty standing before her.

"My very dear friends call me Sher, and since you and I are destined to become the very best of friends, that is what you shall call me," Sher firmly instructed her. "Now go stable Horace."

"Horace?" Rain blurted out in bewilderment.

"A fine and noble name for a fine and noble animal," Sher reasoned. "Now off with you; Henry really should tie up Mr. Thornsby before he wakes up. I don't have time to engage in another altercation; I have a dinner to prepare." Having had her say, Sher spun on her heels and entered the house.

Rain stood there in astonishment before she collected what was left of her thoughts. "Is she always like that?" The blonde asked the chuckling handyman.

"Oh yeah," he responded with a toothy grin. "Come on, Rain. You too, Horace."

"His name isn't Horace," Rain vehemently protested as the horse simply followed Henry into the barn. "Traitor," she grumbled as she threw her hands up in defeat. She followed the pair into the barn and settled Horace into a stall while Henry tied Brett up.

"Have a good night, Horace," she offered once she finished brushing the animal down. Surprisingly the horse seemed to respond to the name. "Great. She's named my horse," she muttered bitterly.

"Need a hand?" she offered as Henry lifted a moaning Brett into the cart.

"No thanks," Henry said with a shrug as he tossed Brett into the cart bed. Brett's head slammed into the back wall as he landed. "I'll see you in the morning, Rain."

"I don't think so," Rain shyly protested; she planned to be long gone by the time the rooster crowed. She had already stayed longer in Stafford then she was accustomed to. Her reaction to Mrs. Jenkins' touch convinced her that it was time to be moving on.

"I'll pick up some extra feed for Horace," Henry added as he climbed up into the cart, ignoring her comment.

"I won't be staying," she argued. Henry simply laughed lightly before flicking the reins and driving off. "I'm not staying," she repeated to herself as she climbed up onto the porch. She wiped her dusty boots off before stepping into the simple yet well decorated home.

"You need a bath," came the sultry purr from behind her.

Rain's heart and stomach clenched as she turned around to find Mrs. Jenkins leaning in the doorway to the kitchen, casting a smoky gaze over Rain's body.

"Mrs. Jenkins, I really do appreciate the kindness that you have shown me over the past few weeks . . . ," Rain began, firm in her convictions to leave this woman's company as soon as possible.

"Sher," the brunette corrected her. "Now I think a bath before dinner would be the wisest course of action."

"Mrs. Jenkins . . . ," Rain began to whine as the taller woman slowly approached her.

"Sher," the woman corrected her once again.

"Fine. Sher." Rain agreed in an exasperated tone. "I haven't set foot in another person's home in more years than I care to think about. I'm not fit company for a lady such as yourself."

Sher studied the agitated blonde for a brief moment before raising her brow in defiance. "Rain, I decide who is or is not welcome in my home," she offered in a calm tone as she placed a comforting hand on the smaller woman's shoulder. Rain couldn't stop the shudder her eager body released. Sher's fingers drifted up the blonde's neck and her fingers began to caress her cheek. "Rain, my late husband was a fine man," Sher explained in a soft voice as her fingertips continued to caress Rain's delicate features. "He was much older than myself and cared for me deeply despite how we met."

"Hmm," Rain sighed as she leaned into Sher's gentle caresses. "Wait," Rain said as she snapped out of her trance. "Mrs. Jenkins, I'll bed down in the barn with Horace and then be on my way. You've already shown me far more kindness than I've seen in a very long time," Rain reasoned as her body screamed at her stupidity.

"And just where is it that you're heading?" Sher asked as her hands came to rest on the small blonde's shoulders.

"Nowhere," Rain confessed as Sher's body brushed against her own.

"Then one more night won't delay your arrival," Sher reasoned as she leaned even closer to the trembling blonde. "I promised to properly thank you and I mean to do just that."

Rain moaned as she felt Sher's breasts brush against her body. Sher leaned in even closer, her breath caressing the blonde's face. Rain felt flush as her body heat began to rise. "Thank you," Sher whispered, her lips almost grazing Rain's as she spoke. Rain's body melted as Sher's full lips brushed against her own.

Rain's eyes drifted shut as she leaned into the kiss and Sher's tongue tickled her bottom lip. She parted her lips and greeted Sher's tongue with her own. They engaged in a sensual duel as they explored the warmth of one another's mouth. Rain's small hands followed the curves of Sher's body as the brunette's hands drifted down her back.

The kiss deepened as Sher's hands cupped her firm backside and Rain's hands felt their way up the taller woman's back. As Sher caressed her bottom, Rain could feel her desire dampening her trousers. Her hips swayed against the brunette's body as their tongues continued to wrestle for control. Rain's nipples tightened as Sher's hand grew more insistent, pressing the smaller woman more tightly against her body.

Rain cursed the need to breathe as the fiery kiss came to an end. "You're welcome," Rain panted as she licked her lips, savoring the remnants of Sher's kiss.

"I'm not through thanking you yet," Sher insisted as she continued to knead Rain's cheeks. "My sweet beautiful savior, I've only just begun to show you my gratitude," Sher whispered hotly in Rain's ear.

Rain moaned as Sher nibbled on her sensitive earlobe. Sher's talented mouth began to feast on her neck as her hands drifted up along the blonde's body. Rain could only whimper as Sher continued to express her gratitude. Rain's head fell back, her hat falling to the floor as Sher cupped her breasts and began to suckle her neck.

Rain's body arched as Sher caressed her aching breasts. Her fingers fumbled to undo the buttons on the back of the taller woman's fine dress. She fought to keep her hands steady as she felt her own shirt buttons being released; Sher's tongue and mouth tasted her newly exposed flesh.

Having freed the buttons down to Sher's slim waist, Rain reached up and untied the ribbon that held her hair up. The silky mass welcomed her fingers as she wrapped them in the raven locks. The soft scent of vanilla mixed with jasmine greeted her. *'Oh God, it was her blanket I was sleeping under. It was as if she was wrapped around me while I touched myself.'* Her mind raced as the erotic image filled her senses.

Rain reluctantly released the silky tresses so Sher could remove her shirt. Sher kissed her shoulders as Rain clasped the taller woman's hips.   Sher ran her hands down the frayed chemise that covered the blonde's breasts before slowly untying it. Rain whimpered as Sher's hands began to caress her stomach.

Sher's hands brushed her breasts as she lowered the undergarment from Rain's body.   The blonde's body was quivering with desire as Sher began to massage her breasts. Rain held Sher's hips tighter as the brunette began to roll and pinch her aching nipples.

Rain gasped in pleasure as Sher captured one of her nipples in her mouth. The brunette's other hand drifted between their bodies and began to undo Rain's belt as she eagerly suckled Rain's nipple. Rain wrapped one arm around Sher's waist as she once again ran her fingers through the brunette's hair.   She arched her body as she pressed the woman's head against her breast, offering more of herself up to the woman's touch.

As Sher's teeth grazed Rain's hardened nipple, the brunette was undoing the buttons on the blonde's trousers. Sher's mouth licked and tasted her way across Rain's chest until she captured her other nipple in her mouth and began to lavish it with the same sweet attention its twin had received. Rain's hips thrust against Sher as her body hummed with a needy desire.

Rain was certain that she was going to explode as Sher began to kiss her way down her body. As Sher made her descent, she tugged Rain's clothing down. Sher's hands clasped her naked backside as she playfully dipped her tongue into Rain's navel.

The blonde's chest was heaving as the scent of her own arousal filled her senses. She steadied herself by clutching Sher's broad shoulders as she urged the brunette to continue her journey. Sher pushed Rain's clothing further down her body; her long dark hair caressed Rain's trembling thighs, further fanning the flames of her passion.

She was covered in sheen of sweat when she heard Sher growling; Rain's boots were preventing her from completely removing the blonde wanderer's clothes. Sher abandoned her quest and Rain felt her thighs being gently nudged apart as the brunette's tongue ran slowly up one of her legs.

Rain opened herself up further as she felt Sher licking away the passion that had painted the inside of her thighs. Rain's breathing grew ragged as she gazed down upon the raven-haired beauty nestled between her thighs. She released a strangled cry as she felt Sher's tongue dip into her wetness.

The blonde clung to Sher's shoulders as the brunette's tongue glided along her swollen nether lips, drinking in Rain's overflowing passion. Sher massaged the blonde's firm round backside as she continued to drink in her passion. Rain's hips thrust forward, silently begging her lover to take all of her.

Sher responded by plunging her tongue deep inside the blonde's center. Rain was panting as she felt Sher's talented tongue curl and plunge deeper inside of her. Sher continued to caress her backside while plunging in and out of her wetness. Rain's hips thrust urgently, matching her lover's sensual rhythm. "Sweet Jesus," Rain cried out as she cupped the back of her lover's head, guiding her to take her deeper and harder. "That's it," Rain groaned as Sher's tongue slipped from the warmth of her center and began to flicker across her throbbing clit.

She felt the hood being teased before Sher suckled her clit in the warmth of her mouth. Rain was losing control as Sher teased her clit with her teeth and her tongue and pressed two fingers against the opening of her center. Rain's hips thrust against Sher's hand as she begged her to be inside of her.

Rain's thrusts grew frantic as the long fingers entered the warm wetness, filling her as Sher suckled her harder. Sher began to move her fingers and tongue in a passionate rhythm that Rain's body moved to match.

Rain lost herself in the sensation of Sher loving her as her knees buckled slightly. Rain fought against the explosion building inside of her, never wanting to feel her lover stop pleasuring her. Sher took her deeper and harder as Rain's body arched and the waves of passion captured her body. The climax ripped through her as she screamed out in ecstasy.

Rain fought to remain standing as Sher kissed her quivering stomach while her fingers remained in her warm wet center. Brilliant blue eyes gazed up at her as she tried to control her breathing. Rain moaned as she felt her lover's touch slip from its cocoon. She watched as Sher licked her fingers clean. As her lover's tongue glided across her fingers, slowly suckling the wetness, Rain cupped one of her breasts and slowly began to roll one of her nipples between her fingers.

Sher released a soft purr as she watched Rain touching herself. "Thank me again," Rain requested in a shaky tone as she guided her lover's head back to her passion. Rain continued to tease her nipple as Sher's tongue once again flickered across her throbbing nub. The sound of Sher's enjoyment was music to the blonde drifter's ears as she watched her lover's tongue darting in and out of her wetness.

Rain's hips swayed as Sher eagerly drank in her nectar. Rain pinched her nipple harder as she felt Sher suckling her clit. The sounds of her climax were already filling the room as Sher's mouth drove her once again over the edge. Rain's body began to collapse. Sher gathered her up in her arms and held her tightly as the aftershocks rippled through the smaller woman's body.

Rain clung to her lover and began to suckle the brunette's nipple through the soft material of her dress. She felt Sher's body arch against her own as she sucked harder on the nipple. Soon the need to feel more of her lover's body had the drifter slipping the woman's dress from her shoulders.

Rain struggled with the buttons and other restrictions the fashionable garment provided. Finally she had managed to slip the dress and Sher's undergarments down to the brunette's waist. They were still kneeling on the floor as Rain raised her lover up to the sofa. Rain ran her fingers down Sher's back as the brunette moaned in pleasure.

With one hand Rain continued to caress the soft skin of her lover's back while she slowly lifted the hem of her dress up to her waist. "Do you want this?" The blonde inquired in a soft sensual tone as both her hands drifted to Sher's slender waist.

"Oh yes," Sher moaned in desire. She gathered her dress up even further while Rain began to lower her bloomers down to her knees.

Rain nestled herself behind her lover, pressing her nipples into the brunette's naked back while her wetness brushed her backside. Sher's hips thrust backward demanding more as Rain brushed her raven hair away from her neck. Rain slowly kissed the nape of her lover's neck as her damp golden curls swayed against her naked cheeks.

"Yes," Sher encouraged her as their hips moved wildly in unison. Rain loved the feel of her lover's skin dancing against her aching clit. "Yes," Sher repeated with an urgent scream as Rain reached around her and began to stroke her clit. Sher's desire coated her fingers as she continued to rock her body wildly.

Rain could feel Sher's thighs trembling as they opened, inviting the blonde further inside of her aching need. Rain lifted her body slightly so she could tease Sher's clit with the pad of her thumb while she entered her with her fingers. Rain's fingers plunged in and out of her lover as her thrusting hips followed the same frantic pace.

"Yes, Rain!" Sher cried out as she exploded under the blonde's body. Sher clung to the plush cushions of the sofa as Rain continued pleasuring her. Soon her lover could only call out her name over and over again until she collapsed. Rain stilled her movements as Sher panted. "Keep going," the woman managed to choke out. "Want to feel you again." Rain held her lover for a moment before slipping her fingers slowly out of her warmth.

The blonde clasped her lover's hips and began to rock against the brunette. Sher moaned deeply as she allowed Rain to ride against her body. Rain was straddling her lover, their bodies gyrating, until their screams rang out as they crossed over the edge.

They held one another in a tender embrace until the beating of their hearts had slowed to a normal level. "Now about that bath," Sher teased her as she kissed her nose.   Rain sighed contentedly as her lover kissed her lips. "I'll need to heat some water," Sher continued thoughtfully.

"You're like a force of nature," Rain noted.

"Oh pshaw," Sher chastised her as she stood and removed the rest of her clothes before tossing them on the floor. "Now get those boots and the rest of your things off so we can take our bath."

"I can't stay," Rain reminded her as Sher strutted towards the kitchen in all her naked glory.

Sher paused along her route to light a couple of oil lamps. "I know.   You're in a hurry to go nowhere," Sher responded in disbelief as she struck another match. "Ouch."   She flinched as an errant spark touched her skin.

"Are you all right?" Rain quickly inquired in concern.

"Yes." Sher shrugged.   "Lesson learned.   There are some things that one shouldn't do naked. Do you still have those boots on? I'm going to have to break you of that habit."

"Sher, I can't stay," Rain protested with uncertainty.

"Right - in a hurry to get to nowhere," Sher conceded with a shrug as she disappeared into the kitchen. "But I haven't finished thanking you yet," the brunette called out.

Rain was struggling to remove her boots as the impact of Sher's statement struck her. "She's going to kill me," the blonde uttered with a hard swallow as her body clenched with renewed desire.

"No, I'm trying to love you," came the sincere response.

Rain looked up to find her hostess once again leaning in the doorway. "You don't even know me," Rain choked out, trying to sound defiant as her sorrow and pain slipped through with her words.

"I understand you better than you think," Sher answered her in a soft honest voice, maintaining her perch in the doorway. "Rain, I'm offering you a bath, a hot meal, a bed to sleep in tonight, and a body to share it with. When you're ready to move on, you're free to go."

Rain just stared at her as she fought against the tears that were threatening to escape. "Now hurry up and get those damn boots off. The water is almost ready," Sher chastised her.

"Already?" Rain responded in amazement. "You certainly do move fast."

"You're just figuring that out?" Sher chuckled. "Now get a move on and while we take our bath I'll tell you all about Horace."

"My horse?" Rain said in confusion as she renewed her battle with her boots.

"No, silly, my husband." Sher sighed as she knelt down and began to assist Rain with her footwear.

"You named my horse after your late husband?" Rain gasped in surprise.

"A noble name for a noble animal," Sher explained. "When I saw him clearing that fence to save me, I knew then that he should be named Horace." Sher continued assisting Rain in removing her clothing. "You see, Rain, I do know you; in fact at one time in my life I was you. But Horace saved me."

"And now you're trying to save me?" Rain grumbled.

"No," Sher corrected her as she assisted the naked blonde to her feet. "I'm trying to love you. Not out of pity, but because I want to love *you*. The water should be ready. I should warn you about something," Sher continued as she led the blonde towards the kitchen.

"You're insane?" Rain commented wryly as they entered the kitchen.

"Tsk," Sher scolded her as she began to pour the water into the claw foot tub in the corner of the room. "No. I plan on getting fresh with you while we bath."

"Oh well, if you must," Rain stammered as she blushed. She watched as Sher tested the temperature of the water. Sher smiled in response as she held out her hand. Rain accepted the woman's hand and her entire body felt the warmth of Sher's gentle touch.

Rain sighed in delight as she lowered herself into the warm water. Sher knelt beside the tub and dipped a cloth into the water and then lathered it with soap. Rain watched her lover's hands foaming with lather and inhaled sharply as she felt the warm soapy clothe run along her body.

Sher slowly ran the cloth down Rain's shoulders, along her

arms, and up the swell of her breasts. The brunette's touch lingered upon reaching her bosom until Rain was moaning with desire. Sher continued to wash her breasts as she climbed into the tub and positioned herself behind Rain's body. "You are very beautiful," Sher whispered in her ear. The timber of her lover's voice sent shivers up and down Rain's spine.

Rain relaxed into her lover's touch as Sher continued to cleanse her body. She loved the feel of the brunette's breasts rubbing against her back. Rain hadn't noticed that Sher had set the washcloth down until she felt the brunette's hands cupping her breasts. Rain's back arched as Sher kneaded her ample bosom playfully. Her eyes fluttered shut as she felt one of Sher's hands drift along the curves of her body.

She moaned as she felt the tips of her lover's fingers teasing the blonde curls of her triangle. She leaned back against Sher's body as a single finger stroked her clit. Sher continued to roll her nipple between her thumb and her forefinger while she teased her nub.

Rain leaned her head back and captured Sher's lips; the blonde could once again taste her own passion on her lover's lips. Sher continued to tenderly caress her nipple and clit. As Rain sank into the feel of the tender kiss and her lover's touch, everything felt right for the first time since discovering her passion for women.

Once again Rain released her passion into her lover's body. The tender kiss continued as Sher wrapped her arms and endless legs around the smaller woman. Rain was smiling as she leaned her head back against her lover's shoulder. "Why?" Rain asked in a small voice.

"Why what?" Sher responded as she nuzzled the blonde's neck.

"Why would you want to love me?" Rain shyly asked.

"Because there's something about you that draws me to you," Sher responded honestly. "Your smile, your laugh . . . I don't know what it is but you have captured my heart. That and you're drop dead gorgeous."

Rain once again found herself blushing. "When I leave . . ."

"If," Sher cut her off.

Rain opened her mouth to respond but words failed her. Everything she had learned in life told her to run. Yet everything she was feeling screamed for her to stay. She was also drawn to this woman and not from the kindness or the intimacy. "I not leaving, am I?" She said aloud as she smiled.

"I don't think so," Sher softly answered.

Rain relaxed in her lover's embrace as she pondered the future while Sher began to tell her about the late Mr. Jenkins. It was a tale that wasn't completed until after the bath and a quick meal Sher threw together. After the meal they retired to Sher's bedroom. Rain had begun to wonder if it was simply the intimacy that was drawing the older woman to her. But that night Sher simply held her. For the first time in years, Rain felt wanted and loved. She was frightened when she realized that she loved the quirky widow as well. As she drifted off to sleep, she promised herself that she would return to her endless journey. She soon lost track of the number of times that she promised herself that she would leave at dawn. And each dawn she would awaken in her lover's arms, knowing that she was going to stay.

The End

JURY DUTY

PART ONE

Walker tapped her fingers impatiently on the counter, waiting for the clerk to check her in. Once she flipped through the long computer printout and checked Walker's identification, she informed the tall brunette to take a seat. Walker grimaced as she looked around at the cafeteria-style tables cluttering the room.   She found a space where no one was sitting and she dashed over. She wasn't looking forward to making idle chitchat with some stranger.

It was bad enough that she was forced to take the day off work.   Not to mention being almost strip-searched when she entered the Cambridge courthouse. Okay, security is very tight these days. Yes, she understood that it was her civic duty and all but still she, like most Americans, hated to be called for jury duty. She knew that she didn't have a reasonable excuse to ditch it. She simply had to grin and bear it. After all, chances were slim to none that she would actually be selected. So now she could just work on the crossword puzzle in The Globe, which was one of her few pleasures in life, and drink her coffee and wait. Soon an elderly gentleman sat at the same table. She smiled up in greeting as she silently prayed that he wasn't a chatterer.

"First time?" He inquired as she glared up from her newspaper.

"Yes," she confirmed as another man sat at the same table. *'So much for peace and quiet,'* she grumbled to herself. Looking at her watch, she grimly discovered that only five minutes had passed since she sat down.

"You know jury duty is a breeze. I've served six times," the elderly gentleman continued.

"Really?" Walker responded.

"Oh yes," the kindly gentleman said as a very attractive blonde sat down and joined them. She smiled at Walker and the gentlemen before retrieving a book out of her backpack. *'Now that's the kind of company, I could enjoy,'* Walker noted to herself as she glanced once again at the crossword puzzle, pretending to listen to the elderly gentleman talk about his grandchildren.

"What ya reading?" the younger man asked the blonde as he leered at her. Walker watched with some degree of annoyance as the petite woman flared her emerald green eyes at him. Shifting uncomfortably in her chair, she held up the book cover for him to read. He pretended to be interested, but Walker could tell that he didn't have the slightest idea what she was showing him. Of course it didn't help his cause when he checked out her ample cleavage instead of the book jacket. "Never heard of it," the dimwitted gentleman said with a shrug.

"I'm not surprised," the blonde brushed him off.

"Is it any good?" he pressed, unaware that his attention wasn't welcome.

Of course Walker figured that out before the blonde sat down. Her gaydar alarm started to scream the moment she laid eyes on the young beauty. Her suspicions were confirmed when she saw the paperback. Walker was well acquainted with Karin Kallmaker's *In Every Port*. Based on how well worn the book was, this wasn't the first time the blonde had read it.

"I enjoy it," the blonde responded to her unwanted suitor.

"Perhaps I could borrow it or you can tell me about it over coffee?" The man suggested.

"No, thank you," the blonde responded in a curt tone.

"You know we're going to be awhile," the man continued.

"We could even end up in siesta together." He continued to leer.

The blonde and Walker rolled their eyes in unison. "You mean sequestered," the blonde corrected him.

"Either way," the man chuckled, somehow thinking he was amusing.

"Not the sharpest knife in the drawer, is he?" The elderly gentleman whispered to Walker. Walker stifled the laugh that was threatening to escape as she flashed a brilliant smile at the elderly gentleman.

"Listen Sparky . . ," the blonde was clearly angry at this point. "I'm not interested."

"Oh come on, you don't even know me," the man pushed.

"And apparently she doesn't want to," the elderly gentleman concluded loudly.

The younger man just scoffed at the interruption. Walker secretly applauded the old man for stepping in. "So what's your name?" The man continued, seemingly unfazed.

"Okay," Walker slammed her hand down on the table. "Enough!" She exclaimed as she stood leaning over him with her imposing six-foot frame. "This isn't a singles bar. Leave the lady alone," she commanded through clenched teeth.

"Hold on, sweetie," the man tried to cajole her. "I was just making friendly conversation with the lady."

Walker thought briefly about wiping that smug expression off his face. *'Why not? It would make me feel better and I bet it's a way to get out of jury duty,"* she pondered wryly.

"Is there a problem over here?" a firm voice said from behind her.

Walker turned to see a dark heavyset woman in uniform glaring at her. *'Could this day get any worse?'* She asked herself. "No problem," Walker muttered.

"Actually there is," the blonde piped in. "This gentleman is bothering me and she was trying to help." The blonde jerked her thumb at the offensive young man.

"That's right, officer," the elderly gentleman added.

"I was just talking to her," the pest argued.

"Is that right?" The officer questioned him dryly.

"Yes," the man reassured her.

"Perhaps you should move to another table," the officer suggested in a bored tone.

"Fine," the man feigned innocence as he stood. "Dyke," he muttered as he glared at Walker.

"Yes," both Walker and the blonde answered.

"Figures," the man spat out.

"You know, you and I should talk," the officer said as she motioned him to follow her.

He seemed surprised as she led him out of the waiting room. "Somehow I don't think he's going to enjoy that conversation." The elderly gentleman chuckled as Walker sat down. "I'm Herman, by the way," he introduced himself.

"Walker," she offered her hand.

"Celeste," the blonde added with a bright smile. "I want to thank both of you for coming to my rescue."

They both muttered that it wasn't a problem as a man in uniform asked everyone to be quiet. He then read off their instructions, which were basically to sit and wait until their names were called.

"Sounds exciting," Celeste mumbled.

PART TWO

The three of them sat there and chatted idly while waiting for their names to be called. One by one they were summoned out of the room. Walker was disappointed that she and Celeste had been separated.

She found herself sitting in a jury box filled with strangers. She filled out the questionnaire they handed her. Based on the questions she was answering, she could only assume that it was a malpractice suit. She was relieved when she was excused and was sent back to wait in the cafeteria-styled room. After finally completing her crossword puzzle, she found herself bored beyond belief. Her thoughts quickly turned to Celeste's firm body.

Glancing around the room she tried to see if either Herman

or Celeste had been sent back. Sadly, she didn't spot either one. She settled back to read her newspaper. "Isn't this exciting," a friendly voice commented dryly. Walker smiled as she looked up into a pair of emerald eyes. Celeste seated herself next to Walker. "Sent you back as well," Walker noted, unable to keep the happiness out of her tone.

"Twice already," Celeste huffed. "How long are they going to keep us locked up here?"

"I have no idea," Walker answered as she took in Celeste's cherubic features.

Then they heard both their names called. "Here we go again," Celeste chuckled. "At least this time we get to go together." Her observation thrilled Walker to no end.

Once again Walker found her long form crammed inside a jury box, filling out another questionnaire after she had been assigned a number. There was a bonus this time. Celeste was sitting next to her. The blonde was teasing her by peeking at her answers. Walker nudged her as she smiled brightly. The large bailiff cleared his throat and glared at both of them.

They blushed in unison. Walker suddenly felt like a schoolgirl who'd been caught passing notes in class. Lowering their heads, both women refocused their attention on the lengthy questionnaire in front of them. This time the questions seemed more complicated. Walker got the uneasy feeling that this case wasn't a simple lawsuit. She groaned as she realized that it was a criminal trial. It could only mean that the jury selection would take much longer. She didn't want to be stuck there. What she wanted was to take off somewhere and get to know Celeste better.

Once everyone had turned in their forms, lawyers pored over them carefully. Walker glanced over at her new acquaintance, regretting that they weren't allowed to speak. The lawyers fussed and fumed and spoke with the judge as Walker shifted uncomfortably in her seat.

"Did you have any plans for afterwards?" Celeste whispered to her. "You know, after we get sprung?"

Walker had intended to sneak over to her office and get some work done before heading back to her empty apartment. Since meeting the bubbly blonde, being alone was the last thing on her mind. "No," Walker answered quietly.

"Would you like to get some coffee or something?" Celeste inquired softly so she couldn't be heard.

"Yes," Walker responded in an equally quiet tone.

Several people were dismissed; neither Celeste nor Walker was among them. The lawyers began to question people directly. More people were sent on their way. Once again Walker and Celeste remained. It was Walker's turn to be questioned. Most of the questions were basic - what do you do, are you married, do you live with anyone, etc.

"Are you familiar with Raymond Carsen?" One lawyer in a bad suit inquired.

"No," Walker answered honestly.

"Really?" The lawyer in the cheap suit smiled. "Have you been out of the Commonwealth in the past few months?"

"Yes," Walker responded truthfully once again. "I've just returned after spending nine weeks in Anchorage on business," she explained as her stomach dropped.

Much to her dismay both the defense and the prosecution accepted her. "If being out of town is a plus then I'm in the same boat," Celeste muttered to her. Suddenly Walker felt a whole lot better. Stuck on jury duty with a beautiful blonde. Yes, life was looking pretty good at the moment.

Her good fortune continued when Celeste was also chosen, apparently for the same reasons. She had a job, lived alone and, since she had been out of the state for what she referred to as *personal* reasons, she had never heard of Raymond Carsen either. Walker was thrilled that Celeste lived alone, but was curious about her personal reasons for leaving the Commonwealth.

"Well, I guess we're stuck with one another," Celeste said as she flashed her a goofy grin.

"Aw shucks," Walker teased in return.

Over the next few hours and after a great deal of debating from both teams of lawyers, the jury and it's alternates were selected and sworn in. Then things took a nasty turn. Perhaps Walker should have paid closer attention to what was going on instead of flirting with Celeste. The defense team was terrified that the media would taint their opinions. They weren't allowed to read the papers (no crossword puzzles!) or watch the news. No easy task in this day and age. So they were to be sequestered.

It wasn't the worst news being locked up with Celeste for an indefinite period of time. But they were instructed that they couldn't socialize with one another. No discussing the case. Not a problem. But there was to be no intimate contact. It was made clear that sort of thing was a major no no.

Walker was dumbfounded. She was to spend twenty-four seven with this beautiful woman and couldn't flirt with her. For the first time in years, she'd met someone nice who seemed to be interested in her as well. And she couldn't do jack about it. *'Life sucks!'* Walker concluded mentally.

Celeste simply sat there with a nasty scowl on her face. Apparently she agreed with Walker's conclusions.

PART THREE

On their first day of jury duty, Walker discovered a few things. First off Raymond Carsen was a bad, bad man who should be locked away for the rest of his life unless, of course, the defense team could prove otherwise. From what she heard that day it appeared that Raymond murdered his elderly landlady who spent most of her free time doing volunteer work. His motive was her Social Security check and she had asked him to turn down his radio after ten o'clock at night. The second thing Walker discovered that day was the fates had nasty sense of humor. Her roommate during the duration of the trial was Celeste.

They looked around the sparse room at the Malden Econo Lodge that had been stripped of its television. There was nothing but two double beds, a bathroom and, of course, each other. "This bites," Celeste grumbled as she collapsed onto one of the beds.

"Tell me about it," Walker concurred.

"Don't get me wrong. I mean, it's our civic duty yada yada yada," Celeste explained in an exasperated voice. "But what the hell! I'd like to think that you and I had, you know . . . kind of hit it off and now we can't even hold hands."

"I'm with you," Walker agreed. "Well, we can spend the time getting to know one another," Walker suggested, trying to make the seemingly impossible situation a little brighter. "You never know, we might not even like each other."

Celeste gave her a doubtful gaze. "What choice do we have?" Celeste agreed halfheartedly. "Given the circumstances of this case . . .," she held up her hand defensively. " . . . I know we can't talk about it. But I know that we can't screw this up because of our hormones."

PART FOUR

Over the next few weeks they spent their days in the courtroom listening to the dullest lawyers on the face of the planet. At night they played cards and talked. The more they got to know each other, the more they seemed to connect. Which made sleep time very trying for both of them. "What did you just ask me?" Walker blushed as she brushed out her long raven tresses. She wondered if the blonde was trying to kill her. Their casual touching or running into one another in the shower was hard enough; on more than one occasion, Walker found herself pruning in the shower after catching a glimpse of Celeste clad in nothing but a towel and a smile. *'Now Celeste wanted to know about that?'*

"You heard me," Celeste said in a husky tone as she wiggled her eyebrows suggestively.

Walker looked over at the blonde who was lounging on her own bed, clad only in a long T-shirt that failed to conceal the firm body that lay beneath. "You want to know how I lost my virginity?" Walker repeated the question.

"Why not?" Celeste encouraged her.

"Why?" Walker teased.

"I just want something to think about tonight," Celeste

answered mischievously.

"Oh, so you can have a good time without me?" Walker tossed her hairbrush at her.

"I can't have one with you," Celeste sighed heavily. "Not yet anyway."

Walker's pulse raced as she drank in the beautiful woman sitting across from her. "Okay, if you tell me your story," Walker agreed against her better judgment.

"Deal," Celeste answered with a smile.

Walker stretched out, leaning on her elbow so she could watch the woman lying on the bed across from her. "It was at summer camp," Walker began. "I was sixteen and a counselor in training. Her name was Monica. She was a little older than I was and we became friends. One night we went for a walk along the beach and, for some reason, while we were walking she held my hand. All of sudden I felt alive and scared to death at the same time. I'd never thought about sex with anyone, much less another girl. She must have felt me shivering. She wrapped her arms around me. There I was looking into her eyes and the next thing I knew we were making out." Walker watched as Celeste's face flushed and her breathing became ragged.

Walker could still recall the sensation of Monica's tongue exploring her mouth for the first time. She had never been kissed before, well never like that. Monica's hands explored her breasts. Her nipples hardened from Monica's touch. "I want you," Monica whispered hotly in her ear. Her mind was spinning as Monica gently lifted her tank top up. Her skin shivered from the cool night air as Monica's hands cupped her breasts. She remembered moaning.

She also recalled trembling with excitement and fear. She didn't know what to do and was too frightened to admit her lack of experience to Monica. If Monica suspected anything, it never showed. Or perhaps she simply didn't care. Monica's skillful fingers worked their way up under her bra. She kissed Walker's neck as she pinched and teased her erect nipples. "Are you wet?" Monica asked her as she continued her assault on her sensitive neck.

55

Walker couldn't recall how or if she responded to the question. She could only remember the feel of Monica exploring her body with her hands and mouth. She remembered inhaling the scent of her long curly red hair. It smelled like peaches. Walker ran her fingers through Monica's hair as the older girl's mouth continued in a downward motion. She didn't know when Monica did it but somehow her bra had been unfastened.

Walker's knees threatened to buckle as Monica captured one of her breasts in her mouth. Walker's body arched in response as her panties grew damper. Monica teased her nipple with her teeth and tongue as Walker struggled to continue standing. Instinctively she pressed the back of Monica's head, encouraging her to take her deeper.

Walker moaned in disappointment as Monica halted her movements. The redhead kissed her deeply as her skillful hands returned to teasing Walker's breasts. Walker wrapped her arms around the other girl, pulling her closer to her body. Monica ended the kiss abruptly. Walker was about to protest when Monica silenced her by pressing a finger against her quivering lips. Leaning in, Monica captured Walker's earlobe in her teeth. Nipping playfully, she further fueled Walker's desire. "God baby, I want to fuck you," Monica growled in her ear as her hand felt it's way down to the waistband of Walker's shorts.

"Huh?" Was the only response Walker could come up with. She knew at that moment that she would do anything this girl asked of her.

Walker remembered Monica undoing her shorts as she dropped to her knees in front of her. She kissed Walker's exposed abdomen, her tongue dipping into her navel as she pulled Walker's khaki shorts down her legs. She could remember feeling exposed, standing there on the deserted beach with her top pulled up and her shorts pooled around her ankles as Monica's fingers spread open her swollen lips.

For the first time in her life Walker felt her clit throb and understood fully what it meant. With a gentle hand she guided Monica towards her wetness. She felt Monica's breath caress her damp dark curls. The intensity jolted through her body as Monica's tongue flicked across her swollen clit. Much to her surprise, her thighs instinctively opened wider.

While Monica groped her backside with one hand, her tongue licked and tasted Walker's lower lips. Monica buried her face deeper inside of her as her other hand moved between Walker's trembling thighs. Walker felt two fingers pressing against her opening as Monica began to suckle her clit.

Walker recalled how her hips swayed as her breathing became erratic. Monica grazed her throbbing clit with her teeth as she plunged her fingers inside of Walker. The young brunette cried out as Monica's fingers curled and teased her sensitive center. Monica feasted upon her as her fingers plunged in and out of Walker's wetness. Monica took her with her mouth and fingers.

Walker found herself clenching the back of Monica's head as she screamed out in ecstasy. Later, they found themselves rolling around in the sand completely naked. Walker fumbled as she tried to pleasure her lover. After it was over, Monica kissed her sweetly as they had dressed. Then she suggested that they should get together again sometime. Walker was confused. Later she would learn that Monica had many friends that she took to the beach. She liked older men and naive women.

At the end of the summer, Walker returned home wiser, a little bitter, less trusting, and completely confused about her sexuality.

Walker could feel her wetness grow from reliving the memory and the sight of Celeste's nipples pressing firmly against the material of her shirt. Celeste's eyes had fluttered shut during the telling of the story. Walker almost laughed when she finished the story. Celeste had her hands clenched tightly and her legs crossed. It didn't take much for her to figure out what was going on in that pretty blonde head. "Okay, your turn," Walker teased her.

"I need a moment," Celeste responded in a shaky tone.

"That's not all you need," Walker added in a rich tone.

"I know," Celeste squeaked. "God that was amazing . . . I . . . Uhm . . ."

"I know," Walker finished for her in a deep voice. "I do too."

"I think I need a cold shower," Celeste groaned.

"You know . . . ," Walker began as she fought the urge to cross the few feet to Celeste's bed, ". . . the Judge said we couldn't touch each other."

"I know," Celeste growled.

"But he didn't say that we couldn't touch ourselves," Walker urged her on, knowing that it wouldn't take much at that moment to drive the smaller woman over the edge. "I mean that's what you were planning on doing." Walker knew that she was playing with fire. Her desires had overwhelmed her senses. She knew that the friendship that had begun to grow between them was great. Yet the desire threatened to consume both of them.

Walker couldn't resist; she needed to release her pent up passion. Slipping her hand up under her nightshirt, she rolled her already erect nipple between two fingers. Celeste's eyes fluttered open and watched her intently. The blonde raised herself up on her knees and started to raise her shirt. Walker's clit began to throb as she spotted the teal panties that lay underneath.

Her mouth went dry as she lowered the collar of her nightshirt to reveal the nipple she'd been teasing. Celeste moaned as her fingers descended into her panties. Walker's breathing became erratic as she watched Celeste's hand move beneath the teal cotton material. All she wanted at that moment in time was to taste this woman.

Walker continued to tease her nipple with one hand as her other hand reached under her nightshirt. She got on her knees as her fingers slipped beneath the waistband of her underwear. Her blue eyes watched Celeste intently as she felt her own wetness greet her fingers.

A sudden knock on the door interrupted them. "Yes?" Walker barked out harshly. "Miss McCormick, your mother's on the telephone," the deputy informed her. Walker's hands quickly removed themselves from her body. Walker suddenly wished that she were an orphan.

"Well, that's a mood killer," Celeste groaned as she collapsed onto the bed. Walker retrieved her robe and took the phone call from her mother. As she reentered the room and found Celeste sound asleep, she knew that the moment had passed. "I can't wait until closing arguments," she muttered bitterly as she climbed into bed, dreading the long lonely night ahead.

PART FIVE

Several more weeks passed and the tension only grew between the two women. Walker found it difficult to focus her attention as her mind wandered to thoughts of Celeste. Finally both sides presented their closing arguments; unlike television, it took three days for them to finish. Once locked away for deliberations, everyone sighed with relief.

It had been hard to spend so much time with people and not talk about the one thing they had in common. "Is it just me or did this guy beg to be caught?" Celeste commented as she plopped down into her chair.

"Oh, how about how his lawyer tried to explain the bloody finger print," another person commented.

"That the print had been there already and blood got on it." Walker snorted. "It certainly didn't look good when their own forensic witness said that wasn't possible."

"Or how about when he tried to cash the landlady's check using her dead husband's ID," another person added.

"At the bank she went to all the time," Celeste added.

Even the jury foreman had to chuckle at that. "Let's face it, Raymond's not the brightest bulb there is," he added. "Who wants to vote and get out of here?"

Everyone agreed eagerly. A vote was taken and, to no one's surprise, Raymond Carsen was found guilty. Walker had tried to give him the benefit of the doubt during the trial but it was clear the guy was guilty. They turned in the verdict and were allowed to go back to the motel to get their belongings. Everyone's mood was brightened by the fact that they were finally free.

Walker couldn't wait and yet suddenly she felt apprehensive. There was no longer anything keeping Celeste and her apart. She tried to hide her nervousness as they entered their room. They had packed their bags that morning in anticipation of leaving. Neither of them had spoken. Walker reached for her bag as her mind struggled for something to say. A small hand covered her own.

Walker swallowed hard as she looked up at Celeste who was trembling slightly. Walker sensed her nervousness and wrapped the smaller woman in her arms. "It feels so good to finally be able to hold you," she said softly. She felt Celeste relax in her arms. Everything felt right. It was funny that they were suddenly shy around each other. Over the past few weeks they had exchanged every detail of their lives. They had laughed and the sexual energy between them had been undeniable.

They stepped slightly apart as Walker looked deeply into the eyes of the woman who had captured her heart. "I know we should take this slow," she said, trembling as she felt the heat from Celeste's body radiating against her own.

"I can't wait," Celeste responded in a husky tone as she reached up and pulled Walker's head down.

Their lips met and melted together instantly. They parted in invitation. The kiss deepened quickly as their tongues danced together. Walker moaned as she pressed her body into the smaller woman. The need to breathe overwhelmed them. "We don't have much time," Celeste gasped. "I know we should wait until we're somewhere more appropriate."

"I need you," Walker uttered hotly in her ear. Her mouth began an assault on Celeste's neck. Her pulse beat wildly just from the taste of her skin. Celeste's hands cupped her backside as she backed her up towards the nearest bed.

Walker grabbed hold of Celeste's hips as she felt herself being lowered onto the bed. They both knew that they had little time to explore their passion. The urgency only seemed to fuel them on. Each began to unbutton the other's pants, kissing deeply as they unzipped them. They lowered the offending material just enough to see one another's panties. Their bodies pressed together as hands began a hurried exploration.

Walker reeled as her fingers slipped into Celeste's wetness. Her thighs opened as she felt Celeste stroke her throbbing clit. They moaned in unison as they teased one another. "Take me," Celeste begged. Walker entered her with two fingers, plunging in and out. Celeste moaned deeply, her own fingers entering

Walker's center. They rode against each other as their bodies trembled. Capturing each other in a passionate kiss, their fingers continued to pleasure the other. Their screams of ecstasy were muffled by their kiss.

They lay trembling on the bed as someone knocked on the door, informing them that it was time to go. They both moaned in displeasure as they quickly stood and adjusted their clothing. They kissed one another quickly.   Grabbing their luggage, they headed towards the doorway. Walker reached out and touched Celeste gently on the arm. "We're not finished," she informed the smiling blonde.

"I hope not," Celeste winked at her. "Trust me. I want more than that from you. I want your heart as well."

"It's already yours," Walker smiled back at her.   "By the way, you never did tell me how you lost your virginity," Walker pointed out.

"I did promise to tell you," Celeste responded thoughtfully. "How about tonight at my place?"

The End

Mavis Applewater

REACHING A VERDICT
(JURY DUTY - PART TWO)

Part One

Celeste Devon looked around her apartment and scowled. While being sequestered away in the motel in Malden, dust had settled, the plants had died, and there was a nasty smell coming from the refrigerator. "This is bad," she grumbled, feeling exhaustion overwhelm her. Her dream woman was coming over and her once pristine home resembled a hovel. She tossed her suitcase in the bedroom, changed into a comfortable pair of worn Levis and a T-shirt, and began to scrub and scour her apartment. "I should have suggested her place," she muttered as she cleaned out what was growing in the refrigerator. "But no. I had to go and open my big mouth."

Celeste had no idea when Walker would be arriving. They'd exchanged phone numbers, and without stopping to think about the long day they'd already endured, Celeste suggested dinner at her place. She gave the tall brunette her address and told to her come over whenever. She knew she hadn't been thinking clearly. Her only thoughts had been about the quick sexual encounter they'd shared and how much she wanted to explore more of what Walker had to offer. It wasn't just Walker's amazing body and the intense sexual attraction; she felt that she and the brunette had connected from the moment they met.

Celeste was tired as she dragged the trash out to the dumpster. She had awoken at seven that morning and been forced to listen to the dry monotone voices of the lawyers deliver the closing arguments. The verdict took no time at all. Raymond Carsen was a guilty guy who wasn't very bright when it came to covering up his heinous actions. The only smart thing he'd done was to murder his poor sweet landlady in a state where there was no death penalty. After rendering their verdict in record time, they then had to wait for the lawyers and judge to be ready for them. After the verdict was read they were loaded into the bus and driven back over the Tobin Bridge to Malden to collect their belongings. She still didn't understand why they'd been lodged so far away from the city.

She smiled as she recalled how the intense sexual frustration had driven Walker to take her on the bed, while a deputy waited outside their motel room. Then it was back on the bus for a long drive in rush hour traffic until they were deposited back at the courthouse, free to go. She was finally free and could touch Walker. The thought of being able to kiss the woman with whom she had shared a hotel room for almost two months made her stomach flutter with excitement. It also frightened her. "What if that pent up sexual frustration is all we have to offer one another?" She wondered.

She deposited her trash and headed back towards her building when she spotted a taxi stopping out front. "No," she whimpered as she spied the sexy brunette exiting the taxi. Walker smiled at her as she approached. "I'm a mess," Celeste blurted out.

"You look adorable," Walker reassured her with a smile. "I take it your apartment looks like mine."

"I forgot how long I've been away," Celeste grumbled as she led Walker into her building. "I'm thankful that the court took care of our landlords but you'd think they would send someone over to water the plants and clean out the fridge," Celeste rationalized as they climbed the stairs up to her apartment. Walker chuckled lightly from behind her as they entered the sparsely furnished apartment.

"This is nice," Walker complimented her as she stepped inside.

"Well, she got most of the furniture," Celeste explained as she closed the door behind them. During their time together Celeste had explained to Walker her reason for being out of town when the murder occurred. She'd broken up with her lover and the blonde had needed some time away to clear her head.

"Tell you what. Why don't I grab us some takeout from that Thai place I noticed on the corner?" Walker suggested. "And you can hop in the shower and relax."

"That would be great," Celeste sighed deeply, feeling completely at ease in Walker's presence. Of course why shouldn't she be? They'd been together twenty-four hours a day for the past seven and a half weeks. Celeste handed the leggy brunette her house keys and went in search of her wallet.

"I got it," Walker volunteered. "I want you relaxed and refreshed. Besides you owe me a story," Walker teased as she wrapped her arms around Celeste.

"Oh no," Celeste blushed.

"You promised," Walker insisted as she kissed Celeste lightly on the cheek.

"I did, didn't I," Celeste offered meekly.

"Hey, relax. I'm just looking forward to spending time with you," Walker offered with a sweet sincerity. "Maybe later we can go for a walk? I never realized how much I would miss the city air until we were locked up."

"That sounds nice," Celeste agreed with a smile and a shy kiss.

Once Walker had left the small blonde opened the windows to air out her apartment. Then she descended on her bathroom - first she cleaned it since it was rather nasty looking after all the weeks of neglect, and then she climbed into the shower, losing herself in the warm spray. The Econo Lodge bathroom had nothing on the heavy-duty shower massage she'd had installed when she moved into the apartment. It felt great to enjoy her shampoo and soaps.

Her thoughts quickly turned to Walker. "How am I going to tell her about my past without scaring her off?" She muttered as she rinsed her body. "After that sweet story she told me about losing her virginity at summer camp, my story is going to seem sleazy." Celeste blew out a heavy breath as she stepped out of the shower and began to dry herself. "Okay, there's no need to panic yet. It's not like I can change the past," she reasoned, recalling all the late night conversations she'd shared with Walker. They had really gotten to know one another and they seemed to connect on so many levels. If Walker shut her out because she lacked discretion in her past, then she wasn't the person she thought she was and she'd be better off without her. *'Please don't be a judgmental jerk,'* her heart pleaded.

Celeste changed into a pair of black jeans and a teal sleeveless tee. Then she blow-dried her short blonde locks, noticing that she needed a trim. All the time she'd spent serving on jury duty had certainly disrupted her life. It was the little things like being able to watch television and get her hair done that she had missed. But spending every waking moment in Walker's company had more than made up for the inconveniences. She had known that there was something special about Walker the moment the tall brunette had jumped to her defense when that obnoxious man had hit on her while they were waiting to be called in for a panel.

She emerged from her bedroom to find Walker setting up the takeout food in the living room. "Hi," she offered with a bright smile as she watched the tall woman's movements.

"Hi," Walker responded with a smile of her own.

"That smells fantastic." Celeste sighed happily as she approached Walker. "After weeks of those cardboard sandwiches I'm really looking forward to this."

"I even got us a nice bottle of wine; it's chilling in the refrigerator," Walker offered with a shy grin. "Hunter Ash, I seem to recall you said that you really liked New Zealand wines."

"I do," Celeste concurred as she wrapped her arms around Walker's waist.

Walker returned the embrace and wrapped her arms tightly around Celeste's body. "This feels nice," Walker murmured softly. "I've been dreaming about holding you since that first day."

"Oh yes, when you defended my honor," Celeste responded softly as she nestled her head against Walker's chest.

"That guy was an ass," Walker snorted indignantly. "Granted, I can understand him not being familiar with Karin Kallmaker but still, what part of 'I don't want to talk to you' didn't he understand?"

"Some men just don't get it," Celeste offered as she inhaled the scent of Walker's skin. "Hmm . . . that's nice. Jasmine?"

"Yeah," Walker responded softly. "I couldn't wait to hop into my own shower and use my body scrub. I hated those little soaps at the motel. But I forgot my own stuff. I was a little flustered with dealing with tying things up at my job and everything else."

"I was the same way," Celeste said as she listened to the steady rhythm of Walker's beating heart. "Well, except for the job part. I can take months off and not worry about it. Still I should start looking for a new assignment," she added with a slight frown.

Celeste was a gifted cinematographer who worked exclusively on documentaries. The work was good and, with the emergence of stations like the Discovery Channel and the Learning Channel, she worked and traveled a lot. She had been smart when it came to investing her hard-earned money back in the days when the pay and work was scarce. So now she worked when she wanted to and on what she wanted to.

"I really need to catch up on work myself," Walker grumbled. "I'll probably been sent off again soon."

Celeste stepped slightly back from the warmth of Walker's body. "Being a geologist must keep you busy these days," Celeste offered as they both took a seat on the sofa. Celeste was thrilled when Walker kept her hand in her own.

"All the major oil companies are certainly keeping us busy," Walker agreed. "I love the traveling. I never thought about it when I first decided to get into the field."

"What made you decide on studying rocks?" Celeste asked

the one question that she'd been dying to ask since she discovered Walker's profession. "And yes, I know it's more complicated than that."

Walker smiled as she released Celeste's hand. The blonde's body instantly missed the contact. "Oddly enough it started my first year in college," Walker explained as she handed the blonde a plate. "I had no idea what I wanted to major in. I was just trying to fill my science requirement," Walker continued as they began to fill their plates and eat.

"This is so good," Celeste moaned as she dug into her plate of curried shrimp. "Okay, so you needed to fill your science requirement?" Celeste encouraged her.

"Right," Walker responded with a nod. "I didn't want to take Biology because I couldn't deal with cutting up a poor little piglet."

"You're squeamish?" Celeste chuckled.

"Just a little," Walker said, defending herself with a slight pout that Celeste found positively endearing. "Anyhoo, I took Geology figuring that since my teammates on the basketball team called it rocks for jocks, it would be a breeze and boost my GPA. I ended up loving it. Of course now I'm more of a team leader and don't get all dirty anymore. I miss that."

They settled into a comfortable conversation as they enjoyed the mountain of Thai food that Walker had purchased. Walker told her about her last trip to Alaska and Celeste shared tales of her trip to Egypt. Celeste felt a niggling fear that the constant traveling and demanding schedules that they both had would be a problem. Celeste cleared away the remnants of the meal and opened the bottle of wine.

She settled down on the sofa next to the very relaxed brunette. "So, Miss Devon, I do believe you owe me a story," Walker stated wryly.

"Yes, I do," Celeste, stammered. Then she took a healthy sip of wine. "Prior to my last relationship, I was very single."

"Yes," Walker responded in a slow careful tone.

"I've had relationships but, well, I did date a lot in my twenties," Celeste continued nervously. "I'm not ashamed of my lack of commitment."

"You shouldn't be," Walker reassured her. "You told me before that you weren't a player but you did date a lot of different women. And you were careful and healthy."

"All true," Celeste confirmed. "While I wanted a relationship I wasn't ready to just jump into one when I didn't feel that it was the real thing. It took me long enough to come to terms with my sexuality that I needed to be in love. Plus the first couple of times I fell in love I ended up being hurt. My last relationship was a good example. Have I scared you off yet?"

Walker released a hearty laugh as she snuggled closer to Celeste. "Not a chance," Walker reassured her. "I certainly explored my options in my youth. Plus with the way both of us have to travel on a moment's notice, it isn't very good for maintaining a marriage."

"I know," Celeste responded sadly.

"What is it, Celeste?" Walker inquired carefully. "We've talked about this before. I think you know that I'm looking for more than what we shared this afternoon."

"So am I," Celeste asserted. "It's just that my first time was a bit unconventional. In the past it's scared away more than one potential suitor."

"It wasn't a farm animal, was it?" Walker teased her.

"No," Celeste laughed as she gave Walker a light swat. "Okay, pour us some more wine and I'll tell you the whole story."

Part Two

For Celeste, doubts regarding her sexuality had begun to emerge during her senior year of high school. By the time she had just about completed her first semester in college she was more confused than ever. She didn't have enough confidence to even talk about it with Joy and Sandra who had become her closest friends during the semester. The two girls were roommates and their room was right across the hall from Celeste's. The three of them hung around constantly and Celeste was drawn to both women.

She was also curious; there were constant rumors about just how close Joy and Sandra really were. One night the three of them were hanging out in Joy and Sandra's room, drinking some cheap rum. As the three of them sat on Sandra's bed, Celeste noticed the constant touches the two other women were sharing. It wasn't the first time she'd noticed the affectionate touching between the two girls. Celeste was fascinated by the interaction; normally she would excuse herself from the scene.

That night, thanks to the rum and cokes she'd consumed, she just sat back and watched. Her body was tingling with excitement. She tried to convince herself that it was caused by the rum and not the sight of the other girls snuggling together and Joy massaging Sandra's stomach. Then Joy reached over and captured Sandra in a lingering kiss.

Celeste's jaw dropped as she watched the kiss deepen and the two women begin to fondle one another. The blonde's body was in turmoil as she found herself excited and terrified. She could hear her heart pounding against her chest as she watched Joy's hands slip up under Sandra's T-shirt. Celeste didn't know what to do. She decided to leave the couple alone and allow them some privacy. As she moved to climb off the bed, Joy turned to her. "Don't leave," the platinum blonde requested in a breathy tone.

Celeste blinked her eyes in confusion, not understanding why she would want her to stay. She looked over at Sandra who smiled at her. "Stay," Sandra encouraged her in a tone that sent shivers up and down Celeste's spine. Before Celeste could respond, Joy cupped her face in her hands and drew her in for a soft kiss. Celeste was lost in the soft feel of Joy's lips exploring her own.

Celeste gave herself over to the feeling as Joy parted her lips with her tongue. She could feel her body being moved. She was now sitting between both women. Joy was exploring the warmth of her mouth with her tongue while Sandra's hands were running up along the sides of her body. She felt Sandra kiss the back of her neck while she cupped her breasts. Celeste moaned from the contact.

Celeste deepened the kiss as her own hands began to explore

Joy's body. Celeste felt hands running up under her shirt. She cried out as she felt both women touching her sensitive breasts. "We both find you attractive," Sandra whispered hotly in her ear.

"I never . . . ," Celeste choked out as she felt her top being removed.

Celeste never finished what she was struggling to say as her bra was removed and Joy suckled her nipple in the warmth of her mouth. Celeste's body arched in response as Joy teased her nipple with her teeth and her tongue while Sandra's hands busied themselves with undoing the buttons of her jeans. Celeste leaned into Sandra's body and the redhead captured her in a fiery kiss.

Celeste's body reacted to every touch both women offered as she turned and found herself pressing her body into Sandra. Joy nestled her body on top of her. Celeste exchanged kisses with both women as they undressed her and themselves. Celeste's naked body was trapped between the two equally naked women. She was excited and frightened. A part of her wanted to stop what was happening. Yet her body craved the feeling of being touched by both women.

Celeste was lost in the feel of Joy's skin and desire melting into her from behind while Sandra's skin and desire caressed her body from the front. She began to kiss Sandra hungrily as Joy began to kiss her way down her back. Celeste kissed her way down Sandra's neck and shoulders while Joy's hands began to caress her backside. Celeste's hips arched as Sandra's hand slipped between their bodies and Joy's hand dipped into her wetness from behind.

Celeste couldn't think as both women pressed fingers against the opening of her center. She parted her trembling thighs as she captured one of Sandra's nipples in her mouth. Celeste winced when both women entered her wetness. She gave herself over to the feel of Joy feasting upon her wetness as Sandra teased her clit. She loved the way Sandra's nipple became erect as she suckled it.

Celeste thrust her hips urgently as they plunged in and out of her in perfect rhythm. She could hear Joy's murmurs of pleasure as Sandra pleaded with her to suckle her nipple harder. Sandra hissed in pleasure as Celeste teased her nipple with her tongue and her teeth. The feel of Sandra's desire pressing against her stomach further fueled her need to touch and be touched by these women.

As Joy and Sandra's rhythm grew wilder, Celeste's head fell back and her body lifted higher. Joy moved behind her and pressed her wetness against Celeste as Sandra once again began to suckle her breasts. Celeste was grinding her hips as she began to cry out in ecstasy. Sandra's head fell back as she ground her wetness into Celeste's body. Joy was groaning as her hips swayed against her backside.

Sandra was quivering beneath her as Joy was trembling behind her. Joy pressed her breasts into her back and leaned over and began to nibble on her earlobe. Joy was whispering lust-filled words in her ear and Celeste felt her thighs trembling. Celeste's head was spinning as she felt her body explode. She cried out as she felt a sudden rush coursing through her entire body.

Before Celeste could understand what had happened, her body's need took over. She began to kiss Joy passionately while she fondled her breasts. Sandra assisted her in fondling Joy's body. Throughout the night both women opened Celeste to a whole new world, showing her everything, and sating desires she never knew existed.

Part Three

Celeste sat there waiting for Walker to say something. The brunette simply stared at her with a stunned expression. "Wow," Walker finally managed to stammer.

"Anything else you want to add to that?" Celeste pushed as she felt her heart drop. Walker simply blinked in surprise. "Walker, I want you to understand something. I don't regret what happened; I just wish it hadn't been my first sexual experience."

"I'm sorry," Walker explained as she recovered. "I can understand why you wished your first time had been different. I felt the same way about Monica. I don't regret what happened, but a part of me wishes that I had waited until I was older and in love."

"So you don't think less of me?" Celeste asked shyly.

"No," Walker reassured her as she wrapped her arms tightly around Celeste's body and pulled her up onto her lap. "Did you think I would because you had a three way?"

"Well, frankly, yes," Celeste retorted as she caressed Walker's shoulders. "In the past when I've explained what happened with Joy and Sandra, most of my lovers thought that I was really into group sex. It either scared them off or they were far too interested."

Celeste felt a sense of relief as Walker chuckled lightly. "Well, as for three ways - been there, done that," Walker offered with a shrug. "And although I enjoyed myself, it's not something I'm interested in at this point in my life."

"I feel the same," Celeste reassured her. "I don't regret my past but it's just that - the past."

"The only thing that bothers me is I get the feeling that Sandra and Joy set you up," Walker offered in concern.

"They did," Celeste agreed as her eyes drifted to Walker's soft full lips. "Did you ever feel that way about what happened with Monica?"

"Yes," Walker confirmed with a heavy sigh. "None of that matters now. If those things hadn't happened we might not be together now. The same goes for Raymond Carsen. If he hadn't murdered his landlady, we might not have met."

"Hmm . . . we can send him a Valentine's Day card every year," Celeste teased while sh Walker's hands caressed her back. Her eyes remained focused on the brunette's lips that were now parted slightly. "Who knew that doing your civic duty could be so rewarding?" Celeste added. Her body trembled from the feel of Walker's fingers slipping up under her shirt. She dipped her head and captured the lips that had been the only thing holding her focus for the last several moments.

Celeste moaned deeply as Walker parted her lips with her tongue. The kiss quickly deepened as their tongues engaged in a sensual duel. Walker's hands began to caress her back, making the blonde shiver. Celeste reached between their bodies and caressed Walker's breasts as the brunette unclasped her bra. Celeste moaned into the warmth of Walker's mouth as her lover cupped her breast.

Celeste reluctantly ended the kiss when the need to breathe overwhelmed her. She ran her fingers through Walker's long silky dark hair while her lover teased her nipples with the palms of her hands. Celeste's body arched in response and she gave herself over to Walker's touch. "Celeste, I want to take this slow," Walker whispered hotly in her ear.

"Do you want to stop?" Celeste panted as Walker began kissing her neck.

"No," Walker murmured against her skin. "I just want to make this moment last."

Celeste tilted her head back, giving Walker more access to her sensitive neck. "So do I," Celeste whispered in understanding. The rushed excitement of the encounter they'd shared earlier that day left both of them with a feeling that something was missing.

Celeste allowed her fingers to enjoy the silkiness of Walker's hair while the brunette slowly kissed her neck and caressed her breasts. Celeste could feel her nipples becoming erect from Walker's touch. Her hips began to grind into Walker's firm body as her lover's mouth moved further down until she was suckling the pulse point on Celeste's neck. Celeste pressed harder into Walker's body as she released a throaty growl.

Celeste pulled slightly away from her lover and stared deeply into her fiery blue orbs. "Bedroom," she said with a soft promise. They exchanged tender kisses before rising up off of the sofa. Celeste took Walker by the hand and led her into her bedroom. Once in the bedroom Walker wrapped her arms around Celeste's body and the two shared tender kisses. Celeste's lips were tingling from the shy exchange. She inhaled deeply and stepped away from her lover. She lit a candle that was by her bedside and then pulled back the bedcovers.

Her body was pulsating and she knew that Walker was watching her every move. Celeste turned to her lover and smiled as Walker kicked off her shoes. She watched as Walker pulled her shirt out of her jeans and began to lift it slowly. Celeste stepped over to her lover and captured her hands. "Let me?" She asked, the heat emanating off her lover's body almost burning her. Walker lifted her arms and allowed Celeste to remove her top.

The blonde took a moment to run her hands along Walker's broad shoulders. She slowly lowered the straps of the black bra Walker was wearing until they were hanging off her shoulders. Celeste kissed the valley between the brunette's breasts as she reached behind her and unclasped the bra. She ran her tongue along the swell of Walker's firm full breasts before removing the garment completely.

She stepped back to admire her lover's beauty as Walker began to reciprocate by removing her top and bra as well. Celeste stepped into Walker's inviting arms and began to kiss her lover. She moaned as her skin melted into Walker's as their breasts brushed against the other's body. Shyly they explored the warmth of each other's mouth as they each caressed the other's back.

"Make love to me," Walker whispered against her lips before reclaiming them. Celeste's heart soared as she ran her hands down along Walker's body. She could feel her lover's skin respond to her touch and it only made her body crave more. Celeste began to kiss Walker's jaw and then down her long neck. Her lover's moans fueled the fire already burning deep inside of her.

Celeste was once again running her tongue along the soft swell of Walker's breasts as her lover caressed her back and ran her fingers through her hair. Celeste's exploration grew bolder as she circled Walker's nipples with her tongue without touching them. Walker whimpered each time she would almost brush one of the rose colored buds. Walker's hands cupped her backside and began to massage her firm cheeks as their hips swayed against one another.

Celeste's wetness was dampening her jeans as she pressed her body against Walker's. She suckled her nipple in her mouth, savoring the taste of her lover's skin. As she teased her lover's nipple she felt Walker slip a hand between their bodies and caress her abdomen. Her skin burned from Walker's touch. She teased her nipples harder, moving from one to the other and then back again.

Walker's thigh parted hers and pressed against her aching center as the brunette began to undo her jeans. She mirrored Walker's actions and began to unbutton the brunette's slacks while she continued to feast upon her breasts. Their bodies separated slightly as they both tugged the other's pants down to their hips. "I need to feel you," Walker panted as she lowered Celeste's panties. Needing to feel the same connection, the blonde once again mirrored her lover's actions.

Both women's pants and underwear hung on their trembling thighs as they brushed their wetness against the other's body. Walker once again caressed Celeste's backside while the blonde buried her face in the brunette's breasts. Each of them slipped a firm thigh between the other's legs. Celeste could feel her lover's desire painting her skin as they began to sway against each other. "You're so wet," Walker moaned as they ground against each other in a slow sensual rhythm.

The urgency of their movements grew as they clung to one another. Walker groaned as Celeste stepped slightly away from the embrace they were sharing. She reached up and kissed the taller woman. Never breaking the kiss, she turned Walker around, backed her up against the bed, and then gently lowered her down. Now lying on top of Walker's long firm body, Celeste melted into her lover's touch. She was breathless as she pulled away from the kiss.

Celeste began to kiss her way down Walker's body, taking her time to enjoy the taste of the brunette's trembling flesh. Walker scooted further up onto the bed as Celeste removed her pants and underwear. She tossed the clothing aside, and while she drank in the sight of her lover lying naked before her, she removed the last of her own clothing. She knew that Walker's eyes were roaming her body as well. "Come here," Walker beckoned her with a sultry purr.

Celeste grinned slyly as she lowered her body and began to kiss her way up Walker's endless legs. The blonde took her time as Walker trembled beneath her. She kissed and licked her calves and the back of her knees as Walker whimpered in pleasure. All too soon Celeste found herself captivated by the scent of her lover's arousal as she kissed the inside of Walker's trembling thighs. Celeste nestled her body between Walker's legs and cupped the brunette's firm backside.

She blew a warm breath in the dark triangle that was moist with desire. She parted her lover and dipped her tongue into Walker's wetness. Celeste murmured in pleasure as she traced Walker's slick folds with her tongue. She drew her lover's center towards her and teased the opening of her center. Walker cried out as Celeste entered her with her tongue. Curling the appendage, Celeste slowly plunged in and out of Walker as the brunette's body lifted up off the bed.

As she fought to hold Walker steady, Celeste began to tease her clit with the pad of her thumb. She could feel Walker nearing the edge so she withdrew from her wetness; Walker groaned in protest. Celeste smiled as her fingers replaced her tongue and she suckled Walker's throbbing clit in her mouth. Walker's body jerked as she cried out in pleasure. Celeste suckled her clit harder, teasing it with her teeth and her tongue while her fingers plunged in and out.

Celeste could feel her own body trembling as Walker's trembled against her. The brunette was groaning and panting; she tried to call out the blonde's name as her body tightened around Celeste. The blonde held onto her lover as her body arched against her, exploding in ecstasy. She tried to drive her lover into a second climax only to have Walker pull away. The brunette moved quickly and swept Celeste up into her arms.

Walker captured her in a fiery kiss as she gently caressed her body. Celeste felt alive as Walker's body melted into her. They rolled around the bed as they kissed and caressed one another. Celeste found herself lying beneath her lover who was suckling her breasts. She arched her back, offering more up to her lover's mouth. The slightest touch from Walker threatened to send her over the edge. Celeste wrapped her legs around Walker's body. Walker rolled them over so Celeste could straddle her body. Walker's hands slowly slid across her skin. The intensity from her lover's touch was driving the blonde insane. She felt that

Walker was a part of her.

She whimpered as Walker's hands moved slower. Celeste looked down into Walker's eyes and almost cried to see the intense emotions she was feeling mirrored in her lover's eyes. Walker smiled as she caressed her hip with one hand and her other dipped into her wetness. The brunette never broke the gaze as she slowly stroked Celeste's throbbing clit. Celeste leaned over Walker's body, allowing the brunette to slowly explore her passion.

The tenderness of Walker's fingers gliding along her slick folds was making her body tremble. As Walker began to tease her clit in slow deliberate movements, she entered Celeste. Walker filled her completely and the blonde could feel the climax already building inside of her. Celeste's body quivered as she gazed deeply into her eyes and her fingers pleasured her slowly. Celeste was shocked as she climaxed quickly and collapsed into Walker's arms.

They climbed under the covers and held one another in a warm embrace. Celeste still couldn't believe how powerful her orgasm had been given how gently Walker had made love to her. Perhaps it was because sharing her heart with Walker was like breathing. As they drifted off to sleep Celeste knew the odds were against them. Because the demands of their respective careers, they both had incredibly bad batting averages when it came to relationships. Yet somehow Celeste didn't doubt that they would make it.

The End

FIELDER'S CHOICE

PART ONE

1953 - St. Louis Missouri

Bobbie stepped off the train and stretched her tired body. She felt like she'd been traveling forever. In truth she'd only been trapped on the smelly train for three days. She grasped her battered suitcase and makeup case tightly as she made her way through the busy depot. It was the start of a new season and Bobbie was eager to begin. It was her fourth season playing for St. Louis Sirens and she felt certain that this would be the year they finally won the pennant.

Of course the excitement was dimmed by the familiar rumors that this would be the last season of the AAGBL. The rumors of the league breakup had been looming over the women since its' start back in the forties. Bobbie knew in her heart that someday the league would disappear and be forgotten by everyone except the women who endured sleeping on the crowded smelly old buses just to make it to the game on time.

Bobbie could never forget the first game she went to as a young girl. Her father had taken her along on a business trip just so she could finally see a game. She had been reading about the league and her one wish was to see a real game. The Peaches had played against the Lassies. The Peaches, who at the time had been her favorite team, lost that day. But for young Bobbie it was a dream come true. It was the day she realized that perhaps someday she could have an opportunity to play the game she loved at a level she'd been raised to believe was impossible. She had been overjoyed the day the scout walked up to her after a college softball game and offered her a chance to try out for the only professional woman's baseball league.

She put everything she had into the tryout. She'd dropped out of college in the middle of her sophomore year just to go racing off to it. Her parents were more than a little disappointed in her actions. She didn't care. She wanted the chance to play with and against the best women in the country. Her efforts paid off and she found herself playing third base for the Sirens. She hated the names the league burdened them with, but she understood that it was designed to drum up business. The names were chosen to be overly feminine or slightly sexy as an added enticement to get men to come and watch them run around in their short skirts.

Still, with a starting pay of fifty-five dollars a week plus another two dollars and twenty-five cents a day for meals, it was a pretty good deal. That and it got her away from home and the prying questions as to why she was still unmarried. Leaving the small New England town she'd grown up in was far from a hardship for Bobbie. She had to get out before she went insane or someone discovered that her desires were definitely for the fairer sex. Out on the road she still had to hide her true nature, but it was easier for her to slip away and meet other women such as herself that would satisfy the fire that raged inside of her.

She walked from the depot to the large two-story house that would once again be her home away from home during the season. "Roberta," Mrs. Griswold, the Sirens' chaperone, greeted her in her usual brisk manner.

The tall brunette rolled her crystal blue eyes at the older scrawny woman who still refused to call her Bobbie. It was a game that they played. Both women seemed to enjoy teasing one another. Bobbie's goal each season was to work the woman into a complete frenzy or to get the rigid woman to crack a smile.

Every season she would prove to be triumphant. She and the rest of her teammates took immense pleasure in playing practical jokes on their chaperone. Despite the fact that Mrs. Griswold was very dedicated to her duties, all of the girls knew that deep down she was a good egg who would cheer them on and occasionally cover up slight lapses in their behavior.

The league's rules of conduct were stricter than a convent and violating them meant being kicked out of the league. To the women who lived to play the game it was a fate worse than death. "Mrs. Griswold. New hair style?" Bobbie commented wryly, taking in the woman's salt and pepper hair wrapped in the same tight bun she always wore. Bobbie's heart beat a little faster when she spotted Mrs. Griswold's lips curling up slightly. Quickly the smile that was beginning to form vanished and the chaperone's lips froze into the same disapproving sneer she always sported when Bobbie teased her.

"Almost got you," Bobbie chuckled brightly. "And the season hasn't even started yet. So where am I bunking?"

"You will be residing in the same room you had last year," Mrs. Griswold informed her crisply.

"The shoebox," Bobbie grumbled, recalling how small the room was. Of course she knew that she wouldn't actually be spending a lot of time in St. Louis since most of the games were played in the Midwest. Most of her days and nights would be spent on the same smelly bus that had been used since the start of the league over a decade ago. "Since Glenda is a married lady now, who am I going to be sharing my palace with this year?"

"You will be sharing accommodations with a new girl this year," Mrs. Griswold informed her in the same brisk voice. "Cherish Goodie."

"Cherish Goodie?" Bobbie blinked in surprise. "You made that up."

"Cherish is a very sweet young lady and will be looking to you for guidance," Mrs. Griswold sternly stated. "Try to set a good example."

"Oh, I'm always good," Bobbie teased her chaperone. "Catch you later, Grizzie," Bobbie added loudly before swatting the startled woman on her backside. Mrs. Griswold yelped loudly; Bobbie sped away before she could receive a lecture.

She halted her retreat when she thought she heard the woman release a light laugh. She spun around quickly in hopes of catching her chaperone laughing at her brash behavior. Mrs. Griswold cleared her throat and glared at her sternly. "A lady walks," she chastised her. Bobbie smirked before bolting up the staircase.

Bobbie was chuckling gleefully, filled with excitement for the new season and seeing her old teammates again. "Bobbie?" a familiar voice called out. Bobbie turned to find the tall catcher bounding towards her.

"Hey Sally," Bobbie greeted her teammate joyfully as they hugged. "Good to see you back again."

"You too," Sally rejoiced. "Too bad about Glenda. I mean Paul is a great guy and I'm thrilled that they got married, but I never thought she'd just chuck it after five seasons. She's been with the league since she was seventeen. I kind of hoped that she would stay. There are other gals who are married and play."

"I know," Bobbie grumbled. "I tried to tell her, but she's in love," she explained. She shrugged, not understanding why Glenda didn't feel that she could do both. "So have you met the new kid yet?"

"No," Sally answered.

The two teammates chatted for a while before they excused themselves to settle into their rooms. Bobbie entered her room; it seemed even smaller than the year before. Seated on the bed that was normally hers was the cutest little blonde she'd ever laid eyes on. "That's my bed," Bobbie informed her directly. The blonde gasped and jumped slightly; she quickly collected the booklet she'd been reading and retreated from the bed. Bobbie rolled her eyes, recognizing the booklet as the Charm School Rules.

"Hello, I'm Cherish Goodie," the petite woman introduced herself as she held out her hand; her emerald eyes darted around nervously.

"Grizzie wasn't pulling my leg. That really is your name," Bobbie noted in amusement.

"Yes, it is," Cherish responded in confusion as Bobbie

brushed past her and tossed her luggage onto the bed. "I didn't see you at the tryouts."

"No, my spot was secure," Bobbie explained absently as her eyes began to wander up and down her new roommate's firm body. "I'm Bobbie Cahill by the way," she finally offered as her eyes drifted to the younger woman's firm full breasts. "How old are you?" Bobbie blurted out. She felt a stab of shame at the way she'd been ogling the younger woman.

"It's a pleasure to meet you, Bobbie, and I'm twenty-one," Cherish explained as Bobbie blew out a sigh of relief. Leering was bad enough, but some of the girls could be as young as fifteen and Bobbie didn't hold any interest in someone who wasn't old enough to vote or drink. Some things in life were just despicable and preying on children topped the list for the brunette.

"So what position are you going to be filling?" Bobbie continued as the younger woman dropped her hand with a look of disappointment.

"Center field to start but I might get a chance to play second," Cherish explained in a hopeful tone.

"You should do fine. I'll work with you," Bobbie offered as she began to unpack.

"Thank you. That's very kind of you," Cherish said, accepting the offer as she sat on the edge of her bed and watched Bobbie carefully.

"No problem," Bobbie responded with a shrug as she emptied her suitcase, wondering if her new roomies politeness was genuine or if she'd taken the charm school rules too literally. "I play third," Bobbie added as she hung up the two simple dresses and her skirts. Then she pulled out her well-worn glove and began to oil it as she relaxed on her bed. "So where are you from, kid?" She asked, unable to call the sweet young thing Cherish.

"Kansas," the girl responded brightly.

"I see - the proverbial farmer's daughter," Bobbie commented in a sultry tone of voice.

"Yes, Daddy is a farmer. How did you know?" Cherish inquired innocently.

Bobbie looked at her roommate with a stunned expression before she realized that her new teammate was just as sweet and innocent as she appeared to be. "Lucky guess," Bobbie quickly threw out as she made a mental note to hide her torrid dime store novels from Cherish's innocent eyes. She watched in amusement as Cherish resumed her study of the sacred manual.

"I never realized that there was a certain way to wash up. But I guess our appearance and conduct are very important," Cherish commented thoughtfully.

"For ticket sales," Bobbie snorted. "They forget sometimes that we're playing a sport and not putting on a show. Look before you accept that thing as the Holy Grail, there are some things you should know. Much of that is pretty basic," she pointed to the long list of rules that included how much lipstick to put on and that you shouldn't raise your voice. "There is one thing in there that you should ignore - that's the part where it says to be nice when strangers approach you because they're just eager fans. If some guy gets out of line with you, and trust me they will, acting like a lady won't save you," she cautioned the naïve farm girl.

"I don't understand," Cherish responded with a wide-eyed innocence.

"Some men don't like to take 'no' for answer," Bobbie tried to explain without upsetting the younger woman. "If someone tries to take advantage of you or touch you without you wanting them to, then you should scream your head off, hit them, and get away from them any way that you can."

"You mean like a masher?" she whispered in a frightened tone. "I've heard about them."

"You didn't get off that farm very much, did you?" Bobbie noted agonizingly, already planning on staying as close to the girl as possible. *'For her own safety,'* Bobbie lied to herself as she once again found herself stealing a glance at her breasts.

PART TWO

Bobbie was trying to read as the bus rumbled along, bouncing harshly whenever it made contact with the smallest bump in the road.   The first month of the season had going very well for the team as they found themselves in second place.   The only trouble seemed to come from Cherish.   The blonde seemed to attract it at every turn.   It wasn't Cherish's fault; she was just too naïve for her own good.   She actually fell for the lame excuses men would hand her to get her alone.   Fortunately Cherish was always under Bobbie's watchful eye and the brunette managed to jump in to save her every time.

Cherish was the shyest sweetest person Bobbie had ever encountered.   The young thing wouldn't even get changed in front of her or anyone else.   That little habit was a major disappointment for the frustrated Bobbie.   Cherish would turn ashen whenever anyone released the mildest of curses.   Bobbie took pleasure in swearing in front of the sweet farm girl just to watch her blush or turn pale.   It was a mean thing to do but somehow Bobbie couldn't help it.   She loved to embarrass the younger girl.   She would even strip naked in front of her under the guise of getting ready for bed, just so she could watch the blonde turn beet red and do anything to avoid looking at Bobbie's naked body.   The brunette found it hard to believe at times that the innocent blonde was only two years younger than herself.

Cherish may have been clueless to the ways of the world and the way she could make Bobbie's body hum with desire but she was a talented athlete.   She proved to be a major asset for the Sirens, catching anything that came at her.   Her hitting was proving to be just as solid.   "What are you reading?" Cherish inquired innocently as Bobbie closed the cheap novel that she'd torn the provocative cover from.

"Just a book," Bobbie responded with a shrug.

"Can I borrow one of your books?" Cherish inquired as she reached for the small stack Bobbie kept nearby, away from prying eyes.

"No," Bobbie responded firmly as she swatted Cherish's eager little hands away.

"But you have so many. I just want one," Cherish protested as her brow crinkled.   "They must be good from the way you just tear into them."

'Oh boy! How do I get out of this one? Of course they're good and they're the only source of entertainment I have since I'm stuck with you twenty-four hours a day.' Her mind raced as Cherish leaned into her body. "You wouldn't like them," Bobbie explained carefully. "They have a lot of cursing in them," she lied, hoping to deter her roommate's interest.

"Oh." Cherish nodded, seeming to accept Bobbie's explanation.

"Why don't we talk about tomorrow's game?" Bobbie suggested, hoping to placate the inquisitive blonde.

They fell into an easy banter and some of the other players joined in as they planned the strategy for the game against the Muskegon Lassies. They played one game six days a week and a double header every Sunday. During the season the team would play between 110 and 112 games, depending on how they performed. They traveled constantly and the bus was uncomfortable.

Adding to Bobbie's discomfort was Cherish's constant nearness. Whenever they traveled overnight on the bus, Cherish would sit and sleep next to her. Each morning Bobbie would awaken to find Cherish curled up against her body. She was well aware of the fact that sleeping next to the blonde on the tiny bus was wreaking havoc with her libido. Yet her constant state of sexual frustration was a small price to pay to play the game she loved so much and now, in her fourth season, she was being paid one hundred dollars a week for the privilege.

The conversation turned to Eleanor Engle who the year before had signed a deal to play AA ball with the Harrisburg Senators. She was the first to break into the men's game. The contract was voided two days later and a rule was passed that barred women from playing AA ball. "I guess we should try and get some sleep. The booklet says that we should be well rested and get at least eight hours of sleep a night," Cherish suggested as the others rolled their eyes.

"Like that's going to happen while we have to ride in this rickety old sardine can," Sally grumbled.

"Cherish has a point," Bobbie defended the pouting blonde. "We need to get some sleep for tomorrow's game."

Everyone accepted Bobbie's stern tone and returned to their seats to try to get to sleep. Bobbie found it difficult to relax with the scent of Cherish's shampoo invading her senses and the little blonde's arm brushing against her own as they tried to adjust themselves to limited space. Finally Bobbie managed to drift off and fell into an uneasy slumber.

A tiny gasp and the feel of someone trembling beside her woke the brunette. Bobbie blinked her eyes open and peered into the darkness of the still traveling bus. She looked around to see that everyone was fast asleep. The one notable exception was Cherish who was wide-awake, clasping a well-worn paperback in her tiny little hands. Her emerald eyes were the size of a dinner plate and her jaw was hanging open.

Bobbie snatched the book away from the mesmerized blonde. She grumbled as she flipped to the steamy passage that Cherish had been reading. She turned her focus on the little blonde who was still trembling; Cherish's mouth was hanging open and she seemed to be struggling for breath.

"*Babes Behind Bars?*" Bobbie whispered angrily in Cherish's ear. "What were you thinking?"

"I didn't know," Cherish squeaked out.

Bobbie's hand quickly flew out to cover Cherish's mouth in an effort to prevent her from waking the others. Bobbie had no idea what she was going to do now. Even Cherish would be able to put the pieces together and there was a strong possibility that she'd reveal Bobbie's secret to the others. "Can you keep your voice down?" She asked the little blonde with an angry growl. Cherish nodded her head. Reluctantly Bobbie removed her hand from the warmth of Cherish's soft inviting lips. "I told you not to read these," Bobbie pressed with a soft moan, fearing that her world was about to collapse.

"I'm sorry, Bobbie," Cherish apologized softly. Bobbie blinked in surprise that Cherish's mannerism hadn't altered towards her in the slightest. "I couldn't sleep and I was curious."

"Why didn't you stop when you realized what you were

reading?" Bobbie asked in a soft pleading tone. "You do know what kind of books these are, don't you?" Bobbie added as she began to wonder if Cherish realized that she was reading a lesbian pulp novel.

Cherish avoided her eyes and began to twirl her long blonde hair nervously. "Not really," Cherish confessed in a shy whisper as Bobbie blew out a sigh of relief. "I just thought it was a shame that Tammy was sent to prison. I wanted to see if she was going to prove her innocence. Plus I don't trust that prison matron or that Susan character," Cherish added in an excited tone.

"Ssh," Bobbie chastised her as she began to rub her now throbbing temple. "You shouldn't trust Susan," she muttered. "What about the other things in the story? How did you feel about what Tammy was doing in the shower with the four other inmates?" Bobbie asked in a hush tone.

"I don't know," Cherish mumbled as she stared at her lap.

"Keep it that way," Bobbie cautioned her as she put the book away, regretting that she couldn't see Cherish's face in the darkness. "And please don't tell anyone what I'm reading; I could get into trouble."

"I'm sorry, Bobbie," Cherish whispered.

"It's okay, kid; just don't do it again," Bobbie warned her.

"Uhm . . . Bobbie, could I . . .?" Cherish began to inquire sheepishly.

"No, you can't have the book back," Bobbie choked out, unable to believe that Cherish was enjoying the risqué paperback. "Cherish, I don't think you really understand what kind of book you were reading."

"I just want to know how it ends," Cherish responded in a pleading tone as she looked up at the flabbergasted Bobbie.

"No," Bobbie responded firmly, knowing she couldn't very well tell the innocent farm girl that Tammy was saved, released from prison, and then had a little orgy with some other inmates she helped prove were innocent. "Now get some sleep. We have a big game tomorrow."

PART THREE

Another month had passed and the team had fallen into third place. It hadn't escaped Bobbie's notice that Cherish's spirits seemed to drop as well. She seemed more distant and distracted at times. Bobbie had tried to get Cherish to talk to her about what was bothering her. Cherish said that she was fine, but Bobbie knew that the girl was lying. The dark circles under her eyes told her everything she needed to know - Cherish had put together what kind of story 'Babes Behind Bars' really was and she realized just why Bobbie enjoyed reading it.

Cherish was distant and moody whenever the tall brunette was around. Bobbie accepted Cherish's obvious need to distance herself from the brunette. She gave up and stopped trying to get the girl to open up. She also stopped teasing her. Bobbie missed the friendly banter and the way they'd felt comfortable around one another. Cherish's rejection wasn't a new experience for her, but it hurt just the same.

They were entering their room at the boarding house in St. Louis when Bobbie noticed the slight limp in Cherish's step. The blonde had won the last game by sliding into home plate. From the look of it the maneuver had injured her, but Cherish insisted that she was fine. Bobbie released a heavy sigh as she closed the door and threw her suitcase on her bed. "You're hurt," Bobbie accused her.

"Nope, I'm fine," Cherish lied as she limped over to her bed and began to unpack.

"Fine," Bobbie spat back bitterly and began to unpack her own belongings.

The silence loomed over them, and Cherish's efforts to conceal her pain were driving Bobbie insane. Once she finished unpacking she slipped off her shoes and pulled off her bobby socks. She watched her roommate struggle against her pain. She'd had enough of the silliness. She threw her socks onto the bed, reached over, and grasped Cherish's thigh.

The blonde cried out in pain and doubled over. Bobbie captured her in her arms and lowered her down onto the bed. "Please don't," Cherish pleaded.

Bobbie jerked away. "Right," Bobbie snapped, fighting against the tears that were threatening to escape. Her hurt and sad reaction surprised her. Normally when she encountered small-minded rejection, her reaction was that of anger not pain. Somehow having Cherish turn away from her made her heart ache. "Heaven forbid I should lay a finger on your precious body, princess," Bobbie spat out bitterly. "Don't worry. I'm not going to touch you, but you need to have that looked at," she fumed as she pointed at Cherish's thigh which she was clutching as tears began to roll down her cherubic cheeks.

"What are you talking about?" Cherish choked out as she wiped the tears away in an angry motion.

"You're hurt and I'm going to get someone you trust to look at your thigh," Bobbie instructed her as the bitterness continued to fill her words.

"I trust you," Cherish sobbed as she fought to control her breathing. "Why do you think I don't?"

"Because you pull away from me every time I'm near you," Bobbie explained as a wave of confusion rushed over her.

"Because you treat me like a child," Cherish confessed as her breathing calmed and she was able to sit up. "You know you're not that much older than I am," Cherish said, pressing her point as she held Bobbie with a steady gaze. "And I should know if I'm hurt or not; I have a degree in biology." Bobbie blinked in surprise, having been completely unaware of Cherish's academic accomplishments. The brunette set aside the information for a moment and pondered what Cherish had said about the way Bobbie treated her. Bobbie sighed with regret as Cherish's words rang true.

"You're right," Bobbie confessed as she took a step closer and knelt beside Cherish's bedside. "Will you let me look at your injury?" she asked respectfully.

"Yes," Cherish agreed as she rolled over onto her side. Bobbie felt a pang of guilt at the way she'd been treating the blonde. She could see that her over-protectiveness had grown out of control. She just couldn't help herself; there was something about Cherish that made her feel like she needed to protect her.

Bobbie climbed up onto the bed, pushing Cherish's belongings aside. "You're just so innocent about things that I keep forgetting that you're a grown woman," Bobbie confessed as she helped Cherish lift the hem of her skirt. "Now lets have a look at your . . .. Ouch!" Bobbie gasped when she discovered the large nasty-looking bruise. "That's quite a raspberry you've got there." Bobbie fought the urge to touch the large purplish mark that marred the beautiful young woman's skin. "I can't believe you have a degree in biology and didn't stop to ask someone to get you some ice."

"It hurts," Cherish confessed with a slight whimper.

"I bet it does," Bobbie agreed, feeling the heat emanating off Cherish's injury. "Why didn't you tell anyone? You know the rules. Hell, you're usually the one preaching them."

"Bobbie, your language," Cherish chastised her.

"Why didn't you say something to Coach?" Bobbie pressed.

"We have a doubleheader tomorrow and I want to play," Cherish admitted reluctantly. "I know that I should have slid the way those nice ladies from the charm school suggested, but I wouldn't have been safe if I did."

"It's okay," Bobbie reassured her. "Those gals don't know diddily about baseball. They expect us to keep our nails well manicured. How are we going to keep the grim off our fingers when we're playing our hearts out?"

"But they're right about some stuff," Cherish argued. "We're in the highest position a girl can attain in this sport."

"I know what the book says," Bobbie scoffed as she took a closer look at Cherish's injury. Her fingers glided along the soft skin as she searched to see if Cherish had pulled a muscle. "It's not only your duty to do your best to hold up the standard of this profession, but to do your level best to keep others in line," Bobbie quoted as her fingers began to enjoy the feel of Cherish's skin. "A load of horse puckey if you ask me. I'm going to get some ice and Mrs. Griswold."

"Please, Bobbie, I want to play," Cherish pleaded.

"If you do you could hurt yourself more than you already

are," Bobbie chastised her. The pouting look she received broke her heart. She forced her eyes away from Cherish's partially exposed body. "Look, I'm not treating you like a kid. I'm treating you like a player, a player that needs medical attention."

"Okay," Cherish conceded just as Bobbie spied two rumpled paperbacks mixed in with Cherish's belongings.

Bobbie quickly snatched up the paperbacks. "Bobbie?" Cherish pleaded as Bobbie held the paperbacks up and began to flip through them. "I just wanted to know what happened. I didn't mean to take your things. I don't know why I did. I've never done anything like that before," Cherish explained hurriedly.

"I can understand you wanting to finish the book. Tammy was in a very tight jam," Bobbie offered with sly grin. "But this is 'She Devil'." She stared in interest at her roommate, as she held up the book in question.

"I'm sorry," Cherish apologized. "I just liked the first one so much, I decided to read a couple more."

"You liked it?" Bobbie choked out as her mind began to spin with possibilities. "How many have you read?"

"All of them except the one you're holding," Cherish explained with a blush.

"We'll talk about this later," Bobbie informed her directly as she started to slip the paperbacks under her pillow. Her movements halted when she noticed that the second paperback still had a cover. None of hers did. She flipped the well-worn book over to find a busty female pirate restraining an equally busty wench. "Uhm . . . that one is mine," Cherish confessed in a shy voice.

"When did you . . .?" Bobbie began to ask, but then she shook her head and shoved both books under her pillow. "Never mind; we'll talk later. In the meantime we need to have you looked at. The sooner you get taken care of, the sooner you can play."

"Hey! My book," Cherish complained as Bobbie stood and made her way to the door.

"You can have it back later," Bobbie informed her briskly.

"When?" Cherish pushed.

"After I get a chance to read it," Bobbie taunted her. "'*Sea Wench*' sounds interesting," Bobbie added with a playful wink before leaving her grumbling roommate.

PART FOUR

Bobbie was dressed in her nightgown, avidly digesting the adventures of the pirate maiden and her unsuspecting wench. Cherish lay face down on her bed with a large bag of ice resting on her thigh. The small blonde was glaring at her. "What?" Bobbie inquired as she returned Cherish's gaze.

"At least you could let me read '*She Devil*'," Cherish grumbled. "After all you're reading my book and I'm just lying here, bored silly, freezing my . . . leg off."

"When did you buy this?" Bobbie finally asked. The question had been nagging at her all night long.

"On my way to the tryouts the train stopped and I was in a store looking for something to read when I noticed the cover," Cherish confessed in a quiet voice as she turned away from Bobbie's prying gaze. "I thought a story about a lady pirate would be interesting. I don't know why I kept reading it once I discovered why the man behind the counter gave me a nasty look when he sold it to me."

"You read it because you liked it," Bobbie said, finally understanding. "Just the same way you liked reading my books."

"Why were you so mad at me earlier?" Cherish inquired as she turned back to Bobbie.

"I thought you'd been avoiding me after you figured out why I read the kind of books I do," Bobbie explained apologetically.

"Oh no," Cherish blurted out quickly. "I've been confused about a lot of things. Being near you seems to add to that confusion. Plus I felt really guilty about stealing your books. I'd put them back when I was done. But I've never done anything so sneaky before. I couldn't help myself. But I was beginning to really resent you for treating me like a child."

"Sorry about that," Bobbie winced. "If I had known I would have gladly loaned you the books."

Bobbie reached under her pillow, reached across the distance, and handed Cherish her well-worn copy of 'She Devil'. "Thank you," Cherish said with a bright smile as she accepted the paperback. "Bobbie?"

"Yup," the brunette responded gleefully, knowing that the frown on the sweet blonde's face was from her lack of good grammar.

"Why do you like reading these kind of stories?" Cherish inquired with a wide-eyed innocence.

"Oh boy," Bobbie sighed, feeling the fear rise in her chest. One look into Cherish's trusting eyes told her to take a chance. "The stories are lacking, I know. But I like the way the women touch each other." She watched as Cherish contemplated what she had just admitted. "Why do you like them?"

"I don't really know," Cherish responded in a distant tone.

"That's okay," Bobbie reassured her as she put the paperback she was reading back under her pillow. Then she got up and checked Cherish's ice bag. "That should do it for tonight," she explained as she removed the soggy bag. "Good thing about being cleared to play tomorrow."

"Second string," Cherish grumbled. "I probably won't get off the bench. I really wanted a chance to play against Racine."

"You'll get your chance," Bobbie reassured her. "Don't forget to hide that," Bobbie instructed her as she tapped lightly on the book. "It could mean a lot of trouble if we get caught," Bobbie warned her before crossing back over the short distance that separated their beds.

"Let's try and get some shuteye," Bobbie suggested as she climbed into her own bed and pulled up her blankets. "We've got church in the morning and then two games."

"Good night, Bobbie," Cherish offered with a soft sigh.

"Good night, Cherish," Bobbie bit back the smirk she always felt each time she said the small blonde's name. *'What were your parents thinking?'* She wondered.

Bobbie left the nightstand light lit so the two of them could continue reading. Bobbie was losing herself in the story of the pirate maiden who enjoyed teaching her feisty wench. The brunette could feel her body beginning to pulsate. She took a cleansing breath as she fought against the constant throbbing of her clit. Normally she would be able to shut off her desire until she had the opportunity to satisfy her needs one way or another. Since Cherish had entered her life Bobbie found it impossible to find the release her body craved more and more.

Her eyes wandered over to Cherish who was lying on her stomach. Propped up on her pillow, the blonde seemed to be completely captivated by the book she was reading. Bobbie watched as her soft pink tongue darted out to lick her lips. Bobbie chewed on her bottom lip in an effort to suppress the moan that was threatening to escape. In the dimly lit room she could see the gentle rise and fall of Cherish's chest, as her breathing grew heavier. The way the light gently highlighted her golden hair was causing Bobbie's stomach to clench. The brunette bolted out of bed and headed towards the door.

"Are you all right?" Cherish asked in concern as she turned to brunette.

"Yeah," Bobbie lied as she lost herself in the emerald gaze. "I forgot to apply my face and hand lotion," she added to enhance the fib. It was true that she hadn't followed the instructed nightly ritual. Of course she never did. She was twenty-three and completely competent when it came to washing her own face. She just wanted to get away from the tempting view of Cherish's well-toned body lying across from her. Bobbie prayed that the communal bathroom would be empty and everyone else in bed so she could do a little self-exploration to steady her nerves.

"Okay," Cherish responded with a hint of disbelief.

Bobbie dashed out of the room, not really caring if Cherish believed her or not. She was not about to look at that angelic face and tell her that she wanted to be alone so she could play with herself. It just wasn't something you discussed with another person, unless they were offering a helping hand.

Sunday night found Bobbie more restless and agitated. Cherish was lying on her bed, devouring the paperback she'd returned to her the previous evening. Bobbie was tapping her foot nervously, waiting for the small blonde to fall asleep. For some unexplainable reason her teammates had possessed very small bladders the evening before and Bobbie hadn't had the privacy to cool the fire raging inside of her.

Now all Bobbie wanted to do was sneak out the window, knowing that Mrs. Griswold was already fast asleep, and go to the little bar two miles down the road. It would be a long walk but Bobbie felt confident that she could sneak away to find a little companionship for the evening.

The Lady Slipper was set back off the main road and looked like the rundown shack it was. If you didn't know that the dank little bar was there, you would pass it by without a second glance. Of course that was the point. It wasn't as if they could hang a big sign out front announcing that there was a lesbian bar hidden away in the proper little community. Now all she needed to set her plan in motion was for Cherish to go to sleep.

Finally Cherish finished the book with a heavy sigh. "Here," the blonde said as she handed Bobbie the paperback. Then she got up, gathered her toiletries, and shuffled off to the bathroom. Bobbie knew that Cherish followed the ritual set up in the charm manual and it would take her a good half hour to come back to bed. First she would use the cleansing cream, mild astringent, hand lotion, skin lotion which should be applied twice, etc, etc, etc. There were even instructions on how to clean up after a game so you would be presentable to the fans. Drying yourself carefully after your shower so you don't chafe your skin. It drove Bobbie nuts. Another thing that made her angry was when some girls weren't chosen because they appeared to be too masculine. It didn't matter if they were straight or not; they all had to look like girls.

Once Cherish returned she climbed into her bed and rested her hands behind her head. "I heard someone talking about the attendance numbers. They're still dropping," Cherish said in quiet concern.

"I know," Bobbie grumbled, knowing that the handwriting was on the wall. Unless something dramatic happened, the league was in trouble. She was tired of the constant moving of the mound and baselines. First they moved them closer so they would hit more home runs. Then they moved them back to where they should be and the women proved themselves to be just as good as the men. None of it seemed to matter. When she stopped to think about these things, she wished she'd stayed in school so she would be more qualified to do more than be an office clerk during the off season.

"Do you think they'll dissolve the league?" Cherish asked in a troubled voice.

"I don't know," Bobbie admitted honestly. "Well, at least you finished college," Bobbie noted. "Why biology?"

"I want to go to medical school," Cherish confessed. "But when I got the chance to play I just knew I had to try. School will still be there when I can't play anymore. I tell you, Daddy about bust a gut when I told him about the scout. He was so proud."

"Sounds like a good man," Bobbie responded gently, feeling a slight pang of jealousy.

"He is," Cherish confirmed with a shy smile.

"Speaking of playing, we sure could have used you today," Bobbie groaned. "We barely squeaked by in the first game and they wiped the field with us in the second. I hope you're feeling better this week when we play the Daisies and the Chicks."

"How do they come up with these names?" Cherish laughed. "I was so happy that I didn't end up playing for the Grand Rapids Chicks. That's what the wild boys in high school called the girls. Why haven't you dressed for bed yet?"

"Not tired and we don't have a game tomorrow," Bobbie blurted out quickly. She had no intention of telling Cherish that she was planning on sneaking out and looking for a nice friendly chick. Cherish gave her a curious look. Little by little Bobbie could see the cracks forming in the blonde's innocent nature. If the brunette had snuck off in the first month they roomed together, she doubted that Cherish would have noticed; she surely would have believed whatever lame excuse Bobbie handed her. Now she was not so certain. "What?" Bobbie blurted out defensively.

"Nothing. You just have the same look on your face that you have when you're sneaking a look at those naughty books you read," Cherish said knowingly.

"You read them too," Bobbie accused as Cherish blushed. "Speaking of which, we need to get rid of them."

"Why?" Cherish blinked in surprise.

"Well, for starters we've read all of them," Bobbie explained in an amused tone. "So it's time to get some more and we can't have them just lying around. You know the rules - no drinking, no smoking, no unladylike behavior, and no contaminating other players. Those books could be considered doing that."

"I don't understand," Cherish responded quizzically.

"I know," Bobbie said. She released a frustrated sigh as she glanced at her watch, wondering if she would be able to make it to Lady Slipper at all that evening.

"What exactly is contaminating other players?" Cherish questioned her in a firm direct tone.

Bobbie braced herself. She had feared the moment when Cherish would start asking these types of questions. She was at a complete loss as to just how much she should reveal to the girl. "Bobbie?" Cherish pressed in a very determined tone.

"Okay," Bobbie blew out. "Well, you must know that what you've been reading is not acceptable."

"Yes," Cherish agreed with a scowl. "I'm not a child."

"I know," Bobbie conceded while she reminded herself that Cherish was an adult. "People might think that by reading those types of books it might mean that you are . . . ," Bobbie began to stammer, " . . . that you might want to do what the women in the books are doing."

"I understand," Cherish reassured her. "Have you?"

"What?" Bobbie stammered as her eyes widened.

"Have you done any of those things?" Cherish asked in a hushed yet excited tone.

Bobbie's jaw dropped as her crystal blue eyes bugged out. *'Now what are you going to say, Cahill?'* Her mind screamed as she continued to gape at Cherish. The blonde rose off her own bed and sat next to Bobbie.

"Have I upset you?" Cherish inquired in concern.

"No," Bobbie squeaked out before she finally clamped her

mouth shut.

"No, I haven't upset you, or no, you haven't done some of those things?" Cherish inquired with renewed interest.

Bobbie turned away, unable to look at the blonde who was now sitting dangerously close to her. Cherish rested her hand on Bobbie's arm. "No, you haven't upset me," Bobbie explained in a quiet painful voice. "I need to get cleaned up for bed," Bobbie added in a strained voice as she stared out the window. Cherish gave her arm a gentle squeeze. Bobbie decided to let the conversation go and allow Cherish to come to her own conclusions.

PART FIVE

Bobbie and the rest of the team paced in the locker room while Mrs. Griswold and Coach Williams argued just outside of the door. Since coaches weren't allowed in the locker room the team would have to wait until they finished to find out whether there would be a practice that day. It was raining and Mrs. Griswold felt that it wouldn't be in the players' best interest or good health to practice. The coach felt they could be doing better and wanted them to practice despite the nasty weather.

Mrs. Griswold was more than a chaperone. She was their confidant, nursemaid, advisor, and parent plus she took care of their equipment. All in all Mrs. Griswold was underpaid and under-appreciated. "What do you think?" Brenda, the pitcher, asked the pacing Bobbie.

"I think Grizzie will get her way," Bobbie noted with a slight chuckle. "Between the weather and the way we played yesterday, she knows we need a break," Bobbie explained as she began to wonder when it was that she started caring so much about other people. Her eyes drifted to the demure blonde who was chatting away with Shelia, another outfielder. Bobbie couldn't help but smile at the way Cherish was so animated. *'Oh yeah, that's when I started to give a damn about other people,'* she noted to herself.

"I think she just wants to take the day off and catch that new Doris Day movie that's playing down at the Bijou," Penny, the shortstop, interjected in a joking manner.

"Maybe," Bobbie noted thoughtfully.

"Yeah, but it's not like she really gets a day off. She still has to baby sit us," Sally added. "Besides I want to see that movie, too."

"Me too," Mary, the first base player and relief pitcher, chimed in.

Bobbie looked over at Cherish who was casting a shy pleading look up at her from her position on the wooden bench that ran the length of their lockers. "Can we?" Cherish pleaded endearingly. Bobbie smiled brightly. She was about to tell the blonde that they could go when she heard a disgusted snort from the other side of the locker room.

"What are you asking her for?" Betty, the second base player, growled. "Can't you even go to the movies without asking for Bobbie's permission?"

The locker room was stunned into silence at Betty's rude comment. Bobbie's anger built and she was well aware that everyone was looking at her to see how she was going to react. "I was asking Bobbie because we're friends and enjoy spending together," Cherish explained with sincerity. Bobbie smiled at the blonde's confident look. Her response was sweet enough but Bobbie recognized the fire in her eyes. She had seen it when Cherish accused her of treating her like a child and she had seen it when an umpire made a bad call against her.

Everyone's focus turned from Bobbie, who was smiling proudly at Cherish, to Betty; she was stunned by the blonde's response. Betty seemed slightly flustered by Cherish's reaction. "So, Bobbie, can little Cherish come out and play?" Betty asked in a mocking tone.

"Betty, what crawled up your ass and died?" Bobbie asked in a slow direct tone as her eyes bored into the platinum blonde second basewoman.

"Language, Bobbie," Cherish chastised her while she wagged her finger at her.

Bobbie smiled slightly at Cherish who was flashing her an appreciative glance.   Bobbie's smile faded as she spied Betty heading towards Cherish.   The blonde stood over Cherish with her hands on her hips and glared down at Cherish. "What's the matter, little girl?   Does hearing adults talking fucking upset you?" Betty challenged the smaller woman.

"Hey," Sally protested as Betty's harsh language took some other players aback.

"That's it," Bobbie flared.   She didn't know what Betty's problem was but she wasn't about to let her take it out on Cherish.

Bobbie started to move towards Betty so she could teach her some manners when Brenda and Cherish jumped up.   Brenda placed her hand on Bobbie's chest. "Don't," the pitcher cautioned her. "You'll be giving her what she wants."

"Betty," Cherish began in a slow careful tone as she stood toe to toe with the larger woman, "I simply find the use of profanity unattractive."

"Listen, you cornbread little . . . ," Betty growled as Cherish stood her ground.

Bobbie tried to move but Mary and Sally jumped up to help Brenda restrain her. "Back off, Betty," Shelia said as she jumped up to defend Cherish who hadn't so much as flinched. Betty lifted her hand to take a swing at Cherish when Penny halted her movement.

"She said back off," the shortstop warned her.

Both Bobbie and Betty were struggling with their teammates to reach their objective as Cherish continued to stand her ground. "Ladies!" Mrs. Griswold's stern voice called out, alerting them to her presence. "Is there a problem?" Mrs. Griswold demanded. Everyone instantly turned their attention to their chaperone. Despite being released from their teammates' grasps, Bobbie knew that it didn't look good for any of them.

"Actually we were just wondering whether or not we would be practicing today?" Cherish explained as she stepped towards Mrs. Griswold.   "Because if we aren't we want to chip in and take you to see the new movie at the Bijou." Mrs. Griswold gave the blonde an incredulous look.   "We wanted to make up for someone gluing your shoes to the floor the other day." Everyone, including Mrs. Griswold, turned towards Penny who was looking around, trying to look innocent.

"Well, then I guess we're going to the movies," Mrs. Griswold accepted graciously yet the stern look on her face informed each of them she wasn't buying the story. "Get changed, girls, and get onto the bus," she instructed them. "And hurry. I do so love Doris Day," she added with a bright smile before leaving the locker room.

"She made Grizzie smile," Bobbie gasped in amazement.

"Tell us what else she can do," Betty snarled from across the locker room.

"That's it. Your head is going in the toilet," Bobbie bellowed as Cherish jumped in her way.

"Don't," Cherish pleaded with her as Brenda and Sally held her back. "Please?" Cherish added softly as she looked up at Bobbie. One look into those amazing emerald eyes and Bobbie could refuse her nothing. Bobbie simply nodded in agreement as she felt Cherish's hands come to rest on her hips.

"I believe I told you ladies to hurry," Mrs. Griswold instructed them as she stuck her head inside the locker room door.

The team quickly changed in silence; the tension looming over them as they rode back to the boarding house. The same mood clung to them as they went to their rooms to get ready for the movie. Bobbie's stomach was tied up in knots. She was proud of the way Cherish handled herself and the situation, yet she still possessed an overwhelming desire to beat the snot out of Betty.

She was tossing things from the top of her dresser into her purse, keeping her back to Cherish. The hair on the back of her neck prickled. She knew without looking that Cherish was standing directly behind her. She felt a gentle hand caress her back. Her eyes fluttered shut from the touch. "Let it go," Cherish whispered against her back as her hands made soothing circles.

Bobbie released a heavy sigh as her shoulders slumped. She turned to Cherish who was looking up at her warmly. "I just don't understand it," Bobbie said as she tried to find some reason for Betty's harsh treatment of Cherish. Bobbie's body trembled slightly as the blonde's hands once again came to rest on her hips.

"Don't you?" Cherish asked as she slightly closed the gap between their bodies by wrapping her arms around Bobbie's waist.

Bobbie was becoming lost in the feel of Cherish's body pressing against her own. "No, I don't," she responded. Her voice trembled slightly and her mind was confused by Cherish's actions. The blonde had always been affectionate with her and others but nothing quite like this had happened before.

Cherish rested her head on Bobbie's chest. "Bobbie, she plays second base and she's in a slump," Cherish offered as Bobbie felt herself pulling the petite blonde closer to her.

Cherish's words rang true. Betty was finding it hard to hit her mark and when Cherish played second base she was on top of everything. Betty was afraid that Cherish was going to take her spot. "I get it," Bobbie agreed as she nuzzled Cherish's hair. When the tall brunette realized that she was standing there drinking in the scent of her roommate's hair she started to pull away. Bobbie's retreat was halted as Cherish tightened the hug she held her in.

At that moment Bobbie was confused beyond belief and she couldn't have cared less. She simply allowed herself to enjoy the feel of Cherish's body pressing against her. Bobbie's heart was racing as they stood there clinging to one another. She felt Cherish's hands wandering up and down her back, slipping lower and lower with each pass. Bobbie's hands were now caressing the smaller woman's shoulders. Bobbie was helpless against the fire that was burning inside her as she felt Cherish's breath through the material of her blouse. The brunette lifted her head and gazed down. Her eyes closed slightly as she found a pair of emerald eyes smiling back at her. Her gaze drifted down to Cherish's pink lips as her lips moved closer.

She could feel Cherish's body swaying against her own as the blonde lifted herself closer until their lips were a mere breathe a part. A loud knock on the door disrupted the moment and

Bobbie jerked her head back as Penny shouted for them to *'Hurry up already!'* Bobbie groaned as she moved to release her tender hold on the smaller woman. Cherish's hands held onto her waist and Bobbie felt a sudden jolt of panic. When she looked down at the blonde the panic was replaced by desire.

Without a word Cherish reached up and cupped Bobbie's cheek in the palm of her hand. The tall brunette leaned into the touch as Cherish reached up and brushed Bobbie's lips lightly with her own. It was a sweet, innocent, and chaste kiss that made Bobbie's toes curl.

Later Bobbie was sitting in the dark movie theatre with her teammates and Mrs. Griswold enjoying Doris Day romping around as Calamity Jane. The only ones who didn't attend were Anne, the right fielder who was Betty's roommate, Shelia, who was expecting a call from her husband, and thankfully Betty. Despite Bobbie's new understanding that Betty was simply afraid that she'd lose her spot on the team, the brunette felt rather certain that she was going lose control and shove the irritating woman head first into the nearest toilet bowl.

The team filled the row of seats and Cherish had ensured that she and Bobbie were seated at the very end against the wall. At first the brunette didn't understand why Cherish had chosen to sit next to the wall, but then she felt a shy hand creeping along her hand in the darkness. As their fingers danced together in the darkness, Bobbie snuck glances at Brenda who was seated to her right; she wanted to make sure that the redhead wasn't watching them.

Bobbie was forced to stifle a moan on more than one occasion, as both women's caresses grew bolder. Bobbie licked her lips and fought to steady her breathing as Cherish's fingertips slowly slid up her arm. The brunette's fingers began to drift lower until they were trailing up and down Cherish's firm thigh. As she felt the soft material of Cherish's skirt in the darkness she could also feel the blonde's thighs parting slightly.

Bobbie crossed her long legs in a futile effort to stop her clit from throbbing as her fingers dipped below the hem of Cherish's skirt. She stole a shy glance over to the blonde who was slowly driving her insane. Despite the fact that her emerald eyes were riveted to the movie screen, the way the blonde was sucking on her lower lip informed the brunette that she was just as flustered as she was.

It took every ounce of strength Bobbie possessed not to simply reach over and wrapped Cherish up in a long lingering kiss while her hand slipped further up her skirt. As her mind pictured the passionate embrace her fingers acted out her fantasy as they moved up along the inside of Cherish's quivering thigh.

A hard swat to her right shoulder startled her. Bobbie's hand quickly retreated and came to rest in her own lap as Cherish released a tiny whimper. Bobbie turned to find Brenda smirking at her. Bobbie rolled her eyes and folded her hands together. As she clenched her hands together in order to prevent them from roaming once again, she heard Brenda chuckling softly. She had long ago suspected that Brenda was a team player in more ways than one. Her overly amused manner regarding Bobbie's frustrated state confirmed her suspicions.

Bobbie's knuckles were white and sore by the end of the movie. No surprise since she'd kept them clamped together for the last twenty minutes of the film. Cherish's hand came to rest on her forearm and the soft caresses continued until the lights came up. The end of the movie could not have come a moment too soon for the frustrated brunette.

As the team stepped into the lobby they animatedly discussed the movie. Bobbie couldn't have cared less that Doris finally won the guy; at that point she had lost all interest in the movie. Bobbie simply wanted to get back cross-town to the boarding house so she could be alone with Cherish. Fate, or whatever powers that be that enjoyed messing with her, had other ideas. Suddenly everyone wanted to go out to dinner at the small restaurant across the street from the theatre.

Bobbie sat between Brenda and Cherish as she picked at her dinner. "Not hungry?" Cherish inquired in concern.

"I'm fine," Bobbie lied, still trying to calm her overheated body. "I'm just a little distracted."

"Okay," Cherish said, accepting her explanation as Bobbie continued to play with her food.

When she felt a hand caressing her thigh, she squeaked and dropped her fork. Everyone except Cherish looked at her, startled by her sudden outburst. "Sorry," she blurted out quickly before turning an angry glare at the smirking blonde beside her. Thankfully Cherish's hand had slipped back up onto the table.

"Bobbie is still upset about what happened in the locker room," Cherish explained.

Bobbie watched in amazement, as everyone seemed to accept Cherish's flimsy explanation. "You okay, tiger?" Brenda whispered in her ear. Bobbie simply blushed and rubbed her forehead. "Cherish, are you picking on Bobbie?" Brenda teased softly as she leaned behind Bobbie so no one could hear the conversation.

"Just a little," Cherish confessed in soft gleeful tone.

"Does anyone want to tell me what really happened in the locker room this morning?" Mrs. Griswold questioned them. The response was a resounding 'no'. Mrs. Griswold nodded in understanding, accepting that they wanted to protect their teammate.

"Speaking of the locker room, Brenda," she said in a hushed tone as the others discussed other subjects, "what did you mean when you said that I would be giving Betty what she wanted if I went after her?"

"Just that since she can't seem to get to Cherish directly, she'll go through you," Brenda explained, maintaining her soft tone so the others wouldn't hear them. "She's scared, and every time Cherish starts at second the more frightened she gets."

"Yeah, but there isn't anything going on," Bobbie asserted.

"Then what the hell were the two of you doing tonight?" Brenda asked.

"Language," Cherish corrected the redhead.

"She doesn't miss a thing, does she?" Brenda laughed.

"I'm beginning to learn that," Bobbie agreed with a smile of her own.

Cherish scooted her chair a little closer as the three of them fell into a conversation about the upcoming games. Even with everything else going on they were still ballplayers. The game meant almost everything to them. "Oh, I forgot to tell you. My Daddy is coming to Ft. Wayne to watch us play against the Daisies," Cherish explained cheerfully.

Bobbie noticed that everyone's attention shifted to the energetic little blonde. News of family or friends visiting always excited everyone since they were all so far away from home. "I really want you to meet him," Cherish added hopefully. Bobbie didn't miss the knowing looks her teammates exchanged. The brunette realized that her feelings for Cherish were not the well-guarded secret she had hoped they were.

"I'd love to meet him," Bobbie responded happily. She was pleased by the looks of approval she was receiving from the others. Yet she wasn't fool enough to think that they could ever be open about their true feelings. And of course she hadn't a clue as to what Cherish's exact feelings for her were. "You never mention your mother. Why is that?"

"She's gone," Cherish responded sadly.

"Way to go, Cahill," Penny grunted at her.

"I'm sorry," Bobbie offered sincerely.

"I was about nine when she left Daddy for some clown," Cherish explained thoughtfully.

"Oh?" Bobbie blinked in confusion, having assumed when Cherish said her mother was gone that the woman had died.

"The really sad part was I really loved the circus. Now it just isn't the same," Cherish explained sadly as everyone choked, stared, or spat out their beverages. "What?"

Bobbie shook her head once again, amazed at how this tiny woman could send her into a complete tailspin. As everyone blankly stared at Cherish, the brunette was putting the pieces of what she had actually said in order. "We're sorry, Cherish. It's just that when you called him a clown I think everyone assumed it was a character description, not his profession."

"Oh," Cherish nodded in understanding before casting a wry glance at Bobbie. The brunette looked at her curiously. "It's true," Cherish assured her. "Bebop the clown; he travels with

Ringling Brothers. I can show you the postcards Mama's sent me from all over the world."

"Sorry," Bobbie apologized mirthfully. "It's just that sometimes I wonder if you're the sweet innocent angel you appear to be or some mischievous imp."

"Maybe I'm both," Cherish responded softly as she wiggled her fair eyebrows. "Eat your dinner, Miss Cahill. You have a game tomorrow."

Much to her teammate's enjoyment Bobbie had no choice but to comply with Cherish's wishes. Mrs. Griswold seemed particularly pleased at the way Bobbie cleaned her plate under Cherish's watchful eye.

PART SIX

They returned to their room at the boarding house. Bobbie was filled with desire and a whole lot of questions. The room was filled with electricity as they removed and hung up their coats. Then they set about removing their flats and stockings. Bobbie kept catching curious green eyes peeking over at her as she slowly rolled each stocking down her long legs. Of course her crystal blue gaze was constantly drifting to the blonde who was mirroring her actions.

Bobbie balled her stockings up, knowing that she should rinse them out. But doing laundry was not her top priority that evening. Cherish removed the belt from her skirt and lay down on her bed, resting on her elbow as she cast a very interesting gaze over at the brunette. "Cherish?" She began slowly as her eyes drifted up and down the blonde's body. "I'm sorry. Do you have a nickname?" She finally asked.

"No," Cherish asserted in a playful manner. "Why does my name amuse you so much, Roberta?"

"Don't go there," Bobbie cautioned her as she watched the blonde remove the ribbon that held her long blonde hair in a braid. Bobbie sighed as she watched Cherish shake her long golden locks free. "Do you have a middle name?"

"I'm not going to tell you," Cherish taunted her as Bobbie rose from her bed, crossed the short distance between them, and sat down on the edge of the blonde's small bed. She leaned over the smaller woman. "Do you know what you do to me?" Bobbie asked in a sultry tone.

"Do I make your stomach feel funny?" Cherish inquired in a breathy voice. "The way mine did the first time I saw you?"

"Yes," Bobbie confessed as she leaned slightly closer to the smaller woman. She could feel the heat radiating off Cherish's body the closer she got. "Do you like that feeling?" Bobbie asked with a slight hint of fear.

"Yes," Cherish confessed, her warm breath caressing Bobbie's face as she spoke.

"Have you kissed a girl before?"

"Yes," Cherish admitted.

Bobbie pulled back slightly, surprised by the blonde's admission. "With my best friend growing up. Alma Sue and I use to practice kissing so we would know what to do with boys," Cherish explained with a shy blush.

"Alma Sue? What is it with you folks in Kansas?" Bobbie teased as she fought against the twinge of jealousy she felt, knowing that another woman had pressed her lips against Cherish's. "Did you like kissing Alma Sue?" Bobbie asked her gently.

"Yes, and she let me touch her," Cherish explained as she began to run her fingers through Bobbie's long dark hair.

Once again Bobbie was surprised and jealous. "Where?" She asked softy as she leaned closer and brushed her lips across Cherish's cheek. She could feel the blonde's breath becoming labored. She kissed her chin. "Cherish?" She whispered as she began to kiss the corner of the blonde's mouth. She leaned back and stared down at the woman who was gradually stealing her heart. The shy look she received told her that Cherish was unable to say where she had touched the other girl. "You can show me if you want," Bobbie suggested hopefully.

Cherish blushed and smiled as her small hand reached up and cupped one of Bobbie's breasts. Cherish's eyes darkened with desire as her smile grew. She gently began to knead

Bobbie's firm full breast. Bobbie's nipple hardened in response as her back arched, pressing more of her bosom into Cherish's tiny hand. "Feels nice," Cherish said in a voice just above a whisper as her hand and fingers grew bolder.

Bobbie lowered her body slightly, brushing Cherish's as she kept her full weight off the smaller woman. She felt their breath mingling and caressing as Cherish drew her closer. As their lips met, brushing shyly, Bobbie had no idea where this moment would lead them; all she was aware of was her need to hold and touch Cherish.

Cherish began to tease her nipple through the soft material of her blouse while her other hand drifted down Bobbie's shoulders to her back. The brunette's lips were tingling from the shy kiss. She quickly reclaimed Cherish's soft lips in an effort to sate her need for more. Bobbie fought with her desires so she would take things slowly and savor whatever Cherish was willing to offer.

The kisses grew more insistent along with Cherish's touch. Bobbie suckled Cherish's lower lip in her mouth as the blonde teased her nipple. She could feel Cherish squirming beneath her as she deepened the kiss and parted her lips with her tongue. Bobbie dipped her tongue into the warmth of the blonde's mouth and began a gentle exploration. As Cherish's tongue danced with her own, she ran her hand down along the blonde's firm body.

Her hand began to caress the blonde's thigh until Cherish yelped and pulled away. Bobbie lifted her body and looked down in concern. "Sorry," Cherish panted. Bobbie was worried that they had taken things too far when she felt Cherish's hands return to her back. "My bruise," the blonde explained as she reached up and caressed Bobbie's cheek. The brunette leaned into the touch.

"Are you comfortable with what we're doing?" Bobbie asked with a mixture of concern and hope.

"Yes," Cherish replied with a promising smile. "When Alma Sue and I did this she wouldn't let me touch her for very long and the kiss wasn't anything like what you did."

"Did she ever touch you in return?" Bobbie asked as began to caress Cherish's hip, mindful of her injury.

"No," Cherish grumbled.

"I take you asked." Bobbie chuckled.

"Many times," Cherish confessed with a heavy sigh. "Then she didn't want to do it anymore," Cherish continued as her eyes drifted to Bobbie's cleavage, her nimble fingers following her eyes. "Bobbie, I've never . . . ," Cherish began to explain shyly as her fingers began to caress the buttons of Bobbie's blouse.

"I know," Bobbie said. "Cherish, we can do anything you want to. And nothing you don't."

"I feel so many things for you, Bobbie," Cherish confessed softly.

"I feel the same," Bobbie reassured her as she prayed that Cherish's feeling ran as deep as her own. "You can unbutton them if you want."

Cherish's eyes met Bobbie's and her face lit up like a kid on Christmas morning. Cherish began to unbutton each tiny button, her eyes focused intently on the task. Bobbie reclined on her side and began to unbutton Cherish's blouse. When the blonde tugged Bobbie's blouse out of her skirt, Bobbie lifted her body and allowed Cherish to remove it. Cherish moaned as she cupped both of the brunette's breasts in her hands.

Bobbie leaned into the touch as she continued to undo the buttons on Cherish's blouse. Cherish's hands continued to roam across her bra as Bobbie began to remove the blonde's blouse. Cherish seemed reluctant to remove her hands from Bobbie's breasts until the brunette tugged on the blouse. Bobbie removed the garment and dropped it off the side of the bed.

They lay side by side and began to slowly caress each other's body. They moved closer and closer as they ran their fingers along bare skin. Cherish's focus once again returned to Bobbie's breasts. They began to exchange tender kisses until Cherish parted Bobbie's lips.

Bobbie pulled her lover closer as the kiss deepened. She could feel Cherish's touch becoming frustrated as the kiss became more passionate. Sensing her lover's need, Bobbie reached behind her and unclasped her bra. Cherish moaned deeply into Bobbie's mouth as she began to lower the garment down Bobbie's shoulders. Cherish's fingers fumbled as she slid her hand between their bodies and tried to feel Bobbie's exposed breast.

Bobbie ended the kiss and stared dreamily into Cherish's eyes as her fingers caressed the smaller woman's back and released the clasp of her bra. They quickly disposed and cast aside their bras. "Sweet Jesus, you are so beautiful," Cherish gushed in amazement as her fingers began to trace the swell of Bobbie's breasts.

Bobbie fought to control her breathing as Cherish's hands began to tease her erect nipples. While Cherish continued to drive her insane by rolling her nipples between her fingers and brushing her calloused hands across them, Bobbie caressed her hip and allowed her hand to drift down to the blonde's firm backside.

She caressed the smaller woman whose body was melting into her own as she lowered the zipper of Cherish's skirt. She rolled Cherish onto her back as she began to lower her skirt down her body. She lifted her lover so she could remove the garment. After she cast it aside Cherish pulled her down for a lingering kiss.

Bobbie cupped Cherish's breast and began to fondle it as her mouth wandered to her neck. Bobbie's thighs trembled as Cherish's nipples responded to her touch. She began to nibble on Cherish's earlobe as the blonde's hands roamed up and down her back. Cherish's body arched as Bobbie suckled her earlobe and dipped her tongue into her ear. "I've never felt like this," Cherish panted as she wrapped her legs around Bobbie's waist.

Bobbie's kisses drifted lower to Cherish's shoulders as her lover pressed against her. She could feel Cherish's excitement painting her skin as she traced her nipple with her tongue. Bobbie brushed away the fleeting thought of stopping before things went too far when Cherish's hips began to thrust against her body. She captured the blonde's nipple in her mouth and began to suckle it eagerly.

She could hear Cherish panting her name as her hips thrust harder against her body and Bobbie teased her nipple with her teeth and her tongue. Cherish whimpered as Bobbie released the sweet bud from her mouth. Then the blonde groaned in ecstasy when Bobbie began to suckle its twin in the same fashion.

Bobbie's thighs quivered as she felt her own desire dampening her panties.

Bobbie was gasping when she finally released Cherish's breast from her mouth. She kissed and tasted the valley between Cherish's breasts as the blonde continued to grind her body against her. Bobbie lifted herself up with her arms, seeking to catch her breath and slow things down. Her reprieve was short lived when Cherish lifted her own body and pulled her back down onto the tiny bed. Before she could protest Cherish's tongue was flickering across her aching nipples.

Her body arched up off the bed as Cherish suckled one of her nipples in her mouth while she caressed the other. Bobbie ran her fingers through Cherish's soft golden locks as her lover feasted upon her breasts. Bobbie's body was straining against her lover's touch. Cherish moved from teasing and tasting one nipple to the other and then back again. Bobbie began to whimper as Cherish's mouth moved down her body. "Cherish," the brunette managed to choke out.

Cherish raised her body slightly and began to lower Bobbie's skirt. "I've wanted to touch you for so long," Cherish whispered. "When you were touching me during the movie tonight, I thought I would burst into flames." Bobbie lifted her body and allowed Cherish to remove her skirt. "I know you probably think it's silly," Cherish continued softly as she began to kiss her way up Bobbie's body. "A couple of naughty books and touching, letting you touch me at the Bijou, but I've dreamt about you holding me, touching me, loving me."

"I've had the same dreams," Bobbie confessed as she pulled Cherish up into her arms and reclaimed her lips. Their nipples brushed as their bodies melted together. As their tongues once again greeted one another, Bobbie parted Cherish's thighs with her own. She pressed her firm thigh against the blonde's center as she cupped her backside.

Bobbie raised her knee so that her lover was straddling it while she guided her closer. Cherish's thigh was now pressing against Bobbie's wet center and their hips began to sway in rhythm. While her mind pleaded with her to stop, she massaged her lover's ass and encouraged her to thrust harder against her.

She could feel Cherish's wetness on her skin as they bucked furiously against each other.

"Bobbie," Cherish panted hotly in her ear as her hips began to thrust with urgency against the brunette's body.

"Cherish," Bobbie moaned in response as her body arched and ground in rhythm with the blonde's. Cherish's body arched up and her head fell back. Bobbie quickly raised her own body and captured Cherish in a passionate kiss. They screamed in ecstasy into each other's mouth as their bodies exploded against one another.

As she felt Cherish collapsing against her, Bobbie cradled her in her arms and lowered her back down onto the bed. Cherish peppered her face with soft kisses. "That was incredible," the blonde choked out.

"You are incredible," Bobbie responded as she caressed her body.

"Bobbie, is it normal to want more even after something so amazing?" Cherish asked as her hands began to roam along the curves of Bobbie's body.

"Yes," Bobbie moaned as she felt herself melting into the blonde's touch. "But we should stop," Bobbie uttered reluctantly.

"Why?" Cherish asked in confused frustration.

"Because right now you can walk away still innocent," Bobbie said, trying to reason with her.

"I don't want to walk away," Cherish reassured her firmly. "Do you?"

Bobbie stared down into Cherish's passion-filled eyes and found her answer. "No," Bobbie admitted as she ran her fingers along Cherish's cherubic face. Bobbie brushed away her fears and doubts as she lowered her body and began to kiss her way down Cherish's body. She savored each moment as she felt her lover's passion caressing her body. She playfully dipped her tongue in and out of Cherish's navel causing the blonde to giggle. Then she ran her tongue along the waistband of her panties as she caressed her thighs.

Bobbie took her time lowering the cotton panties down her lover's body as she drank in the sight of her newly exposed flesh and listened to her whimpers of desire. Bobbie gasped when she removed Cherish's underwear and looked down upon her lover's glorious naked form. Bobbie cast aside Cherish's underwear before removing her own. She smiled as she watched Cherish's eyes drink in her body.

Bobbie knelt down on the small bed that was not designed for two people and began to kiss her way up Cherish's quivering thighs. She nestled herself between Cherish's thighs and then draped the blonde's legs over her shoulders. The musky aroma of her lover's arousal filled her senses as she began to lick the passion from the inside of the blonde's thighs.

Cherish's wetness caressed her cheek as she moved closer to the source of the blonde's passion. Bobbie blew a gentle breath across the damp blonde curls. "What are you . . .?" Cherish began to question as Bobbie dipped her tongue into her wetness. Her body arched up off the bed. Bobbie held her steady as she ran her tongue along her sex. "Is that your tongue?" Cherish asked as Bobbie began to flicker the appendage across her clit.

"Uhm hmm," Bobbie moaned before she suckled the throbbing nub in her mouth.

Bobbie teased Cherish's throbbing clit with her teeth and her tongue as Cherish clutched at the bedding. Bobbie took her lover harder, fighting against her need to be inside of her. She felt Cherish's body trembling against her skin. Bobbie's rhythm increased as she drove the blonde nearer to the edge. Cherish's body was covered in a sheen of sweat as it arched higher. Thankfully the blonde had the sense to bury her face in her pillow as she screamed out in pleasure. Bobbie was certain by the way Cherish's body was clenching her own that her cries would have woke up the entire household.

Bobbie gently lowered her lover's spent body down onto the bed, crawled up, and wrapped her long arms around the smaller woman. She held and kissed Cherish as her body continued to tremble with pleasure. "We should try and get some sleep. We have a game tomorrow," Bobbie said reluctantly once she felt Cherish's breathing even out.

Bobbie leaned down to kiss her lover goodnight. "Stay?" Cherish invited her.

"Yes," Bobbie agreed with a promising kiss. They curled up under the covers and Bobbie wrapped Cherish up in her arms.

"Bobbie?" Cherish asked, her breath caressing Bobbie's neck as she spoke.

"Yes?" Bobbie responded as her body tingled from the feel of Cherish's naked body pressed against her own.

"There was something in one of the books . . . ," Cherish said in a breathy tone as her hand drifted down between them. "It sounded really nice," Cherish continued as she began to kiss Bobbie's neck and her fingers began to tease the curls of the brunette's mound. Bobbie's thighs parted as Cherish's fingers journeyed lower. Bobbie moaned when Cherish's fingers gently explored her slick folds. Bobbie parted herself even further as she felt Cherish's fingertips gliding across her clit. She clung to her lover as Cherish's fingers teased and stroked the aching nub. Bobbie's hips thrust up off the bed as her lover entered her. Cherish's fingers moved with a shy slowness at first as her thumb teased her clit. The blonde fumbled occasionally but soon Bobbie was moaning and thrusting with pleasure as Cherish plunged in and out of her wetness. All too soon it was Bobbie's turn to bury her face in a pillow as she cried out in pleasure.

When she felt Cherish's fingers retreating, Bobbie gently clasped her wrist and kept her inside of her while the last waves of ecstasy slipped through her trembling body. As the last of the aftershocks dissipated, she released Cherish's hand. The blonde was smiling with a look of amazement. "That was nice," Bobbie said softly before placing a gentle kiss on Cherish's lips.

Cherish curled back up in her arms as Bobbie's breathing steadied. "Cherish, what are you going to do after the season is over?" Bobbie asked the woman nestled in her arms, fearing the answer.

"I don't know," Cherish answered softly. "I was planning on going home."

"Oh," Bobbie responded in disappointment.

"But now I'm waiting for a certain third base player to ask me to join her for the off season," Cherish explained as she nestled closer.

"I usually travel around and get a job somewhere," Bobbie explained with a shy smile. "Now I don't know. Where would you like to go?"

"Are you asking me to join you?" Cherish teased her.

"Cherish, will you stay with me after the season is over?" Bobbie asked as her eyes drifted shut.

"Yes," Cherish agreed.

The End

Mavis Applewater

HERE COMES THE BRIDE

PART ONE

Katie sighed deeply as she watched the group of women grow rowdier and rowdier with each passing moment. She collected their drinks from the bartender and made her way over to the screaming women who were eagerly stuffing bills in the male dancers' g-strings. "I hate bachelorette parties," the petite blonde muttered softly under her breath.

'Of course if these gals realized that most of these guys are gay and have a sock stuffed down their g-string, they probably wouldn't be in such a hurry to part with their money,' Katie thought gleefully as she placed the round of cocktails before the screeching women.

"Thank you," came the soft response from the one woman whom still seemed to possess a modicum of dignity. Katie had noticed the tall brunette sitting quietly while her friends had lost all control.

"You're welcome," Katie said as she smiled at the attractive woman.

Katie suddenly gritted her teeth as she felt a hand groping her backside. She spun around and brushed the grinning redhead's hand away. "No touching," Katie chastised the drunken woman.

"Toni!" the brunette choked in disgust.

"Lighten up, Lori," the redhead slurred. "It's about time that you started having some fun."

"I'm sorry about my friends," Lori apologized to Katie in a soft tone.

"Don't worry about it," Katie responded as she leaned closer to Lori. "A few shots of tequila and women are worse than men. No one's safe." She pulled away slightly and drank in the brunette's chiseled features and crystal blue eyes.

The blonde could feel her heart beating just a little faster as Lori returned her gaze in the smoke-filled nightclub. "So I take it you're the babysitter tonight," Katie offered in a teasing tone as Lori took a sip of her club soda. Lori simply nodded in agreement. Katie grimaced as she spied one of Lori's friends standing behind her, holding up a crisp bill, waving one of the male strippers over. "Duck," Katie cautioned her before getting out of the way of the muscle-bound blonde surfer boy. He planted a sloppy kiss on the unsuspecting Lori before she could pull away.

Steve snatched his tip away from Lori's friend before dancing away. Lori was scowling as she wiped her mouth. "I tried to warn you," Katie snickered in the brunette's ear.

"Isn't he a good kisser?" Toni chimed in as Lori continued to wipe her mouth.

"No," Lori growled as she took a healthy sip of her soda water.

"We need more shots," the redhead exclaimed. "Lori isn't having fun yet."

"I don't . . . ," Lori began to protest.

"Lori," another one of her friends chastised her, "loosen the bone, will you? Join the party."

"Okay," Lori conceded.

"Seven shots of Cuervo," one of the women instructed Katie as she dropped two twenty-dollar bills on her tray. "Keep the change," the ebony woman added with a playful wink. "First the shots and then a little something that will get Lori into the swing of things," she shouted as her friends cheered.

"I don't like the sound of this," Katie muttered as she made her way to the bar. "Now they're tipping? I have a feeling I know where this is heading. Not that I haven't done it before, and Lori is very good looking," she reasoned as she collected the round of shots and headed back towards the drunken women.

Katie's suspicions were confirmed when she spied Lori sitting in the corner ignoring her companions; the other six women were huddled in a group cackling and snickering like schoolgirls. The dark woman who had ordered the shots cut Katie off as she approached the table. "Hi," the woman began with a sly smile. "I was here a few months back with a few friends and you delivered a round with a little something special."

"Uh huh," Katie responded wryly as the woman pressed two one-hundred-dollar bills in her hand.

"Would you mind delivering Lori's shot to her personally?" The woman asked with a sly wink as Katie stuffed the money in her bra.

"Body shot and a lap dance?" Katie questioned with a smile, actually looking forward to performing for Lori. "And how will your friend react to this?"

"I'm honestly not certain. I just want her to relax and have some fun," the woman said sincerely.

"No problem," Katie agreed. "But if she objects or looks uncomfortable, the show is over."

"Understood," the woman conceded. "I'm not trying to make fun of her and I don't want to upset her."

Katie placed the tray on the table and passed the tequila around to the other six women. She took Lori's shot and some salt and limes over to Lori. The brunette smiled up at her.

"I guess I'm going to have to join in," Lori grumbled.

"You could say that," Katie teased her as she set the items down on the table beside Lori. The tall woman was reaching for the tequila when Katie's hand stopped her. "I've been asked to give you special service."

Lori gave her a quizzical look as Katie began to unbutton her blouse to her navel. Katie smiled as she watched Lori's crystal blue eyes casting a hungry gaze over her slightly exposed body. Katie hiked up her skirt slightly and straddled the stunned brunette's lap. "Ever do a body shot, Lori?" Katie inquired in a breathy tone, spoken just loud enough so the brunette could hear her over the thumping bass of the music.

Lori shook her head as Katie leaned her smaller body into the brunette's while Lori's friends cheered them on. "If you don't want to do this just say so," Katie whispered in her ear.

"Just tell me what to do," Lori choked out as her hands came to rest on Katie's waist.

Katie leaned back, her thighs tightening their hold on Lori's body while she reached over and picked up the large shot of tequila and salt. "When doing tequila it's important to remember three things. Isn't that right, ladies?"

The women cheered as they rubbed wedges of lime over the backs of their hands and then applied a light layer of salt. "The three things you need to remember are lick, shoot, and suck," Katie explained huskily as she rubbed some lime on the swell of her breast. Then she sprinkled some salt over the damp spot. Her body tingled as Lori's fingers began to caress her body. As Lori's friends continued to hoot and holler their encouragement, Katie tucked the shot glass in her cleavage. She held up a thick lime wedge as Lori stared at the shot glass nestled between her breasts.

"Are you ready?" Katie teased the blushing brunette. "First *lick* the salt," she instructed Lori as she wove her fingers through long dark hair and drew her closer to her breast. Katie squirmed in Lori's lap, enjoying the feel of the taller woman pressing against her clit. Katie bit back a moan when she felt Lori's tongue slowly lick the salt from her skin. She felt tiny drips of tequila splashing on her skin.

Katie was enjoying the feel of the seam of Lori's jeans pressing into her center as she ground against the taller woman. Katie could feel her desire growing as Lori's talented tongue licked away the last granules of salt from her breast. "Now it's time to shoot," Katie offered in a low voice as she placed her small hands on Lori's broad shoulders, raised her body up, and pressed her ample bosom into Lori's face.

She heard the brunette gasp as she shuddered against Katie. The blonde pulled back slightly and drank in the flushed features of the woman she was straddling. Lori's hands drifted away from her hips. Katie swallowed hard as the tips of Lori's fingers gently glided across the swell of her breasts. Katie stared deeply into Lori's amazingly blue eyes as the brunette reached for the shot glass tucked away in the blonde's cleavage.

"Oh no you don't," Katie chastised the surprised looking woman. "I liked your hands where they were," she explained as she watched crystal blue orbs widen in confusion.

"How am I . . .?" Lori stammered as her hands drifted along Katie's body then up under her skirt and once again cupped the blonde's firm backside.

Katie smiled wickedly as she lifted her body closer until the shot glass was resting against Lori's trembling lips. Katie ran her fingers through Lori's silky tresses. "If you don't want to, then I can stop this now," Katie explained in a low tone that only Lori could hear.

"Come on," one of Lori's friends whined.

"Let's do it," Lori said with a throaty growl that sent a shiver down Katie's spine.

The blonde nodded in agreement as she smiled down at Lori. "Shoot," she commanded as she arched her back and guided Lori to drink the golden shot from her cleavage. Lori captured the shot glass in her mouth, spilling a little of the tequila down Katie's cleavage. The blonde smiled as she felt the warm liquor trickling down her skin as Lori's head tipped back and she consumed the liquor with the glass carefully nestled between her lips.

Katie watched carefully as Lori drank a little more than half the shot. Katie carefully took the glass from her lips before she began to choke. The other women had already slammed down their shots and were sucking on the limes. "Now suck," Katie demanded as she placed a wedge of lime between her lips with the pulp side facing out.

Katie almost pulled away when she saw a brief look of panic flash in Lori's eyes. The look faded and Lori pulled her down and began to suckle the fruit that was clenched in the blonde's teeth. Katie's clit throbbed as Lori eagerly sucked on the wedge of fruit. Katie moaned, as she tasted the citrus mixed with the tequila. The others cheered loudly as Lori sucked harder.

Katie could feel Lori's tongue trying to remove the offending piece of fruit. The blonde was panting heavily as she took the fruit from her mouth and tossed it onto her tray. Lori leaned in and began to lick the last remaining pulp from Katie's quivering lips. The blonde's lips parted, inviting Lori's tongue to deepen its exploration. She wrapped her tongue around the brunette's as her hips ground in rhythm with the music.

The kiss deepened as she felt Lori's fingertips shyly slipping up under her panties. Katie reluctantly ended the fiery kiss, knowing that she had to get back to work. She felt lightheaded as she stared deep into eyes that were now dark with desire. Katie licked her lips, savoring the taste of lime and tequila mixed with the taste of Lori's lips.

Lori's friends cheered and applauded loudly as the brunette blushed. Katie's hips were still grinding in rhythm with the music as Lori matched her movements. Katie was about to remove herself from the delightful feeling as the other women turned their attention back to the scantily clad men dancing for them. Feeling suddenly bold and very amorous, she held up the shot glass. "You didn't finish," Katie teased her. Her heart pounded in her chest as she waited for the other woman's reaction.

Lori grinned up at her as her fingers continued to caress Katie's firm backside. The blonde moaned as Lori's fingers kneaded her flesh. "Set it up," Katie instructed her as she kept hold of the shot glass, which was less than half full. The blonde leaned back; Lori reached over with one hand while the other remained nestled up under Katie's panties.

Lori squeezed the lime over one of Katie's breasts. The blonde's body arched as she felt the cool liquid paint her breast. Lori's hand trembled as she placed the lime onto Katie's tray and picked up the salt. Lori paused for a moment and Katie feared that she had pushed things too far, and then Lori's fingers neatly tucked some money back under the lacy material of Katie's bra.

"Wouldn't want you to lose that," Lori explained softly as her fingers drifted into Katie's bra. The blonde moaned as Lori's fingers lightly brushed her nipple.

"Thank you," Katie managed to choke out as her body ached to feel more. Regrettably Lori's fingers retreated from her bra and the brunette sprinkled some salt on the wet spot on her breast. Katie's body trembled as she felt the granules dance against her skin.

"Lick, shoot, suck?" Lori inquired as her voice trembled slightly.

"Yes, but this time you're going to drink all the tequila, including what you spilled earlier," Katie instructed her.

Lori slowly licked away the salt and then began to lick away the drops of tequila that had spilled down Katie's cleavage earlier. The blonde's body was trembling as Lori's mouth teased the valley between her breasts. She could feel Lori moaning in pleasure against her skin.

When Lori lifted her head, Katie leaned back and poured the remaining tequila down along her firm abdomen. She flexed her muscles so that most of the liquor would pool in her navel. Lori dove in and began to lick the tequila off Katie's body. The blonde leaned back, wrapping her legs tighter around Lori's body and her head almost touching the floor.

Katie felt Lori's hands holding her up as she feasted upon her stomach. She bit back a deep moan as Lori's tongue dipped into her navel and sucked every last drop of tequila. Lori's exploration began to drift lower. Katie was tempted to just give herself over and let the woman make love to her right then and there. "Go, Lori!" One of the women shouted, snapping both women back to reality.

Katie lifted her body back up as Lori's hands drifted to her back and held her steady. Katie took a wedge of lime and ran it along her breast, dipping into her bra and dangerously close to her aching nipple. "Suck," Katie offered in a needy voice as she lifted her arms over her head. Lori's mouth and tongue quickly captured her skin. As Lori's tongue dipped into her bra, Katie clasped the woman's shoulders and drew her closer.

"Yes," Katie hissed as she felt Lori's tongue tease her nipple. Katie looked around to see that everyone else in the nightclub was focused on the dancer dressed like a firefighter. She turned her attention back to Lori who was pulling down the top of her bra with her teeth. Katie placed her hand on the back of Lori's head and guided her to continue her exploration. The blonde's body trembled and her desire grew when Lori sucked her nipple into the warmth of her mouth.

Lori teased her nipple with her teeth and her tongue while Katie slipped one of her hands between their bodies and cupped the brunette's mound. Lori suckled her harder while Katie stroked Lori urgently with the heel of her hand. Lori nipped at her breast while her hips rocked against Katie's insistent touch.

Katie was about to explode when she reluctantly pulled away. "I need to get back to work," she explained with a whimper as she began to adjust her clothing. Her hands were shaking as she buttoned her blouse. Lori nodded mutely as Katie climbed off her lap and straightened her skirt. Katie blew out a heavy breath as she began to clear away the glasses. Once her tray was full she bent over the trembling brunette. "Any way you can ditch your friends?" Katie inquired, not feeling certain that she should continue crossing the line with this woman.

She watched as Lori took a deep swallow. "I . . . Uhm," Lori stammered as she struggled to breathe.

"Katie?" The manager called out and motioned for her to get back to her other patrons.

"Gotta go," Katie said with a shrug before making her way over to her other tables. Her legs were still shaking as she took more drink orders.

"Wow, that was some show you put on," Kenny, the bartender, teased her as she collected her orders. "I've never seen you get into it like that. Usually you just bump and grind for a couple seconds and let them do a shot on your neck."

"Did you see her?" Katie laughed. "I asked her to ditch her friends."

"What?" Kenny squealed. "That isn't like you. But then again I'd hop the fence for her. So what did she say?"

"Nothing; the boss caught me," Katie shrugged, feeling more than a little disappointed that Lori hadn't accepted her uncharacteristic offer. "Speaking of putting on a show, are you responsible for John's new outfit?" She nodded at the buffed man dressed in leather chaps and a cowboy hat dancing for the screaming women.

"You like?" Kenny grinned. "Later he's going to rope and tie me."

"Pig," Katie snorted before returning to her customers.

As she continued to wait on tables her eyes kept drifting over to Lori who was still seated in the same chair while her friends continued to hoot and holler. She smiled each time she looked over and found Lori watching her every movement. It was finally last call, and despite the fact that Lori's eyes never left her, the brunette still hadn't said anything, even when Katie would rest her hand on her shoulder.

Katie approached Lori's party last; they seemed upset that the show was over. "Last call, ladies," Katie announced, resting her hand once again on Lori's shoulder. The group of women complained about the night coming to an end.

"Set them up again," Lori offered in a rich tone as she placed a couple of twenties on Katie's tray. "And I'll have a Cuervo Sunrise."

"No way, Lori; you can't pay," the ebony woman who paid Katie for the lap dance protested.

"It's the last one," Lori protested. "Besides you spent all your money on these young stud muffins and my special shot," she teased her friends.

Katie nodded in agreement as she went to the bar and placed their orders. "I hate women," Roger, one of the other waiters, complained to Kenny. Most of the servers were men who were scantily clad in tight black pants and white vests. Katie was one of the few women that worked on the nights when *Men In Motion* performed. "All night long they grope me and then stiff me. It's not right."

"Oh, I don't know," Katie teased him as she pulled the two one-hundred-dollar bills from her bra and waved them in front of him.

"Not fair," Roger grumbled while Katie placed her order and paid Kenny for the round, tucking the extra twenty and the other bills into her bra. "I let that big gal over there feel my package and all I got was a five."

"That's because you don't wait to see the money up front," Katie chastised him as she collected her last order of drinks. "I'm not going to miss this place if I get that job."

"When is your big interview?" Roger inquired as he collected his order.

"Tuesday," Katie sighed with relief. "I'm so sick of having a degree I can't do crap with. I thought after I got my PhD I would at least get a teaching position. But it's slim pickings out there."

"Slim pickings in here," Roger grunted as they made their way over to the tables.

Katie delivered the last of the drinks to the tipsy women. She purposely saved Lori's for last, still hoping the brunette would respond to her earlier invitation. Their fingers brushed as Katie handed her the drink. "Thank you," the brunette said softly. "For everything," she added with a shy smile as she began to sip her drink.

The others quickly consumed their cocktails as Lori and Katie simply smiled at one another. "Come on. The limo's waiting," Lori finally said, breaking the intense gaze they'd been sharing. "Get your gag gifts together." Katie laughed as an array of condoms and vibrators were stuffed into bags. Katie hadn't missed the penis straws the women had been using all night. She watched as the redhead who had groped her earlier tossed the veil onto her head.

"How do I look?" The woman slurred.

"Lovely," Katie said with an amused smirk. "Enjoy the wedding, ladies," she said as she reluctantly left Lori's side.

Katie busied herself collecting glasses as she watched the wedding party stumble out the door. She grimaced slightly, feeling a sense of disappointment that she wouldn't see Lori again. Once her tables were clear and the last of the rowdy women finally ejected, Katie began her cash out. As she was sorting her money, she unfolded a twenty-dollar bill to find a napkin neatly folded inside. She opened it slowly with nervous anticipation. *'Courtside Marriott 1N Room 312'* was all the pristine written note offered. "Please be from her," she whispered as she quickly counted her earnings.

Katie tipped out Kenny and made a mad dash for her car in the back lot. She was shaking as she started her beat-up Toyota and drove towards the hotel that was only a short distance away. Katie made her way to Room 312, her body tingling as she stood before the door. She ran her fingers through her short blonde hair and smoothed out her clothing, feeling grungy from her shift and the tequila that had been poured over her body. She wiped her sweaty palms on her skirt and knocked on the door as she whispered a quiet prayer that it would be Lori waiting for her on the other side.

PART TWO

Katie's prayers were answered when the door opened and she found Lori shyly smiling at her. "Hi," she said as Lori stepped aside, allowing her to enter the hotel room.

"Hi," Lori responded as she ran her fingers nervously through her long dark hair. Lori turned and closed the door behind Katie. Katie took a moment to take in the brunette's appearance. She had showered and was now dressed in a long white terry cloth bathrobe. Katie smiled as she contemplated how adorable the taller woman looked.

Katie watched as Lori began to fidget. "That was some party. Your friends really seemed to enjoy themselves," Katie offered. She stepped closer to the tall woman who was making her body pulsate with desire.

"Yeah, well, we don't let loose very often," Lori explained with a light laugh as she neared Katie. "Actually, I never do. This just isn't something that I do," she added in a slightly embarrassed tone.

"Neither do I," Katie confessed as she closed the gap between them. "I mean I've done the lap dance thing before but not the way I did with you tonight."

"I've never done anything like that before," Lori continued as her voice trembled. "I can't believe how good it felt to touch your body," she added distantly.

"I liked the way you touched me, too," Katie reassured her as she placed her small hands on the curve of Lori's waist. Katie smiled; the differences in their heights granted her a full view of Lori's cleavage. Katie couldn't help noticing that Lori was probably naked under her bathrobe. She felt Lori's arms encircling her as she leaned in and placed a soft kiss on Lori's neck.

She could feel the taller woman trembling against her. "Do you want to touch me again?" Katie asked before placing another kiss on the moaning woman's neck. Lori whimpered in response. "Do you want me to touch you?" Katie inquired as she began to nibble on Lori's neck.

"Yes," Lori gasped on a needy breath as her hands began to roam down Katie's back.

Lori's hands once again cupped Katie's firm backside as the blonde kissed her neck, working her way up to her chin. Lori bent down giving the eager blonde more access while her hands began to pull up Katie's black skirt. "But . . . ," Lori protested in a weak voice as Katie's lips inched closer.

"Ssh," Katie silenced her before running her tongue along Lori's quivering lips.

"If you don't want this, I'll go," Katie offered softly against Lori's lips. Lori's response was to brush Katie's lips with her own while her hands ran up under the blonde's skirt. Katie reclaimed her lips and deepened the kiss; she poured all of her desire into the fiery kiss while her hands caressed Lori's hips.

Lori's lips parted, inviting Katie in; they began a sensual duel as their tongues caressed one another. Katie could feel Lori's hands growing bolder as the brunette began to lower her panties. Katie's body melted into Lori's as she guided the taller woman backward towards the bed. The blonde cocktail waitress lowered the taller woman down onto the bed as she felt Lori's hands moving out from under her skirt.

Katie kicked off her shoes. She felt Lori lowering the skirt's zipper while they continued to explore the warmth of one another's mouth. Reluctantly Katie ended the kiss as she rolled over onto her side. They were both breathing heavily as two sets of hands began to remove Katie's skirt. Once the garment was lowered far enough Katie reached down and completely removed her skirt and tossed it across the room.

Lori pulled her down and captured her lips once again as Katie pressed her body against Lori. Katie cupped one of Lori's breasts and began to massage it gently through the thick material of the robe. Lori's hands drifted back to Katie's panties as the blonde deepened the kiss. They were both gasping for air as the kiss came to an end and Lori lowered Katie's underwear even further down her hips. "I could feel you at the club," Lori panted. "I could feel how wet you were as your body touched mine. It drove me crazy knowing that I was doing that to you."

"And did it make you wet?" Katie moaned as she slipped her hand underneath Lori's robe. "Did you want me as much as I wanted you?" Katie teased as her hand slipped between Lori's thighs. The brunette's thighs parted, allowing Katie to explore her further.

"Yes," Lori confessed as Katie's fingers brushed her damp curls.

Katie's clit throbbed as she parted her lover and dipped into her wetness. "Did you want more?" Katie encouraged the brunette as her fingers glided slowly along her slick folds.

"Yes," Lori groaned as her fingers began to caress Katie's aching need. "I wanted to be inside of you," Lori gasped as she continued to stroke Katie's clit with her fingers. Katie continued teasing the brunette as she straddled her body.

With her free hand Katie began to unbutton her blouse while Lori teased her. Katie reached down and untied Lori's robe and gently pulled it open as her fingers teased the brunette's pulsating nub. Katie drank in the sight of Lori's well-toned body. "You are so beautiful," Katie said in pure amazement.

Lori blushed at the comment as she lifted her body. Katie was now straddling the brunette as she had earlier in the evening. Lori began to kiss and taste Katie's skin as she struggled to remove the blonde's blouse. Katie assisted her lover in removing of her top and then her bra. Lori's eyes darkened with desire as she gazed at Katie's breasts.

The blonde shifted back and away from her before removing Lori's hand from her wetness. Lori looked at her in confusion. Katie leaned in and kissed the brunette deeply as she brushed her clit against Lori's. Her lover's moans urged her on as their hips began to thrust urgently. Katie leaned forward, offering her breasts to Lori. The brunette began to kiss her skin once again before suckling her nipple in her mouth.

Katie was clutching her lover as their clits rubbed together while Lori teased her nipple with her teeth and tongue. She could feel Lori's hands slip between their bodies and once again dip into her wetness. Katie pulled back slightly as Lori whimpered and began to tease the blonde's clit. Katie buried Lori's face in her breasts as she felt the brunette's fingers pressing against her center.

"You still taste like tequila," Lori whispered as she licked her skin and her fingers entered Katie's wet aching core.

"You need to finish your shot," Katie grunted as she began ride against Lori's hand while the brunette teased her nipples with the tip of her tongue.

Lori began to suckle her nipples harder; moving from one to the other while her fingers plunged in and out of Katie's wetness. "Harder," Katie pleaded as she thrust harder into Lori's touch. Lori granted her request as her hand and mouth took her higher while her thumb began to stroke her clit. Katie's thighs trembled as her head fell back. Katie screamed out in pleasure as the waves of ecstasy ripped through her small body. Lori's fingers stilled inside of her as she kissed Katie tenderly on the neck.

Katie's heart was racing as she removed herself from her lover's touch and gently guided Lori onto her back while she removed her robe. "I want to feel all of you," Katie explained as she tossed the garment aside. The blonde began to kiss her way down Lori's body, drinking in the salty taste of her sweat-covered body.

Lori squirmed beneath her as Katie's mouth descended lower until the blonde found herself kneeling on the floor before the beautiful brunette. Katie kissed and tasted the desire that painted the inside of Lori's trembling thighs. "Please," Lori pleaded as Katie draped the brunette's long legs over her shoulders.

Katie took a moment to inhale the musky scent of Lori's desire before she blew a warm breath through the dark curly patch she'd been fanaticizing about. Katie cupped Lori's firm backside as she pulled her closer and dipped her tongue into the brunette's passion. Katie murmured in pleasure, as she tasted Lori for the first time.

Tasting the taller woman was pure bliss. She buried herself deeper inside Lori's wetness as she ran her tongue along the slick folds. Katie licked and tasted Lori slowly while the brunette begged for more. Lori's hips arched up off the bed as Katie ran her flattened tongue along her sex. Lori's thrusts lifted her higher as Katie pressed her tongue against the opening of her center. She could hear Lori's muffled screams as she curled her tongue and entered the brunette's warm inviting center.

Katie plunged in and out of Lori as the brunette ground her body against her. Katie's body began to tremble as she dipped deeper inside her lover. She heard Lori protest as her tongue slipped from inside of her. Lori's cries quickly turned to pleasure when Katie suckled her clit in her mouth and her fingers replaced her tongue. She fought to hold Lori steady as she suckled her clit harder while her fingers wiggled and plunged deeper inside of her. "God yes," Lori screamed as Katie grazed her clit with her teeth.

The hotel room was filled with the scents and sounds of their passion as Lori climaxed. Katie continued to feast upon her as her fingers stilled inside of her lover. Katie used her shoulders to keep her lover from trapping her between her trembling thighs while she drove her once again over the edge. Katie felt Lori pulling her up onto the bed. Katie almost exploded as Lori pulled her in for a lingering kiss.

Katie moaned as their nipples brushed and their bodies melted together. Lori rolled her onto her back and began to kiss her way down her body. She lifted her hips so Lori could remove her panties. She felt Lori's breath on her skin as she hovered over her. The sight of Lori's glorious backside just above her greeted Katie as the brunette began to kiss her thighs.

Katie caressed Lori's backside as the brunette began to feast upon her wetness. Katie parted her thighs as Lori buried herself between her legs. As Lori suckled her clit Katie slipped her two fingers deep inside the brunette's center. Her hips thrust urgently as Lori suckled her harder. Lori's legs parted as she rode against Katie's touch. Encouraged by Lori's urgent thrusts, Katie added another finger inside of her lover. Lori bucked urgently in response as Katie gave herself over to the feel of the brunette's tongue feasting upon her.

Katie's body lifted higher; she cried out while Lori screamed into her wetness. Both women continued to pleasure each other until they collapsed onto the bed. Katie had barely enough time to catch her breath before she felt Lori kissing her way back up her body. The blonde's body was tingling as Lori's mouth worshiped her skin. Soon they were once again wrapped up in one another's arms, rolling across the bed.

Katie needed to feel and taste every inch of this amazing woman. Lori seemed to be filled with the same uncontrollable desire as they found themselves locked in an intense kiss while their thighs pressed against the other's center. Katie was lying on top of Lori while they thrust against each other in a sensual rhythm. She was panting as Lori's hands drifted up and down her body. The blonde reached over to the nightstand and grabbed the gift bag she'd seen earlier at the club.

"What are you doing?" Lori moaned as she rode harder against the blonde's thigh. Katie smiled down at her lover when she found what she was looking for in the bag. She knocked the bag with the rest of its contents to floor as she pulled away from Lori. She held the small purple phallic shaped vibrator up and pulled off the cap. Katie twisted the top and felt the small vibrator buzzing in her hand. "Is that how that works?" Lori asked in amazement as Katie pushed her thighs open.

Katie snuggled up against Lori's long body and rested her head on the brunette's chest. She lowered the vibrator to Lori's clit and held it gently against the aching nub. Lori held her tightly while her body gyrated in response. Katie captured one of Lori's nipples in her mouth as she continued to pleasure her with the vibrator. She tugged on Lori's nipple playfully with her teeth while the brunette climaxed.

Katie turned the toy off and cast it aside. "I've never felt this alive before," Lori confessed in a hoarse tone as she wrapped Katie up in her arms. They snuggled closer and gently caressed one another until they were once again lost in a passionate kiss. Soon Katie found herself lying on her stomach as Lori pressed her wetness into her. "Oh yes," Katie murmured as she lifted her hips to feel more of Lori.

Katie's clit was once again throbbing as she matched Lori's urgent thrusts. "You feel so good," Lori moaned as her breasts danced across Katie's back. The bed rocked as they moved in perfect rhythm driving each of them closer to the edge. Katie felt Lori exploding against her. The brunette began to kiss her way down Katie's prone body. The blonde opened herself up, as her lover tasted her from behind. Her body began to sway as Lori's tongue dipped into her center. Katie clutched at the bedding as Lori plunged deep inside of her.

Katie whimpered in protest as she felt Lori's mouth leaving her body. Lori guided her down onto her back. Katie reached for her only to have her hands captured by Lori's and lifted above her head. The brunette held her wrists above her head with one hand while she stroked her aching clit with the other. Katie's body was thrashing; she felt Lori inside of her while her thumb teased her clit. She stilled her body and found Lori looking down upon her while she pleasured her. The intensity of the brunette's gaze quickly sent the smaller woman over the edge.

Katie pulled Lori down and began to caress her body. Her breathing was still erratic, as her exploration grew bolder. "The sun is up," Katie panted as Lori began to kiss her neck. The brunette simply hummed in response as she began to suckle the pulse point on Katie's neck.

Suddenly Lori's head snapped up and she crawled away from Katie to stare out the window. "What?" Katie asked in confusion.

"The wedding," Lori explained in a horrified tone as she turned away from the stunned blonde and pulled on her bathrobe.

"Oh." Katie laughed as she pulled herself up and began to search for her clothing. Her knees were weak and her mind a little foggy as she pulled on her skirt. She noticed the large garment bag hanging on the clothing rack. "I don't know why you gals insist on partying the night before the wedding," she teased, feeling uneasy when Lori wouldn't look at her. "So you're a brides maid?" She asked as she continued to dress, hoping that Lori would look at her.

"No," Lori choked out in a fearful tone.

"Maid of honor?" Katie continued, feeling her anger rise when the other woman wouldn't look at her.

"No," Lori sobbed, still keeping her back to the confused blonde.

Katie pulled on her bra as her brow crinkled in confusion. Her emerald eyes suddenly widened as she walked purposely over to the garment bag. Her body was trembling as she reached for the zipper.

"Please don't," Lori pleaded as she jumped off the bed.

It was too late. Katie had already begun opening the bag, her heart pounding as the delicate white lace was revealed. She stumbled backward as the gown was finally in full view. "You're the bride?" Katie choked out in horror.

She turned to see the frightened look in Lori's eyes and knew it was the truth. "I have to go," Katie stammered as she frantically began to search for the rest of her clothes and her car keys. Lori collapsed onto the bed. Katie fought against the urge to go to her and offer some comfort. But what could she say or do? Katie stood there as her emotions stormed inside of her. On the one hand she knew she had nothing to feel guilty about. On the other hand, she was angry that Lori had used her. Katie also felt a deep-seated need to comfort the woman who was weeping uncontrollably. There was a loud knock on the door and a familiar voice demanded that Lori wake up.

Katie recognized the voice and knew it belonged to the woman who had started this entire fiasco. She threw open the door and found two brown eyes staring at her with a very surprised look. Katie yanked the woman into the hotel room and slammed the door shut. The woman's shocked gaze bounced between Katie and Lori. Katie felt a surge of anger rush through her, as the woman looked at her half clad body with a snarl.

The dark-skinned woman's jaw dropped in horror. "Oh my God," the woman stammered. "You slept with the cocktail waitress?"

"Yes," Lori choked out, still unable to look at either of them.

"I have a name," Katie fumed as her anger reached the breaking point. Lori turned to her with a sad expression and Katie's heart sank when she realized that Lori didn't know her name. "Katie," she added weakly as she crossed her arms over her chest, suddenly feeling ashamed of her actions. The blonde fought back the tears that were threatened to escape. She turned to the stunned African American woman who was still staring at both of them. "Let me guess. You're the maid of honor," Katie spat out.

"Natasha," the woman stammered.

"Look, she's freaking out," Katie quickly explained. "You're her best friend. I suggest you do something to help her."

"What can I do?" Natasha stammered as Katie snatched her blouse off the floor.

Katie flashed the bewildered Natasha a sneer. "You started this," Katie accused her. "Why did you set her up like that?"

"I didn't . . . I mean, I didn't know . . . ," Natasha tried to explain.

"But you suspected," Katie accused her. "That was the real reason for the lap dance, wasn't it?"

"I . . . Uhm," Natasha stammered as her eyes took a sudden interest in her shoes. "Yes, I suspected but I never thought that this would happen," Natasha blurted out as she looked up at Katie, looking guilty.

"What?" Lori fumed as she jumped off the bed and stormed over to a stunned Natasha. The brunette towered over the frightened woman. Even Katie jumped back as she felt the anger pouring out of Lori. "What did you suspect?" Lori demanded with a growl.

"Lori, I'm sorry," Natasha blurted out fearfully. "I know that you care for Brian. But I never felt that you were in love with him, and for sometime I suspected that maybe you were denying . . ."

"Denying what?" Lori shouted. Katie and Natasha cringed from the harshness in the woman's voice.

Natasha stood there in stunned silence as Katie quickly scrambled to find her shoes and car keys. She snatched up both items and made a mad dash for the doorway. "Wait," Natasha called out to her in a pleading tone.

"For what?" Katie flared at both of them. "You're her friend; you help her," Katie shouted as she tucked her shoes under her arm and reached for the doorknob. "I think I've done everything that I can," she added bitterly.

A deafening silence filled the room as Katie began to open the door. The hairs on the back of her neck stood on end as she felt Lori approach her. "Katie?" Lori offered in a soft tone that sent a shiver down the blonde's spine. Katie took a deep breath and collected her last ounces of courage before turning to the tall brunette. Katie looked up at Lori with a cold stare. "I'm sorry," Lori said sincerely as she reached out to the smaller woman. Lori's hands froze in midair before she could touch Katie. "I'm really sorry for all of this," Lori added sadly as her crystal blue orbs filled with tears.

"So am I," Katie responded curtly before walking out of the room and bolting down the hallway to the staircase. She didn't care that she was fleeing the hotel in a state of undress. She just needed to get away. She didn't stop running until she was nestled safely in her own apartment.

PART THREE

The following Tuesday Katie was sitting in the outer office of the assistant director's office at one of the most prestigious museums in Boston. She was wearing her best suit and she tapped her fingers nervously, praying that she wouldn't do anything that would ruin the opportunity for landing her dream job.

The past few days had been hell for the small blonde. She felt angry, guilty, used, and like a fool all at the same time. She was sorry that Lori was confused with her sexuality but she was angry that both Lori and Natasha had used her.   Then again she willingly went to the beautiful brunette's hotel room without questioning anything.   Not even taking the time to practice safe sex.   Katie knew in her heart that knowing that Lori was to be married the following morning was the only thing that would have stopped her from going to that hotel room.

Katie shook her head in an effort to vanquish the troubling thoughts and questions that still plagued her.   *'I need to focus. I'm more than qualified for this job.   I have the right experience with my internships and studies overseas.   I have the right recommendations.   I can do this.   Soon I'll be doing what I love most - studying the past,'* Katie thought, giving herself an internal pep talk as the secretary motioned for her to go in to see Ms. Beauchamp.

Katie smiled confidently as she collected her portfolio and entered the small yet elegant office.   Her confidence vanished when she spotted Natasha standing behind the desk.   The one saving grace was that Natasha seemed equally as stunned as she was.   The sound of the secretary closing the office door jolted both women back to reality.   "Please have a seat," Natasha offered in a slightly flustered tone.

Katie nodded agreeably as she sat in the chair.   The blonde reminded herself that all was not lost.   Hopefully Natasha was ethical enough to overlook the events of a few days ago.   "Dr. Keefer," Natasha began in a professional tone, while her voice quivered slightly.   "Katherine Keefer," Natasha muttered as she rubbed her temple nervously.   "I had no idea," Natasha stated, a look of despair on her face.

"Of course not," Katie responded dryly.   "I was just a cocktail waitress."

"With your credentials, why are you working there?" Natasha inquired in bewilderment.

"Money," Katie retorted flatly.   "I have loans to repay and the money is good.   It's only temporary until I can start working in my field.   And it appears that I will continue working there for awhile longer," Katie added in a defeated tone as she began to gather up her portfolio.

"Wait," Natasha halted her firmly. "You don't understand what the problem is."

"Yes, I do," Katie retorted bluntly. "I'm a slutty cocktail waitress who screwed your friend and therefore not qualified to set foot in this fine institution. Despite my impressive resume. I guess it's time to start faxing my resume to other parts of the country."

Katie hung on to her calm demeanor despite the fact that anger was rapidly growing inside of her. She'd just lost the position she'd spent most of her life working to attain because she had slept with the wrong person.

"No, you don't understand," Natasha addressed her as she stood. "You're the top candidate for this position. This meeting was supposed to be just a formality to ensure that you weren't some kind of flake who only looked good on paper."

"You know you're giving me excellent grounds for a lawsuit," Katie cautioned her, feeling completely confused by the turn of events. *'Did I misjudge her?'* Katie questioned herself as she reclaimed her seat in front of the other woman's desk.

"The problem is . . . ," Natasha began hesitantly as Katie braced herself for a brush off. "The final decision is going to be made by the director, Dr. Milner."

"I'm very confused right now," Katie confessed. "I get the feeling that you're telling me the job is mine but I'm not going to get it."

"The problem is . . . ," Natasha repeated with a trembling voice, "that Dr. Milner won't be making her decision until next week when she returns from her *honeymoon.*"

Katie broke out in a cold sweat as her emerald eyes bugged out in horror. "Oh my God," she responded slowly. "Lori?"

"I'm afraid so," Natasha responded in a sorrowful tone.

"She married him?" Katie mumbled in a distant voice, confused as to why she cared.

"Yes," Natasha answered her in a hurt tone. "She almost didn't," she continued.

"It's none of my business," Katie cut her off as she once again collected her portfolio and stood to leave.

"This is my fault," Natasha muttered angrily. "I've been trying to push her for years to realize the truth. I should have stopped when she got engaged."

"Again, none of my business," Katie responded curtly. *'Damn! My only one night stand and it cost me everything I've spent my entire life working for.'*

"Hold on," Natasha interrupted her thoughts. "Lori is a very honorable person."

"Yes?" Katie snapped back in a sarcastic tone. "I could tell by the way she bedded me the night before her wedding."

"Hey!" Natasha flared defensively.

"What?" Katie responded with a heavy sigh.

Natasha took a deep breath of her own before continuing. "I don't think Lori will refuse to hire you for this position because of what happened."

"How can she hire me now?" Katie argued. "How can she work with me? How can I work for her?"

Katie simply shook her head, knowing that Natasha was asking herself the same questions. Katie turned and walked out of Natasha's office, feeling like her world had just come crashing down around her.

PART FOUR

The crowd seemed rowdier than normal, which wasn't helping to lift Katie's spirits. Her co-workers' constant inquiries as to what was wrong and how her big interview had gone didn't help either. She had been faxing her resume out across the country without much success. It wasn't as if anthropology was a booming field these days. It had been over a week since her big interview and her mood was growing darker with each passing day.

She delivered a round of drinks to a group of drunken women who were celebrating one of the ladies' fortieth birthday. Katie kept her distance, vowing never to fall into the same trap again. Unfortunately her aloof demeanor was affecting her tips.

She turned around to wait on her next table when she spotted her standing at the bar.

Katie's heart raced and her palms began to sweat. She almost dropped her tray when she found herself lost in a sea of blue. Even from across the crowded nightclub Lori's presence was wreaking havoc on her emotions and libido. Somehow she managed to take the order.

She brushed past Lori, hating her body when it tingled as she moved by the tall brunette. "Excuse me," Katie said curtly, trying not to look at the other woman.

"I need to talk to you," Lori offered quietly as her hand came to rest on Katie's forearm.

Katie shrugged away from Lori's touch; it sent a jolt through her body. "I'm working," Katie responded icily, her eyes drifting to Lori's amazing hands. She felt an unexpected surge of anger when she spotted the large diamond ring and gold band on the brunette's ring finger. "You know, if you'd bothered to wear that rock the last time you were here, we wouldn't be in the mess," Katie accused her bitterly.

"I left it with my parents so nothing would happen to it," Lori explained shyly.

"How very thoughtful," Katie snapped.

"I need to talk to you," Lori repeated, fidgeting with her wedding band.

"And I told you that I was working," Katie repeated harshly, noticing that Kenny was watching the entire scene. "I need a Sex On The Beach, a Kahlua Mudslide, a Tom Collins, a Midori Sour, and a Long Island Ice Tea."

Kenny nodded, slightly stunned by the harshness in Katie's voice. "You should be working for me," Lori asserted firmly. Katie's jaw dropped as she stared at the brunette with a bewildered expression. "You deserve the position. It would be wrong for you not to get it or take it because of something . . . because of my mistake. I don't understand why I did what I did."

"Sure you do," Katie responded frankly. "You wanted it to happen, Lori, and now you just want to pretend it didn't. That you didn't feel the way you did. That you didn't enjoy what we did. But you did."

She could see the fear in Lori's eyes as the brunette struggled to catch her breath. Katie grimaced at the reaction she'd caused with her callous words. She collected her order and left the confused Lori standing at the bar. Katie was grinding her teeth when she returned to the bar and found Lori still standing there. "Please leave me alone," Katie pleaded after she placed her order. "I need this job."

"You have a job in your field waiting for you," Lori pushed. "You earned it. You deserve it. You and I will rarely cross paths. I won't bother you. I won't harass you. I will simply let you do your job and I will never allow what happened between us to affect my ability to be objective when it comes to your position. Take the job, Katie. Don't hurt yourself because I'm a total jackass."

Katie tried to ignore her but Lori's words were getting through. During the night Lori remained perched at the bar, and each time the blonde cocktail waitress approached, she implored her to accept the position. Katie was thankful when closing time approached and Lori would be forced to leave. The brunette thrust her business card onto Katie's tray. "Call me," Lori asserted before walking out of the smoky nightclub.

"Want to talk about it?" Kenny pried as Katie counted out her meager earnings. Her head slumped as she released a sob.

"You're not going to believe it," she cautioned him as she looked up with tears falling down her face. A long dissertation and several Margaritas later, she woke on Kenny's sofa with a nasty hangover. As her head pounded, she dialed Lori's office number and reluctantly accepted the position.

PART FIVE

Several months later Katie felt like a new woman. Lori had kept her word and stayed away from her. They only saw one another when it was absolutely necessary. And when they did meet both women managed to keep things on a strictly professional level. Of course it didn't stop Katie's mind from wandering back to the delightful memories of the one night they'd shared. She often found herself wondering if Lori ever thought about that night. Then she would mentally kick herself for even thinking about those things. She did notice that when she and Lori would pass one another in the museum that the brunette often seemed lost in thought. Once again she chastised herself for even pondering what was going on in the brunette's mind. "None of my business," she reminded herself.

One night Katie was working late on a new collection that had just been received by the museum. The tapestry she was examining was so captivating that she was lost in the design. "Amazing, isn't it?" The sultry voice whispered in her ear. Katie yelped in surprise as she jumped and clutched her heart.

"Sorry," Lori quickly apologized as she took a shy step backward.

"You scared me," Katie chastised the brunette playfully. "I was so wrapped up in this I never heard you come in."

"Should I start wearing a bell or something?" Lori teased her with an amused smirk.

"That could help." Katie laughed. The laugh suddenly died as she found herself once again captivated by Lori's eyes. When she realized that she was staring at the other woman, she immediately broke the gaze and turned her focus on her work. "Sorry," she mumbled as Lori took a seat next to her.

Katie's body began to tremble in reaction to Lori sitting so close to her. "How's it going?" Lori inquired as she began to examine the tapestry.

"Good," Katie explained proudly. "I should have the dating completed by tomorrow. From everything I can see it's authentic."

"Good to hear," Lori congratulated her. "You're doing a great job."

Katie almost missed Lori's comments as she watched the brunette's fingertips carefully dance across the rich threads of the tapestry. Katie's eyes drifted shut and her stomach clenched as memories filled her mind. Suddenly her eyes snapped open when she realized that something was missing. She stared down at Lori's hands and discovered what was missing. Instead of the gold band and large diamond ring, there was only a dim tan line on Lori's ring finger.

Before she could stop and think about what she was doing, Katie captured Lori's hand and looked at it as a wave of confusion rushed over her. It wasn't until Lori shyly removed her hand from Katie's grasp that the blonde realized what she'd done. "Separated," Lori offered quietly in response to Katie's unspoken question.

They sat there in the dimly lit room that was Katie's lab, each seemingly struggling with the rush of emotions. "Do you want to talk about it?" Katie finally offered as she tried to ignore the constant throbbing of her lower anatomy.

"It was a mistake," Lori offered grimly. "But I guess you already knew that."

"I didn't," Katie lied. She instantly regretted the lie. "The night we met I never would have guessed that you were the one who was getting married. I thought it was the redhead who grabbed my ass." Lori laughed at the memory. "I mean, she was wearing an engagement ring and put the veil on," Katie continued to explain. "Plus I thought you were . . ." She began to chew on her bottom lip nervously, wondering if she should be the one to say this to Lori.

"Gay," Lori concluded for her.

"Yes," Katie admitted, "I thought you were gay."

"Did you think that before or after I licked tequila off your body?" Lori inquired nervously.

"Before," Katie confessed as her hand unconsciously grasped Lori's. When she realized that she was holding the brunette's hand, she went to release it. Her movement was halted when she felt the light squeeze Lori offered in response.

"I didn't," Lori responded sincerely. "Natasha did. She said that she'd known it for years. I mean, I guess I suspected and I've had urges, but I guess that I'm really good at lying to myself."

Katie wrapped her fingers around Lori's as she allowed the woman to proceed at her own pace. Katie was fighting against the overwhelming urge to reach out and kiss Lori as she drank in the brunette's chiseled features. "When I touched you, it felt right," Lori continued thoughtfully. "My body never felt that way before."

Katie's mind went blank as she reached out and cupped Lori's cheek in her hand. Lori smiled at her as she leaned into the touch. Katie wasn't certain which of them moved first or if they moved in unison. She wasn't aware that they'd somehow closed the gap that was separating them until she felt her lips melting into Lori's.

Katie cast aside all sense of reason as she parted Lori's soft full lips with her tongue. She moaned as Lori's tongue parted her eager lips in the same manner. Katie soon became lost in the sensation of their tongues wrapping around one another. The blonde's hands began to roam across Lori's broad shoulders, as the kiss grew more passionate.

Both women were gasping with desire as they finally released one another. "Why do you have to be such a good kisser?" Lori asked in wonderment as she captured Katie's face in her hands.

"Why do you?" Katie responded with smile as Lori drew her closer and reclaimed her lips.

Things quickly escalated as their hands began to roam across one another's bodies. "This is happening too fast," Katie panted as she pulled Lori up and guided her over to her desk.

"I know," Lori groaned as she began to remove Katie's lab coat and unbutton her blouse.

"This is wrong," Katie continued to reason as she lowered Lori down onto her desk. Her nimble fingers quickly undid the buttons of Lori's blouse while the brunette opened her blouse and began to caress Katie's breasts.

"We shouldn't be doing this," Lori added as Katie began to open the brunette's slacks.

Katie was about to add another reason why they should stop when she felt Lori teasing her nipples and suckling her neck. "God, I want you," Katie moaned instead of arguing against touching one another. She felt her blouse fall to the floor. Lori fumbled slightly until she finally released the clasp on Katie's bra. While Lori quickly removed the garment, Katie was pulling the brunette's slacks down her hips.

Katie's body arched as Lori captured her nipple in her mouth. The blonde's hands moved quickly up the brunette's body and began to remove her lover's blouse and bra. Lori's mouth teased her nipples while Katie fondled her lover's breasts with her small hands. Lori moaned against her skin when Katie began to pinch and tease the brunette's nipples.

Lori pulled away from her slightly and looked up at Katie with a smoky gaze. "Katie, I don't want just this," she offered softly. "I mean, I want this, but it isn't just your body that draws me to you."

"I feel the same," Katie confessed, suddenly feeling a sense of freedom by finally admitting that there was more to her attraction than just Lori's stunning good looks. "We can still do this right?" she added playfully.

"Yes," Lori responded huskily.

Katie drew Lori's slacks and underwear down her long legs as she sank to her knees. Then she removed the last of Lori's clothing and cast it aside. Kneeling beside her desk, Katie nestled her body between Lori's thighs and draped her long legs over her shoulders. Katie sighed as she drank in the aroma of her lover's passion. She parted Lori's lips and dipped her tongue inside of the brunette's wetness. Lori's body arched as Katie's tongue glided along her sex. Katie pulled Lori's body closer as her tongue began to flicker across her swollen nub. Katie suckled Lori's clit into the warmth of her mouth while she pressed her fingers against the opening of her lover's warm wet center.

She could hear Lori's frantic pleas as she entered her. She felt the walls of Lori's center tighten around her fingers. She allowed her lover's body to adjust to the feel of her touch as she suckled her clit harder. Katie knew that the intensity of their long denied feelings would overwhelm both of them quickly. She couldn't slow her pace as she began to plunge in and out of Lori's wetness while she teased her clit. She needed to feel Lori exploding against her and she silently prayed that they would have time in the future to take things slower.

The uncertainty of their future did nothing to stop Katie from taking her lover completely as her hand and mouth moved in perfect rhythm. She felt Lori's body trembling as she neared the edge. Urged on by her lover's pleas Katie took her harder and deeper until she felt Lori's body thrashing wildly. Lori was crying out her name as she climaxed against Katie.

The blonde's fingers stilled inside of her lover, allowing the last drops of passion to slip through her trembling body. Katie slowly licked Lori's passion from the inside of her quivering thighs. She gradually slipped her fingers out of the warm cocoon and rested her head on Lori's stomach. "I adore you," Katie confessed as she placed soft promising kisses on Lori's skin.

"Katie," Lori whispered, as the blonde looked up and found that she was staring into crystal blue orbs filled with what she hoped was love.

The thought frightened her as she stood and Lori pulled her closer. The fear slipped away as she felt Lori's tongue teasing her erect nipple while her hands busied themselves with lowering the blonde's pants and underwear. Katie's head fell back as her lover's fingers explored her wetness. She parted her thighs as Lori entered her. Soon her hips were thrusting against Lori's touch while the brunette suckled her nipple greedily.

The feel of Lori plunging in and out of her while her thumb teased her clit was quickly driving Katie over the edge. "Come for me," Lori pleaded against her skin. Katie's body erupted as she cried out and clung to Lori. The brunette wrapped her up in a warm embrace as Katie tried to calm her trembling body. Katie lifted her head and brushed back Lori's hair from her brow.

"We have a lot to talk about," she whispered before placing a gentle kiss on Lori's brow.

"I know," Lori agreed before kissing Katie lightly on the lips. "Do you think we could go somewhere and talk?"

"Yes," Katie accepted with a smile.

They dressed and Katie locked down her lab. She offered her hand to Lori who accepted it with a bright smile. Still fearful of what lay ahead of them, Katie led Lori out the door on what would be their first date. The feel of Lori's hand resting comfortably in her own gave her a sense of reassurance and courage.

The End

ROLL OF THE DICE

Kerry rolled her shoulders in an effort to alleviate the tension that was steadily building. In the past years the junket to Las Vegas for the annual Consumer Electronics Show was a lot of fun. But that was before the economy and her relationship decided to take nosedives. This year it was a room full of desperate looking salesmen and designers trying to their level best not to look as if their jobs depended on the success of the new products. The truth was that for most of them their careers were indeed riding on whatever masterpiece they'd developed.

Kerry wasn't as worried as most. The educational software she'd developed was not only user-friendly but so was the cost. She had already confirmed orders with several elementary school systems; the trip was a success. But there were a few notable drawbacks. Larry and Charlie never seemed to leave her side and couldn't understand why she didn't want to go to a topless bar with them. She had no problem going to a strip show. She and Stacy had gone whenever her lover accompanied her. But now she and Stacy had called it a day and she didn't want to hang out with the men in plaid.

Charlie and Larry were sweet enough, but they really needed someone in their lives to tell them how to dress. It wasn't the first time Kerry considered designing software that would help the fashion-challenged computer geeks she worked with. The other thorn in her side was the boys' behavior. Despite the fact that they were well educated and probably two of the brightest minds in the country, they behaved like a pair of pimply-faced adolescents whenever they got out of the lab and got to play in a place like Las Vegas. Every time an attractive woman passed by she had to wonder if they'd ever seen a pair a breasts. Not that she'd seen that many up close since she was terminally shy. Her height didn't help much since she stood just less than six feet tall.

She continued to explain the benefits of her new software to an elderly man from Comstock who was the principal of a private school. She pushed her wire-rimmed glasses up once again, cursing herself for not putting in her contacts. The older man, who was easily old enough to be her father, was flirting with her despite the fact he was sporting a wedding band. *'Ugh! What is it about this town?'* she mentally groaned as she continued to outline the benefits of the software in a polite professional manner. In the past years she would simply shrug it off when someone flirted with her or treated her like a piece of meat. This year was the first time in a long time that she was single, and the unwanted attention was starting to get on her nerves.

When the man finally agreed to place an order, she thankfully turned him over to Brian, one of the salesmen. "I'm so glad that I'm going home tomorrow," she muttered to Charlie and Larry who were giggling.

"Oh come on, Kerry, I think he likes you," Larry teased.

"Knock it off, Larry," Charlie chastised him. Kerry was well aware that Charlie had had a crush on her for many years. Since he understood he didn't have a snowball's chance in hell, she could deal with it. "Why don't you come out with us tonight?" Charlie suggested hopefully.

"What are you two demons doing tonight?" Kerry asked as she started to fold up her materials, knowing her time at the booth was coming to an end.

"Tittie bar," Larry responded proudly.

"Larry!" Charlie gasped as he blushed.

"What? I've heard Kerry say that," Larry defended himself

as he brushed what was left of his hair back.

"True, but it's different when you have a pair," Kerry teased both of them. "I'll pass on joining the two of you."

"Come on, Kerry," Larry pushed. "Don't lock yourself up in your room again tonight. We could go to a gay bar if you want."

"Huh?" Charlie squeaked.

"Charlie, she needs to get out," Larry explained. "Kerry, ever since you and Stacy broke up, your life is duller than ours."

"Hey!" Kerry fumed as both men pouted.

"It's true, Kerry," Charlie shyly confirmed.

"You said that you and Stacy split up because you both felt as if something was missing," Larry continued hesitantly. "You're not going to find what you're looking for by locking yourself up in your room."

Kerry could feel the anger swelling inside of her. The only thing that stopped her from thumping Larry upside his balding head was that she knew he was right. "I'm just not up to it. Plus I'm flying out in the afternoon," she grumbled. "You boys have fun tonight." She packed up the last of her belongings as the two men continued to pout. "If I change my mind, I'll call your cell," she added in hopes that they would stop giving her heart wrenching, injured puppy dog looks. They smiled. "I'm done for the night," she added before making her departure.

Later Kerry sat in her hotel room bored out of her mind. She'd read everything about gambling and watched all the infomercials on television. The mathematics of the whole process was fascinating to her analytical mind. Yet based on the odds and the inevitable outcome, she wondered why people would risk hard earned money on games designed to beat them. After she read and watched everything, she flipped through the channels on the television. Finding nothing of interest she read the room service menu, checked the escape route posted on her door, filed her nails, repacked her clothes, checked her airline tickets, and finally sat on her bed looking at the design on the ceiling.

After the boredom and Larry's words had driven her almost completely insane, she got up, showered, and changed into a pair of jeans and a simple white sleeveless T-shirt. She put in her contact lenses and headed down to the casino to find out what all the fuss was about. She took one hundred dollars down with her; that would effectively keep her from getting caught up in the mania. Not that she expected to be swept away. After doing the math she realized she would probably return to her room quickly minus the one hundred dollars.

She felt a slight thrill as she entered the hoopla of the casino. Stacy had never wanted to gamble, thinking it was a foolish waste of money. Instead they'd always gone to see Zigfried and Roy or went sight seeing and shopping. Every once in awhile they'd gone to a strip club. She made her way past the endless rows of slot machines, already thinking that they were a waste of time.

She decided to try games where the playing field was a little more level. She had studied the games in the book she found in her hotel room. She opted to start with blackjack. The rules and betting seemed simple enough. The one thing Kerry really enjoyed about Las Vegas was that she didn't stand out quite so much with all the leggy showgirls around. After a few hands of carefully played blackjack, studying her cards and weighing the odds much to the anger of her fellow players and the dealer, she had lost thirty dollars and she decided it was time to move on.

She turned to the roulette table, again because the rules and odds were simple. The excitement of the people surrounding her failed to get her into the mood as she lost yet another thirty dollars. She gathered up her remaining chips and contemplated going back to her room. Then Kerry noticed the crowd surrounding the craps table. She had studied the rules, but for the life of her she still couldn't grasp the way the game was played.

Kerry fiddled with her chips as she debated whether she should go over and watch the game in an effort to understand it better or simply cutting her losses and go back to her room. She was just about to head back to her room when she spotted a flash of golden hair at the craps table. Kerry moved over to the table to get a better look. Using her height, she managed to move in next to the petite blonde who was rolling the dice and losing.

Kerry's body tingled slightly as her shoulder brushed against the smaller woman. "Craps - a loser." There was a collective groan around the table as the blonde scowled.

"Sorry," Kerry apologized, fearing that the slight brush against the other woman had caused her to throw a bad roll.

"Not your fault," the blonde said with a smile that warmed Kerry's body. "I've been on a bad streak all night." Kerry simply nodded in understanding as her crystal blue eyes scanned the blonde's firm body. Kerry's stomach clenched as she took in the leather mini-skirt and the short top that revealed the blonde's firm abdomen.

"I've been having the same luck," Kerry quickly stammered out.

"Hey, are you going to roll the dice or talk?" a surly gentleman barked from behind Kerry.

"Why don't you give it a try?" The blonde encouraged her as she handed her the dice.

"Maybe I'll bring you luck," she encouraged her as their fingers brushed slightly.

"I'm not sure what to do," Kerry managed to choke out as her mouth went suddenly dry.

"I'll show you everything," the blonde responded with a slight purr.

Unable to form a complete sentence, Kerry simply nodded in response and placed a bet down. The blonde caressed her hand as the stickman called out that there was a new shooter. Kerry blew out a heavy breath and she shook the dice furiously before letting them fly across the green felt table. She wasn't able to focus on what happened to the dice; her attention remained on the pair of emerald eyes staring up at her.

"Seven - a winner," the stickman called out as everyone cheered.

"What?" Kerry blinked in surprise as the blonde's hand caressed the small of her back.

"I guess your luck is changing," the blonde complimented her. "Let it ride."

"Okay," Kerry mumbled in agreement as she accepted the dice once again, knowing that she would agree to anything the smaller woman suggested at that moment.

The blonde continued to caress Kerry's back as she once again tossed the dice down the length of the table. Once again she was a winner and the crowd cheered. "Let it ride," the blonde instructed her once again; her caresses grew slightly bolder as her hands drifted down to Kerry's firm backside. The tall brunette swallowed hard and her palms began to sweat. She shook the dice furiously and once again cast them down the table. She won once again; she was rewarded with enthusiastic cheers and the feel of her new companion's free arm wrapping around her waist.

"Looks like you got yourself a real good luck charm," the surly man congratulated her.

"Yeah, I guess I do," Kerry agreed as she stared deeply into the blonde's smoky green eyes. "So, my little good luck charm, what should I do now?"

"Let it ride," the blonde repeated with sly smile.

Kerry leaned slightly closer to the blonde; she fought to keep the dice from slipping from her grasp since her hands were sweaty and shaking. She tossed the dice and won once again. Kerry was lightheaded from the sight of her growing stack of chips and the feel of the blonde's hand caressing her backside while her other hand drifted to her thigh.

Kerry's knees threatened to buckle as her winnings continued to increase and the blonde's caresses grew even bolder. Caught up in the thrill of winning and the excitement of the crowd rooting her on, she continued to play. When someone shouted that her good luck charm should blow on the new dice she'd been handed, the tall brunette uncharacteristically held the red cubes out to the blonde. The smaller woman blew a warm breath across her palm and then grazed her fingers gently with soft lips. Kerry threw the dice without looking, as her focus remained captured by a fiery gaze.

Kerry was confused when she won. "What does that mean 'I won the hard way'?" She asked her good luck charm.

"I'll explain it to you later," the blonde offered in a breathy tone.

Kerry's lower anatomy pulsated with desire at the promising

tone. "Should I keep going?" Her voice quavered as she spoke.

"Yes," her good luck charm encouraged her as her small hand slipped between Kerry's quivering thighs.

Kerry stifled the deep moan that threatened to escape as she tossed the dice once again. As the red cubes tumbled down the green felt table, she felt her good luck charm cup her mound. Kerry wrapped her arm around the blonde's shoulder in an effort to remain standing. The blonde leaned into her touch as she won another large stack of chips.

The blonde once again blew on her dice and kissed her long fingers; this time her tongue teased the back of Kerry's hand. The tall brunette tossed the dice and her other hand drifted down the blonde's back. She won again and the crowd went crazy. The sounds of excitement that surrounded her were lost as her good luck charm began to grind the heel of her hand against Kerry's throbbing clit.

Kerry's nipples hardened as her excitement grew. Her body was pulsating with need and her wetness soaked through her underwear. The excitement was overwhelming her normally reserved personality as she ran her hand up under the cool leather of the blonde's skirt. Kerry gasped slightly as she felt the silk of her companion's panties. As Kerry rolled the dice one more time she wondered how much longer she'd be able to control the passion raging inside her.

The blonde pressed her body closer and her hands grew more insistent. She reached up to cup Kerry's face and drew her down to her own as she won once again. "One more roll and then it is time for you to collect your winnings." Her hot breath caressed Kerry's skin as she spoke. The brunette's eyes drifted to the pair of full lips that were dangerously close. Kerry parted her lips to respond. Words failed her as the blonde's hand increased its rhythm.

Kerry didn't look as she rolled the dice one last time and her good luck charm captured her lips in a fiery kiss. She moaned as the blonde parted her lips with her tongue and invaded the warmth of her mouth. Kerry's fingers dipped shyly beneath the stranger's panties while the blonde's hand teased her clit urgently. "A winner!" was called out and the room erupted. Kerry didn't notice at first since she was too involved with exploring the warmth of her good luck charm's mouth. Both women were breathless when the kiss reluctantly came to an end. "You won again," the blonde stated as they stepped slightly away from each other.

"Yes, I did," Kerry panted in response.

The crowd was chanting, encouraging the weak-kneed Kerry to continue playing. "Time to collect your winnings," the blonde instructed her as she took the dice from her trembling hands and passed them off. They collected the sizeable stacks of chips and carefully carried them over to the cashier's window. Kerry's excitement and concern grew as the cashier counted her winnings.

"Are you staying at the hotel?" The blonde inquired as she wrapped her arm around Kerry's waist.

"Yes," Kerry squeaked out.

"You need to fill this out," the cashier instructed her as she slid a form through the slot.

"What's this?" Kerry asked in confusion as she looked over the document.

"It's for the IRS," the cashier explained in a bored tone. "Just fill it out and I'll get you a check."

Both she and the blonde blinked in surprise. "How much did I win?" Kerry asked as she began to fill out the form.

"Twenty-six thousand four hundred seventy-five dollars," the cashier explained in the same bored manner.

"Whoa!" Kerry choked as the blonde looked at her watch.

"You were playing for almost two hours," she exclaimed in surprise.

"I wasn't paying attention," Kerry confessed with a slight blush as she slid the document over to the cashier.

"Neither was I," the smaller woman smiled in response as her emerald eyes roamed across Kerry's body. "I'm Leigh," she offered as she wrapped her arms around Kerry's waist.

"I'm Kerry," the brunette responded. She chuckled lightly when she realized they hadn't bothered to exchange names. "Nice to meet you, Leigh," Kerry responded softly as she began to caress the blonde's shoulders.

The tall brunette's mind went blank and her body trembled from the feel of Leigh's body pressed against her own. Once again Leigh reached up and captured Kerry's face in her small hands and drew her closer. Kerry moaned as Leigh reclaimed her lips with a soft sensual kiss. Her hands began to roam along Leigh's body as the kiss deepened. The sound of the cashier clearing her throat brought the promising kiss to an end.

Kerry snatched up the check as Leigh took her by the hand and captured her in a smoky gaze. Kerry swallowed hard as Leigh led her away from the crowded cashier's window. Neither woman spoke as they walked out of the casino and headed across the hotel lobby towards the elevators. Kerry caressed the back of Leigh's hand with her thumb. As they stepped into the elevator Kerry dismissed the fleeting thought that said this wasn't such a good idea. One look at her smiling companion completely washed away all her fears. Kerry pushed the button for her floor.

Kerry released a soft moan as Leigh wrapped her arms around her body and guided her to the back of the empty elevator. Leigh began to softly kiss Kerry's neck as the brunette ran her hands down the blonde's back. Leigh's lips began to descend further down Kerry's neck as the brunette slipped her hands up under the blonde's skirt.

As Kerry cupped Leigh's backside, she felt a rush of desire that she hadn't experienced in a very long time. Leigh began to suckle her aching nipple through the cotton material of her shirt. Kerry released a hiss as her head fell back. As the elevator continued to rise, Leigh suckled her nipple harder while Kerry lowered the blonde's underwear.

Kerry's body arched. She ran her fingers along the firm flesh of Leigh's backside while the blonde tugged the brunette's shirt out of her jeans. Leigh's hips thrust against her as Kerry groped her firm flesh. "God, you're so beautiful," Leigh groaned as she slipped her hands up under Kerry's shirt.

Leigh cupped Kerry's breasts as the brunette felt the blonde's desire coat her fingers. Leigh caressed her breasts as she ground her body into Kerry's. Both women were panting with needy desire as the loud ping announced that the elevator doors would be opening. They adjusted their clothing before departing the elevator. Kerry's heart was racing as she felt Leigh's presence following close behind her.

Leigh snuggled against Kerry's body from behind as the tall brunette fumbled with the keycard to her hotel room. Her hands trembled as she slipped the card into the lock and Leigh caressed her body. Thankfully Kerry finally managed to open the door; she stepped aside and allowed her small blonde friend to enter her room.

Kerry felt feverish as she closed the door behind them. This was possibly the most rash and exciting thing she'd ever done in her life. "You know, I've never gambled before," she said as she watched Leigh sit down on the bed.

"This really was your lucky night then," Leigh offered softly as she beckoned her closer with a wave of her finger.

A sudden wave of shyness rushed over the tall brunette as she slowly approached the bed. Leigh's smile grew broader as she pushed aside Kerry's suitcase, which had been resting on top of the bed. "Leaving soon?" Leigh inquired as she leaned back and watched Kerry's approach. Kerry's body quivered from the hungry look she was receiving.

"I'm flying out tomorrow afternoon," Kerry explained as she stood before the attractive blonde.

"I'm flying out in the morning," Leigh said as Kerry knelt before her.

"Too bad we didn't meet sooner," Kerry offered as she ran her hands up along the soft stockings Leigh was wearing. Her hands continued up until she was fondling the straps of the black garter belts that were holding the stockings in place.

"I'm only in town for tonight," Leigh responded softly as Kerry unhooked the snaps of her garter belt.

"I guess it really is my lucky night," Kerry responded as the blonde kicked off her high heels. The brunette slowly rolled down one of the black stockings, her fingers enjoying the feel of the blonde's skin responding to her touch.

"Mine too," Leigh whispered as Kerry tossed her stocking across the room. Then the brunette repeated the slow sensual action as she removed the other stocking.

Kerry lowered her head and began to kiss Leigh's thighs as the blonde whimpered. Leigh ran her fingers through Kerry's long dark hair. The scent of Leigh's desire invaded Kerry's senses as she continued to kiss her thighs while lifting her leather mini-skirt higher.

She could feel her lover's body lie back on the bed as she trembled. "I want you, Kerry," Leigh pleaded as Kerry traced the inside of her thighs with her tongue. Kerry slipped her hands beneath Leigh's body and undid the zipper on her skirt. The scent of Leigh's arousal mixed with leather was driving Kerry insane with desire. The need to touch and be touched by this blonde-haired beauty was her only thought as she lifted her head.

Leigh raised her body and stared deeply into Kerry's eyes. There was no mistaking the look of pure lust in the small blonde's fiery green eyes. Kerry stood slowly, never breaking eye contact with her lover as she removed her shoes and lowered herself into Leigh's warm embrace. Leigh lowered her body back onto the bed, pulling Kerry down along with her.

Kerry reclaimed Leigh's lips, the kiss instantly igniting with unbridled passion. She felt Leigh's hands pulling her shirt up as Kerry cupped the blonde's breast and explored her mouth with her tongue. Kerry was panting as she broke away from the kiss and raised her body. Leigh climbed up and straddled her lap while she urgently pulled the brunette's shirt up and off her body.

Leigh began to suckle Kerry's neck as she reached around the brunette and unclasped her bra. Kerry's clit was throbbing as her bra was removed and Leigh's hips thrust against her body. She ran her fingers through Leigh's long blonde hair as her lover captured her nipple in her mouth. Kerry cried out as Leigh teased her aching nipple with her teeth and her tongue. Kerry arched her back in an effort to offer more of herself to her lover.

Kerry's body was on fire as her hands drifted down Leigh's body and began to pull the blonde's shirt up. The blonde reluctantly released Kerry's breast from the warmth of her mouth and allowed the brunette to remove her top, which was quickly followed by her bra. They shifted to a more comfortable position as they caressed one another's breasts. They exchanged promising kisses that quickly deepened.

They pinched and teased each other's nipples while their tongues battled for control. The need to feel more of her lover's body overwhelmed Kerry as she lowered the blonde down onto the bed. Both women were gasping for air as the kiss came to an end. Kerry rolled her lover over onto her stomach. She ran her fingers across the exposed skin of her lover's back, smiling as she felt tiny goose bumps emerge wherever she touched Leigh.

Leigh's body squirmed beneath her as her touch drifted lower and she caressed the blonde's leather-clad hips. Kerry slowly removed Leigh's skirt. She then slowly removed the blonde's garter belt and black silk panties and cast them aside. Then she kissed her way up Leigh's body as her lover murmured in pleasure.

She lifted her lover's hips as she kissed her firm round cheeks. Leigh rose up on her hands and knees and parted her thighs as Kerry's tongue dipped into her wetness. She feasted upon her lover's wetness as Leigh's hips swayed, inviting Kerry to explore her completely. Kerry accepted the invitation eagerly as she plunged her tongue deep inside Leigh's center. The blonde's hips bucked in response as Kerry plunged in and out of her.

The brunette could feel the walls of her lover's center tighten around her tongue. Leigh whimpered as Kerry removed her tongue from deep inside of her and began to lick her desire from the blonde's quivering thighs. Kerry knelt behind her lover and ran her hands along her firm backside. Leigh released small gasps of pleasure as Kerry's hands drifted lower and lower. Kerry glided her fingers along Leigh's slick folds, savoring the feel of the blonde's desire caressing each finger.

Leigh parted her thighs even further as her hips swayed. Kerry leaned closer, pressing two fingers against the opening of Leigh's wet warm center as her nipples brushed across the blonde's back. "Oh yes," the blonde moaned as Kerry entered her. Kerry filled her lover as Leigh's hips bucked once again with urgency. Kerry wiggled her long fingers inside her lover before slowly gliding in and out of her.

Kerry's pulse was racing and the rhythm of her touch grew wild.   Leigh's hips thrust in unison as Kerry filled her completely.   Kerry could feel her lover's body shaking as she neared the edge.   She pressed her long body against Leigh's quivering form.   Enjoying the feel of their bodies rocking wildly against each other, Kerry took her lover harder.   Leigh cried out as her body convulsed against Kerry's touch.

Leigh collapsed as her body exploded in ecstasy.   Kerry waited until she felt her lover's tremors ease before slipping from her center.   Leigh rolled over and pulled Kerry down to her, capturing her eager lips with her own.   Kerry moaned as Leigh unzipped and lowered her blue jeans.   The brunette allowed her lover to roll her over onto her back.   As Leigh hovered above her, Kerry caressed her breast.

Kerry's body was on fire as Leigh began to kiss her way slowly down her neck.   Leigh kissed the valley between her breasts before her mouth moved to the swell of her breasts. Leigh teased Kerry's nipples with her tongue before suckling one of the erect buds in the warmth of her mouth.   Kerry's body arched as Leigh feasted upon one nipple while she teased its twin with her nimble fingers.

Kerry's hips thrust with need as Leigh's mouth and fingers moved from one breast to the other and then back again.   The brunette was lost in the feel of Leigh's mouth teasing her as her naked body covered her.   Leigh's mouth moved further down her body and Kerry trembled from her touch.   "This really is your lucky night," Leigh promised against her quivering skin. "Because I'm going to make love to you until you beg me to stop."

Kerry released a whimper of desire at Leigh's sultry promise and the feel of her jeans being pushed further down her body. Leigh kissed her body as her skin was exposed.   She could hear Leigh's soft murmurs of pleasure as she removed Kerry's jeans and then her underwear, tossing the garments across the room. Kerry clutched at the bed covers as her lover's tongue ran up her long legs.

Kerry parted her thighs as Leigh nestled her body between her legs. Kerry's entire body pulsated with desire as Leigh's mouth caressed the inside of her thighs. "Please," Kerry begged her lover who blew a warm breath through her damp dark curls. She draped her legs over her lover's body as Leigh parted her swollen lips and dipped her tongue into her wetness. Kerry cried out as she felt Leigh's tongue running slowly down along her sex.

As Leigh suckled her throbbing clit in the warmth of her mouth, Kerry pleaded with her lover to grant her the release her body craved. Leigh's response was to tease her clit with her teeth and her tongue. Kerry cried out as she climaxed against her lover's mouth. Leigh continued to pleasure her as Kerry's body rocked against her. Soon the brunette's body exploded once again.

Kerry wiggled out from underneath her lover and wrapped her in her arms. They began to exchange passionate kisses as their bodies melted together. Kerry was lost in the feel of Leigh's nipples brushing against her own as their clits caressed one another. They fondled one another as they rocked against each other with a desperate aching need. They screamed into the warmth of the other's mouth as they climaxed together.

Kerry gave in to the need for more as they teased each other's clit. Both women teased the other as they straddled each other's thigh. The dark hotel room was filled with the sounds of their passion as they plunged in and out of the other's wetness. Kerry felt her body moving in unison with her lover's as they clung to one another. They exploded once again in unison before collapsing together.

Kerry fought to control her breathing as Leigh began to caress her once again. Kerry returned her lover's caresses as they slowly explored each other's body. Kerry felt alive as they made love slowly until she was sated and spent and begging Leigh to stop. The blonde kissed her deeply as she curled up in her warm embrace and the two drifted off to sleep.

Kerry was awakened a short time later to find Leigh scrambling around the room, trying to find her clothes. "Morning," the blonde greeted her with a smile as she climbed up onto the bed and kissed the exhausted brunette.

"Leaving?" Kerry asked in confusion as Leigh pulled herself off the bed and continued dressing.

"I'm going to miss my flight if I don't go now," Leigh grumbled with a hint of disappointment.

"Catch a later one," Kerry reasoned as she climbed out of bed and wrapped a sheet around her body.

"Can't," Leigh sighed as she made her way to the door.

Kerry wrapped the sheet tighter around her body as she stumbled to the door. She opened the door and leaned against the door jam. "Uhm . . . ," she stammered, uncertain what she should say after spending the night making love to this beautiful stranger who was smiling up at her.

"Thank you," Leigh whispered as she reached up and caressed Kerry's face. She pulled Kerry down and captured her in a soft sensual kiss that left Kerry breathless. "Perhaps your luck will hold out and we'll see one another again," Leigh said softly before leaving the stunned Kerry standing in the doorway. Kerry watched the blonde make her way quickly down the hallway. She turned to find Larry and Charlie staring at her with shocked expressions.

"Hey boys," she gloated before retreating back into her hotel room.

Once Kerry looked at the rumpled bedding, her heart dropped. "Damn! Why didn't I get her number or email address?" She berated herself. Her eyes widened in surprise when something on the nightstand caught her attention. She shuffled over to find her airline ticket sitting there. "I didn't leave this out," she noted with a slight sense of dread. She looked around to find everything else where she'd left it.

Later that day Kerry boarded her connection in Chicago, threatening Charlie and Larry so they'd stop asking her about the previous evening. She reclined in her seat, thankful that the boys were seated several rows behind her. She put on her sunglasses and yawned heavily. She didn't listen to the preflight instructions. Kerry leaned her head back and tried to catch some much needed sleep. She did buckle her seatbelt and kept her eyes closed as the plane took off. The beeping sounds and the captain's voice informed her that they were in the air and heading back east. She kept her eyes closed as she unsnapped her seatbelt.

Kerry could hear the busy airline attendants taking care of her fellow travelers. *'If I just keep my sunglasses on and my eyes shut, maybe they'll just let me sleep,'* she pondered as she thanked her good fortune that no one was seated next to her.

"Excuse me, Miss; would you like a beverage?" a familiar voice whispered hotly in her ear.

Kerry's body stiffened. She ripped her sunglasses from her face and found a flight attendant grinning at her. "Leigh?" She choked out as the blonde winked at her.

"So tell me, is Boston your final destination?" Leigh inquired hopefully.

"Yes," Kerry responded with a brilliant smile.

"Mine too," Leigh answered softly. "Of course, I had to do a lot of bargaining to get on the same flight as you."

"My ticket," Kerry said, suddenly understanding. "Good thing I was traveling on the airline you work for."

"It seems your lucky streak is still running hot," Leigh teased her as she leaned closer to Kerry. "Tell me, Kerry, are you familiar with the Mile High Club?"

Kerry's body filled with renewed desire as Leigh caressed her arm. "I'll be back later," the blonde whispered before leaving.

"This is my lucky day," Kerry said with a sly smirk.

The End.

STARTING OVER

Randy sat at the bar with a confident look on her face. She didn't really feel as calm and collected as she appeared to be, but in her heart she knew that she needed to do this. Amy was gone and the tall brunette needed to prove that she was still attractive. Randy looked around the small women's bar looking for the right woman to help mend her broken heart. She could feel the phallus that she had strapped on brushing against her as she shifted on her barstool.

None of the women present really appealed to the brunette. Randy grimaced slightly, wondering if she was wasting her time. Maybe she should just go home and enjoy the new toy hidden beneath her faded Levis by herself. "I can do this," she reassured herself. She felt more than a little silly sitting in a crowded bar knowing that she was packing and looking for a one nightstand. The last time she'd had a date was over four years ago. Now she was cruising a sea of women like some twenty-year-old kid.

Yet here she was nursing a Sex on the Beach after spending the last few weeks doing nothing but going to work and then returning exhausted to an empty apartment. She couldn't eat. She couldn't sleep. She was miserable and felt worthless. It hadn't helped that Amy had used every bad cliché in the book when she'd ended their relationship. When Amy threw in the old *'it's not you, it's me,'* Randy almost threw a fit.

Now Randy was determined to get on with her life. A meaningful relationship was something she would seek at a later date; tonight she needed to feel alive again. She needed to prove that she was still attractive and that her relationship with Amy had been a mistake.

Randy's crystal blue eyes were drawn to the pool table in the corner. There was a group of women laughing there and one of them made Randy's broken heart skip a beat. She was a petite blonde with an amazing body. Thankfully the short black mini-skirt accented by a cropped black baby doll T-shirt clinging to her ample breasts gave Randy and every other woman in the bar a clear view of her attributes. Randy couldn't stop staring at the attractive woman as a pair of emerald eyes met her own.

The blonde's eyes twinkled in response to Randy's smoky gaze and she flashed an inviting smile at the suddenly nervous brunette. Randy inhaled deeply and tried to collect her thoughts as she spied the small woman heading towards the bar. In an effort to regain her cool façade, she adjusted the phallus and donned a bored expression. The blonde ordered a round of drinks from the bartender as Randy's eyes drifted down the small woman's body.

The blonde's legs and well-toned abs captivated Randy as the small stranger collected her large drink order. Randy tossed some money towards the bartender in an attempt to pay for the blonde's drinks. "No thanks," the blonde quipped with a confident smile as she pushed Randy's money back towards her and paid for the drinks herself.

Randy sighed deeply as her lips curled in understanding; the only woman she'd found attractive that evening had just shot her down. "I know that look," the blonde said softly as she collected her drinks.

"Do you?" Randy quipped as she wondered if she looked as pathetic as she felt.

"Yes," the blonde stranger asserted confidently before she calmly turned away.

Randy allowed the scowl she was sporting to grow as she stared at her lukewarm cocktail. She wondered if she should just tuck her tail between her legs and go home. She started to stand so she could make a quick exit and go home when a warm hand came to rest on her shoulder, halting her movement. "Giving up so easily?" A hot breath whispered in her ear. The feel of the blonde's breath against her skin made her stomach clench. Randy was confused as the same woman who had just brushed her off slid next to her at the bar.

Randy simply stared at the attractive woman leaning against the bar. "I think you should stay and do what you came here to do," the blonde informed her as Randy's brow crinkled in confusion. "After all you did come prepared," the blonde emphasized as she ran her hand up along Randy's thigh and cupped the phallus hidden beneath her jeans. Randy squeaked in surprise as she felt the strap-on device press against her clit. "Feels nice," the blonde added in a breathy tone as she continued to press against the dildo.

Randy swallowed hard; the blonde continued to caress her as she waved for the bartender. Randy's head was spinning as the surreal situation continued to play out. "Two woo-woo shots," the blonde ordered quickly before returning her gaze to a very confused Randy. "This is what you came here for, isn't it?" The blonde teased her. "You want to prove that she's a fool and you're better off without her. And that she'll end up regretting letting you go?"

Randy's jaw dropped as the blonde continued to caress her. She tried to speak but the feel of the phallus and the blonde's smoldering gaze made it impossible to get the words out. "I told you that I know that look," the blonde answered her unspoken question. "You just got dumped and now you're looking for someone to make you feel like you're still worth something. But you're only looking for one night," the blonde continued. She paid the bartender for the drinks while her hand remained between Randy's now trembling thighs.

"Here," the blonde said with a smile as she slid a shot glass over to the still stunned Randy.

Randy's heart was racing as she accepted the drink and raised it as the blonde raised her own. "Here's to moving on and finding someone who deserves you. Because whoever she is, she *is* a fool for letting a beautiful woman like you go." Randy clinked her glass against the blonde's before drinking the shot. Randy's desire grew as the blonde kept caressing her. She opened her mouth to speak but the blonde halted her words by pressing her fingers against Randy's quivering lips. "Don't," the blonde hushed her. "I don't want to hear about her. For tonight the only thing I'm interested in is this," she explained in a sultry tone as she pressed the phallus harder against Randy's throbbing clit.

Randy moaned as she kissed the blonde's fingertips. Her lips tingled as the blonde's fingers left her mouth. "I feel like I just won the lottery," Randy said to the beautiful woman who had just offered her everything she wanted for the evening.

"Well then, isn't about time you collected your winnings?" The blonde purred as she captured Randy's lips in a lingering kiss.

Randy's hips swayed as the blonde continued to rub her hand against her center while Randy explored the warmth of her mouth with her tongue. Randy parted her thighs as the mystery woman's caresses grew more demanding. She turned slightly as the blonde nestled her body between her thighs as their kiss deepened.

Randy's back was pressed up against the bar as the blonde began to undo her jeans. She was gasping for air as the kiss came to a reluctant end and her lover slipped her hand into her jeans. "I want to feel it," the blonde panted hotly in her ear. Randy ran her hands up under the blonde's leather skirt and cupped her firm backside. The blonde stroked her phallus while she began to nibble on Randy's earlobe.

The brunette responded by slipping her fingers under her lover's panties. Randy's fingertips tingled from the feel of the blonde's flesh. Her lover moaned into her ear before dipping her tongue inside. The blonde was pressing her center against the phallus as she cupped one of Randy's breasts. The sound of the bartender clearing her throat behind them alerted Randy that she was about to ravish this beautiful stranger right there at the bar. Randy looked down into the blonde's smoky green eyes as the other woman continued to grind herself into the brunette's phallus. "I need you now," the blonde pleaded as they both looked around for someplace more suitable to continue their exploration.

Randy smiled as she noticed that the door to the outside deck was open. With the cooler weather approaching this time of year, the deck would be dimly lit and only used by women seeking privacy. Randy slipped her hands out from the blonde's skirt. Her soon-to-be-lover pulled her skirt back down as Randy pulled her zipper back up, careful not to catch her new toy.

Randy took her lover by the hand and led her across the room. As they stepped out onto the deck, Randy prayed that this wasn't a dream or some kind of cruel joke. Her prayers were answered as the blonde pushed her up against the outside wall. In the darkness she could still see her mystery woman's long blonde hair and fiery green eyes. The blonde quickly lowered the zipper of Randy's jeans and began to tug them down the brunette's hips.

The blonde began to stroke the phallus urgently as her lips drifted down Randy's neck. Randy's desire was painting the inside of her thighs as the blonde's mouth drifted lower. "Do you want me?" The blonde whispered against her skin.

"Yes," Randy growled in response as she once again slipped her hands up and under the leather skirt. This time she felt her way to the elastic waistband of the blonde's panties and quickly lowered them as far as she could reach. Randy then cupped the woman's backside, enjoying the feel of her cool skin reacting to her touch.

"You are so beautiful," the blonde whispered as she pressed her center against the phallus while her hands moved up Randy's body and began to pull her white cotton T-shirt up. Randy trembled from the feel of the night air and the blonde's wetness brushing against her skin. "I want you to fuck me," the blonde confessed boldly; Randy felt the heat rise inside her.

She clasped the mystery woman's hips and drew her closer as the blonde unclasped Randy's bra. Randy's breathing caught as the blonde ground her body against Randy's. "Not yet," the blonde whimpered. "First I want to make you wetter than you've ever been in your entire life," the blonde panted in a needy tone.

'*I already am,*' Randy's mind screamed as the blonde's tongue circled her nipple. She clasped her lover's hips tighter as her nipple became erect. Randy was certain that she must be dreaming; a beautiful blonde stranger was offering her wild sex out on the deck behind the club. Out of the corner of her eye, she spied another couple pleasuring one another in the darkness. After years of enduring the stagnation of her so-called marriage and Amy's mind games, she was losing herself in the raw passion her mystery woman was offering her.

"They're watching us," her mystery lover murmured against her breast. Randy knew that she was talking about the other two women cloaked in the shadows.

"I know," Randy moaned in response. Randy's hips jerked in response as her lover tugged on her nipple with her teeth. Another jolt reached her aching clit as her lover began to pinch and tease her other nipple with her fingers. Randy's desire grew as she watched the other couple's groping increase as they watched them.

The blonde's hips were grinding harder into her body as she suckled Randy's nipple eagerly. Randy's knees began to tremble as her hands moved up under the tiny black shirt that was clinging to the blonde's body. "I need to feel you," Randy moaned as she unclasped the smaller woman's bra. "I want to take you," Randy added with a feral growl as her hand felt its way around and cupped the blonde's breasts.

"I'm yours," the blonde promised, her breath warming Randy's skin as she spoke. The blonde leaned her body back slightly and once again began to stroke Randy's phallus. "I want you to take me right here," she emphasized each word as she stroked the phallus harder. "Then I want you to take me back to my place and I will do *anything* you want."

Randy was certain that she'd died and gone to heaven as the woman reached between their bodies and dipped two of her fingers into her wetness. "And I do mean anything," the blonde promised as she raised the fingers coated with her wetness to Randy's lips. "I'm healthy," she added as she offered her fingers to Randy's trembling lips.

"So am I," Randy reassured her lover before her tongue reached out and swirled around the blonde's fingertips. Despite Amy's protests that there wasn't another woman, Randy hadn't believed her she'd been tested for every STD under the sun.

Randy swooned as she licked the blonde's passion from her fingers; she sucked one into her mouth, savoring the taste of her mystery lover. Her own desire grew as her lover moaned deeply and pressed her center tighter against Randy's body. The blonde was squirming against her as Randy cleaned her fingers thoroughly running her teeth along her fingertips before releasing them.

"I can taste you?" The blonde panted excitedly as she pressed her mound against the phallus.

"Yes," Randy reassured her before she pulled the woman's small shirt up over her breasts and brushed her bra up. Then she began to kiss her way down the smaller woman's neck to the swell of her firm full breasts.

Randy ran her tongue slowly along her lover's breasts as the blonde continued to tease her clit with the phallus. Her wetness grew as the leather straps of her phallus tightened against her body. She heard cries of passion from the other couple. Apparently she wasn't the only one turned on by her mystery woman's boldness. Randy suckled her lover's nipple in her mouth; the blonde's body arched in response and her head fell back.

The sight of her lover offering her breast up to her, her long golden hair flowing in the moonlight, made Randy's body pulsate even harder as she fought against the climax that was already threatening to overtake her. The blonde parted her hips and wrapped her legs around Randy as far as she could given the restraints of their clothing. "Condom?" The blonde gasped as she began to stroke the phallus even harder.

"It's new and clean," Randy explained quickly before once again lowering her mouth to one of the blonde's erect rose-colored nipples. She suckled her harder as her lover's hips thrust against her urgently.

Randy was surprised when the blonde pulled away from her and stumbled backward. The intense gaze the blonde gave her set her body on fire. Randy allowed her body to sink harder against the cool brick wall of the building as the blonde sank to her knees before her.

Randy ran her fingers through her lover's long silky hair as her jeans were lowered to her ankles. She gasped as the blonde ran a single finger along the inside of her quivering thighs and up along the straps of her phallus. Randy's crystal blue eyes darkened as she watched her lover collecting her wetness and paint the tip of the phallus.

Randy almost exploded as she watched the blonde's soft pink tongue snake out and slowly circled the tip of her phallus. "I want you," the blonde murmured as she slowly licked away Randy's passion from the tip. Randy watched her repeat her actions. She stole glances at the other couple, pleasuring each other as they watched Randy and her mystery lover.

Every fiber of Randy's being was filled with a needy desire as her lover took the phallus deep in her mouth and began to suckle it. Randy pressed her lover harder into her as she felt the nub on the end of her phallus rub against her throbbing clit. Randy's hips swayed in response as her lover took her eagerly. The younger woman's words were echoing in her ears as she watched her avidly suckle her new toy, only stopping to paint it with Randy's wetness before returning it to the warmth of her mouth.

Unable to control her need any longer, Randy guided her lover away from the phallus. She moaned as she watched the blonde capture the long phallus between her breasts. "Please," the blonde pleaded. Randy simply nodded in response, knowing that her lover's need for release was as desperate as her own.

"Turn around," Randy instructed her; they both moaned in response.

Randy knelt down on the hard flooring of the deck as her lover turned away from her and supported herself on her hands and knees. She raised the blonde's skirt up to the blonde's waist before pulling her panties down her thighs. The aroma of her lover's desire filled her as the blonde parted her legs. Randy ran her hands along the blonde's exposed body.

The blonde whimpered and moaned as Randy caressed her backside. The brunette placed a light slap on the white cheeks her lover offered up freely. The blonde cried out in pleasure. "Do you belong to me?" Randy questioned her with a sultry purr as she gently pressed the phallus between her lover's thighs.

"Yes," the blonde cried out as she thrust her hips against the phallus.

Randy slipped one of her hands against the blonde's wet mound as she gently rubbed the phallus against her slick folds. Randy fought against the urge to touch her own desire as her lover rocked against the phallus, silently urging Randy to enter her. Randy continued to lubricate the phallus with the blonde's passion as she teased her clit between two of her fingers.

"Please," the blonde begged as she thrust herself harder against Randy's touch. "Please, baby," she continued in a needy tone.

Randy removed her hand from the warmth of her lover's wet mound and clasped one of her shoulders as she gently guided the tip of the phallus to the opening of the blonde's center. Her lover bucked against her as she pleaded with Randy to take her. The blonde's thighs parted even further as Randy gently slid the phallus inside of her. She was careful as she entered her, allowing the smaller woman to become comfortable with the feel of the toy inside of her.

"Take me," the blonde demanded as she tried to ride against the phallus. "Fuck me, baby," the blonde pleaded as Randy smiled and clutched her shoulder tighter. Normally Randy hated that word unless she was actually doing it and then it drove her insane with desire. She answered her lover's pleas and thrust her hips against the smaller woman, filling her completely.

They became lost in a haze of lust as they rocked against one another in a wild rhythm. With one hand still clutching the smaller woman's shoulder and the other planted firmly on the blonde's hip, Randy plunged in and out of her lover with a desperate need. Randy's body quivered as the blonde matched her movements. "Come for me," Randy demanded. She was nearing the edge as their bodies rocked against one another in a frenzy.

Randy's body was quivering as she rode her lover harder and the blonde cried out in ecstasy. She could see her lover's hands trying to clutch the floor as her body exploded and Randy took her harder. She continued to plunge in and out of her lover until the waves of ecstasy consumed her and she exploded against the smaller woman.

They collapsed onto the floor but continued to sway against each other as another climax consumed them. Panting heavily they finally stopped and Randy covered her lover's body with her own as the last waves of pleasure filtered through them. Fearing that she was crushing her lover, Randy finally lifted her body and gently removed the phallus from the warmth of the blonde's center.

Randy brushed the blonde's hair back from her sweaty brow as she leaned back. Her lover curled up in her arms and began kissing her neck. The tender caresses of the blonde's mouth refueled Randy's desire. Unexplainably her body, which had been completely sated moments before, was once again pulsating.

Randy pulled the smaller woman up onto her lap. The blonde's head fell back as she straddled Randy's body and the brunette began to pinch and tease her nipples. Randy paused for a moment when she saw something hauntingly familiar in the smaller woman's emerald eyes. *'Of course you know and understand the look in my eyes. You possess the same look,'* she suddenly realized. Knowing that her lover's needs truly mirrored her own, Randy more than ever wanted to pleasure the beautiful woman whose body was melting into hers.

"Do you know how beautiful you are?" Randy asked in a sultry tone as her lover returned her lustful gaze with a shy smile. Randy reclaimed the blonde's lips fiercely and began to explore the soft wanting they offered as she continued caressing the smaller woman's breasts. Randy's tongue wrapped around her lover's as she glided her hands down along the blonde's overheated body. Clasping her lover's hips Randy pulled the blonde closer to her. She griped the phallus with one hand as she gently grasped her hip with the other. Her lover's hips thrust forward in a demanding motion.

Randy responded urgently as she entered her lover with a powerful thrust. Her lover tore her lips away from Randy's as she cried out. "Yes!" The smaller woman pleaded as she rocked her hips against Randy's touch. The brunette's hands clasped her lover's thrusting hips. She guided her lover's body as her mouth began a sweet exploration down the blonde's neck to the swell of her breasts.

As her lover thrust urgently against her Randy captured one of her nipples in her mouth. She continued to urge the woman's hips to ride her body harder. She could feel the blonde's wetness brushing against her skin as she suckled her urgently. Her lover's blunt nails dug into Randy's broad shoulders, as the blonde seemed lost in a wild frenzy.

The blonde's body exploded as she climaxed against the tall brunette. Randy captured the smaller woman in her arms and held her close to her body as she trembled in her embrace. Randy was startled at how right it felt to hold this stranger. As her lover's breathing calmed Randy heard the sounds of approaching footsteps. Carefully they gathered themselves. Both women swayed as they stood. Randy watched her lover as they both quickly adjusted their clothing. There was no mistaking the fire in the small blonde's eyes.

"Do you have a car?" Randy asked quietly as she brushed a lock of hair off the blonde's brow.

"No. I came with some friends," the blonde explained as she caressed Randy's hip.

"Will they be worried?" Randy inquired as she leaned into the smaller woman's touch.

"No," the blonde responded flatly, confirming Randy's suspicion that she wasn't the only one who was nursing a broken heart.

"My car's in the lot if you still want me to take you home," Randy offered, leaving the decision entirely in her mystery lover's hands.

"Let's go," the blonde said firmly as she took Randy by the hand and led her back into the small bar.

They didn't stop as the blonde made a determined path to the front door. The cool night air enveloped Randy's overheated body as they stepped out into the parking lot. Randy gave her lover's hand a quick squeeze before she led her over to her car. She quickly kissed her on the cheek before opening the passenger side door for her and helping her into the SUV. With a bounce in her step the tall brunette quickly made her way over to the driver's side and poured her body inside.

Her hands shook slightly as she put the key in the ignition. A fleeting panicked thought clouded her mind, as she was just about to start the car. She turned to her lover and found herself lost once again in a smoky emerald gaze. All of her fears quickly faded as she pulled the small woman towards her and lost herself in a lingering kiss.

Randy and her lover were gasping for air when the kiss ended. She started the car and they put on their seatbelts before Randy put the car in gear. As Randy followed the directions to the blonde's home they began to caress one another's thighs. Randy's body quickly heated from the small blonde's touch. Unable to resist exploring her lover, she reached over and slipped her free hand back up under the blonde's leather skirt.

Her lover moaned and parted her thighs as Randy's hand drifted higher. The wetness that greeted Randy's touch sent a delightful shiver throughout her entire being. She pressed her fingers against the blonde's damp underwear and began to tease her clit through the silky material. Randy could barely keep her eyes on the road as her lover undid her seatbelt and raised her skirt up to her waist. Fueled by the blonde's actions, Randy's fingers teased her gasping lover harder.

When Randy stopped at a red light her lover quickly closed the gap between them and pulled the brunette's T-shirt up just high enough to reveal one of her breasts. Randy slipped her fingers into the blonde's panties as her lover suckled her nipple through the material of her bra. Randy ran her long fingers along the blonde's slick folds while she tried to keep an eye on the traffic light.

Regrettably the light changed and her lover's mouth abandoned her breast. Randy maintained her touch in her lover's wetness. The blonde released a deep moan while Randy dipped deeper inside of her.   Soon Randy had captured her lover's throbbing clit between her fingers. She teased her lover as one hand gripped the steering wheel tightly and her eyes focused on the empty streets.

"Look for a parking space," her lover managed to choke out as her hips swayed against Randy's touch. Somehow Randy managed to park her car without causing an accident as she continued to pleasure her lover. She quickly threw the car into park and shut off the engine. Then she tore off her seatbelt with one hand while she maintained the steady rhythm with the other. Randy closed the gap between them and practically crawled onto the heaving blonde as she quickly lowered her panties. Her lover growled with desire as Randy entered her.

The blonde was frantically trying to grip anything inside the car as Randy drove her over the edge. Randy gently withdrew her touch from her panting lover. The brunette drank in her lover's flushed features as she struggled to breath while Randy slow licked the blonde's nectar from her fingers. "That was insane," the blonde finally managed to squeak out as Randy released a proud throaty chuckle.

"Ready to take me to your place so we can go completely crazy?" Randy suggested in a promising tone.

"Yes," the blonde confirmed as she quickly pulled up her underwear and lowered her skirt.

The race from the car and up to the blonde's apartment was a blur. They kissed one another deeply as the blonde fumbled with her keys. Once the door was finally open the blonde pulled Randy into the dark apartment and slammed the door shut. Before Randy had a chance to get her bearings, the blonde pushed her up against a wall and began removing Randy's clothing. Randy gave herself over to her lover's demanding touch as her clothing went flying off into the darkness.

Randy's heart was pounding as her lover knelt before her and began to undo the straps of her phallus. Her new toy also went flying off into the darkness. Randy struggled to control her breathing as her lover parted her and then ran her tongue along her sex. "I want to make you feel as good as you made me feel," the blonde offered with a promising husky tone before she ran her flattened tongue against Randy's clit. Randy cried out as her lover began to feast upon her.

Randy felt more alive than she had in years as the stranger suckled her clit in the warmth of her mouth and entered her with two fingers. Randy's hips bucked in response and her lover murmured with pleasure while she drank in the brunette's desire. Each time Randy felt her body was ready to explode, her lover slowed her movements, making the brunette whimper with need. "Oh God, please!" Randy finally cried out as she guided her lover deeper into her wetness.

Her lover gave in to her urgent pleas as her mouth and fingers took Randy harder. Randy's body rocked against her lover's touch as the smaller woman plunged in and out of her while she teased Randy's aching clit with her teeth and her tongue. Randy's ears were buzzing as her mind filled with crimson images and her body shook. She cried out as her body exploded against the blonde.

Her lover continued to pleasure her as Randy's body pressed harder against the wall. She rocked her wetness against her lover as her body soared. Quickly she felt her body crash into the abyss. As she fought to remain standing and regain her ability to breathe and think, her lover tenderly ran her tongue along the inside of her thighs. Once she could breathe without choking, she assisted the blonde to her feet and kissed her deeply. Tasting her own desire on the smaller woman's lips sent Randy into a tailspin. Quickly Randy removed her lover's clothing and tossed the articles off into the darkness. Her lover guided her further into the apartment to the bedroom; they never broke the fiery kiss as they stumbled into the darkened room.

Randy finally ended the kiss so she could remove the last of her lover's clothing and guide her down onto the bed. She groaned in pleasure as she lowered her body down onto the blonde's and their skin touched for the first time. They quickly wrapped themselves around one another and allowed their passion to consume them. Randy ran her hands along her lover's body, afraid that if she stopped touching her the spell would break and she would awake to find that it all had been a dream.

Randy pressed her thigh against her lover's center while the blonde mirrored her actions. Soon their bodies began thrusting against each other as they kissed once again. They rolled around the large bed as they caressed one another and their bodies became one. Crying out once again, they climaxed in unison. Exhausted and sated they somehow managed to climb under the covers.

The blonde nestled her body on top of Randy's and they clung to one another while they drifted off into a peaceful slumber. When Randy awoke she finally felt free of the demons Amy had left behind. Yet there were a couple of problems facing her in the morning light. The first was that it felt far too good holding the stranger in her arms and they both knew that it was only to be for one night.

Randy understood that they were both reacting to a recent heartache and now it was time for her to go. The second problem was that it was morning and nature wasn't simply calling - it was screaming like a banshee. Randy needed to get up without awakening the woman whose beautiful body was draped across her since she was wary of the awkward conversation that would follow. Then of course there was the problem of trying to find the bathroom. She hadn't seen much of the mystery woman's apartment when they arrived. In fact she hadn't seen the apartment at all; they'd simply stumbled through the darkness and ravished each other.

The blonde murmured and squeaked in her slumber as Randy gently rolled her off her body and slipped out of bed. She pulled the blankets back up over the blissfully sleeping woman. Then she quickly looked around and grabbed a quilt that was lying on the floor and wrapped it around her body just in case the blonde had roommates. She doubted that anyone else lived in the apartment since they'd made enough noise to wake the dead during the night and no one had come running.

Bleary-eyed, Randy stumbled out of the bedroom back into the living room. "Okay, bathrooms are usually near the kitchen," she reasoned as she passed the kitchen, which was separated from the living room by a simple breakfast bar. She tripped over the clothing they'd tossed across the room and opened the first door she found. The door opened to a broom closet. She grumbled as she closed it and tried the next door she found. She smiled when she found the tiny bathroom waiting for her on the other side.

Randy was just washing up when she heard voices in the other room. *'What the hell happened here?'* a woman, whose voice she didn't recognize, demanded.

'What are you doing here, Susan, and why the hell would you bring your new girlfriend here?' the blonde shouted.

"This is bad," Randy mumbled as she dropped the quilt and wrapped her body in a short bathrobe hanging on the back of the door. She could hear Susan explaining that she was there to get the last of her things.

"You could have called first," the blonde shouted as Randy quietly exited the bathroom, noticing the redhead with empty boxes in her hands facing the blonde. The other woman in the room made Randy feel sick as she leaned against the outer wall. Her mystery lover was the only one who saw her and the small blonde's face paled.

"Oh, come off it, Shay," Susan scoffed. "It's not like I'm interrupting anything."

Randy felt the anger shoot through her as Susan spoke to the blonde in such a dismissive tone. Feeling bold at the fact that Susan hadn't noticed her yet and that she knew Susan's new love all too well, Randy decided it was time to really heat things up.

"Well, I was just going to make breakfast and I'd really like to know how many people I'm cooking for," Randy offered cockily as everyone turned to her.

"Randy?" Amy choked out in disbelief.

Randy simply cast an icy glare at her ex-lover who just a few weeks ago had sworn up and down that she wasn't leaving her for another woman. Shay, who was wrapped in a bed sheet, simply looked at her in surprise. Susan's jaw dropped as her dark eyes ran up and down Randy's half-naked body.

Randy was amused by the absurdity of the situation and decided to add more fuel to the fire. She brushed past the stunned trio and walked into the kitchen with an air of confidence. Pretending that she'd been there many times Randy set about making coffee.

"Wait! You're cooking for her?" Amy spat out jealously.

Randy simply rolled her crystal blues in disgust. Amy really did lack the ability to focus on what was really happening around her at times. *'What did I ever see in her?'* her mind wondered as a strange sense of freedom and relief washed over her. *'I'm actually glad she left me,'* her mind quickly processed as she turned on the coffee maker.

"Shay darling, will our guests be staying or going?" Randy asked innocently.

"Going," Shay spat out vehemently.

"Wait! I need my stuff," Susan argued.

'Another rocket scientist. She and Amy are perfect for each other,' Randy thought as she continued to act as if she'd been Shay's kitchen on a regular basis.

"Then next time you'll call," Shay fumed. "Not that I should be surprised since you didn't even bother to tell me that you were leaving. No note; no nothing. After five years I find out that it's over between us when I come home from work one day and find your half of the closet empty."

"You didn't tell her that you were leaving her?" Amy blurted out.

"I . . . Uhm . . . ," Susan stammered.

Randy could understand Amy's sudden concern. The two of them must have been planning this for months since they were already living together and it takes a lot of time and effort to find a decent apartment these days. *'That's quite a catch you dumped me for.'* Randy silently chuckled.

The room filled with an eerie silence; Susan and Amy stared at each other and Randy looked at Shay in concern. "We should leave. You can come back another time," Amy finally reasoned. Susan opened her mouth to protest, but as she looked around the living room she must have realized that she was seriously outnumbered. She tossed the cardboard boxes she held onto the floor and began to follow Amy out of the apartment. Amy and Susan halted their movements when they stumbled across the phallus that was lying on the living room floor. Randy didn't miss the jealous look that flashed across both women's faces before they stormed out of the apartment.

"That was the smartest thing she's done in years," Randy offered thoughtfully.

"Thank you," Shay offered quietly as she pulled the sheet tighter around her body and walked over to Randy.

"You're welcome, Shay," Randy offered, thinking it was nice to finally know her mystery woman's name.

Shay laughed at the absurdity of the moment. "So what are the odds that they would be together?" Shay finally offered playfully.

"Slim to none," Randy reasoned. "It probably would have killed them to find out that we didn't even know each other's names until they showed up." Randy didn't miss the shadow that crossed over Shay's face. "How about I make us breakfast? We can get to know one another and maybe become friends," Randy suggested hopefully.

"I'd like that, Randy," Shay agreed with a shy smile.

Over breakfast Randy was pleased that she and Shay really did seem to get along. Also the fact that they'd slept together seemed to vanish as they fell into a comfortable conversation.

A year later Randy was trapped in another dilemma. The morning after should have been the end of the story. Except she and Shay did end up becoming friends. They rarely spoke about the one night of passion they'd shared despite the fact that Randy often liked to replay the night in her mind. They had moved passed it as they fell into a comfortable friendship. Both women had even started dating other women.

That was the problem Randy now faced. She and Shay weren't just friends. They had become good friends and now, a year later, Randy was more than aware that her feelings for Shay ran deeper than friends. She had fallen for the energetic blonde. She couldn't seem to spend enough time with Shay and it drove her insane whenever Shay met someone new.

Randy was seated at the bar in the restaurant she had agreed to meet Shay at for dinner. She was firm in her conviction that she needed time away from the blonde. She didn't sense that Shay shared her feelings and she didn't want to lose the friendship that had formed between them.

"Now what has you so deep in thought?" A familiar voice questioned her.

Randy was surprised when she looked up to find Amy looking at her. Despite the breakup Randy was now able to be at least civil to her ex-lover. "Nothing," Randy lied as Amy seated herself next to her. "Meeting people?"

"Date," Amy responded with a shrug.

"Yeah, sorry to hear about you and Susan breaking up," Randy quipped in a snide tone.

"Right," Amy scoffed. "So what's new with you?"

"Just meeting Shay for dinner," she explained, trying desperately to sound blasé about the entire situation.

"How's that going?" Amy asked sincerely.

"I've told you before we're just friends," Randy grumbled in response.

"You're a terrible liar, Randy," Amy responded seriously.

"It's the truth," Randy protested.

"So you haven't told her then?" Amy quickly inquired.

"Told who what?" Randy asked in bewilderment.

"Shay," Amy said in a flat tone, "You haven't told her that you're in love with her."

"Don't be ridiculous," Randy argued. "We're just friends."

"Still an emotional coward," Amy grunted bitterly.

"Excuse me?" Randy flared.

"You forget how well I know you," Amy noted as she placed a comforting hand on the brunette's arm. "Randy, you asked me to live with you before you had enough courage to say I love you."

"So?" Randy shyly mumbled.

It was hard enough for Randy to realize that she had fallen in love with Shay, but to have Amy of all people counseling her about the bizarre situation was more than the brunette could handle.

"Tell her," Amy offered in a comforting tone.

Randy's mind was spinning. Could it be that Amy was right?   She and Shay had met under extremely odd circumstances. Randy went to the bar to meet and have sex with a stranger after her lover left her. Shay's friends dragged her out to the bar for the same reason. They'd met, and without even taking the time to introduce themselves, they'd shared a wild night of passion. In the morning they'd been greeted by both of their ex-lovers who were living together. *'Not exactly a story you can tell your grandkids,'* Randy's overactive mind quipped.

"Amy, thank you for your advice, but the fact that Shay and I became friends is strange enough," Randy reasoned.

"How did the two of you meet?" Amy suddenly inquired. Randy groaned, feeling a throbbing headache forming.

"We picked each other up in a bar," Randy confessed as she watched her ex-lover's face cloud over with a disappointed look. "Oh what? You're the last person I need a lecture from," Randy scolded her. "You were cheating on me with Susan."

"That was the biggest mistake of my life," Amy offered in a hurt tone as she leaned closer to Randy. "I should have never let you go."

Randy threw her head back as she laughed. She reached over and tucked her fingers under Amy's chin. "We weren't meant to be," Randy offered gently as she watched Amy's brown eyes fill with regret.

"You're in love," Amy responded with a smile as Randy stared into her eyes. She wondered how Amy could see how much she truly loved Shay and the blonde who held her heart was completely clueless.

The hair on the back of Randy's neck stood on end as a familiar sense washed over her. While Amy's hand still rested on her shoulder and Randy's fingers remained under her ex-lover's chin, the brunette turned to see a pair of very angry emerald eyes glaring at her.

"Shay?" Randy squeaked, suddenly feeling a sense of guilt as she quickly removed her fingers from Amy's face.

Shay's face turned a brilliant shade of red as her eyes darkened with anger. Randy felt helpless and confused as Shay spun on her heel and stormed out of the restaurant. Her jaw hung open as she stared blankly at Shay's retreating form.

"What just happened?" Randy blurted out once Shay had vanished.

"Go after her," Amy demanded. "And tell her how you *really* feel about her. Don't argue with me and don't stop and don't overanalyze things. Trust me. This isn't easy for me. I would give anything for you to look at me the way you look at her. But you never did."

"Thank you," Randy offered as she stood, still feeling confused by what was happening.

"Oh, and Randy? If for some reason she doesn't feel the same way, I'll be waiting for you," Amy said sincerely.

Randy stared at Amy as if she'd sprouted a third eye. Finally she shook her head clear and made her way out of the restaurant. Randy's hands were shaking as she climbed into her car and started it up. Amy had been so kind and sincere, just as she'd been back when she and Randy had first started dating. Randy was touched by Amy's willingness to help her follow her heart. She also knew Amy well enough to know that her sincerity would be very short-lived.

As Randy approached the door to Shay's apartment her knees were trembling and her palms were sweating. She was still confused as to why Shay had looked at her the way she did and why she'd bolted out of the restaurant. Randy knocked on the door to the apartment she'd visited many times over the past year. Images of nights watching movies while sharing popcorn and late night chats filled her mind. She also recalled how she would sit across from Shay, trying to wish away her feelings of love and desire for the small blonde.

Randy knocked once again on the door, this time with more urgency. The brunette felt that her future was hanging in the balance as she waited for Shay to answer the door. She'd seen Shay's Mazda parked out front so she knew that the blonde was home. Just as Randy's heart began to shatter and she was ready to give up and walk away, the door opened.

Shay looked lost as she stared up at Randy. "Hi," Shay greeted her in a quiet voice.

"Can I come in?" Randy inquired carefully.

Shay simply nodded as she opened the door wider and allowed Randy to step inside. Randy felt an uncomfortable chill as silence engulfed them while Shay closed the door. "Shay, why did you run out of the restaurant?" Randy asked her, maintaining a calm that she didn't really feel as she spoke.

"It looked like you had other plans for the evening," Shay responded coldly as she shrugged.

Randy blinked in confusion as she watched Shay move as far away from her as possible. Randy was stunned as Shay rested her body against the breakfast bar and folded her arms against her chest. "Have I ever blown you off?" Randy asked, still keeping her voice level.

"No," Shay responded as she stared at her feet.

"I know you don't like Amy," Randy continued, still feeling a strange sense of guilt. "I don't blame you. She isn't one of my favorite people either, but I don't see a reason not to be polite to her. Its has been over a year since we broke up."

"I know," Shay mumbled while maintaining eye contact with her shoes. "Did you know that she and Susan split up?"

The question was so soft that Randy almost didn't hear the small blonde's words. "I heard." Randy shrugged, still confused as to why Shay was acting the way she was.

"Why was she touching you?" Shay demanded suddenly.

"We were talking," Randy responded defensively. "She was meeting a date."

"Then why was she touching you?" Shay asked again in a firmer tone.

Randy's mouth hung open. The question sounded more like an accusation. "She wants you back," Shay muttered bitterly. "She's told everyone that will listen that she made a mistake and wants you back."

"So?" Randy scoffed at the notion. "First, she only thinks she wants me back. Secondly, Hell would have to freeze over and the Red Sox would have to win the World Series before I would even consider trusting her again. You know that, don't you? Remember that night a few months ago when we were talking over that pizza? We agreed that Susan and Amy had done us both a favor by dumping us? That neither of us were really happy in our relationships and it took them leaving us to realize just how miserable we were?"

"Yes," Shay conceded with a heavy sigh as she finally met Randy's gaze. "I'm sorry. It's just that I ran into Susan today and she gave me an earful about how Amy wanted you back."

"You saw Susan?" Randy blurted out as a sudden surge of jealousy rushed through her. "What did she want?"

"The same thing Amy wants," Shay laughed as she smiled at Randy. "I told her to go away."

"Good," Randy responded flatly.

Randy smiled in response to the bright smile Shay was giving her. "I guess both of them are rebounding and thought we'd be stupid enough to give them a second chance," Randy finally offered as she moved across the room and leaned against the breakfast bar next to Shay. Randy's heart started to beat faster as she felt the warmth emanating off Shay's body. Randy swallowed hard as her mouth became suddenly dry.

"I'm sorry I acted like an idiot," Shay said softly. "I'm over Susan. I have been for a long time. Seeing her again and then seeing you with Amy just brought up a lot of the old hurt feelings."

Randy summoned up her courage for what she knew she had to do. She was worried that she was about to make things more difficult for Shay. Her mind tried to form the right words to tell her how she felt - that Amy never truly held her heart. That spot belonged to Shay. "There's just one thing," Randy began slowly as fear gripped her heart. "Amy didn't ask me to come back to her."

"She will," Shay said in disgust.

"Well, she did," Randy, continued as she watched Shay's brow crinkle in confusion. "But only if the woman I'm interested in shoots me down. She said that she would wait for me if this woman didn't share my feelings."

"She's priceless," Shay grumbled. "So you're interested in someone?"

Randy prayed that the hint of disappointment she heard in the blonde's voice was because she shared her feelings. "I met her a while ago," Randy began to explain as she watched Shay's face carefully. "It's really strange. It was a one-night stand. It felt so right holding her in my arms when I woke up in the morning. I've never felt so complete."

"Does she know how you feel?" Shay asked in a supportive tone.

"Not a clue," Randy confessed. "You see, we're friends and I'm terrified that I'll lose her friendship."

"I know what you mean," Shay responded absently as she pushed her body away from the counter and wandered over to the kitchen.

Randy watched her as the blonde began to make some coffee. It was a familiar ritual they shared whenever they found themselves beginning a heavy conversation. "I don't think you do," Randy continued as she fought against the fear that was threatening to consume her. "It's you," Randy finally confessed in a strong voice. She felt her body constrict as she stared at Shay's back and the petite blonde halted her movements. "I fell in love with you," Randy finally admitted, knowing that she had just risked everything.

Randy watched in agony, as Shay remained frozen. After what seemed like an eternity the brunette clutched her key ring tightly and started to walk towards the front door. *'Well, that answers that. Goodbye, Shay,'* she cried silently as her heart shattered.

"Where are you going?" Shay blurted out as she dashed out of the kitchen.

Randy's shoulders slumped as she felt Shay's hand on her arm. The touch sent a shiver up and down her spine. It was Randy's turn to remain frozen in place. It had been hard enough to confess her feelings to Shay. The last thing she wanted to do was sit up all night and talk about how they could still be friends.

"Giving up so easily?" Shay echoed the challenge she'd offered the first time they'd met. "I know that look," she echoed once again as she gently wrapped her arms around Randy's waist and turned her towards her.

Randy was stunned when she looked down into Shay's brilliant emerald eyes and saw that they mirrored her own. "Do you?" Randy responded in a breathy tone as Shay reached up and cupped her face.

"Yes," Shay confirmed. "I think you should stay and do what you came here to do."

"And what's that?" Randy asked softly as she leaned into Shay's touch.

"You came here to tell your best friend that you fell in love with her and you want to make love to her," Shay pleaded as her body brushed against Randy's.

"What else do I want?" Randy encouraged her as she ran her fingers through Shay's long blonde hair.

"You want to hear her say that she loves you too and that she wants more than the close friendship you already share," Shay offered as she traced Randy's chiseled features with her fingertips. "I'm in love with you, Randy. I have been for a long time, but I convinced myself that I could be happy just being your friend since it was all you seemed to be offering me.

Randy blew out a sigh of relief as she allowed her body to relax into Shay's touch. She had prayed that Shay shared her feelings or that maybe late one night they would find themselves together in bed one more time. In the blink of an eye everything had changed. Shay's body was pressed against hers so tightly that she felt the blonde's nipples against her chest and she knew that she was finally happy.

"Make love to me?" Shay requested in a breathy tone that was unlike the uncontrolled passion her voice had possessed the first night they met.

Randy felt her heart swell with joy as she wrapped her arms around Shay's slender waist. Shay reached up and guided Randy to her. Randy's body pulsated as she watched her lover's lips part and Shay's warm inviting breath caressed her face. Randy brushed her lips against Shay's and felt the warmth spread through her. Her heart pounded rapidly as she held Shay tighter against her body and reclaimed her lips. This time the kiss quickly deepened as the blonde parted her lips with her tongue. Randy invited her lover in for a sweet exploration as she began an exploration of her own.

Randy's tongue engaged in a sensual duel with Shay's as she caressed the blonde's hips. Shay moaned into her mouth as the blonde's hands explored Randy's body. Randy felt lightheaded as she reluctantly ended the kiss. "I've been waiting for over a year to kiss you again," Randy whispered against Shay's skin as she kissed her neck.

"Oh Randy, it was so hard not to touch you," Shay confessed with a deep moan. Randy nibbled her way up along Shay's neck until she was suckling her earlobe. Shay's soft murmurs of pleasure warmed Randy's heart and body. She could barely stand as her mouth reclaimed Shay's lips and they lost themselves in the fiery kiss. Shay began to tug her blouse out of her slacks as Randy's hands slipped down the blonde's body to cup her firm backside. She massaged Shay's bottom as the blonde slipped one hand up under the light material of the brunette's blouse.

Randy pulled Shay closer; her skin tingled from the feel of the blonde's fingers dancing up her body. She wanted to continue exploring the warmth of Shay's mouth yet the need to breathe was too great. They were both gasping as the kiss ended. "I love you," Randy repeated as she held Shay against her body.

"I love you too," Shay murmured in response as she returned Randy's warm embrace.

Randy inhaled the soft scent of Shay's shampoo as they stood there holding onto one another. Finally Shay took a shy step back, took Randy by the hand, and led her over to the sofa. "I need to sit," Shay confessed with a smile as they climbed up onto the sofa. Randy gave Shay's hand a reassuring squeeze before she pulled the blonde into her arms. Randy smiled as Shay nuzzled against her body.

Randy smiled at how good it felt to finally be holding Shay in her arms without feeling guilty about touching her. Randy looked down at the blonde who was smiling up at her. They began kissing once again. Each kiss was soft and promising as they nestled against one another. Soon the tender kisses began to grow deeper as lips parted and hands began to roam. Randy soon became lost in the feel of Shay as she began to unbutton the blonde's blouse.

Once she had undone the last button Randy brushed the blouse open and began to dance her fingertips across Shay's firm abdomen. She could feel Shay's movements growing bolder as the blonde's hand once again slipped up under her blouse. Her skin burned as Shay caressed her body. Randy cupped one of Shay's breasts and moaned as she felt the blonde's nipple harden from her touch.

As their tongues danced together Shay unclasped her bra and Randy caressed the blonde's breast. Randy's hands moved slowly along Shay's body and began to slip the blonde's blouse down her shoulders. Shay's hands moved to Randy's breasts as she pulled the brunette's bra up.

The kisses ceased for a moment as they stared deeply into one another's eyes. Randy ran her fingers along Shay's lips and along her jaw before she slowly removed the blonde's blouse. Randy took a lingering glance at Shay's half exposed body while the blonde gently caressed her breasts. "It's funny. After everything we did the first time we met, I feel suddenly shy about touching you," Shay confessed as the palms of her hands brushed across Randy's nipples.

"That night was incredible," Randy said softly as she continued to run the tips of her fingers along Shay's skin. "But that intensity doesn't hold a candle to what I'm feeling for you right at this moment."

Shay smiled at her and Randy trembled as she felt the blonde's hands retreating from her body. Shay's smile grew broader as she reached behind her back and unclasped her bra. Randy watched her intently as Shay slowly slipped her bra straps down her shoulders and arms. Her crystal blue eyes drank in every curve of Shay's body as she continued to glide her fingers across her skin. She smiled as she felt her lover's skin respond to her touch.

While she tenderly caressed Shay's skin the blonde undid and removed Randy's blouse and bra. Randy's touch only left Shay's body when she needed to move so the blonde could undress her. Randy's eyes moved to lips that were slightly parted. Soon she was kissing the blonde once again as their half-naked bodies melted together. Randy's desire intensified as she felt Shay's erect nipples brushing against her skin.

The need for more quickly became demanding as Randy lowered Shay down onto the sofa. Randy's hand came to rest on one of Shay's hips as they continued to kiss. She moaned as she felt Shay's body moving beneath her and the blonde's thigh parted her long legs. Randy's hand drifted along Shay's hip as she pressed her center against the blonde's thigh.

Randy's clit rubbed against Shay's thigh as she slipped her hand between their bodies and undid the blonde's slacks. She felt her lover's movements quicken as she lowered the zipper of Shay's slacks and brushed them open. She ran her hand along the elastic waistband of Shay's panties as the blonde pressed her thigh harder against her aching need.

Randy released Shay's lips and lifted her body up. She supported her body with her arms as she straddled Shay's thigh tightly and began to rock her hips slowly. She looked down at Shay's flushed features as the blonde's hands clasped her hips, guiding her body against her thigh. Randy lowered her head and began to tease Shay's nipple with her tongue while the blonde encouraged her hips to increase their rhythm.

Randy was lost in a haze of desire as she captured Shay's nipple in her mouth. She suckled her lover eagerly as her hips increased their sensual rhythm. She could hear Shay's soft murmurs as Randy's thigh greeted the blonde's center. Soon they were melting together as their hips swayed in a perfect rhythm.

They wrapped themselves around each other as Randy's mouth blazed a tantalizing trail between Shay's breasts and mouth. Randy was lost in the feel of Shay's body moving against her own. She was only dimly aware of Shay lowering her pants and underwear until she felt the blonde's hands massaging her now exposed backside. "Randy? Baby, can we move this into the bedroom?" Shay choked out as Randy lifted her body.

"Yes," Randy responded with a soft smile.

Randy wanted to slow things down and make love to Shay before they became lost in raw desire. She assisted her lover to her feet and wrapped her arm around her waist. She loved the feel of Shay's body next to her own as they stumbled over their loose clothing towards the bedroom.

Shay turned on the light as they stood beside the bed. Randy brushed Shay's cheek with back of her fingers. They took a moment to exchange gentle touches before Shay guided Randy down onto the bed. Randy rested on her hands as she watched her lover undress her. Now completely naked Randy found that she felt totally at ease as she lie before Shay and offered her hand to the blonde.

Shay climbed up onto the bed and straddled Randy's body. Once again they kissed. Randy rolled Shay onto her back and finished undressing her. As Randy exposed Shay's beautiful body she kissed every inch of newly exposed flesh. She could feel Shay's eyes watching her every movement as she kissed her way up along the blonde's legs until she was nestled between her thighs.

"Make love to me," Shay offered as Randy blew a warm breath through her damp golden curls. Randy responded to her lover's request by parting her and dipping her tongue into Shay's wetness. The blonde lifted her body as Randy cupped her backside and drew her closer. Randy ran her tongue along Shay's sex, savoring the nectar of the blonde's desire.

Randy could feel her own wetness growing as she ran her tongue along the blonde's slick folds before she began to flicker her tongue across Shay's clit. The sound of her lover moaning her name as she suckled her throbbing clit in her mouth made Randy's body tremble in response. Randy was nearing the edge as she feasted upon her lover. Her mind was lost in the feel of Shay's body responding to her touch.

Randy held her lover steady as Shay's body arched up off the bed, trembling uncontrollably. Soon Shay was crying out and Randy was kissing her way back up the blonde's body until she was holding the blonde in a tender embrace. As Randy held her lover she felt the spark of raw passion that they'd shared the first time they'd touched building inside of her.

Shay must have felt the same spark as she began to caress and kiss every inch of Randy's body. Randy's body melted into Shay's as they rolled around the bed and fondled one another. Randy hissed in pleasure as Shay entered her while she suckled her nipples. Randy wrapped her legs around Shay's body as the blonde plunged in and out of her wetness while Randy begged her for more.

Randy reached between them and cupped her lover's wetness. She cried out as Shay pleasured her while she ground her desire against Randy's hand. The brunette's hunger ran deep as they gave themselves over to the feelings that they shared. During the night Randy pleasured Shay in ways that she had only allowed herself to dream about. Well after the sun had risen, Randy finally collapsed onto her stomach with Shay straddling her from behind.

"I don't think I can move," Shay choked out as she kissed Randy's neck.

"Good thing it's the weekend and we don't have to go anywhere," Randy mumbled into the pillow.

Shay released a sated sigh as she lifted her body off Randy's. The brunette echoed her lover's sigh as she rolled over and they climbed under the covers. "I love you," Shay said, yawning as Randy spooned her body.

"I love you too," Randy responded as she smiled, lost in the wonderful feeling of holding Shay in her arms.

The End

TRADING ROOMS

PART ONE

Ellie Baxter folded her arms across her chest and glared at her older sister. "Not in this lifetime," she spat as her sister pouted. "Suck it up, Tina."

"Ellie, I really want to do this," Tina pleaded.

"Why?" Ellie snorted in disgust. "And why didn't you tell me that you entered us?"

"Because I knew what you would say," Tina explained flatly. "Don't you want to be on television?"

"No," Ellie retorted as she rolled her crystal blue eyes. "And I don't want Roger and Barry redecorating our kitchen. I can only imagine what those two creatures will do to it."

"Ellie, we need to have the kitchen redone and this way it will be done for free," Tina reasoned. "Plus we get to be on television," Tina added with a gleeful squeal. Ellie groaned; she hated it when her older sister acted like a teenager.

"Yeah, and you get to suck up to Barry," Ellie teased her sister, knowing that Tina had a crush on the older of the two brothers living next door to them.

Whenever Tina was attracted to some guy, the six-foot dark-haired beauty turned into a girlie girl. It never ceased to amaze and amuse Ellie who was two years younger and half an inch shorter than her normally sane sibling.

"Knock, knock," an overly cheerful voice beckoned them from the front door of their modest little house.

"It's Sara," Tina gushed as she rushed to the door.

Ellie shook her head in disbelief as she watched her sister act like a teenager. "I can't believe that's the same person who just last week threatened to set the paper boy on fire for missing the porch." A sudden panic filled Ellie as she realized that she was going to be on a television show.

"Oh crap! I've got to find a way to get out of this," Ellie muttered as her sister ushered Sara Dearborn, the host of *Trading Rooms,* into the living room. Ellie had watched the show with her sister many times. It was simple. Neighbors exchanged keys and each couple redecorated a room in the other's home. Despite her grumbling Ellie did enjoy the show; she just didn't want to be on it. Every time she watched she wanted to see someone go completely ballistic over what their neighbor had done to their home.

"You must be Ellie," the hostess chimed. "I'm Sara Dearborn and this is . . ." The perky dirty blonde spun around, looking for someone. Just then a small blonde stumbled in and yawned. Ellie smiled at the attractive woman who was hiding behind dark sunglasses and clutching a paper coffee cup. "There you are," Sara continued in an annoyingly perky tone. "This is Carrie Carson, the designer you'll be working with."

'Things are looking up,' Ellie thought as her eyes traveled up and down Carrie's firm body. The blonde yawned once again and then jerked her head up. She tore off her sunglasses and stared at Tina and Ellie. "Whoa! Dueling Amazons," she gasped. Sara's jaw dropped at Carrie's comment as Tina and Ellie chuckled. Since both sisters stood almost six feet tall they were well accustomed to people reacting strangely to them. Both of them stared down at the demure Carrie who wasn't any taller than five foot four.

"Carrie?" Sara gasped in horror.

"Oh, lighten up," Carrie retorted as her eyes wandered to Ellie. "I just spent four hours circling the airport because the fog I thought I left in England apparently decided to follow me." Ellie smiled, not missing the twinkle in the blonde's eyes as their eyes met.   Carrie took a sip of her coffee as she cast an appreciative glance at Ellie. "And let me tell you, my last job was a real bitch. Material Girl my ass. She has more money than God and is planning on keeping every penny of it."

"Carrie, your language," Sara cautioned her with a horrified look. "Don't forget the cameras will be rolling soon."

"You want to hear bad language?" Carrie snorted. "You should hear Miss Like-A-Virgin if she catches you trying to slip one of her little darlings a Pop Tart. You would think that someone who dated Warren Beatty would have a sense of humor."

"You met her?" Tina gushed as Sara's mouth hung open; apparently she was disgusted by Carrie's behavior. "What's she like?" Ellie rolled her eyes at her sister who normally was the portrait of control.

"She's okay but one hell of a business woman," Carrie yawned. "If you want Italian marble then you're going to pay big bucks for it. Why is that so hard to understand? Any chance of getting more coffee?" The blonde added as she stared at her now empty cup.

"I'll make some," Ellie volunteered, thankful for the opportunity to get away from her suddenly star-struck sister.

"Thank you," Carrie offered with a slight purr.

"Uhm . . . Carrie, can I have a word with you?" Sara stammered as she tugged on the petite blonde's arm.

"This is so exciting," Tina gushed as she followed Ellie into the kitchen. "Carrie Carson has been on the show a couple of times. She's worked for some major stars."

"Just when did you become a star-struck goober?" Ellie grunted as she began to make coffee.

"Oh, like you're immune?" Tina teased her. "You couldn't wait to make coffee for her."

"That has nothing to do with the celebrities she's worked

for," Ellie explained with a wry smirk.

"Then why?" Tina began to question. "Never mind. I get it. Small blonde with big . . ."

"Hey," Ellie cut her off.

Tina folded her arms across her chest and glared at Ellie with a confident smile. "So we're going on the show and maybe we'll both get what we want," Tina encouraged her.

"Do I have to wear one of those ugly smocks?" Ellie grumbled.

"Ladies!" Sara's overly perky voice beckoned them back into the living room.

Ellie's eyes widened in surprise as Tina actually bounced into the outer room. "I wish I had a camcorder. Mom and Dad would laugh themselves senseless if they could see this." Ellie laughed as she followed her sister into the outer room.

"Okay, girls. I'm just here for a quick Q&A and then you can chat with Carrie," Sara rambled on excitedly. A loud snore diverted everyone's attention to the small blonde who had fallen asleep on the sofa. "Jet lag," Sara offered with a helpless shrug. Ellie couldn't help but smile at the sight of the tiny blonde snoring away with her mouth hanging open and her hands still gripping the empty coffee cup she'd arrived with.

"First, the two of you are sisters and the guys next door are brothers. Any romance happening there?" Sara gushed excitedly.

"No," Ellie stated firmly while Tina simply blushed.

Sara continued to ask them questions, which Tina seemed to eat up and Ellie found inane. Still, Tina did seem really happy and Ellie tried to play along. Ellie's spirits lifted when Carrie finally woke up. The blonde snorted loudly before loudly exclaiming, "Oh yes, baby." There was no mistaking the sensuality in her voice as she cried out. The blonde blushed furiously when her eyes snapped open and found three very amused women looking at her. "Oops," she apologized as her blush turned even redder.

"Well, it seems Carrie took a trip to naughty land without us," Sara teased the embarrassed decorator.

"Pity," Ellie whispered with a sly grin as Carrie cast a wary glance over at her. "I'll get you some coffee," she offered as she made a quick retreat into the kitchen, feeling Carrie's eyes watching her every movement.

PART TWO

Ellie sat on her living room sofa; Sara had left the three them alone to talk about what they should do to Barry and Roger's home. "Now for the fun part," Carrie stated as she took another sip of coffee. Ellie was amazed by the amount of caffeine the small woman had consumed, not to mention that each cup was loaded with far too much sugar. "So tell me about Barry and Roger. What room will we be redecorating?" Carrie inquired exuberantly. Ellie wasn't terribly surprised by the woman's sudden boundless energy. Between the sugar and caffeine, the small blonde must have had a good buzz going. "Are they a couple?" Carrie added in a serious tone.

"No," Tina quickly corrected her. "They're brothers."

"I get it, and the two of you are sisters." Carrie nodded in understanding. "The show loves cute things like that. Okey dokey. What room are we doing?" The blonde asked as she pulled out a sketchpad and a notebook.

"Their living room," Tina explained.

"What does it look like now?" Carrie continued as she scribbled something on her notepad.

"Hell," Ellie offered.

"It's not that bad," Tina lied.

"Two straight guys living alone? I'm guessing it is a cross between a sty and a sports bar," Carrie noted.

"Something like that," Ellie smirked.

"Yeah," Tina reluctantly agreed.

"Believe it or not, that could work," Carrie said thoughtfully.

"I was thinking of something lighter with maybe a hint of a period look to it," Tina suggested as Ellie rolled her eyes.

"You just described your living room," Carrie responded absently as she continued to take notes. Ellie chuckled at the observation. "You need to keep in mind that the guys are the ones who will be living there. Okay, do they have a fosse ball table and mismatched chairs?"

"You've seen it?" Tina asked.

"No, just thinking about my kid brother's place," Carrie explained dryly. "Why are you letting these bozos redecorate a room in your home?" Carrie asked in amazement.

"Tina wants to be on television," Ellie said, teasing her sister who grimaced at her comment. "Be thankful I'm leaving out the part about you wanting to knock boots with Barry," she whispered so only Tina could hear her. Her older sister swatted her.

"And what do you want?" Carrie inquired softly, her emerald eyes glinting mischievously as she spoke.

Ellie's stomach clenched slightly at the decorator's seductive tone. One thing was certain, Carrie Carson wasn't a shy lass. "I'm looking forward to the *experience,*" Ellie offered in a sultry tone as she held the blonde's fiery gaze.

"I hope I don't disappoint you," Carrie teased in response.

Ellie's lips curled seductively as her heart beat just a little faster. "Now let's talk some more about the boys next door," Carrie said, changing the subject and breaking the intense gaze they shared. As Tina and Carrie spoke, Ellie's head began to spin at the over exuberant blonde. More than once during the conversation Ellie found herself wondering if Carrie ever took a moment to breathe. She also found herself wondering if Carrie was equally energetic in bed.

Later, after Carrie had left to look at Barry and Roger's living room, Ellie threw her arms around her sister. "Thank you," she gushed.

"Get off me," Tina shrugged her sister away. "And get your mind out of the gutter. I can't believe the way that you shamelessly flirted with that woman."

"She wants me," Ellie boasted with a brilliant smile. "And I wouldn't go casting stones, missy. I noticed how you want to redo that living room like you're planning on moving in."

"You think every woman wants you," Tina chastised her. "I wonder who will be working with Roger and Barry on our place?" she pondered.

"Who cares?" Ellie responded with a dismissive wave. "So long as it isn't that Federico guy. He paints everything pink."

Just as she finished expressing her opinion, Sara returned with Federico in tow. "I am not letting him turn our kitchen into a bottle of Pepto Bismol."

"It will be fine. We'll just tell no the boys no pink," Tina reassured her.

PART THREE

The following morning, with cameras rolling, Sara gleefully exchanged house keys with Tina, Ellie, Roger, and Barry, explaining that they had two days and a five hundred dollar budget. Ellie wasn't thrilled about the orange smock she was forced to wear or the fact that they'd be sleeping at Roger and Barry's bachelor home. But the thought of spending almost forty-eight hours with Carrie made her pulse race.

When they stepped into the boy's living room, Ellie shuddered at the worn-out chairs, water-stained coffee table, and the St. Paulie Girl poster on the wall. Other than that the room had nothing to offer. "We have quite a project on our hands," Carrie mugged for the camera. "First, let's clear all this out and then we can get started," she brightly explained to them. As they hauled the beat-up old chairs out to the front lawn, Ellie realized that on television all the hard labor was shown in fast motion. In reality, moving the guys' beer-stained furniture was breaking her back.

Once everything had been cleared out, Carrie announced that they would be painting the walls and staining the floor. Carrie revealed the paint and stain they would be using, explaining that she was going for the look of a gentleman's study. Ellie tried to imagine just how they were going to pull that off with their limited amount of time and money.

Ellie tried to look happy about doing all the hard work as they began to lay tarps. She tried to get close to Carrie whenever she could, but with the cameramen constantly following them, it made the task difficult. Just as the camera crew was about to take a break, Carrie informed them that she had to pick up supplies for the project and meet with Crafty Carl, the show's resident handy man. He could build anything the designers scribbled out for him on a napkin.

Ellie grumbled as they began to paint the walls. "Get over it," Tina scolded her. "You're just mad she isn't flirting with you the way she did yesterday."

"Am not," Ellie said as she pouted like a small child.

The painting and staining took hours and Ellie's body was aching. Just as she was about to collapse, Carrie and the camera crew returned. "Now, ladies, while the floor is drying I have a couple of special projects for you," Carrie explained brightly.

"Oh goodie," Ellie grunted as Carrie flashed her a cautioning look.

"I knew you would be enthused," Carrie quipped with a smile. "Tina, I need you to work on the curtains."

Ellie was left alone, literally watching paint dry, as Carrie took Tina and the others off somewhere. Ellie's heart leapt when Carrie returned alone. "Hi," Carrie greeted her somewhat shyly.

"I'm in trouble, aren't I?" Ellie said with a grimace.

"I understand that you're only doing this to make your sister happy," Carrie began seriously. "But if I do well, I get work and sell books."

"Understood," Ellie said. "I'll play nice in front of the cameras."

"Thank you," Carrie responded sincerely as she caressed Ellie's arm. "There's something else."

Ellie swallowed hard as she felt her skin burning from Carrie's light touch. "There's always an unspoken competition between the designers that at times borders on all out war. I'm not going to lose to Federico," the blonde added firmly. "Want to help me show up the Pink Wonder?"

"You lead, I'll follow," Ellie conceded with a smile as Carrie took her by the hand.

"I do so like to lead," Carrie responded huskily.

Ellie's clit began to throb in a steady rhythm as she watched the sway of Carrie's hips as she walked back outside. Helplessly Ellie followed her. "Ready?" Carrie whispered in her ear just as they were about to step out into the front yard.

"You have no idea," Ellie gulped as she felt a shiver pass through her.

Much to Ellie's displeasure, which she somehow managed to hide from the cameras, her project was to construct three large bookcases. She began work with a plastic smile plastered on her face. Several hours later she had finished the difficult project and her body was screaming from lifting and screwing the heavy wood together. Carrie had come back to check on her with the camera crew in tow.

"Looks great," Carrie complimented her.

"Thank you," Ellie accepted the compliment as she blew out a sigh of relief, looking forward to a reprieve.

"Now we can stain them," Carrie said with a bright smile.

Ellie's crystal blue eyes widened in horror as Carrie handed her a paintbrush and a can of stain. "Oh, I see. By we, you mean me," Ellie teased. "Do we need to sand them first?" Ellie joked, not looking forward to more hard labor.

"Carl did that before you started to put them together," Carrie explained as the crew departed for another break.

"Why do they get so many breaks?" Ellie grumbled.

"Union," Carrie explained with a shrug.

"Unlike being slave labor like me," Ellie conceded.

"Poor baby," Carrie teased her as the blonde's tiny hand came to rest on Ellie's hip.

"So why didn't good old Crafty Carl put these suckers together?" Ellie asked as she jerked her thumb towards the large bookcases.

"He's working on other projects for both Federico and myself," Carrie explained as her fingers began to caress Ellie's jean-clad hip. "How are you holding up?"

"I'm sore in places I didn't know existed," Ellie confessed as she leaned slightly closer to the attractive smaller woman. "How's my sister doing?"

"Sewing and flirting with Barry," Carrie responded as she pressed her firm body into Ellie's. "Tell me, are you interested in one of the boys?"

Carrie's perfume invaded Ellie's senses as their bodies brushed slightly against one another. "What do you think?" Ellie answered softly.

"I think . . . ," Carrie said softly as her body melted into Ellie's, her breath caressing the tall brunette's trembling body. "I think I need to get back to work inside," Carrie apologized as she pulled away from Ellie's touch. "I have a shot set up with Sara."

PART FOUR

Much to Ellie's dismay and increasing frustration, once she finished staining the shelves she was assigned more arduous tasks that kept her away from the attractive blonde. She was about to throw in the towel and call it quits when she and Tina had to move the heavy shelves into the house. Carrie came rushing out as they fought to carry the heavy shelves. "Let me help," the blonde sputtered. "Someone was supposed to move these for us," she apologized as the three of them struggled to maneuver the shelves into the living room.

Once they managed to move all three shelves inside and set them up the way Carrie wanted, Ellie was ready to drop from exhaustion. She looked around the living room, thinking that it really didn't look much different. Sara chose that moment to pop in. "We're off," she announced to Carrie.

"See you in the morning," Carrie responded with an exhausted wave.

"So we're done for the day?" Tina yawned as Ellie gave the small blonde an expectant look.

"No," Carrie confessed. "There's a lot that you don't see on a half hour television show. First, we need to hook up the doors and then put the guys' toys inside."

"Doors?" Ellie groused.

"I finished them earlier and all we have to do is put them up," Carrie explained quickly. "Why don't we do that and Tina can hang the curtains she made this afternoon?"

"Tina made curtains?" Ellie choked out in surprise.

"Bite me," Tina flared.

"She made slipcovers too," Carrie added with a conspiratorial whisper.

Installing the doors on the bookshelves proved to be an exercise in self-control for Ellie. The doors went in easily enough; it was Carrie that was driving her insane. Well, not so much the blonde, but her constant touching tested Ellie's willpower. Their fingers brushed when exchanging tools, and Carrie's hands would inevitably find their way to some spot on Ellie's body. Deciding that she'd had enough teasing, the brunette decided to fight fire with fire.

As Carrie was screwing one of the doors on, Ellie held it steady for her. She reached over the smaller woman and held the door in place, pressing her hips into the blonde's firm backside as her breasts melted into the smaller woman's back. She bit back a laugh as Carrie's hands trembled and the blonde released a tiny whimper.

"That's what you get for teasing me," Ellie whispered hotly in the smaller woman's ear once the door was secured.

"I wasn't teasing," Carrie softly choked out.

"Huh?" Ellie stammered.

"I'm done," Tina called out as she climbed down off the ladder she'd been using to hang the simple curtains. "They really did brighten up the room."

"Great!" Carrie responded brightly. She brushed past Ellie as if nothing had happened. "Why don't we set up the boys' electronic stuff in their new entertainment center and then we can call it a night."

"That's Ellie's department," Tina smirked. "I am heading off to bed."

"You mean you're going to snoop through Barry's stuff," Ellie quipped.

Tina stuck her tongue out at her younger sibling before darting up the staircase. "What did she mean 'that's your department'?" Carrie inquired with a genuine interest.

"I'm an electrician," Ellie explained with a shrug.

"Now you tell me," Carrie groaned.

"Why? Did you want to put in track lighting?" Ellie teased.

"No," Carrie scoffed at the notion. "But we could have really done some fun stuff."

"Such as?" Ellie inquired as she and Carrie lifted the boy's large television into the entertainment center.

"Wouldn't you like to know?" Carrie taunted her in response, their fingers brushing slightly as they moved the large television into place. Ellie inhaled sharply from the contact.

They finished hooking up the electronic equipment - the cable box, the VCR, the DVD player, Nintendo, and a host of other toys. Ellie was pleased when Carrie slipped behind the shelves with her to assist with the wiring. The close space and the scent of Carrie's perfume made Ellie's palms sweat. "Now I know why you didn't want a back put on the shelves," she offered in an effort to make conversation and steer her thoughts away from the attractive woman standing dangerously close to her.

"One man's bookshelf is another's entertainment center," Carrie boasted, her fingers grazing across Ellie's arm as she spoke. The tall brunette shivered as she fought to control her breathing. The feel of Carrie's fingers dancing across her skin was intoxicating. The tiny blonde leaned closer as her hands began to drift further along Ellie's body. The tiny space they were trapped in made it impossible for the tall brunette to move.

"Are you always this . . . ," Ellie stammered for the right words as her body trembled with desire.

"Touchy? Forward?" Carrie cut her off with a knowing smirk. "When I see someone I like and I think the feeling is mutual then yes, I'm direct. I travel a lot so I'm not allowed the luxury of taking my time."

"What if I want to take things slowly?" Ellie inquired directly, trapping the energetic blonde with her crystal blue eyes.

"Then I guess I'll be taking a long cold shower and making a lot of trips back here to . . . Where am I anyways?" Carrie asked in confusion.

"At the moment you're trapped behind a bookcase in some guy's apartment," Ellie teased as they both squirmed in the tight space.

Carrie released a light laugh that completely melted Ellie's heart. "Not the strangest position I've ever found myself in," Carrie joked as she took Ellie by the hand and began to gently caress the back of it with her thumb.

"Do tell?" Ellie quipped as she assisted the decorator out from behind the entertainment center.

Carrie stumbled as they emerged from behind the cumbersome furniture. Ellie reached out and captured the smaller woman by her hips just as the blonde's face landed between her breasts. Ellie looked down at the blonde head nestled between her breasts and grinned with amusement. "So much for taking things slowly," she teased with a wry chuckle.

"Sorry," Carrie apologized as she took a shy step back in retreat.

"No you're not," Ellie taunted her as she noticed that the blonde's emerald eyes were still fixed firmly on her chest.

"Okay, I'm not," Carrie smirked. "Perfect height," she added with a mischievous grin.

Unaware of what she was doing, Ellie's hands began to caress the smaller woman's hips as Carrie's focus remained on her ample bosom. Carrie released a needy sigh before taking a tentative step backward. "We need to push the shelving closer to the wall. I know that with all that wiring we can't get it flush but we need to get it as close as we can," the decorator explained with a slight frown, her emerald eyes finally meeting Ellie's inquisitive blue gaze.

Unable to speak since her body was burning with desire, the brunette simply nodded in agreement and reluctantly released her hold on the small blonde. They'd already secured the three bookshelves together into one unit. They closed the doors before they each took one end to move it.

Once the shelving was in place they took a step back and Ellie was amazed that the room was now looking more like the gentleman's study that Carrie had described that morning. "Amazing," she uttered in appreciation. "I still don't know how you're going to pull the rest of it off."

"Trade secret," Carrie teased her as she folded her arms across her chest. "I guess we're done for the night," Carrie offered quietly.

Ellie was taken aback by Carrie's sudden standoffish behavior until she realized that the blonde was giving her what she had asked for. The only problem was that the dark-haired electrician was no longer certain she could take things slowly with the smaller woman who would more than likely walk out of her life the next day. Suddenly feeling disappointed, Ellie began to look around the room for a distraction. The room was empty with the exception of the bookshelves, the ladder, the curtains Tina had hung, and some paint tarps scattered across the floor. Ellie released an exasperated sigh as she tried to reconcile her feelings.

"What's wrong?" Carrie inquired softly as she stepped slightly closer to Ellie.

"Nothing," Ellie lied, her courage suddenly failing her.

"Second thoughts?" Carrie whispered against her skin. Ellie jumped in surprise, not realizing that the blonde had moved so close to her. The brunette's hands instinctively reached out for Carrie and encircled her waist.

"It's just that I'm not into the casual thing," she tried to explain as her hands began to roam up the cropped shirt Carrie was wearing.

"I can't make any promises," Carrie confessed with a hint of regret as her small hands reached up and her fingers wrapped themselves in Ellie's long raven tresses. "I should go," Carrie whimpered as she nestled herself against Ellie's body.

"Why?" Ellie panted as the desire for Carrie swelled inside of her.

"Because if you're feeling half of what I am, if we start anything I doubt that either of us will be able to stop," Carrie murmured against her body.

Ellie felt a shiver run through her as Carrie's hot needy breath penetrated the material of her T-shirt and warmed her skin. The confused brunette knew that Carrie was right, but her body couldn't resist the feel of the blonde she was holding tightly in her arms. Unable to stop herself, Ellie pulled Carrie closer to her. She moaned deeply as the blonde's thigh pressed against her aching center. Her mind urged her to pull away as both of them began to run their hands up and down the other's body.

Ellie's mind and body were lost in an all out war until she felt Carrie's soft warm lips teasing her neck. Ellie's head fell back, offering more of her sensitive neck up to Carrie's insistent touch as the brunette's hands drifted down to the blonde's Capri pants and cupped her firm backside. As Carrie kissed and tasted her way along Ellie's neck the brunette massaged her backside, their hips swaying against one another in a sensual rhythm.

Ellie's knees buckled slightly as Carrie's kisses grew more determined and their hips thrust urgently against one another's body. The brunette felt lightheaded as her desire began to pool between her legs. Ellie arched her body against Carrie's as she guided the blonde's hips to meet her urgent rhythm. Carrie had been right; now that they'd started they wouldn't be able to stop.

"I want you," Carrie whispered against her skin as the blonde's hands drifted up and under the back of her shirt. Ellie could only moan in response. "Just say the word and I'll stop," Carrie continued as she began to fumble with the clasp of Ellie's bra. Ellie was far too lost in the heat of their passion to refuse as she reached between their overheated bodies and began to undo Carrie's pants.

Carrie growled in frustration as she continued to fumble with the clasp of Ellie's bra. "I'm never good with these," the blonde confessed in a defeated voice as she tugged insistently at the garment. Ellie released a throaty growl as she took a step back and pulled her white T-shirt up and over her head. She cast the unneeded garment aside before reaching behind her, undoing her bra before quickly disposing of it as well.

There was no mistaking the look of pure desire in Carrie's eyes as they rushed into each other's arms and lost themselves in a fiery kiss. Their hips thrust urgently against each other. Ellie could feel her clit pulsating as her faded jeans became damp with desire. Carrie's small hands cupped her breasts and began to caress them as Ellie's attention returned to lowering the blonde's pants.

Ellie released a deep moan as she felt Carrie pinching and teasing her nipples while she lowered the blonde's pants down her hips. Carrie tore her lips away from the passionate kiss and began to kiss her way down Ellie's exposed flesh. The brunette struggled to remain standing as she lost herself in the feel of Carrie's mouth tasting her skin. The brunette's body was humming with pure lust as she slipped her fingers beneath the blonde's panties. Her fingertips burned as she felt the firm flesh responding to her touch.

Ellie was panting heavily as Carrie's tongue traced the swell of her breasts. The electrician was unable to control her passion as she urgently lowered Carrie's underwear needing to feel more of her lover's body. Ellie's body arched and she released a passionate hiss when Carrie captured one of her nipples in her mouth, suckling it with a fiery intensity.

Ellie parted the blonde's knees with her thighs as her hands began a heated exploration of Carrie's body. She caressed her firm abs with one hand while the other drifted up under the blonde's top and quickly released the clasp of her bra. Carrie was grinding herself against the taller woman when Ellie's fingers dipped into her wetness.

Ellie gasped as her fingers were painted by the blonde's wetness. "Oh my God, you are so wet," Ellie managed to choke out as Carrie suckled her nipple harder, teasing it with her teeth and her tongue. They stumbled backwards as Ellie ran her fingers along the blonde's slick folds. Carrie's mouth moved to her other nipple as Ellie's knees finally gave out and she guided them down onto the floor.

Pulling the blonde on top of her body, Ellie was lost in the feel of Carrie's wetness as she began to tease the blonde's clit. With her free hand Ellie began to pull Carrie's top up. The blonde reluctantly released Ellie's breast from the warmth of her mouth as the brunette removed her top and bra. Ellie tossed the garments across the empty room as Carrie straddled her hips.

Ellie pulled Carrie's body up and captured one of her nipples in her mouth while her fingers dipped deeper into the blonde's wetness. Carrie's body was thrusting above her with an urgent need; Ellie pressed two fingers against the opening of her center and suckled her nipple harder. "Please," Carrie pleaded as her hips pressed harder against Ellie's long fingers.

Unable to resist her lover's urgent plea, Ellie entered her warm wet center. She could feel the walls gripping her fingers as Carrie's body arched in response. Ellie groaned in disappointment as the rose-colored bud was torn from her mouth. Hips thrust against her touch as Ellie's fingers wiggled inside the blonde. Carrie's eyes were glazed over with desire as she looked down at Ellie.

The sight of her half-naked lover straddling her made Ellie's pulse race as she began to plunge in and out of the blonde's center. Carrie's body moved in unison with Ellie's fingers as the brunette began to tease her throbbing clit with the pad of her thumb. Ellie took her harder and deeper as Carrie rode her hand and begged her not to stop. She cupped Carrie's firm ass and began to tease the blonde as she plunged deeper inside of her.

Carrie's desire painted her abdomen as she rocked against Ellie. The brunette was lost in the feel of Carrie's thighs trembling against her. Needing to feel her lover explode against her body, she added another finger inside the blonde. Carrie cried out as her head fell back. The blonde's thighs tightened around Ellie's body, trapping the brunette beneath her as she exploded.

Ellie's fingers stilled, allowing the waves of ecstasy to wash over her lover. She looked up in amazement; she drank in Carrie's flushed features while the blonde struggled to control her breathing. Carrie's entire body was quivering as Ellie began to stroke her clit. Soon Carrie's body was thrusting against her touch as Ellie began to pleasure her once again.

Carrie's body fell over her and Ellie began to flicker her tongue across her nipples while her fingers filled her completely. "Yes," Carrie cried out as her tiny body trembled. She collapsed against Ellie and began to suckle her neck urgently as the aftershocks trickled through her body.

Ellie held her lover in a warm embrace as the blonde trembled and gasped against her body. Finally, when she felt

Carrie's body calming, she removed her fingers from the warmth of her center. Carrie rolled over onto her side and watched Ellie slowly licking her fingers clean. Carrie caressed and teased her breasts as Ellie feasted on the glistening desire coating her long fingers.

As Ellie savored the sweet ambrosia of Carrie's passion, the blonde removed the remainder of her clothes. Ellie watched as her lover revealed all of herself to her. The brunette drank in the sight of Carrie's firm abdomen and thighs along with the gentle swell of her firm round breasts. "You are so beautiful," she gasped in wonderment as Carrie lowered herself and began to slowly remove the last of Ellie's clothes.

Carrie kissed her way down Ellie's body as she removed her faded blue jeans. The brunette felt a shiver of pleasure shoot through her with each brush of the blonde's lips. Ellie's body arched up off the hard floor when she felt Carrie's tongue circling the back of her knee. Ellie released sharp needy gasps as Carrie's mouth explored her long legs. "Tell me what you want," Carrie pleaded against her trembling thighs.

Ellie opened her mouth to speak just as she felt Carrie's tongue tease the inside of her quivering thighs and the words failed to emerge. Her hips jolted up off the floor as Carrie's warm breath teased the damp curls of her mound. "Anything!" Ellie cried out in a promise as Carrie cupped her backside and drew her wetness to her mouth.

Ellie cried out incoherently as she felt her body lifted higher; Carrie tightened her hold on her as the blonde's tongue dipped into her wetness. Ellie's head fell back; she tried to clutch at the hardwood floor as Carrie ran her tongue along her aching sex. "Anything?" Carrie murmured into her wetness as she pressed her tongue against the opening of Ellie's center.

"Yes," Ellie cried out as her hips thrust against her blonde lover.

She could feel Carrie tightening her hold on her hips as she plunged her tongue deep inside of her center. Carrie curled and twisted her tongue as she began to tease Ellie's clit with her fingers. Ellie couldn't stop her body from rocking urgently as Carrie's tongue sunk deeper inside of her. Her body thrashed urgently as Carrie plunged in and out of her.

Ellie could feel her climax steadily building as her lover murmured in pleasure. The brunette thrust harder, demanding more of her lover's touch as her thighs clenched around the blonde's body. "No," Ellie protested as she was about to fall over the edge and Carrie withdrew her touch.

Carrie wrapped a comforting arm across her stomach as she suckled Ellie's throbbing clit in her mouth. Ellie's body instantly arched once again and thrust against Carrie. The blonde suckled her clit harder as her fingers entered Ellie's center. Ellie's body rocked wildly as Carrie's mouth and fingers moved in perfect rhythm, taking her higher with every touch.

Ellie felt the room spinning as Carrie feasted upon her. She begged her lover for release and the blonde responded by taking her harder and faster. Ellie's eyes snapped shut and her ears began to buzz as her body arched against her lover. The climax tore through her as Carrie continued to pleasure her. She quickly felt the waves of ecstasy recapture her as her body exploded.

Ellie was gasping for air as she felt Carrie move up her body and wrap her up in her arms. The desire still coursed through her body as she captured the blonde in a lingering kiss. Carrie's breasts brushed against her own as their bodies melted together. They rolled across the floor as both of them pressed a firm thigh against the other's wetness. Ellie's clit was throbbing as she felt Carrie's wetness paint her thigh. They rocked against each other as their hands roamed across one another's body.

The thrusts grew more demanding until they were crying out into the warmth of the other's mouth. Sated and spent, they collapsed against each other as they fought to regain the ability to breathe normally. Ellie could feel the rapid beating of Carrie's heart as she held her in her arms. Ellie winced slightly as she moved. "Muscles still hurting?" Carrie inquired softly as she ran her fingers along Ellie's broad shoulders.

"Yeah," the brunette confessed shyly.

"Roll over," Carrie instructed her as she removed herself from Ellie's embrace. The brunette gazed curiously at the blonde. Carrie ignored her questioning gaze as she stood, teetering slightly as she walked over and retrieved some of the tarps.

Carrie laid one out on the floor and motioned for Ellie to lie across it. The brunette opened her mouth to protest but the gleam in Carrie's eyes quickly silenced her. Ellie lay down on her stomach across the tarp, the material scraping her sensitive body, and Carrie tucked a folded tarp under her head. Ellie sighed deeply as she folded her arms and rested her head on the second tarp. "Not the best idea but we can work with this," Carrie whispered. Ellie's body trembled as the blonde's hot breath teased her ear.

The tremble exploded into quivering as she felt Carrie straddling her hips. She moaned deeply as Carrie's hands gently kneaded her aching shoulders. Ellie was lost in the feel of Carrie's hands roaming across her back, gently working the knots out of her tired muscles. She moaned as she felt Carrie brush her hair back to begin working on her neck.

Ellie gasped as the blonde's erect nipples brushed across her back and the damp curls of her mound grazed her backside. Ellie couldn't stop her body from reacting as the massage grew more sensual and Carrie's body began to sway against her. Ellie lifted her hips, needing to feel Carrie's wetness against her. She could hear her lover moaning from behind her as the blonde pressed into her harder.

Ellie lifted her hips higher as Carrie began to thrust against her. Shamelessly Ellie lifted her body so that she was balancing herself on her hands and knees. Carrie accepted the invitation as she reached around the brunette and cupped one of her breasts. Carrie moaned as she rocked against the brunette while she pinched and teased her nipple. The feel of Carrie's desire grinding against her as the blonde's nipples teased her back was driving Ellie insane.

Ellie's clit pulsated as her hips matched Carrie's urgent rhythm. She rocked harder against Carrie's body as the blonde moved both of her hands to clasp Ellie's hips. Carrie guided her hips as they ground together with raw desire. Ellie felt her soul shattering as they exploded against one another and collapsed on the floor.

PART FIVE

Ellie awoke to find that she was still lying on the filthy tarp with Carrie's naked body on top of her. She smiled as she turned her body and carefully lifted her sleeping lover. Carrie's eyes blinked open and Ellie held her breath, anxiously waiting to see what the blonde decorator's reaction was going to be. Carrie's warm smile melted her heart. "Good morning," the blonde offered softly before gently kissing Ellie.

"Good morning," Ellie echoed before reclaiming Carrie's soft inviting lips.

From above them she could hear her sister moving around. "Reality sucks," she grumbled as she and Carrie stumbled to their feet.

"Doesn't it though," Carrie agreed as they quickly threw on some clothing. "Ellie?" The blonde began in a shy voice. "Before we get cleaned up and the camera crew invades, I was just wondering if you had any plans for tonight?"

Ellie found the blonde's sudden shyness endearing. "Well, other than killing my sister, I hadn't really scheduled anything," she offered teasingly. "What did you have in mind?"

"Dinner?" Carrie offered in a hopeful tone.

"I'd love to," Ellie accepted with a brilliant smile.

"Really?" Carrie responded with a slight blush. "God, I love your smile," she added absently. Then she shook her head clear. "Okay, we need to shower and get back to work."

"Slave driver," Ellie quipped as they darted upstairs.

As the day progressed and the work on Barry and Roger's living room progressed, Ellie found herself getting caught up in the excitement of finishing the job. She even found Sara's excessive perkiness slightly infectious. Of course when the cameras were absent, Tina took pleasure in teasing her about the noise that had kept her awake. Ellie couldn't find it in herself to argue; she could only blush at her sister's teasing.

"This is amazing," Sara gushed as Carrie explained what they'd done and how they'd done it. Ellie was pretty impressed by the outcome. Carrie had turned the guys' dumpy living room into a gentleman's study. She even managed to hide the fosse ball table with a table that Crafty Carl had constructed; a table that was painted to look like a chess board that would slide away when the guys wanted to play fosse ball. The slipcovers were plush and dignified and made the beat-up armchairs look elegant. Carrie had sanded down and stained the coffee table so it matched the new entertainment center.

All in all, the place looked really spiffy but comfortable. It also, much to Tina's disappointment, screamed that it was a man's place. Tina managed to get over her disappointment when she saw how much Roger and Barry loved the changes. It also helped that Barry was so impressed that he hugged her.

Soon they were standing in their kitchen with their eyes closed. "Okay, open your eyes," Sara chirped.

When Ellie blinked open her eyes, she was instantly assaulted by the sight she found waiting for her. Her jaw dropped open as she took in the horror that was now her kitchen. "I like it," she lied, knowing that the cameras were watching their reaction. It was cluttered and very pink. Not just pink - it was neon pink. She looked over at the guys and Federico smiling in appreciation. Out of the corner of her eye, she caught the horrified look on Carrie's face.

"What the hell were you thinking? Tina screeched out suddenly as she stormed over to the three stunned men. "This sucks. I said no pink. This sucks." Ellie couldn't stop laughing as her sister grabbed the stunned decorator by his cheesy ascot. "Are you insane?" Tina continued to flare as she started to strangle Federico.

"Cut," Sara cried out frantically as the crew rushed over to save poor Federico.

Ellie felt Carrie's arms wrap around her waist. "I've always wanted to see that happen on this show," Ellie noted as she leaned into Carrie's touch.

"He ruined your kitchen." Carrie chuckled.

"You wouldn't know a good decorator I could call, would you?" Ellie offered hopefully as Tina continued her assault on Federico.

"We can discuss it over dinner," Carrie suggested as she took Ellie by the hand and led her away from the mayhem.

The End

THE BEACH

PART ONE

Daryl looked around the beach house suspiciously. "Jeremy?" She called out as she wondered what her brother was up to. "Come out from wherever you're hiding before I hunt you down and beat the snot out of you," she added with a menacing growl.

"My, aren't we cranky this morning," Jeremy taunted her as he emerged from one of the back bedrooms.

"Ugh," Daryl grunted in disgust at her brother's cheerful tone. She was now completely convinced that he was definitely up to something. "What is going on, you little goober?" she asked, not happy about spending her morning off driving all the way up the coast to visit her older brother at the family's dilapidated beach house. Her icy blue stare made the man shrink back in fear.

Anyone watching the scene would had found it amusing since, despite Daryl's almost six foot stature, Jeremy stood a good half foot taller and possessed the body of a lumberjack. Still, the younger of the two could always make her larger sibling tremble with fear. "Jeremy, why did you drag me all the way up here on my day off?" Daryl demanded.

"I'll get us some coffee from Duffy's," he offered

sheepishly.

"I've had my coffee. Now out with it," Daryl demanded as she wondered if another cup of coffee might not be a good idea. She decided to make Jeremy sweat a little more before sending him down the road for more coffee.

"Loosen the bone, will you, Wilma?" Jeremy grunted as he folded his arms across his large chest. His crystal blue eyes were filled with concern as he stared down at Daryl. She couldn't help the small smile that emerged on her lips. It had been a difficult time for both of the siblings over the past few years.

"I'm sorry," she offered quietly. "So why all the mystery?" She added in a softer tone.

"I just thought it would be nice to spend some time together," Jeremy offered in a tender voice that didn't match his size. "The past few years have been hard on both of us. First, there was my divorce and then you and Shannon broke up as well. Then losing Mom and then Dad so soon afterward - it's been hell on both of us."

"That it has," Daryl agreed as she wrapped her arm around his waist. "So why here?"

"Well . . . ," he began slowly. "Are you sure you don't want me to run down to Duffy's?"

"I don't like the sound of this," Daryl concluded. She glared up at the taller man who seemed suddenly uncomfortable.

"I was just thinking . . . ," Jeremy began shyly.

"Never a good sign," Daryl grumbled.

"I want to fix this place up and I was hoping that you might want to help me," Jeremy finally blurted out.

"That's it?" Daryl inquired in confusion as she wondered why her brother had suddenly regained interest in the beach house.

"If we work together on weekends and nights, we could get this place back in shape by Memorial Day weekend," Jeremy offered hopefully.

"It would be a lot of work," Daryl responded thoughtfully.

"Think about it," Jeremy urged her eagerly. "We loved coming here when we were kids. And then later when I was in college and Mom and Dad stopped coming up here, we really had some good times here."

Daryl felt her face flush slightly as she recalled one memory in particular. "Yeah, you and Lesley use to throw some great parties," she said absently as she felt her body temperature rise slightly. "It was nice of her to come to Dad's wake. I always liked her."

"Me too," he confessed with a shy smile.

"Not that I didn't like Carol," she added quickly, referring to her brother's ex-wife. "I guess I just always thought that Lesley was going to be the girl you married."

"So did I," he said as his smile grew a little brighter. "But what did we know then? We were just a couple of college kids."

There was something in his tone that alerted the brunette that there was more going on than he wanted to admit. "Uh huh." She chuckled softly. "She's divorced as well, isn't she?"

"Yes," Jeremy muttered quietly. "So what do you think? Can we get the old place fixed up?"

"It'll be a lot of work," Daryl said wryly. "Let's go to Duffy's for some caffeine, then we'll look this place over and see what needs to be done."

"I've already started a list." Jeremy beamed as he gave her a heart felt hug.

"Oh goodie." Daryl chuckled with a hint of fear.

PART TWO

The project of repairing the beach house quickly proved to be a massive undertaking. Daryl and Jeremy soon found themselves spending all their free time up at the beach house. Everything had fallen into disrepair. The work had already gone past Memorial Day and now, in mid-June, they were nearing completion.

Daryl loved every moment of the time with her brother. Over the past few years they had leaned on one another and at the same time distanced themselves. The renewed closeness proved to be good for both of them. Daryl had longed suspect the other motive behind Jeremy's interest in fixing up the old beach house. She was hoping that her suspicions were right and that Jeremy and Lesley had rekindled their romance.

"You think it's ready to have people up?" Jeremy inquired hopefully as they laid the last of the new carpeting in one of the two bedrooms.

"Are you thinking of anyone special?" She teased him as the burly man blushed. "I thought so." She chuckled. "So when did you start seeing Lesley again?"

"I Uhm . . . ," he stammered. "I talked to her a couple times after Mom died. First just to thank her for the flowers she sent. Then after Dad's wake, we went for coffee and, I don't know, it was like nothing had changed."

"I'm happy," she reassured him. "So I guess I'll get this room and the two of you get the one with the fireplace." She groaned.

"We're taking things slowly," he said with a slight chuckle. "But I was hoping that we could invite her up next weekend. Being back here would be nice."

"So if she turns you down, I get to share the room with fireplace with Lesley. Cool," she teased him.

"You wish, Miss Stud Muffin." Jeremy laughed. "Sis, can I ask you something without you getting upset?" He added in a serious tone.

"Probably not," Daryl snickered.

"Why did you stop coming up here?" Jeremy inquired as he tacked down the last of the carpeting. "It was really strange. Right around the time you came out, you just seemed to disappear from our lives. The three of us had always been close since Lesley and I started dating back in high school. I wondered if maybe you had a thing for her."

"Eww," Daryl choked out in disgust. "Trust me. Hitting on Lesley would be like hitting on my sister. It wasn't her. It was . . .," her words suddenly caught in her throat as she recalled the weekend her life changed forever.

"Sis?" Jeremy said in concern as he put his tools down and sat down next to her.

She lay down her own tools and leaned against the wall they had painted the weekend before. She didn't want to get into this but Jeremy deserved an explanation. She had always been close to her older sibling until that weekend. "Well . . . ," she began slowly, unable to meet his gaze. "It all started Fourth of July weekend back in 1989 . . ."

PART THREE

It was July 3rd 1989 and Daryl had gone to the beach house to enjoy the holiday with her brother, his girlfriend, and a large group of their friends. Her boyfriend, Brian, had been unable to attend. She was disappointed when she drove up to Cape Ann. After she arrived, Brian had vanished from her thoughts completely. Just out of high school she found herself surrounded by Jeremy and Lesley's friends from college. The only person she really recalled meeting that weekend was Carrie.

Carrie had long golden blonde hair, stood five-foot-four, and Daryl instantly thought that she was the most fascinating person she had ever met. Carrie was Lesley's roommate. She and Daryl were instantly joined at the hip from the moment the tall brunette had been introduced. They spent the day swimming, playing volleyball, and then drinking around the bonfire that night.

Maybe if Brian hadn't completely slipped Daryl's mind, or if she had mentioned him just once to Carrie, things might have turned out differently. Then again, Daryl reasoned in hindsight, meeting Carrie was meant to be. It was late and the two women were slightly buzzed as they sat with the rest of the group around the bonfire. Daryl had already convinced herself that her flushed features was due to the fire blazing before her and not the feel of Carrie's knee brushing against her own.

She had also managed to convince herself that the rapid beating of her heart was from the excitement of the day and not from the casual brushing of their bodies. Of course she had no explanation as to why her stomach clenched tightly when Carrie leaned over and whispered in her ear, suggesting that they go for a walk along the darkened beach. Daryl only nodded eagerly in response, strangely unable to speak.

She would never forget the way Carrie's hair glimmered in the glow of firelight or how her emerald eyes sparkled when Daryl accepted her offer. Unnoticed by the rest of the partygoers, the two women got up and walked off into the darkness. The sounds and scent of the ocean filled Daryl's senses as they abandoned their footwear to walk in the surf. Their fingers brushed as they walked further away from everyone. Carrie's smaller hand wrapped around her own and Daryl's stomach began to quiver.

Still the brunette dismissed what was happening as her hand clasped Carrie's tighter. Daryl found that she was watching Carrie's movements as they strolled slowly down along the pounding surf. The small blonde was wearing cut-off jean shorts and a black tank top that covered her teal bikini. Earlier that afternoon Daryl had stared at the blonde when they arrived at the beach and Carrie revealed her skimpy bathing suit. Carrie had an amazing body and now Daryl found herself admiring the way her hair flowed as the wind swept off the ocean.

"Moon light suits you," Carrie offered as she smiled up at Daryl. "But then again, watching you on the beach this afternoon was nice too," the blonde continued in a delightfully husky voice.

"Thank you," Daryl responded as a wave of confusion washed over her. The tall brunette looked down at her khaki shorts and plain powder blue T-shirt that were covering her black bikini and thought she didn't look all that special. She turned to find herself locked in a smoky emerald gaze and suddenly she felt very special. There was something about the way Carrie was looking at her that made her heart beat just a little faster and her lower anatomy pulsate in a steady rhythm.

Her mind was muddled as Carrie led her behind some large rocks. She could no longer see the bonfire and the voices of the rest of the partygoers were a faint whisper. Her mind tried to will her to say something about rejoining the others but her body had other plans as she found herself stepping into Carrie's arms. Somehow she convinced herself that she was only seeking shelter from the cool ocean air as she wrapped her arms around the smaller woman's waist.

Her mind questioned her actions as Carrie wrapped her long raven tresses around her fingers and she found herself leaning into the smaller woman's touch. Instead of walking away, Daryl pulled the blonde closer so that their bodies were touching. She felt the dampness growing between her trembling thighs as Carrie nuzzled her neck. She gasped as she felt the light feathery touch of Carrie's lips caress her neck.

Her mind protested as she wrapped her fingers through Carrie's hair and her hips swayed against the small blonde's firm body. While her thoughts were screaming for her to run, she groaned in protest as Carrie's lips left her neck. "I've been wanting to do this all day," Carrie said dreamily.

Daryl looked down in confusion, unable to comprehend what it was that the blonde was talking about. The fiery gaze from Carrie's eyes explained everything to her. Instead of pulling away, she dipped her head as Carrie reached up. Their lips brushed and Daryl trembled from the heat. While her mind begged her to stop, she parted her lips and Carrie's tongue slipped into the warmth of her mouth.

Her tongue greeted the blonde's while her inner voice continued to protest. She shut the voice out as she felt Carrie's small hand cup her breast. She became lost in the sensation of their tongues wrapping around one another as she cupped the smaller woman's firm backside. Her clit was throbbing as Carrie's firm thigh pressed against her center.

Daryl felt Carrie pull her T-shirt up and, instead of halting the blonde's actions; she caressed the smaller woman's backside. Carrie stepped back slightly and pulled Daryl's shirt up and off her body. Instead of protesting, the brunette quickly reclaimed the blonde's lips. She knew that she should put a stop to what was happening when she felt the ties for the top of her bikini being undone. Instead she undid the zipper on Carrie's shorts.

As she felt the top of her bathing suit being tugged off her body, she pulled the blonde's shorts down to her hips. She allowed Carrie's shorts to fall to the sandy ground as the blonde's lips began to once again caress her neck, working their way slowly down to the valley between her firm full breasts. Daryl moaned deeply as Carrie's tongue traced the swell of her breasts.

'Just what in the hell are you doing?' her inner voice asked as she began to lower the bottom of Carrie's bathing suit down her hips.

She ignored her inner voice. Her back arched when Carrie began to swirl her tongue around her nipples. It was a slow tantalizing torture as the blonde's tongue circled her now erect nipples - first one then the other, but never touching the swollen buds themselves. Her chest heaved as her breathing became ragged. Daryl cupped the flesh of Carrie's firm backside and began to knead it gently.

The blonde moaned against her breasts before pulling one of her nipples into the warmth of her mouth. Daryl cried out as her eyes fluttered shut. As if it had a mind of it's own, one of her hands drifted up Carrie's back. Her fingers fumbled to undo the ties to the top of Carrie's bathing suit while the blonde suckled her breast.

Daryl growled in frustration as the knots of Carrie's top refused to yield, having tightened from their swim earlier in the day. Carrie's teeth grazed across her nipple, sending a jolt through her body. The surge of desire was too much for her to endure. She needed to feel Carrie's skin. She tore the straps of the bathing suit as Carrie's mouth moved to her other breast while her fingers captured Daryl's now neglected nipple.

Daryl was panting hungrily as her hands moved quickly from Carrie's back to her well-toned abdomen. The tips of her fingers burned as she felt Carrie's skin respond to her touch. Carrie suckled her nipple harder as Daryl cupped the blonde's breasts. She allowed herself to simply enjoy the weight of the smaller woman's breasts.

Daryl felt her knees buckling as she cupped Carrie's breasts and brushed her palm against the blonde's nipples. The feel of Carrie's nipples hardening from her touch made her wetter than she had ever been in her entire life. Carrie moaned deeply against her skin as she began to pinch and tease the blonde's erect nipples. Daryl felt Carrie's hips pressing against her own and she couldn't stop herself from grinding her center against Carrie's thrusting hips.

The brunette's body trembled in disappointment as Carrie

stepped slightly away from her. "Do you have any idea how hard it was to be around you all day and not touch you?" Carrie said to her in a needy tone as she began to remove her top. Both the tank top and the bra of the swimsuit went flying off into the darkness. Daryl was a mass of confusion as she drank in the sight of the half-naked woman standing before her, bathed in the light of moon.

Her confusion and her excitement grew as she watched small hands begin to lower the rest of Carrie's swimsuit further down her hips. Daryl didn't realize what she was doing when she sank to her knees in front of Carrie. She clasped the blonde's hands tightly and halted her movements. She looked up into Carrie's passion-filled eyes and took over the task of removing the rest of the smaller woman's clothing.

Everything happened in a blur of excitement. It wasn't until Daryl found herself kissing Carrie's naked hips that she realized what she had done. The musky aroma of Carrie's desire filled her senses and threw her into a lustful haze as she dipped her head down to drink in the tantalizing scent of her lover's passion. She felt Carrie running her fingers through her long dark tresses. The feel of Carrie's fingers massaging her scalp invoked another moan. Her eyes began to flutter shut when she heard Carrie's voice. "Tell me what you want," Carrie offered in a breathy tone. "I'll do anything . . . to you . . . for you," Carrie promised in a voice dripping with desire.

Daryl's eyes snapped open as she realized she didn't know what she wanted. Until Carrie had spoken she was completely unaware of what she had done. She was torn by the confusion screaming through her thoughts and the temptation of the damp golden curls that were a mere breathe away from her lips. As she struggled with what was happening, Carrie lowered her body down onto the sand.

Daryl could feel Carrie's breath on her face just before she reclaimed Daryl's lips. Once again, instead of resisting, Daryl found herself plunging her tongue into the warmth of Carrie's mouth. As the brunette explored every inch of Carrie's mouth she felt her body being gently pulled down onto the sandy beach. Carrie's breasts brushed against her own and, instead of pulling away, she melted into the body that was now covering her own.

Daryl's body sank deeper into the sand as Carrie began to kiss her way down her torso. The brunette felt the last vestiges of her clothing being removed and, as each article of clothing left her body, Carrie's mouth quickly caressed the newly exposed skin. Instinctively Daryl parted her thighs as Carrie settled her body between them. The brunette released a feral growl as she felt Carrie's tongue caress the inside of her thigh.

Never before in her life had she felt such an aching need to be made love to. Shamelessly she raised her hips up to Carrie's eager mouth. She felt the blonde cup and lift her backside to bring her closer. Daryl draped her long legs over the smaller woman's shoulders. She lifted her head so she could watch Carrie drink in her passion. A warm breath blew gently through her dark damp curls. She clutched frantically at the sand as the blonde's tongue dipped into her wetness.

Daryl struggled to keep her eyes open as Carrie's tongue glided slowly along her swollen nether lips. The brunette pressed her wetness deeper into Carrie's touch; her mind was reeling as she lost herself in the pure ecstasy of the moment. She reached down and wrapped her fingers in Carrie's long blonde hair as she guided her to take her deeper.

She shuddered Carrie's fingers pressed urgently against the opening of her center. She cried out in pleasure as the blonde entered her and suckled her throbbing clit in her mouth. "Yes," she demanded as she thrust her hips against Carrie's mouth. Her thoughts were filled with a deep-seated need to pleasure Carrie as she was now pleasuring her.

Emerald eyes twinkled up at her through the darkness. Carrie murmured with pleasure as she feasted upon Daryl's overflowing passion. Daryl's thighs trembled as her eyes slammed shut. She clutched wildly at the sand beneath her hands as Carrie's fingers plunged in and out of her wetness filling her completely. "Ca . . . Car . . . ," she choked out, unable to speak coherently as her body exploded.

Carrie held her steady as she continued to pleasure her wildly with her mouth and her fingers. Daryl's mind filled with crimson images as Carrie's teeth grazed her clit and she added a third finger inside of her. Daryl's body heaved as the climax tore through her. She felt herself going higher and higher; Carrie's fingers stilled inside of her while her tongue flickered across her nub in a steady rhythm.

Daryl's body threatened to trap Carrie's as the blonde's fingers began to slowly slip in and out of her center. Daryl fell over the edge once again, the feeling of pure ecstasy filling her completely as she once again cried out. Her body collapsed onto the sandy ground as the last waves of pleasure filtered through her.

Carrie nestled her head on her stomach, kissing her gently before slipping her fingers from the warm wetness of Daryl's center. The brunette struggled to control her breathing while Carrie's tongue ran slowly across her stomach. In a haze she looked down at her lover; the sight of the blonde lying there dipping her tongue into her navel made her body tremble with a desire.

Before she could think about what was happening, she managed to wrap the smaller woman up in her arms and roll her onto her back. Carrie pulled her down on top of her and captured her lips in a fiery kiss. She slipped her thigh between Carrie's and felt the blonde's wetness caress her skin.

Carrie slipped her thigh between Daryl's legs and cupped the brunette's backside. Daryl tore her lips away, gasping as she and Carrie rocked urgently against one another in a sensual rhythm. "God, yes," Carrie groaned as Daryl began to suckle the pulse point of her neck. There was something exciting about the way their bodies melted together and the feel of Carrie's pulse beating steadily against her lips was driving the brunette insane with desire.

Her need to feel and taste every inch of the blonde's body was her only conscious thought as her mouth and lips began to trail across Carrie's milky white shoulders. Daryl slipped one hand between their swaying bodies. She moaned deeply as she captured Carrie's breast in her mouth while her fingers glanced across the damp blonde curls. "Can you feel what you do to me?" Carrie implored her as her hands guided Daryl's backside to thrust against her harder.

Daryl suckled the blonde's nipple eagerly as she dipped her fingers into the sweet wetness of her passion. Uncaring of the sand and the cold that was surrounding them, Daryl plunged her fingers deep inside her lover while she teased her nipple with her tongue and her teeth. She could feel the walls of Carrie's center grip her fingers while their hips continued to thrust against one another. "Come for me," she said, encouraging Carrie as her thumb teased her throbbing clit.

Carrie cried out in pleasure as she gripped Daryl's body tightly. The brunette released her nipple from the warmth of her mouth and raised her body. She watched in amazement as she plunged her fingers in and out of the smaller woman. The sight possessed her and soon she found her tongue flickering along the blonde's clit while her fingers continued to fill her.

For the first time in Daryl's young life she found herself climaxing simply from the feeling of her lover climaxing from her touch. It was truly amazing and frightening at the same time. During the night she lost herself in the fiery exploration as they pleasured one another. Carrie showed her everything that night and she gave herself freely.

Daryl awoke as the morning sun peered through the clouds. She panicked when she realized that she was naked and had her arms around a naked woman. The realization of what had transpired the night before came crashing down upon her. Carrie lifted her head and smiled sweetly at her. "Good morning," Carrie greeted her brightly as Daryl simply stared at the woman. Carrie blinked in confusion as she lifted her glorious naked body up off of Daryl's. "I have sand in some very interesting places," Carrie teased in an effort to lighten the mood. "Do you think anyone will notice if we slip into the shower together?" She suggested playfully as she leaned in for a kiss.

Daryl jerked away quickly. "Daryl?" Carrie's voice trembled as she called out to her. Daryl quickly scrambled to gather up her clothing. The brunette began to dress quickly, keeping her back to the young blonde. She was terrified to look at Carrie. "What's going on here?" Carrie demanded from behind her. Daryl couldn't answer, the words stuck in her throat as she finished putting her clothing back on. She hadn't bothered with her bathing suit; she just need to get dressed and run.

"Fine," Carrie snapped from behind her. Daryl's heart was pounding as she turned to find Carrie dressed in her shorts and tank top, holding what was left to her bikini in her hands. "Let me guess. You have a girlfriend and this was just a fling. I have the worst taste in women," the blonde grumbled.

"No, you don't get it," Daryl spat out, uncertain at just who it was she was angry with. "I have a boyfriend."

"What?" Carrie gasped. Her face turned ashen and she sank to her knees.

"I was drunk last night. You should have never taken advantage of me," Daryl accused her. Her body trembled and her mind screamed that she was a coward.

"You're straight," Carrie muttered absently as a crestfallen look clouded her delicate features.

"Of course I'm straight," Daryl screamed as Carrie stared thoughtfully down at the tattered remnants of the top to her swimsuit. "I was drunk last night and didn't know what I was doing," Daryl lied, knowing that she was slightly buzzed but was by no means intoxicated when she found herself begging Carrie to take her again and again.

She watched as Carrie stood up on unsteady legs. When the blonde looked over at her, she knew that the lie was clearly written across her face. Carrie tossed the bathing suit top at the brunette. "You keep telling yourself that," Carrie said coldly before storming off. Once Daryl had regained what was left to her composure, she raced back to the beach house and packed her bags. She scribbled a quick note to Jeremy before driving home.

PART FOUR

Jeremy was still looking at her, waiting for Daryl to say something more. She'd been lost in the memory and now it was finally time to share it with someone else. "Do you remember that fourth of July weekend just before I came out?" She said hesitantly. Jeremy nodded, silently encouraging her to continue.

"Brian couldn't make it here for the holiday. I can't recall why but I do remember not being overly disappointed by his absence. I was really looking forward to spending time with you, Lesley, and all your college friends. The parties you guys threw were always a lot of fun and, since I was about to start college in a few months, it was a thrill to hang out with an older crowd."

"We weren't that much older," Jeremy scoffed as he gave his younger sibling a playful nudge.

"Hey, I had just turned eighteen," she countered playfully. "Back then those couple of years seemed like a big deal."

"What happened that weekend?" Jeremy asked in a quiet voice. "You left the day after you arrived. At the time I wondered if you were missing Brian."

"The day arrived I met Lesley's roommate and best friend for the first time," she continued as a small smile emerged on her lips.

"Carrie?" He asked her with a hint of curiosity.

"Carrie," she confirmed, as her smile grew brighter. "I didn't know she was gay. Of course back then I had no idea that I was gay so the thought hadn't occurred to me." Jeremy laughed lightly at her comment. "Sounds silly now, I know." She laughed at her own naivety. "Anyhoo, from the moment I met Carrie I was quite taken with her. Only I didn't know it. I was so naïve I didn't think twice about the fact that she and I were practically joined at the hip from the first moment we met. That night during the party around the bonfire, we went for a little walk along the beach. Let's just say that by the time the sun came up I was a lot less naïve."

"You and Carrie?" Jeremy responded with a smile of admiration. "Carrie's a great girl."

"I know," Daryl confessed with a blush. "The next morning I was confused and I totally freaked out. I swore up and down that I was straight and that she took advantage of me while I was drunk."

"She didn't, did she?" Jeremy flared with an overprotective growl.

"God no," Daryl reassured him instantly. "Even when I was

saying it, I knew it was a lie. So did she," she added grimly. "I just couldn't face her after that. If I thought she would be around, I avoided being with you guys. By the time I had dealt with my confusion and decided to swallow my pride, it had been a few years and I came up here for that last weekend you guys spent here. Carrie was with her girlfriend and pretty much avoided me like I was a bad memory. Which I guess I am."

"That was right before Lesley and I split up," Jeremy added thoughtfully. "I never did like that girl Carrie was seeing back then. Neither did Lesley."

"Well, Carrie seemed pretty fond of her," she stated bitterly as she recalled walking in on the two of them necking in the kitchen. "It bothered me seeing them together. All I wanted to do was tell Carrie the truth. Instead, I packed my bags and took off again just like I did the last time I had seen her."

"I wish I'd known this before," Jeremy said thoughtfully. "You know, Carrie dumped her before the weekend was over. They left not long after you did. Will it be a problem seeing Carrie again?" He inquired carefully. She stared back at him in confusion. "She and Lesley are still very close."

"Peachy," she grumbled. "I'll cross that bridge when I get to it. In the meantime, dear brother, we need to get back to work if we want this place presentable before the end of the summer." Having said that, the siblings returned to their labors.

PART FIVE

A week later Daryl pulled up alongside the beach house. She looked the house over and was pleased by all the work she and Jeremy had done. Her car was loaded down with groceries and a few household items she'd picked up over the past week. Jeremy's truck and another car occupied the driveway. There wasn't anyone she'd wanted to invite to the first party at the house. She frowned slightly, knowing that the other car was Lesley's. She was excited about seeing Lesley again but she worried about being a third wheel.

She reached into the backseat of the car and retrieved a

couple of boxes. Her view was blocked by the packages but she was determined not to make too many trips. She stumbled as she rounded the corner to the back porch. "I should have just let them come up here by themselves," she muttered under her breath.

"I was just thinking the same thing myself," a hauntingly familiar voice said.

Daryl's breath caught as she lowered the boxes to see who had spoken to her. Her heart leapt when she saw her lounging on the back steps. Her hair was shorter and her body even firmer than she remembered. She noted the pensive look on her face as she waited for Daryl to say something. *'I'm going to kill him,'* her mind growled. She noticed the blonde's lips curling up into a hardened smirk and she realized that she hadn't spoken. "Carrie," she finally greeted the woman warmly. "It's good to see you," she added sincerely.

Carrie lowered her sunglasses and studied her carefully, searching for any signs of deceit. "Nice to see you as well," Carrie responded as she pushed her sunglasses back up. Daryl could still hear the wariness in the smaller woman's voice.

"Where are the lovebirds?" Daryl asked as she shifted the packages in her arms. "Or shouldn't I ask?" She added playfully.

"They went for a walk," Carrie responded lightly as she stood. "Let me give you a hand."

"Thanks. If you could just grab the top one," Daryl said, relaxing slightly. "So they just left you here?" Daryl continued as they made their way into the house. "In the kitchen," she instructed her guest.

"Please," Carrie scoffed. "Sitting around contemplating my navel lint was much more fun than watching the two of them making goo goo eyes at one another. I felt like we were back in college." Carrie laughed as she placed the box she'd been carrying onto the counter.

"Yuk," Daryl groaned as she put her load down on the table. She turned to find Carrie giving her on odd look as she drummed her fingers on the top of the box she'd carried in.

"Daryl?" Carrie began in a dry tone. "Are you trying to tell me something?"

Daryl stared at her curiously as Carrie continued to drum her fingers in a steady rhythm. It wasn't until Daryl finally noticed the new toaster oven she had unwittingly given to Carrie to bring in that she fully understand. She howled with laughter as she crossed the room to join Carrie. She was pleased when the blonde giggled along with her. "Well, I guess I do owe you one of these," she said once she'd finally managed to stifle her laughter.

"Really?" Carrie inquired with a bold smile.

"Oh, look at how proud you are," Daryl teased the blonde. "Come on. Give me a hand with the rest of the stuff," she added with a playful nudge. "I'm surprised that Lesley never told you that I came out," she added as they stepped outside.

"She may have wanted to," Carrie said shyly. "I came out to her not long after we started our freshman year and she never had a problem with it. But after that night, whenever your name was mentioned I kind of made a mad dash out of the room."

"Oh?" Daryl said curiously.

"I just felt so terrible about not being supportive that morning," Carrie explained as they began to unload packages from the car. "I didn't know it was your first time with a woman."

"You have nothing to apologize for," Daryl responded firmly. "I should have told you and I shouldn't have accused you of taking advantage of me. It was a lie. I was just scared and confused."

"I can only imagine," Carrie said with a heavy sigh as they made their way back into the house. "I never told Lesley. I did wonder if I had taken advantage of you."

"Carrie," Daryl said firmly as the put the last of their cargo away. "Trust me. I didn't do anything that night that I didn't want to. My only regret was the way I acted towards you that morning. I wanted to tell you this years ago but the last time I saw you . . . well, you were otherwise engaged."

"Ugh . . . her." Carrie groaned. "Once again it was proof that I have no taste in women."

"Thank you," Daryl scoffed with a slight chuckle.

"Well, not to be insulting, but a straight teenager with a boyfriend," Carrie pointed out.

"Yeah, what were you thinking?" Daryl continued to tease her.

"I was thinking '*wow, she is hot*'." Carrie responded with a playful nudge.

"Thank you," Daryl responded with a shy smile. "I need some air. Want to go out onto the porch? The sun should be setting soon."

"I brought a bottle of wine," Carrie suggested.

"I always liked you," Daryl responded happily. "I brought glasses and a corkscrew."

They gathered up the wine and the glasses and headed out to the back porch. They sat on the swing she and Jeremy had hung a couple of weeks earlier. As they chatted, Daryl could easily see why she had fallen for Carrie the first time. She was beautiful, smart, witty, and charming. "So I get this message on my voicemail," Daryl continued, explaining what had happened between her and Shannon. "She's canceling again." She emphasized the last word. "I don't recall what we were planning on doing but there was something in the way her voice cracked. You know, the sound like you just woke up but it isn't that. It's the 'I've just had really hot sex and now I need to drink a gallon of water' tone."

"Ouch," Carrie responded with a cringe.

"After three-and-a-half years she couldn't tell me the truth when I confronted her about it," Daryl continued. "In the end she handed me the old 'it's not you, it's me' line of crap. She moved in with her new girlfriend right away."

"Bitch," Carrie added in support.

"Cheers," Daryl offered as she refilled their wine glasses.

"My last girlfriend neglected to tell me that she was crazed psycho who was wanted by the police," Carrie offered as she sipped her wine.

"What?" Daryl choked on her wine. "You're making that up."

"I swear it's true," Carrie said. "I had no idea until I came home one day about three months ago to find that she'd cleaned me out. Just as I was about to call the police, they showed up at my door looking for her. It seems she liked to pass checks that were either stolen or worthless. I don't even know how the cops got my address since we weren't living together."

"Women," Daryl scowled. "Who needs them?"

"We do." They both giggled in unison.

"So do you like being an EMT?" Daryl inquired as she leaned slightly closer to Carrie.

"I love it," Carrie responded brightly. "Despite the crazy hours and the bad things you see, it's worth it." Daryl lost herself in the steady rhythm of Carrie's voice. "What about you? Social Services isn't exactly a walk in the park," Carrie inquired.

"Like you said, the hours are crazy and you see a lot of things that will stay with you. But it's worth it," Daryl responded proudly. "I forgot how quiet it is up here," she said softly as she absently caressed the back of Carrie's hand.

"Hmm," Carrie responded with a contented sigh as she captured Daryl's hand in her own.

Daryl felt a sense of warmth as she held the smaller woman's hand. They listened to the crashing waves as they fell into a comfortable silence. Daryl turned and watched Carrie looking blissfully out at the darkened sea. She placed her wine glass down without releasing her hold on Carrie's hand. The blonde turned to her and Daryl was lost in emerald eyes that twinkled at her in the moonlight.

She reached over and brushed a stray lock of hair from Carrie's brow. "I must look like a mess," Carrie said softly.

"No," Daryl responded with equal tenderness as her breathing became shallow. "I think you're beautiful." She was mesmerized by Carrie's shy smile as they both leaned slightly closer to one another. "I've . . . ," she began. Suddenly words failed her as she felt Carrie's breath caressing her face. She took the glass of wine from the blonde's hand and placed it next to her own.

Carrie leaned in and nuzzled Daryl's neck, feeling the beat of her heart. Daryl sighed happily as she captured the sweet scent of Carrie's hair. "This is nice," she said softly as she slowly caressed Carrie's shoulder. The sigh transformed into a moan as Carrie's lips kissed the side of her neck. She ran her hands down Carrie's back while the blonde placed soft delicate kisses along her jaw.

She looked down and found herself lost in a smoky lustful gaze. Their lips brushed slowly. Gone was the urgency of their youth, yet the fiery passion still smoldered. Daryl's lips were still tingling from the brief contact when she reclaimed Carrie's lips. The second kiss was just as brief yet seemed to linger. They caressed each other's faces with their fingertips before kissing once again with a slow promise. The kiss deepened as their hands began to slowly explore.

As their tongues met, their hands grew bolder. Daryl began to unbutton the blonde's blouse as Carrie's hand slipped between her thighs. She moaned into Carrie's mouth as the blonde cupped her mound. She slipped her hand under the lacy material of Carrie's bra while the blonde used the palm of her hand to tease Daryl's throbbing clit. She felt the zipper of her jeans being lowered as she began to roll Carrie's nipple between her fingers.

The sound of someone clearing their throat startled them and they froze. Carrie giggled as she buried her face in Daryl's shoulder. Daryl turned to find Jeremy and Lesley watching them with amused expressions. "Lesley!" Daryl greeted her old friend brightly and was about to stand when she realized that her hand was still firmly buried in Carrie's bra.

"That's okay. Don't get up," Lesley laughed. "We'll see the two of you inside."

Jeremy and Lesley were laughing heartily as they went inside, leaving the embarrassed couple on the porch swing. Carrie was laughing against Daryl's shoulder. "She looks good, don't you think?" Daryl quipped as Carrie's head fell back in gales of laughter. Daryl couldn't resist the sight and quickly claimed Carrie's lips. She plunged her tongue into the warmth of the blonde's mouth while she teased her nipple with her fingers. Carrie's hand reclaimed its nest between her thighs and quickly resumed its steady motion.

The swing creaked beneath their wild rhythm and they broke apart gasping for air.   "We have to stop," Daryl panted reluctantly.

"I know," Carrie whimpered in return.

Daryl stole one last kiss before the couple straightened their clothing and joined the others.   The four of them enjoyed a simple dinner and chatted nonstop.   All the while she and Carrie exchanged knowing glances that further fueled Daryl's growing desire.   By the end of dinner, the tall brunette could barely walk. The one saving grace was that she noticed Jeremy and Lesley exchanging the same teasing looks.   She offered to clear the dishes and Carrie eagerly offered to help.

While they were washing the dishes, Daryl couldn't resist brushing against Carrie's body.   The tiny whimpers and moans that escaped from the blonde made her body pulsate.   Finally, as they were drying the last of the dishes, Jeremy and Lesley excused themselves and retired to the back bedroom.   "I thought they would never leave," Carrie huffed as she tossed down her dishtowel and pulled Daryl in for a searing kiss.

Daryl melted into the kiss, recalling that the last time she'd felt this alive was the last time she'd held this woman in her arms.   She pulled Carrie's shirt out of her pants as she backed the smaller woman up against the kitchen counter.   They broke apart when the need to breathe became too urgent.   "Stay with me tonight," she whispered hotly into Carrie's ear before dipping her tongue inside.

"Yes," Carrie hissed in response.

It was all the encouragement Daryl needed before sinking to her knees.   She quickly undid and lowered Carrie's jeans, pulling her underwear down at the same time.   Carrie with her pants down around her ankles leaned back against the counter and opened herself up to Daryl.

The musky aroma of her lover's desire filled the brunette's sense as she dipped her tongue into Carrie's wetness.   "So wet," she groaned before slowly licking away each drop of passion. Carrie's hips rocked forward, begging for more as Daryl clasped her firm backside.   She felt Carrie clutching her shoulders as she plunged her tongue inside of her center.   She plunged in and out of the blonde as Carrie's hips thrust in a wild rhythm.

She drove her lover higher and then, just as she felt the blonde's thighs trembling against her face, she withdrew. "No," Carrie whimpered in disappointment. The whimper evolved into a deep moan as Daryl's fingers replaced her tongue. She suckled her lover's clit in her mouth as her fingers plunged in and out of her wetness. Her mouth and hand moved in unison, quickly driving the blonde over the edge. Daryl clung to her lover, needing to pleasure her again.

Carrie gently pushed her away. Daryl looked up with desire and found her lover's gaze mirroring her own. "Bed," Carrie said urgently. Daryl nodded in agreement as she reluctantly removed herself from the warmth of her lover's passion. Somehow the couple managed to stumble into Daryl's bedroom, stealing kisses along the way.

Once the door was closed the kisses grew in intensity while they slowly undressed one another. They tumbled onto the bed naked and their bodies melted together. Daryl's body was pulsating as she pulled Carrie's naked form down on top of her. They kissed hungrily as their fingers explored every inch of the other's body. Their wetness painted skin and soon they were exploring one another's mouth as fingers entered wet cores. As her lover's fingers filled her and her thumb teased her clit, Daryl's hand mirrored Carrie's actions. Soon they were screaming in pleasure. They replayed every memory from their first time together and created new memories as the night wore on. Daryl was lost in the feel of Carrie's body as the blonde straddled her, offering all of herself up to the brunette's touch.

For the second time in her life, Daryl awoke to find Carrie's naked body covering her own and this time she felt at peace. Carrie looked up at her with a smile. "Good morning," Daryl offered with a soft purr before kissing Carrie's sweet inviting lips.

"Good morning," Carrie responded softly against her lips.

"I don't think Jeremy or Lesley are in any hurry to get out of bed this morning," Daryl said in a breathy tone as Carrie's body arched against her. She ran her tongue along the blonde's neck.

Carrie pulled away slightly and captured Daryl's face in her hands. "No running away this time," she cautioned her.

"Not a chance," Daryl reassured her before capturing Carrie's lips in a slow sensual kiss.

THE END

Mavis Applewater

STORM WARNING
(THE BEACH - PART TWO)

Carrie snuggled against Daryl's naked body. As she ran her fingers along the soft inviting curves of the brunette's body, she fully expected to wake up and find that the night before had been nothing more than a dream. It wouldn't be the first time her overactive imagination had conjured up a passion-filled night that featured Daryl. As she felt Daryl's skin respond to her touch, she knew that it wasn't a dream. The other fear she faced when she awoke that morning was that Daryl would prove once again to be the same angst-ridden, issue-burdened girl she'd been twelve years earlier.

Once again Carrie was delighted to find that just wasn't the case. Daryl bore no resemblance to the frightened teenager she'd been the first time they had been intimate. That girl was long gone and in her place was a strong confident woman, the type of woman that Carrie could easily find herself falling for. Her gentle caressing paused for a moment as the blonde quickly pushed the premature thought aside. Mission accomplished, she once again began to caress Daryl's naked body.

Her lover moaned softly as Carrie brushed the palms of her hands lightly across the brunette's nipples. Carrie smiled as she watched the rose-colored buds pucker in response to her touch. Carrie shifted her body so that she was now straddling her lover. She knew that her desire was painting her lover's skin. "You're driving me insane," Daryl groaned from beneath her.

"Good," Carrie whispered as she flashed the tall brunette a confident smirk.

"Trying for another toaster oven?" Daryl teased her as the brunette's hands found their way to the firm flesh of Carrie's naked bottom.

"Not this time," Carrie responded with a purr as she wiggled her body against the brunette's squirming form. Daryl moaned as Carrie continued to press her clit against the brunette's taut stomach. "This time I'm going for something much more pleasurable," Carrie explained as she captured Daryl's erect nipples between her agile fingers.

"Such as?" Daryl panted in a needy tone.

"This time I want to make love to you until you forget your own name," Carrie whispered before lowering her head and tracing one of Daryl's nipples with the tip of her tongue. The strangled whimper her lover released informed the small blonde that she was well on her way to fulfilling her promise.

"Carrie," Daryl choked out as the blonde captured her nipple in the warmth of her mouth while she continued to grind her wetness against her lover's body. Her hands massaged Carrie's flesh, guiding her to rock harder against Daryl's body. Carrie suckled Daryl's nipple eagerly as she teased its twin with her fingers. She knew that her desire was flowing along her lover's body as she became lost in the taste and feel of the brunette's skin.

Carrie's mind filled with images of the first time she'd made love to Daryl. The image of two youthful bodies rolling around in the sand further fueled her desires. Carrie teased Daryl's nipple with her teeth and her tongue before lavishing the same attention on its twin. She felt the brunette's body arching up off the bed. Carrie's thighs trembled as Daryl moved in a sensual rhythm beneath her.

She reluctantly freed her lover's breasts from the warmth of her mouth and raised her body. She stared into Daryl's lust-filled crystal blue eyes as she continued to grind her center against the brunette's body. She smiled as her lover's breathing became labored while Carrie cupped her own breast and began to tease her nipple. "You like?" Carrie teased as she began to perform the same act on her other breast.

"Uh huh," Daryl squeaked out as Carrie's hands began to drift lower down her body.

Daryl's hands moved to assist the blonde in her exploration. Carrie gently brushed them aside. Her lover's body rocked harder against her as Carrie parted herself with two fingers and dipped into her wetness with her free hand. "Please," Daryl pleaded as Carrie began to pleasure herself. Carrie cast her lover a mischievous grin as she dipped deeper into her wetness. She felt Daryl's wetness grinding against her hand in an urgent motion. Carrie's eyes began to flutter shut as the sensation of her touch threatened to overwhelm her. Daryl's body lifted as Carrie raised her passion-covered fingers to Daryl's trembling lips.

Carrie inhaled sharply as Daryl's tongue reached out and began to flicker across the blonde's trembling fingertips. Her body tingled as Daryl slowly cleansed each finger, scraping her teeth along the tips before releasing them. Carrie needed to steady her pulsating body for a moment before returning her attention to her lover. Every look, every gesture she received from the brunette, only drove her nearer to the edge and she wanted this moment to last. Once again the petite blonde began to glide her fingers along Daryl's body; this time her mouth and tongue followed each caress.

Each whimper, gasp, and stifled moan confirmed that she was driving Daryl insane. Once again Carrie was feasting upon the brunette's breasts as she nestled her body between Daryl's thighs. She could feel her lover's desire growing as the brunette's center brushed against Carrie's body. Urged on by the feel of her lover's body arching beneath her and her own growing desire, Carrie began to kiss her way down Daryl's body until she was inhaling the musky scent of the brunette's passion.

Carrie became lightheaded with the aroma and sounds of Daryl's need as the brunette draped her long legs over the blonde's shoulders. Carrie blew a warm breath against the damp dark curls as Daryl lifted her body slightly higher. "Soon," Carrie offered with a breathy promise as she cupped her lover's backside and brought her closer. Carrie dipped her tongue inside of Daryl's wetness and slowly traced the brunette's slick folds. Carrie savored each drop of her lover's passion as she feasted upon her slowly.

Daryl's body bucked and pressed closer in an attempt to encourage Carrie to fill her completely. The blonde continued to slowly pleasure her lover despite Daryl's urgent pleas. She flickered her tongue across the brunette's throbbing clit, suckled it until Daryl was ready to explode, and then she would retreat leaving her lover wanting. Carrie continued the slow torture as she lost herself in the taste. Daryl was begging for release as Carrie kissed the inside of her trembling thighs. Once again she buried herself in her lover's wetness, her own desire also demanding release. Carrie pressed her center against the mattress as she eagerly began to suckle her lover harder. As Daryl's body lifted higher off the bed, Carrie pressed two fingers against the warm wet opening of her center. "Yes," Daryl cried out as she thrust her body against Carrie's touch. The blonde could feel the walls of her lover's center tighten the moment she entered her.

Carrie fought to hold her lover steady; the brunette rocked harder against her touch as the blonde filled her completely. Carrie wiggled her fingers inside of her lover while she teased her clit. She could feel the sweat pouring off Daryl's body as she plunged in and out of her. Carrie's hand and mouth began to move in perfect rhythm as the she ground her own body against the mattress. She felt Daryl's body trembling against her own as the blonde increased her sensual rhythm. Daryl's body tightened around Carrie's fingers as she cried out.

The blonde continued to pleasure her lover as the brunette begged her for more. Daryl was gasping for air as Carrie's touch withdrew. The blonde nestled down beside the panting woman and leaned up on one elbow while she cleansed her fingers with her tongue. Daryl's breathing grew heavy as she watched the blonde lick away her wetness. Then Carrie parted her own thighs and slowly began to tease her clit. Daryl released a deep gasp as Carrie painted her own nipple with her wetness.

"That's it," Carrie whimpered as Daryl began to feast upon her nipple, urgently licking away her wetness.

Carrie pressed her body into Daryl's and their hips began to sway together. "Harder," Carrie encouraged her lover as her back arched and she pressed the brunette's head closer to her breast. They began to rock against one another wildly while they straddled each other's thigh. As their bodies melted together, their movements became frenzied until Carrie pulled away from her lover. Daryl was panting heavily as she looked at the blonde with a glassy-eyed expression.

Carrie licked her lips slowly before she guided her lover onto her stomach. Then Carrie covered her lover's body with her own, pressing her wetness against the brunette's firm backside while she straddled her. Daryl's body lifted in response as Carrie pressed harder against her. Daryl managed to support her body on her hands and knees while Carrie continued to thrust against her. Carrie was lost in a haze of pleasure as they moved in rhythm. She fumbled slightly as she reached between them, searching for her lover's clit. Once she found the pulsating bundle she teased it with her fingers while they continued to rock against each other wildly.

Daryl cried out beneath her as Carrie felt her own body nearing the edge. As Daryl clutched at the bedding, Carrie entered her, drawing out her climax as she continued to ride her lover's quivering body. Daryl exploded once again and this time Carrie followed her over the edge. They collapsed into a heap on the mattress, neither able to speak or breath.

Finally Carrie steadied her breathing and began to kiss Daryl's shoulders. "You are amazing," the brunette murmured into her pillow as the annoying chime of the William Tell Overture filled the room.

"Damn," Carrie grumbled as she recognized the sound. "That's my cell," she apologized, knowing that no one would be calling her if it weren't an emergency.

Still feeling weak in the knees, the blonde stumbled as she climbed off the bed. "Let it ring," Daryl grumbled.

"Can't," Carrie choked out, her voice still raw from screaming all night long. She searched frantically in the pile of clothing they'd strewn about the bedroom during the night. She discovered the small gray cell phone and answered it quickly. She paced to the other side of the room and spoke in a hushed tone, not wanting to explain to Daryl the complications her life consisted of. "When?" Carrie grumbled as she began to gather her clothing. "I'm on my way," she responded as she began to pull up her pants. "I love you too," she concluded before disconnecting the call.

She tossed the phone onto the bed and looked over at her lover who was casting her a very wary glance. "I have to go," she explained quickly as her heart sank.

"Apparently," Daryl responded coldly.

"It's not what you think," Carrie tried to explain as she quickly dressed.

"Right," Daryl said in the same cold voice.

"Honestly," Carrie pleaded as she gathered up her things. "I'll explain it to you later. Right now I don't have the time. Can I call you when you get back to the city?"

"Don't bother," Daryl snapped as she climbed off the bed, wrapping the bed sheet around her body.

"Daryl, wait," Carrie called out as the brunette stormed out of the bedroom.

Carrie understood; from what Daryl had heard, she'd jumped to the wrong conclusion. She just didn't have the time to explain things to her. Carrie gathered her belongings and ran out to her car. Sensing that something like this would happen, she'd insisted that she and Lesley take her car up to the beach house. "Damn you, Phoebe," Carrie fumed as she started her car and drove away, praying that she hadn't blown it with Daryl.

Carrie was too angry to call Lesley and explain what had happened; she simply drove, thankful that it was early morning and there wasn't much traffic. By the time she reached the Beverly Police Station she was ready to ring Phoebe's neck. As she stormed up the steps to the small police station, her cell phone went off once again. She didn't bother to check the caller id; she knew who it was. "Yes, Mom," she bellowed into the phone.

"How soon can you get there?" her mother sobbed.

"I just arrived," Carrie grumbled as she entered the police station. "I was in Ipswich so it didn't take long. Did she tell you what she did this time?"

"Well, no," her mother hedged. "I'm certain that it's just a misunderstanding."

"Yeah, like all the other times," Carrie spat out.

"Now, Carrie," her mother began to chastise her.

"Ma, you can't keep treating her like a child," Carrie argued as she walked up to glass wall that separated the inside of the station from the public. "I've got to go," Carrie said as she approached the glass and got the attention of the officer working on the other side.

Carrie snapped the cell phone shut, knowing that trying to talk to her mother about Phoebe was a lost cause. "Hello, Officer. I'm here about Phoebe Riley. I believe she was arrested last night," Carrie explained, knowing how these things worked since Phoebe had put her in this position on more occasions than the young EMT could count.

"And what is your relationship to Ms. Riley?" The officer yawned as he looked up the information on the computer.

"I'm her sister," Carrie admitted in embarrassment.

"I'm sorry," the older man grunted as what appeared to be Phoebe's extensive rap sheet popped up on the computer screen.

"Tell me about it," Carrie responded with a deep sigh. "What did she do this time?"

"Breaking and entering, resisting arrest, assaulting a police officer, and she was in possession of a controlled substance when she was arrested," he explained dryly.

"Oh goodie, we can add drugs to the list," Carrie said as her head throbbed. "Can I bail her out?"

"Nope," he answered. "She has to be arraigned first."

"Cool," Carrie beamed, hearing the first good news she'd received since her mother interrupted her morning with Daryl. Secretly Carrie loved it when Phoebe was held over. She always hoped that the time would give both her mother and younger sister a chance to think about Phoebe's actions. It never did any good, but Carrie always held out hope that one of them would awaken to Phoebe's problems. "Maybe she'll finally get jail time," she whispered hopefully.

"You can see her if you want," he suggested in a bored tone.

"I wish I could say no," she sighed as she agreed to visit with her sister.

Carrie drummed her fingers on the cheap table as she waited in the sterile interview room. It wasn't the first time she'd waited to visit her younger sibling in such a place, and she feared that it wouldn't be the last time either. A burly policewoman escorted her younger but taller sibling into the room in handcuffs. Phoebe sighed as she took a seat across from the irate Carrie. "So are you going to bail me out?" Phoebe asked in a bored tone.

"Not right away," Carrie informed her as she glared at her. "Your arraignment isn't until tomorrow morning."

"What?" Phoebe shouted. "Can't you do something about that?"

It was typical for Phoebe to act that way. She never thanked Carrie or apologized to her; she simply demanded. And since she was the baby and had managed to give their mother a grandchild, whatever Phoebe wanted Phoebe got. Carrie on the other hand was the oldest and was expected to be the responsible one; since she was a homosexual she would never have her mother's respect. If it weren't for Debbie, her adorable niece, Carrie would have walked away from her family years ago. The one thing Carrie wanted as much as she wanted her sister to clean up her act was to get custody of her niece; that would keep her away from Phoebe's bad habits and her endless stream of loser boyfriends.

It would never happen since, despite everything, Phoebe really did love her daughter and Carrie's mother would never allow her grandchild to be raised by someone like her. The irony of the situation didn't escape Carrie's notice. "So you want to tell me what happened?" Carrie finally asked her sibling.

"The cops made a huge deal out of nothing," Phoebe explained in a disgusted tone.

"Don't hand me the line of garbage you're planning on shoveling out for Ma," Carrie snapped. "Tell me the truth."

Phoebe simply shrugged in response. "Fine. I'll see you in the morning."

"Yeah whatever," Phoebe shrugged once again. "Do you think you could spring for a lawyer this time?"

"I can't afford it," Carrie responded honestly.

"Come on, I know you must have money stashed away," Phoebe persisted.

It was true; Carrie had her savings, which Phoebe had already cleaned out on more than one occasion. But since her last girlfriend had turned out to be just like her sister, Carrie was tapped out. The only money she had put aside was in a trust she'd set up for Debbie's education. Carrie had been smart, setting the money up so that no one but she or Debbie could touch it. There was no way she would allow Phoebe to get her hands on the money so she could put it up her nose or give it to the new love of her life.

"What could you spend your money on?" Phoebe sneered in disbelief.

"Well, what you didn't borrow or steal, Sara took," Carrie responded honestly. "The rest goes towards living expenses for Debbie and I," Carrie added, knowing that Phoebe and her mother seemed to forget that it was Carrie who paid for her niece's upbringing. Carrie cringed as she realized that Phoebe's bail was going to put yet another strain on her already tight budget. Hopefully her mother's rent wouldn't go up again this year and Carrie could get ahead of the game once again.

"Fine. I'll just deal with a public defender," Phoebe grumbled as she pouted like a child.

"Anything else?" Carrie groaned, weary of spending time with her sister; her mental list of things to do grew larger with each passing moment. Phoebe just sat there, staring off into space. "I'll see you tomorrow. Oh, and thanks for ruining the first weekend I've had off all year."

"Whatever," Phoebe grunted as Carrie stood and knocked on the door, alerting the guard that she was ready to go.

Carrie sat in her car and started making the calls she needed to so she could be in court tomorrow to hand over her hard earned money. She switched her shift with a friend so she wouldn't have to go in until late afternoon. That would give her time to go to court and still be able to pick her niece up after school. Now she had to drive to her mother's and pick Debbie up, knowing that her elderly mother wasn't physically capable of taking care of the overactive six-year-old. Had she known that Phoebe was going to leave Debbie with her mother last night she would have taken her niece with her to Ipswich.

As she drove to Brighton she thought about how she was going to explain things to Daryl. She didn't want to burden the brunette with her problems. Daryl also worked for Social Services; she might feel obligated to blow the whistle on Phoebe. Debbie would be taken away from her sister and it would only lead to a custody battle between Carrie and her mother. "What am I going to do?" She grumbled as she found herself in the sudden influx of traffic along Rte. 128.

After arriving at her mother's, Carrie endured a barrage of questions and an argument regarding Debbie. Carrie finally convinced her mother that her niece would be better off with her since the six-year-old had her own room at Carrie's house. At her mother's apartment, Debbie and Phoebe were forced to share a room. While Carrie's mother scolded her for not getting Phoebe out on bail, Debbie eagerly packed her stuff up. Each time the little girl stayed with Carrie she brought more and more of her belongings to leave there. Even though the little girl was only six, she seemed to understand her mother's shortcomings. She loved her mother but constantly expressed a desire to live with her aunt.

"I still think she should just stay here," Mrs. Riley protested as Debbie emerged from the tiny bedroom she shared with her mother.

"Ma, I live closer to her school," Carrie argued. "I can drop her off before I leave for court and pick her up when she's done and bring her back here before I go to work."

"I suppose," Mrs. Riley finally agreed.

Carrie blew out a sigh of relief, knowing that Debbie's morning routine took its toll on her aging mother. "Now, what about Phoebe? Could you possibly pay for a lawyer?" Her mother said in a scolding tone.

"No," Carrie flatly refused. "Don't worry. It will probably go just like all the other times. The D.A. will throw out the drug and resisting arrest charges and she'll end up on probation. Think of it this way - she'll have to get a job."

"She's been looking," her mother argued.

Carrie let the comment slide; she looked over at her niece whom seemed eager to get going. "Ready, squirt?" Carrie offered as Debbie collected her bags and raced to the door. "Say goodbye to Grandma," Carrie scolded the little girl who came rushing back and hugged and kissed her grandmother.

"I'll see you tomorrow," Carrie said as she stood. She lingered for a moment, waiting for her mother to say something other than goodbye. Just once a 'thank you' would be nice. Realizing that no gratitude was coming from her mother, Carrie left with her little niece, clutching her hand tightly.

Later that night, as she was tucking Debbie into bed, the little imp captured her in a big hug. "Thank you," the little blonde offered brightly.

"For what?" Carrie asked in confusion as she stared into Debbie's dark brown eyes.

"For everything you do," Debbie offered innocently.

"How old are you?" Carrie asked, surprised once again by the child's wisdom.

"Six and a half," Debbie explained proudly.

"Oh, that must be why you're so wise," Carrie complimented her before placing a kiss on the little girl's forehead. "Good night."

"Good night, Auntie Carrie," Debbie squealed as she snuggled up against her pillow.

"Door open or closed?" Carrie inquired as she stood.

"Open, please," Debbie requested.

Carrie sat in her living room and finally drew up the courage to dial Lesley's cell phone number. She prayed that her college roomie was too preoccupied rekindling her romance with Jeremy to answer.

"Hello?" Lesley answered.

"Hey, it's Carrie," she explained with a heavy sigh.

"What happened?" Lesley blurted out.

"Phoebe happened," Carrie responded wearily.

"I should have known," Lesley grumbled.

"By any chance is Daryl willing to speak to me?" she asked fearfully. Her question was greeted by an uneasy silence. "Lesley?" Carrie prodded as her heart raced.

"She left this morning," Lesley explained with a heavy sigh. "Look, I'll call her and explain everything."

"No, she should hear it from me," Carrie grumbled as she mentally cursed her sister for once again screwing up her life. "Plus I can't tell her everything."

"Why not?" Lesley asked in confusion.

"She's a social worker," Carrie explained. "I don't want to start things off with her having to choose between me and her job."

"There are worse things than you getting custody of Debbie," Lesley blurted out.

"I'd love to have her living here fulltime," Carrie responded. "But it would only lead to a legal battle with my mother and Debbie could get hurt or end up with strangers."

"Do you want her number?" Lesley offered.

"Yes," Carrie sighed with relief. "I can only imagine what she must be thinking. From what she heard when I was on the telephone with my mother, she must think I'm cheating on my lover."

"Oh brother," Lesley groaned. "I'd love to see you guys work this out. Daryl is a doll. And after what Sara put you through . . ."

"My fault, I should have known better then to date someone Phoebe introduced me to," Carrie grunted. "They were probably running the check scam together."

Lesley agreed with her conclusion; she gave her Daryl's telephone number and a promise not to say anything to the brunette until Carrie had the chance to explain things. Once she ended the conversation with Lesley, she took a calming breath and dialed Daryl's apartment. Not surprisingly she got the brunette's answering machine. "Daryl, if you're there please pick up," she said in a soft voice. She waited and received no response. "Okay, I'm sorry I had to run off this morning but I had a family emergency. I'd love to explain it to you." She waited once again and once again was greeted by silence. She ended the conversation by leaving her home phone number and her cell phone number. She sat up for another two hours, sipping tea and waiting for the telephone to ring. Finally she climbed the staircase and checked on her niece before going to her bedroom and climbing into bed.

The following morning Carrie fed, dressed, and dropped Debbie off at school before she drove up to Beverly. As she predicted, Phoebe was released on bail, which took a huge chunk out of Carrie's savings.   She drove her sister back to her mother's, and without so much as a thank you, Phoebe hopped out her car and rushed into the apartment building. Then she drove over to Debbie's school so she would be early and her niece wouldn't be forced to wait around. Carrie suspected that happened to her niece quite often. She drove her niece home after praising her for the gold star she'd received in school.

By the time Carrie arrived for her shift she was exhausted. The night was insane and she was eager to get home. When she was halfway home, she realized that she'd shut her cell phone off when she went into the courthouse that morning. She flipped it on once she pulled into her driveway. She was delighted to find a message from Daryl who still sounded a bit wary. "Damn, I missed her call," she moaned as she rushed into her home.

She immediately checked her answering machine and was once again delighted to find a message from Daryl. She dialed the brunette's number and held her breath until she heard Daryl's voice. "Hello?" Daryl answered.

"Daryl, it's Carrie," she said nervously.

"Hi," Daryl responded and Carrie's heart dropped. She still heard suspicion clouding the brunette's voice.

"I'm so sorry about yesterday," she apologized. "That was my mother who called and something happened with my kid sister."

"Is everything all right?" Daryl asked in concern.

"It will be. I hope," Carrie responded, feeling slightly relieved. "Look, I really had a great time with you. And I was wondering . . . well, I was hoping, if you wanted to . . . would you like to go out to dinner or something?" She managed to stammer out.

"Yes," Daryl responded brightly.

"Really?" Carrie blurted out.

"Yes, really," Daryl answered her with a light laugh.

They talked for several hours and Carrie felt great. Unfortunately it took another three weeks before the conflicts in their work schedule would bring about their first date. Carrie was excited and nervous, as she was getting ready for her first date with the tall brunette. She checked the short black dress she was wearing and smiled. Just as she was getting her coat and heading out the door, her telephone rang. "Hello?" Carrie answered, knowing by the displayed number that it was her mother.

"She's gone," her mother said in a tense voice.

"Who? What's happened?" Carrie demanded fearfully.

"Phoebe," her mother choked out.

"How long has she been gone?" Carrie asked sternly.

"Three days," her mother confessed shyly.

"She jumped bail?" Carrie fumed.

"We don't know that," her mother said.

"Her trial is next week," Carrie argued. "Of course she jumped bail."

"Could you come over?" her mother asked softly.

Carrie's heart sank as she looked at her watch. "Maybe in the morning?" Carrie offered hopefully.

"Debbie is very upset," her mother coaxed her. "I'm sorry, Carrie; I just can't get her to calm down."

"Fine. I'm on my way," Carrie agreed before disconnecting the telephone. "I can't believe this is happening," she said with a heavy sigh as she dialed Daryl's number. She tried to explain that she had another family emergency. Although Daryl accepted the explanation, Carrie detected a hint of disbelief in the brunette's tone. Carrie felt miserable as she drove over to her mother's apartment. Her heart broke when she saw that both her mother and Debbie were overwrought.

Once she managed to calm them both down, Carrie sat her mother down for a long overdue talk. "You look very nice," her mother commented in a slightly snide tone. "What's her name?"

"Daryl," Carrie informed her as she cradled Debbie on her lap.

"Really?" Her mother responded excitedly.

"Relax.   Daryl is a woman," Carrie corrected her assumption.

"But that's a boys name," her mother said in a perplexed tone.

"I'll be sure to mention that to her if I ever get another date with her," Carrie grunted. "Look, Ma, we have to talk. I've checked with all the hospitals and the police and she wasn't in an accident."

"That we know of," her mother interrupted.

"Ma, she took off," Carrie stated bluntly. "And it's not the first time. But it is the first time she could go to jail for it."

"I don't understand how she ended up this way," her mother said in bewilderment. "Both of you were such good kids."

"I still am," Carrie protested.

"I know that, sweetie," her mother agreed softly. "I do know that. And I love you. I just don't understand how you could be . . ... you know."

"It's not a bad thing," Carrie tried to argue. "I'm gay."

"Ssh," her mother scolded her.

"Look, I think that Debbie should stay with me," Carrie asserted.

"No," her mother disagreed vehemently.

"Ma, I have more room and I can take care of her," Carrie argued.

"No," her mother flatly refused. "Phoebe will be back."

"Fine, but maybe both of you should live at my place," Carrie offered, hoping that her mother would agree. "Just until we find Phoebe."

"I like where I'm living," her mother refused. "And I don't want Debbie exposed to certain things."

"I can't believe you," Carrie choked out.

"I'm sorry; it's how I feel," her mother explained. "Take her for the rest of the weekend, but then she's staying here."

"Fine," Carrie agreed, knowing that they would fight about this again at a later date.

Carrie rose with her niece cradled in her arms. "She already has everything she needs at my house," Carrie explained as she balanced the sleeping child in her arms.

"Carrie, the bail money?" her mother inquired tearfully.

"It's gone unless she shows up for her court date or gets caught," Carrie explained flatly.

"How much?" her mother asked.

"Five thousand," Carrie responded.

"I'll pay you back," her mother offered sadly.

"Don't worry about it." Carrie waved her off, knowing that on her mother's limited income she wouldn't be able to keep her promise. "I need to get the squirt to bed. We're going to talk about this again," Carrie added sternly.

"I know," her mother conceded with a slight smile. "I love you."

"I love you too," Carrie said with a smile.

"And Carrie, thank you," her mother added. Carrie blinked in surprise. "Debbie told me that I should tell you that," her mother added proudly. "I do appreciate everything you do. It's just hard admitting that I need to ask my child for help."

Carrie blinked back the tears as she carried her niece out to her car. In the weeks that followed, Debbie was shuffled between the two households. Despite the fact that the little girl made it clear that she preferred to live with Carrie, Mrs. Riley refused to allow her daughter to become her guardian. The added responsibility added a new dimension to Carrie's life. The change effectively eliminated any chance of having Daryl in her life. She couldn't explain to the brunette why she was unable to get together with her. The excuses were growing more and more flimsy until the brunette simply stopped returning her calls.

Carrie didn't have time to nurse her broken heart; she had her niece and mother to take care of. One night she was just finishing her shift when Bob, one of her co-workers, came running over. "Carrie, we just got a call. It's your mother," he explained in a harried tone. Before he could say anything else, Carrie was in her car rushing over to her mother's apartment. Years of being an EMT hadn't prepared her for the sight of an ambulance with its lights flashing in front of her mother's home. She rushed over. "I'm her daughter," she explained to the EMT who was loading her mother into the back of the ambulance.

His face turned grim when he took in her dark blue uniform, which looked exactly like the one he was wearing. "She's had a stroke," he explained as gently as he could. "We've got her stabilized." Carrie nodded in understanding as her heart hammered in her chest. "We're taking her to St. Elizabeth."

"Good, I just need to get my niece," she stammered.

"Uhm, she's upstairs with Social Services," the man explained hesitantly. "She called 911. Bright kid, but the operator figured something was up with her mother not being around. I have to go."

"Go," Carrie said, knowing her mother's life depended on it. She raced up to her mother's apartment and prepared to do battle with some bureaucratic fat head.

"Auntie Carrie," Debbie squealed as Carrie entered her mother's kitchen. She was shocked to see who was sitting at the table chatting with her niece. Carrie wrapped Debbie in her arms as she looked down at Daryl. "I heard you were a very brave girl," Carrie complimented her niece as she cradled her in her arms.

"She was," Daryl agreed with a smile. "She called 911 and told the operator all the right things. She told me her Auntie Carrie told her how to do that."

"How is Grandma?" Debbie asked fearfully.

"I don't know yet," Carrie informed her softly. "We'll go to the hospital just as soon as we can. First, I think Miss Temple has a few questions to ask me."

"I'm sorry, Carrie," Daryl confirmed as Carrie put Debbie down.

"Squirt, go pack one of your overnight bags while I talk to Miss Temple," Carrie said gently as her emerald eyes began to fill with tears. Debbie nodded and shuffled quickly off to her bedroom. "Don't take her away from me."

"I won't," Daryl promised. "I just need to clear some things up, then I'll drive the two of you over to the hospital."

"Thank you," Carrie choked out.

"Where's Debbie's mother?" Daryl inquired carefully.

"I don't know," Carrie confessed. "Phoebe jumped bail. I found out the night I was supposed to meet you."

"How about her father?" Daryl gently asked.

"I don't know," Carrie admitted.

"You don't know where he is?" Daryl asked softly.

"I don't know who he is," Carrie said with a tremble. "I doubt that Phoebe is certain who he is either. What else do you need to know?" Carrie asked, hoping to finish the conversation before Debbie heard anything she shouldn't.

"No," Daryl offered in a comforting tone as she stood. "I'll work this out. I can't work the case directly but I'll find some way to make this work."

"Thank you," Carrie choked out as Daryl wrapped her arms around her.

"We'll work this out," Daryl promised softly. "Can you drive?"

"Yes," Carrie responded in confusion.

"Why don't you give me your address and your house key and I'll look after Debbie," Daryl offered. Carrie tensed, fearing that she was being duped. "A hospital ER is no place for a little girl, especially at this time of night. I'll stay with her at your place," Daryl explained as Debbie stepped into the kitchen.

Carrie quickly explained to the precocious six-year-old that Daryl was going to look after her until she got home. Debbie seemed fine with the idea, already taking a shine to the tall brunette. Carrie gave directions to Daryl on how to get to her house and gave her the key before rushing off to the hospital. It was almost dawn when Carrie returned to her home. She looked at her key for a long agonizing moment before she realized that Daryl had the key. It felt strange to knock on the door to her house.

Daryl opened the door quickly, wrapped her arms around Carrie, and ushered her inside. "How's your mother?" Daryl asked quickly as she seated Carrie on the sofa.

"Stable," Carrie explained as she released an exhausted sigh. "We'll know more in the next couple of days. But it looks good. Well, as good as it can be. How's Debbie?"

"Okay," Daryl responded thoughtfully. "She's sound asleep. She was a little worked up over everything that happened last night, but I had a long talk with her. That child absolutely idolizes you," she added with a chuckle.

"I wanted to bring her here," Carrie explained as Daryl guided her to rest her head on her shoulder. "Not just when Phoebe split this time, but before."

"It seems that she would be happier here," Daryl responded in understanding. "I made some calls and there's no reason why she can't stay with you."

"Thank you," Carrie responded softly as she snuggled closer to Daryl. "You have no idea how much everything you've done means to me."

"Anytime," Daryl offered as she kissed the top of Carrie's head. "It's nice to know that you had a good reason for standing me up. I should have believed you."

"Please," Carrie scoffed. "If someone blew me off as many times as I did you, I would have assumed that they were a worthless wench."

"Well, you're not worthless or a wench." Daryl chuckled as she caressed Carrie's shoulder.

"I could be a wench if you wanted me to be," Carrie responded playfully as she looked up into Daryl's eyes.

Without knowing who moved first, Carrie found herself locked in a passionate kiss as their bodies melted together. Both women were gasping for air as the kiss came to a reluctant end. Carrie stood and held out her hand to the brunette. The look of love she saw in the brunette's eyes reassured her that she was making the right decision. Daryl's hand slipped into Carrie's as she stood. "We'll have to be quiet," Carrie cautioned to the taller woman as she led her upstairs towards her bedroom. She paused for a moment and checked on the slumbering Debbie. She rejoined the smiling Daryl in the hallway.

"You're a natural," Daryl said with a brilliant smile. Carrie blushed in response as she reached up and kissed Daryl gently.

Carrie led the brunette into her bedroom and locked the door behind them. "Does this mean I finally get a date with you?" Daryl teased as she caressed Carrie's face.

"Yes," Carrie sighed as she leaned into the taller woman's touch. "But I'm afraid it will have to be somewhere less than romantic."

"I can do Chuck E Cheese," Daryl said with a soft promise before reclaiming Carrie's soft lips.

"You don't know what you're getting into," Carrie cautioned her as the kiss ended.

"I think I do," Daryl reassured her as she began to slowly undress Carrie.

"Are you sure?" Carrie inquired carefully as she also began to undress her lover.

"Yes," Daryl confirmed. "We can do this."

Carrie understood that Daryl was referring to the complications in the blonde's life. She could see it in Daryl's eyes; she was at least going to try to make things work between them. They continued to undress one another while stealing kisses. Once they were naked, Carrie led her lover to her bed and pulled back the covers. She kissed Daryl deeply as she lowered the tall brunette down on the bed. As Carrie climbed into bed next to her and wrapped the blankets around them, she knew that they both understood that physical and emotional exhaustion weren't going to allow them to explore the all consuming passion that they'd shared the other times they'd made love.

They melted into a gentle embrace as the kisses grew deeper and each pressed a firm thigh against the other's wet center. They continued to kiss and caress as they rocked in a slow gentle rhythm. Carrie's heart soared as she felt her lover's desire greet her skin. Each began to tremble and they released a soft cry as their rhythm increased steadily. Soon they climaxed in unison. Daryl wrapped her arms around Carrie's body as the blonde snuggled against her and drifted off to sleep.

When Carrie awoke she was thrilled to find that she was still nestled against Daryl's body. "Still haven't scared you off?" She asked as she looked up to find her lover casting an amused grin down at her.

"No, but you keep trying," Daryl teased her in response before kissing her gently.

"As much as I would love to stay here all day, I need to take care of Debbie and get over to the hospital," Carrie explained as Daryl caressed her back.

"We should get up then," Daryl explained softly. "I've already taken the day off from work so I can help you out any way that you need."

"You're amazing," Carrie choked out.

"Finally you've fallen for my charms," Daryl teased as they climbed out of bed.

"Daryl, I fell for your considerable charms that first day on the beach," Carrie confessed.

The End

THE PROMISE

PART ONE

Amsterdam 1939

Glenna looked over at her companion with an amused grin. The tall slender redhead with the brilliant blue eyes sipped her tea thoughtfully. Helga was the portrait of elegance. She had a slender body, long legs, and a swan-like neck. Back home in the states she would have been easily mistaken for a movie star or royalty. If you passed Helga on the street you would never suspect that the statuesque beauty was a madam. Not just any madam. Helga was a brilliant businesswoman who ran a very discreet operation for those with enough class and money.

"What is it that you are smiling at, my friend?" Helga inquired curiously, her rich accent rolling off her full lips.

"You, my friend," Glenna responded happily.

"I delight you?" Helga inquired with a slight purr.

"You know that you do," Glenna agreed. "I was just thinking what a strange friendship we share."

"You mean because we . . . how do you Americans say, fucked?" Helga inquired playfully. "Such a vulgar term."

"True," Glenna agreed. "But somehow the way you say it

brings a certain elegance to the term."

Helga flashed a sly grin at the tall American and Glenna was just about to expand on her thoughts when a petite strawberry blonde entered Helga's luxurious apartment. Emerald eyes stared curiously at Glenna who smiled in response. The small girl blushed before shyly scampering out of the room. Glenna turned to see the warning glare Helga flashed at her. The small blonde's name was Dodi. Other than that and the fact that Helga kept her way from her business and clients, Glenna knew nothing about the girl.

"If you will excuse me?" Helga offered politely as she stood. "I need to see to Dodi."

"Of course," Glenna said with a slight nod. "I'll just enjoy my tea and reminisce about how we met."

"You mean when you entered my theatre for the first time. Such a pleasant memory," Helga added before she left the room.

"Hmm," Glenna sighed as her thoughts drifted once again to the mysterious Dodi. "Who is she?" Glenna pondered thoughtfully. Although she had known Helga for six years, she hadn't a clue as to who the young girl was.

PART TWO

Six years ago Glenna was on her honeymoon. She was a blushing young bride and her husband, William, was bordering on senility. Not surprising since her groom was nearly a half century her senior. It was a good match in many ways. Glenna's family needed her to maintain her station in high society and William needed a wife. Since he was a rich old codger it seemed like an ideal match for the young woman. After all, Glenna reasoned that William really wasn't going to be on this earth much longer. She truly liked the older gentleman who was far too busy amassing a fortune to wed and he was only cognizant of their marriage on rare occasions. She of course would perform her duties. She was stunned that at those times Horace would display uncharacteristic stamina. Her only fear was that she would send her elderly husband to his grave before she had the chance to give him an heir.

It wasn't the money that she sought; she truly wanted to have a child.   Of course William's millions didn't hurt.   But underneath it all she was simply a socialite that needed to hide her true sexuality.   They honeymooned in Europe and delighted in the grand old architecture and arts.   When they arrived in Amsterdam Horace was weary and Glenna was thankful.

After some discreet inquiries, a chambermaid informed her of a little known place that would appeal to Glenna.   Chez Elle was described to her by the chambermaid as the spot she should go.   The name explained it all to the eager Glenna.   The brunette didn't doubt the information the maid had passed along to her since she had already bedded the woman.

Chez Elle was hidden away on a dark side street.   It was, for all intents and purposes, a theatre.   Certainly not the kind her old schoolmates from Vassar would have approved of since the main attraction was the live sex shows consisting mostly of a female entourage.   Glenna felt like a gangster when she knocked on the dark doorway and gave the password.   The tall burly man examined her closely to ensure she was dressed appropriately, and then allowed her to pay the hefty entrance fee when he was assured that her pedigree was appropriate.

Glenna walked into the bright theatre and was amazed by the wealthy women and men floating about.   She surveyed the plush booths and elegant décor.   If it weren't for the three naked beauties pleasuring each other on stage, she would have thought she was at one of New York's finer establishments.   A young woman dressed in a long flowing gown approached her.   The woman began to speak and Glenna held up her hand.   "English, please," Glenna implored her, feeling far too weary to translate.

"An American," the woman said excitedly.   "We have so few visiting us these days with all the troubles. Welcome!   Are you alone?"

"Yes," Glenna responded with a shy smile as the woman removed her wrap.

"If you wish companionship you need only to tell your server," the woman explained as she led Glenna down the aisles past several booths where couples were engaged in some very interesting activities. "And if you wish your server, simply ask," she explained as she seated Glenna at a small private table. "If someone approaches you that doesn't interest you, a simple no will end the encounter. Enjoy your visit; everything will be added to your bill. Simply pay the cashier on the way out."

Glenna nodded, slightly stunned by the casual atmosphere. Her server was an attractive woman with an ample bosom that pressed against her tight dress. Glenna ordered a bottle of champagne and watched the show. She sipped the champagne as she delighted in the performances.

A slender redhead seated herself at Glenna's table without introduction. The woman's sparkling eyes captivated Glenna. "Are you enjoying your visit?" the woman inquired in a rich accent that Glenna instantly realized was German.

"Very much," Glenna responded as the woman slid closer to her.

"I'm Helga," the woman introduced herself. "I would like to enjoy your company, if it pleases you?"

"Glenna," the brunette responded eagerly. Helga captured her hand and ran her long fingers along the back of the brunette's hand. "Would you like some champagne?" Glenna offered. Helga simply nodded in response.

"And where is he this evening?" Helga inquired as she ran her finger along Glenna's large diamond wedding band.

"Sleeping," Glenna responded with a light laugh as Helga waved the serving girl over.

Glenna could feel her pulse racing as the girl placed another champagne flute on the table. Helga brushed the girl's lips lightly with her own as she ran her hand up the back of the girl's dress. Glenna purred with excitement as she watched the scene. Helga quickly dismissed the girl and sipped her champagne as Glenna drank in her body. The black silk pantsuit fitted Helga's slender frame perfectly.

"Pity," Helga said as she placed her glass on the table.

"What is?" Glenna inquired, thoroughly intrigued by this beauty sitting next to her.

"That someone so young and beautiful has to sneak away from her husband," Helga explained as she ran her fingers along

Glenna's firm jaw. "Are you simply curious?"

"No." Glenna laughed lightly as she leaned into Helga's touch. "He's not so young and I passed the stage of curiosity quite some time ago."

"Ah, he is rich," Helga said with a knowing smile.

"Very," Glenna confessed as she ran her fingers along her companion's thigh.

"Clever girl," Helga said with a saucy wink. Glenna's hand continued to enjoy the feel of silk while Helga's hands drifted down the front of Glenna's evening gown. They watched the show as Glenna's desire deepened. Her hand grew bolder and soon she was caressing the inside of Helga's firm thigh. Her blue eyes widened when she felt the hard bulge between her companion's thighs.

Helga sighed deeply as she captured Glenna's trembling hand. The redhead moved Glenna's hand deeper between her legs. Glenna moaned as she cupped the woman's mound and felt the hardness pressing against her palm. "Would you like to see?" Helga invited her in a husky tone.

"Yes," Glenna gasped.

Glenna licked her lips eagerly as Helga unbuttoned her slacks and pulled them down slightly to reveal her creamy white hips and the phallus strapped to her mound. Helga's eyes glazed over as she guided Glenna's hand down to touch the phallus. Glenna lost herself in the feel of it while she stroked the phallus slowly. Never in her previous escapes had Glenna been treated to such a delightful encounter. Soon touching the phallus wasn't enough. She shifted in the velvet-covered booth and lowered her mouth.

Eagerly she took the phallus into her mouth; Helga moaned in pleasure while she ran her fingers through Glenna's long raven tresses. Their passion grew steadily until Helga pulled Glenna up to her and captured her lips in a fiery kiss. Soon Helga was leading Glenna away from her table. As the strolled through the theatre, she noticed the respect that was accorded Helga by each person she encountered.

Glenna understood many things as they made their way up to Helga's private booth. First, Helga was the driving force behind

Chez Elle. Secondly, her attractive companion's desires weren't limited to women. Helga, she would learn later, found pleasure in beautiful people regardless of their gender. Helga led her to her private booth; it contained a large bed that could provide comfort while giving the guests an unobstructed view of the stage without the patrons being able to observe Helga's activities.

Glenna and Helga undressed one another while exchanging passionate kisses and soon Glenna found herself lying beneath the beautiful redhead. Glenna wrapped her long legs around Helga's body and allowed her to fill her completely. Helga took her to new heights that evening. After their encounter ended and before Glenna was in the taxi heading back to the hotel room she shared with her husband, Helga offered to assist Glenna in finding companionship whenever she was in the area.

Glenna knew that Helga wasn't offering herself but was more than willing to broker any recreation that Glenna might seek. That was the way it had begun. Glenna became one of Helga's clients and once a year visited Amsterdam whether or not William could accompany her. Somehow the two women struck up a mostly unlikely friendship. She knew that Helga was closer to her than her other clients. She also knew that, despite their closeness, neither of them wanted a romantic relationship with the other.

She even corresponded with Helga and learned a great deal about her foreign friend. Helga was a cunning businesswoman and very well educated. She had left Germany when the politics changed. She built her business up quietly and, since her clients were very well connected throughout the continent and she was discreet, she was allowed to keep her business thriving.

The only thing Glenna didn't know about was Dodi. She remembered the first time she saw the shy young woman. At first Glenna thought she was a child but when she looked closer she knew that Dodi was probably only a few years her junior. Helga made it clear the first time she saw Glenna admiring Dodi that the petite woman was not on the menu. Dodi was kept away from anyone that had anything to do with Helga's business. Glenna respected her privacy regarding the matter and never questioned her.

For a brief moment she thought that perhaps Dodi was Helga's child but quickly realized that the girl was far too old. It was strange that Glenna knew Helga's favorite sexual position and her dreams for the future but hadn't a clue as to who the young girl was. She would have asked Dodi but the girl wasn't allowed to speak to her and all they shared were a few smiles and curious looks.

PART THREE

"Such an interesting look on that beautiful face," Helga commented merrily. Glenna blinked before noticing her friend grinning at her.

"I was just reminiscing about how you seduced me," Glenna teased her friend.

"I seduced you?" Helga responded with a hearty laugh. "It was a nice evening. Your body wrapped around my own while we made love watching those two young women performing the same act on stage."

"It was so very kind of you to invite them to join us after their performance," Glenna added with a wry smile.

"I am always a gracious hostess," Helga commented softly. "Plus I was granted the pleasure of watching those two beautiful creatures fulfill your every desire." Glenna blushed deeply at the memory. "That evening I knew that you would be a wonderful client. Then you took me by complete surprise and invited me for tea the following afternoon. At first I was worried that you might have, how do you say, a crush? Such harsh words in your language for such beautiful sentiments." Glenna listened carefully as her friend spoke. She always found Helga's voice captivating. "But that afternoon we talked about everything from art to the state of the world. None of my other clients would even speak to me on the street, but you invited me to your home and offered your friendship. You didn't offer your bed, knowing that it wasn't what either us sought from the other, and for that, my friend, I am in your debt."

271

"Helga, I treasure our friendship," Glenna quickly explained. "It is so nice to have another woman to speak to about life. Unlike so many women I know, you don't hide your intelligence nor do you ask me to hide mine. I love your letters. And I will always hold the memory of sharing my passion with you very close to my heart. We both know that our feelings for one another are not romantic."

"You have been visiting Amsterdam for a few months now. Are you enjoying your stay?" Helga inquired casually.

"Yes, very much so," Glenna responded, slightly bewildered by the sudden change in the conversation.

"How much longer will you be staying in my adopted country?" Helga continued as her eyes drifted to the door where Dodi had exited a short while ago.

"Not very much longer I'm afraid," Glenna responded with regret. "The climate is changing and William is insistent that I return to America."

"I trust it is not the weather that you are referring to," Helga said thoughtfully.

"No," Glenna responded sadly. "The world is changing, my friend, and I fear that my husband is correct. I should return to my home, and to my husband of course," she added with a smile as she spoke of her husband.

"If he only knew how you spend your leisure time, you would certainly send that old man to his grave." Helga laughed. "But he is correct. The world is changing and this will not be a safe place for very much longer. You should go as soon as you can."

"I will be leaving in a few days," Glenna responded, seeing the worry in her friend's eyes. "I will miss you."

"And I shall miss you as well," Helga said with sincerity. "You are the only client I've brought to my home and the only one that has ever seen Dodi. You are curious about her?"

"Yes," Glenna answered honestly. "But I respect your privacy."

Helga looked at Glenna sadly. "She is my sister," she explained proudly.

"I thought I saw a resemblance," Glenna added. "At first I thought she might be your child."

"I am far to young to have a child her age," Helga scoffed indignantly. "She is twenty-seven."

"I had figured that much out," Glenna reassured her. "What happened to your parents?" She inquired carefully.

"You've heard about what is happening in Germany?" Helga began slowly.

"I've heard rumors," Glenna shuddered as she thought of the unbelievable stories she had heard.

"They are true," Helga said in a heavy tone. "Our parents died helping us flee our home. I brought Dodi here thinking that we would be safe, but I was mistaken."

"Then perhaps the two of you could accompany me back to my home?" Glenna suggested earnestly, not fully understanding just why these two young women would be in danger.

"You mean that?" Helga asked cautiously.

"Yes," Glenna said firmly as she reached over and squeezed Helga's trembling hand.

"Thank you," Helga responded as she squeezed Glenna's hand in return. "Dodi has finished the university. I've set up money for her in New York. I am planning on following her as soon as I can, but I need to get her there first."

"Why is that a problem?" Glenna asked, clearly confused as to why the two women couldn't just leave Amsterdam.

"We are Jewish," Helga explained flatly. Glenna stared at her blankly, still not understanding why that would be a problem. "This makes us targets. Not so long ago we could have simply moved on. Now, because we are Jewish, we are no longer free to leave. I need to ask you a favor, my friend."

"Anything," Glenna asserted earnestly.

"It could be dangerous," Helga warned her.

"Anything," Glenna repeated more firmly.

"Take my sister with you," Helga said in a pleading tone.

"You should come with us," Glenna insisted urgently.

"I can't," Helga responded heavily. "I wish I could. I will get there as soon as I can," she added with a promise. "You will

273

take her there?"

"Yes," Glenna agreed, regretting that Helga was going to remain behind.

"I am trusting you with the dearest person in the world," Helga cautioned her. "Promise me that you will get my little sister to safety."

"I promise," Glenna vowed.

PART FOUR

A few days later Glenna checked out of her hotel. She had both her bags and Dodi's, which Helga had delivered, sent to the train station. Nervously she sat at the café awaiting Helga and Dodi's arrival. Helga's long black car pulled up in front and Glenna quickly dashed outside the moment the driver opened the door.

Inside the car, she found a nervous Helga and a very agitated Dodi. "I was beginning to worry," Glenna said, hoping to ease the tension in the car.

"Someone was being difficult," Helga explained as she glared at her younger sibling.

"I'm not a child," Dodi responded firmly as she rolled her eyes in exasperation.

"Here are her papers. " Helga handed a large bundle to Glenna.

"An American passport," Glenna said thoughtfully. "I'm impressed." Helga simply shrugged. "Dorothy Grayson," Glenna read aloud.

"Grayson?" Dodi said in confusion.

"Would you prefer Frankel and get arrested at the train depot?" Helga fumed.

"It's my last name," Glenna quickly explained. "According to this you are my niece."

"Yes, and you behave for your Auntie Glenna," Helga ordered her younger sibling. "And try not to speak, but when you do remember . . ."

"Sound like an American," Dodi finished for her. Glenna smiled at the bland tone that rolled off the blonde's lips. Helga looked at Glenna in question.

"That was very good," Glenna reassured her. "No one will question her. Besides I'll be the typical obnoxious rich American and no one will even notice her."

"I wish the two of you would stop pretending that I am not here," Dodi groused while still maintaining her Yankee accent.

"I'm sorry, Dorothy," Glenna apologized, recalling what it was like to be left out of conversations whenever her parents bothered to be around.

"Thank you," Dorothy accepted. "It's nice to know that someone realizes that I have an adult name."

"Dodi," Helga teased her.

"No," the blonde protested as the car came to a stop. "Dodi is a name for a little Jewish girl. It's not safe," she explained as tears welled up in her emerald eyes. "Why can't you come now? Or I could wait until we can travel together."

"I am sorry. It is safer for you to go now," Helga choked out as she hugged her sister tightly. "I will be joining you in America before you know it," she promised. Glenna's heart sank, as both she and Dorothy feared that Helga might not be able to keep her promise. "Glenna will take care of you," Helga said as Glenna stepped from the automobile. Dorothy joined her as Helga wiped the tears from her eyes. "I promise," Glenna reassured her friend. "She will be eating hot dogs and watching baseball when you arrive."

Helga pulled her into a tight hug. "Thank you," the redhead whispered into Glenna's ear. "Just one more thing," Helga began firmly as she released her hold on Glenna. "Just remember that she is my baby sister. Auntie Glenna, do not do anything that I would be forced to hunt you down and torture you for." Glenna swallowed hard as her friend captured her in a murderous gaze. "Do you understand?" Helga said slowly. "Do not touch her."

"Helga!" Dorothy shouted out in embarrassment.

"Ssh," Helga hushed her sister. "Glenna, do you understand?" she repeated venomously.

"Yes," the tall brunette squeaked out.

Later, Glenna sat nervously on the sofa in the sleeper car that she and Dorothy would be sharing for the next three days. She was surprised by the way their papers were checked over and over again. That was until Glenna started acting like the grand dame. She played the spoiled rich American heiress to the hilt, shouting at everyone and throwing her weight around. The guards simply shoved their passports at them and allowed them to board the train.

"Your act was very convincing," Dorothy said as the train left the station.

"I've had a lot of practice," Glenna explained. "I was born a spoiled brat and have managed to remain so well into my adulthood."

The attractive blonde sat down next to Glenna. The brunette pulled away slightly and Dorothy laughed lightly. "I cannot believe that she threatened you like that."

"Oh well, you know she is just worried about your welfare," Glenna explained. She had no intention of revealing to this sweet girl that her older sister used to hire female companions to sleep with Glenna.

"She trusts you with my life but not my virtue," Dorothy said in an amused tone. "Now why is that?" Glenna's mouth went dry as she tried to think of some reasonable explanation. She was at a complete loss. "Should I inquire as to how well you are acquainted with my sister?" Dorothy said as her accent slipped slightly.

"I Uhm . . . we . . . err," Glenna stammered like an idiot.

"I see," Dorothy said in a knowing tone as the smile slipped from her cherubic features. "Chez Elle." Glenna looked with a stunned expression at the naïve-looking girl. Dorothy held up her hands, stopping Glenna from responding. "I know. Helga doesn't think I know but I know all about the club and what happens there. My sister thinks that I am a little girl who would never question how we arrived in Amsterdam with nothing but the clothes on our backs and ended up living in a luxurious apartment with more money than our parents made in a lifetime, all with in a very short period of time."

"I see," Glenna said as she released a sigh of relief. "Does it bother you?"

"Yes," Dorothy answered honestly. "But I understand that she did what she had to do to keep us both alive. What I don't understand is why you would go to a place like that."

"It served a purpose," Glenna answered with a shrug.

"You paid my sister for sex?" Dorothy asked in confusion.

"I never paid your sister to sleep with her," Glenna explained quickly. It was the truth since Helga never charged her for the first night at the club.

"But you did pay her to arrange for others to sleep with you?" Dorothy asked in bewilderment.

"Yes," Glenna confessed, suddenly feeling very dirty.

"I do not understand," Dorothy continued.

"I really don't wish to discuss this any further," Glenna snapped as shame washed over her.

"I am sorry," Dorothy apologized. "I never understood why someone would need to pay for intimacy. Certainly not someone as attractive as yourself."

"Can we please change the subject?" Glenna begged.

"I am sorry," Dorothy repeated. "You are risking your life for me all because of your friendship with my sister, and I repay you by trying to pry into the details of your sex life. Forgive me."

Glenna nodded her head in agreement. She was thankful that the questions had ended but suspected that Dorothy had a very inquisitive mind; the subject would come up again. She studied the young woman carefully. Her soft features and firm body were certainly appealing to Glenna's baser instincts. "Yes?" Dorothy challenged her in a sultry tone.

"Why do I think that you are not as innocent as Helga thinks you are?" Glenna said with suspicion.

"Helga thinks I am a virgin." Dorothy chuckled. "I have tried to tell her the truth but for someone as, shall we say, worldly as my sister, she can be amazingly naïve when it comes to me. Before you ask, the answer is no. My tastes are not as varied as my sister's."

"Meaning?" Glenna pried before she could stop herself.

"Helga loves freely," Dorothy responded honestly. "She finds beauty in the person. Although I do appreciate beauty, my vision is limited to only one gender and I am far more selective in my choices. I also need more than a pretty face to win my favors."

Glenna contemplated what her traveling companion had just told her. Dorothy was by no means a loose woman but she was human. The only question left in Glenna's overwrought mind was which gender the young blonde favored. Glenna shook her head clear of any further exploration as she recalled the murderous gaze Helga had cast upon her.

"Here are your papers," Glenna said as she handed the packet over to Dorothy. "Your bank account in New York is all set up. You should be able to settle anywhere." She watched as Dorothy's eyes widened at seeing the figures. The large amount had surprised Glenna as well before she realized that it was everything the two women had.

"Chez Elle is not a seedy brothel," Glenna explained. "Helga ensured that everything was very high class. You not only had to have the right amount of money to enter but the manners as well. And so you know your sister never sold herself. She only sought enjoyment with people who interested her."

"You make it all sound almost respectable," Dorothy said grimly.

"In some ways it was," Glenna continued. "Helga provided a safe environment for consenting adults whose passions are illegal. Yes, she arranged for people to meet but sex was never a guaranteed part of the arrangement. Sometimes it was simply a date. A nice dinner with someone who shared similar interests."

"On your dates, did any of them end with a simple handshake?" Dorothy pried suspiciously.

"Yes," Glenna answered honestly.

"But most of them ended in the bedroom, didn't they?" Dorothy pushed.

"Yes," Glenna once again answered honestly.

"I am not judging you, but it is a brothel," Dorothy asserted. "A very expensive one from what I can see," she emphasized as she held up the papers from the bank.

"And where am I to go to find companionship?" Glenna argued. "I am a homosexual. Nowhere on this planet is that legal. I could be jailed or worse for simply loving a woman."

"Trust me; I do understand," Dorothy said softly. "Or did you not understand our earlier conversation? What is it that *we* are called in your country? Queer?"

Glenna cringed at the term. "There are some words in English that you do not need to learn," Glenna chastised her. "Lesbian," she corrected her.

"Of course. Sappho and her island," Dorothy concurred.

"Yes, but I wouldn't say it very loudly," Glenna cautioned her. "At least you don't have to lie about being Jewish after you get settled in New York."

"Really?" Dorothy choked out as her eyes filled with tears. "I barely remember what that is like."

"I have friends back home who are Jewish. They can show you around and take you to temple," Glenna offered.

"You make it sound so simple," Dorothy said in wonderment.

"It is that simple," Glenna reassured her. "Trust me. There are still some blockheads there but since you have more than enough money," Glenna emphasized her point by tapping the bank statement," no one is going to give a hoot. That is the American way. Well, that and always remember to root for the home team."

"Yes, baseball!" Dorothy shouted excitedly. "You must teach me about baseball." Dorothy tugged on Glenna's arm eagerly. "I want to be a real American by the time Helga arrives."

"All right," Glenna laughed at the younger woman's excitement. "We have three days on the train and then an ocean voyage ahead of us. I think I can fill you in on all the basics of the game by the time we dock."

"We are not flying?" Dorothy asked curiously, her accent

growing thicker with each passing moment.

"No. With everything going on, my husband said that he felt better if I sailed home," Glenna explained.

"You are married?" Dorothy said in confusion. "I think that I am going to understand baseball more quickly than I will understand what goes on in there," she said as she poked her finger against Glenna's forehead.

"Oh, you don't want to go there," Glenna laughed as she captured Dorothy's finger. "Okay, let's start. There are nine men on the field at one time . . ."

"No women?" Dorothy challenged her.

"No," Glenna answered.

"Why?" Dorothy pressed.

"Why what?" Glenna asked in bewilderment.

"Why are there no women?" Dorothy asked in dismay.

"Because there aren't," Glenna said.

"Why?" Dorothy pushed.

"I don't know," Glenna conceded in frustration. "Now where was I? Right. Nine *men* are on the diamond at the same time . . . "

"They play on a diamond?" Dorothy asked seeming to enjoy the frustration she was causing Glenna. "I like diamonds."

"Well, that's one thing you and Helga have in common," Glenna teased.

After an exhausting attempt to explain the rules of baseball to her energetic companion, Glenna finally decided to give up for the night. "Dinner," she groaned in exhaustion as she rang for the porter who arrived quickly. Glenna smiled, knowing that her wealth did provide privilege no matter where she traveled. "Could you set up the beds while my *niece* and I are in the dining car?" Glenna instructed the older man.

"Yes, Madame," he responded in broken English.

"Come along, Dorothy," she beckoned her companion as if she was a small child. She was amused by the harsh glare she received from the younger woman.

"Yes, of course, Auntie Glenna," Dorothy chimed in

response, sounding like a teenaged American girl as she skipped out of the car. Glenna bit back her laughter as she watched the girl walk down the aisle of the crowded train.   Her smile vanished as she found herself captivated by the gentle sway of the young woman's hips. "Why do you have to be so beautiful?" She muttered as she followed her companion.

Over dinner they fell into easy banter despite the fact that Dorothy was careful not to speak very often, fearful that her accent would slip. Dorothy reached for Glenna's wine glass and took a sip.   Glenna had teased the younger woman by not allowing her to order any wine with dinner. "Naughty girl," she taunted the blonde as she retrieved the wine glass from her grasp.

Dorothy was glaring at her once again when Glenna noticed a young man smiling suggestively at Dorothy. The brunette cast an icy blue stare at the man as her jaw clenched. "Jealous?" Dorothy questioned her in an annoying tone.

"Whatever do you mean?" Glenna scoffed in return. "After all, you are my niece and I value my life," she added the last part of her statement softly so only Dorothy could hear her.

"Then why were you staring at my ass earlier?" Dorothy whispered hotly in her ear as Glenna choked.

"My, you have learned some very interesting vocabulary," Glenna managed to choke out as she felt the blush creeping up to the tips of her ears.

Dorothy released a throaty laugh as her head fell back, causing her long strawberry blonde hair to cascade down across her face. The younger woman quickly snatched away the wine glass. "Never play with fire, young lady," Glenna warned her as the blonde sipped her wine.

"Why? Are you going to spank me?" Dorothy said in husky tone.

"Have you no shame?"   Glenna laughed lightly, knowing that she was being played. "Or do you hold my well-being with such little regard? Helga will hunt me down and rip my heart out of my chest if she even knew we talked in such a manner."

"She will make it out, won't she?" Dorothy asked fearfully as she leaned back in the booth, brushing her hair out of her face.

"Yes," Glenna reassured her as she leaned over to brush the

few remaining strands of hair off Dorothy's brow. Glenna's fingertips traced the soft outline of the blonde's face before coming to rest under her chin. She tilted Dorothy's face up gently and found herself lost in her emerald eyes. "She will be joining us before you know it. And who knows? Maybe the Germans will stay out of Amsterdam. Now finish your wine; it's late," she added as she reluctantly released Dorothy's face.

Glenna noticed how the tips of her fingers were tingling from the brief contact. Sitting back in confusion, she watched the blonde slowly sipping her wine until her eyes caught the same young man still ogling Dorothy. This time a fierce growl accompanied her icy stare. "Come along, *Auntie*. It is past your bedtime," Dorothy mocked her as she rose from her seat and offered her hand to the tall brunette.

Glenna shot the young man one last glare before taking Dorothy's hand and walking back to their car. As they entered, Glenna noticed that both sleeping berths had been opened and turned down. She grimaced as she looked at her companion and realized the drastic differences in their height. Normally she took the lower berth since she almost always traveled alone.

"I could give you a boost," she suggested to her companion who was busy gathering up her sleeping attire.

"I am not climbing up there. I will never be able to get back down," Dorothy laughed as she padded off towards the bathroom.

Later that evening Glenna was sound asleep in the upper berth while Dorothy slept in the lower. The sound of whimpering woke the brunette. Confused by the darkness and the movement of the train, she rubbed her head searching for some answers. Then she heard a stifled sob coming from below her. She stumbled out of the bed, crashing to floor. "Damn it to Hell!" Glenna cried out as she rubbed her injured backside. She saw the startled blonde head shoot up, tears streaming down her cheeks. "I'm sorry. You were crying and I misjudged the distance."

"Bad dream," Dorothy sniffed. "I didn't know . . . sorry I woke you."

"Ssh," Glenna hushed her as she crawled over to the blonde's bed. "Do you want to talk about it?" she offered tenderly as she brushed away the tears with her thumb.

"Sometimes I dream about my parents," Dorothy explained. "We were there when they were . . ."

"It's all right," Glenna reassured her as she gathered the smaller woman in her arms. She rubbed Dorothy's back as the blonde clung to her.

"Hold me," Dorothy pleaded.

Against her better judgment, Glenna crawled into the tiny bed and wrapped the smaller woman up in a warm embrace. Dorothy snuggled against Glenna's chest and clung to her tightly. Something about holding this woman in her arms felt right. The scent of Dorothy's shampoo invaded her senses as she felt the blonde's heart beat against her chest. The strange sense of comfort she had felt quickly vanished as Glenna felt herself becoming aroused.

Sleep eluded Glenna that evening as she enjoyed the feel of her companion's body pressed against her. She was only aware of the passing of time when the sunlight peeked through the tiny windows of their room. She felt Dorothy running her fingers across the lace along the collar of her nightgown. "Thank you," Dorothy whispered. Glenna kissed the top of her head in response.

Dorothy shifted and lifted her head slightly. Once again Glenna found that she lost in a sea of green. The look in Dorothy's eyes mirrored her own desires. Both women turned away quickly, breaking the spell that seemed to be binding them. Dorothy climbed off Glenna body and made her way into the bathroom.

They spent the rest of the day in their car, talking about baseball and America. They ignored the events of the previous evening and the early morning. They left their quarters only for meals. All too soon it was once again time for bed. Glenna was nervous about how Dorothy would sleep. "Will you be all right?" She inquired carefully. Dorothy simply nodded in response as she climbed into the lower bunk.

"You don't seem very sure," Glenna pushed despite her need to distance herself from the intoxicating blonde. Dorothy opened her mouth to speak and then just as quickly snapped it shut.

Glenna rolled her brilliant blue eyes as she knelt down beside the lower bunk. "Move over," Glenna said in a calm voice. Dorothy quickly moved to the back of the bunk as she held the blankets up for Glenna to crawl under. Glenna snuggled under the blankets as Dorothy wrapped her arms around her. "I'll just hold you until you fall asleep," she whispered in the darkness as her body once again responded to the small blonde's closeness.

As she tightened her hold on Dorothy, Glenna knew that she had been fooling herself. She hadn't climbed into the tiny bunk solely to comfort her companion; something deep inside of her needed to hold this woman. She stopped fighting with herself and allowed herself to simply enjoy the feel of Dorothy wrapped up in her arms. She sighed contently as Dorothy nuzzled closer.

She was beginning to drift off to sleep when she felt soft lips run along her neck. Her eyes flew open as her heart began to race. "We can't," Glenna moaned as Dorothy's tongue traced her chiseled jaw line. Despite her words, her hands slid slowly down Dorothy's back. "We shouldn't," she protested weakly as Dorothy's kisses grew more insistent.

She could see Dorothy's eyes twinkling at her in the darkness as her breath caressed Glenna's face. The brunette parted her lips in an effort to offer one last protest when Dorothy's soft lips brushed against her own. The warmth spread throughout her entire being as she deepened the kiss. As Dorothy parted her lips with her tongue, Glenna was helpless to stop her.

She wrapped her fingers in Dorothy's long silken locks and pulled her closer as their tongues teased one another. She felt a small hand cup her breast as she explored the warmth of Dorothy's mouth. Glenna moaned, trying to convince herself that kissing this woman would be enough for her. Glenna's body arched as Dorothy massaged her breast in a slow torturous motion.

Glenna was gasping for air as the kiss ended. Her mind spun as Dorothy suckled her neck. She tried to tell the blonde to stop but she couldn't bring herself to say the words. Instead she found herself lifting Dorothy's nightgown up her body. The blonde raised her body and she removed her nightgown and underwear. She tossed the garments across the room as her eyes looked down upon Glenna's quivering form.

Glenna was so lost in the vision of beauty lying on top of her that she was barely aware that Dorothy was now undressing her. Somehow in her lustful fog, she managed to assist in the removal of her clothing. Dorothy pulled the blankets down and snuggled down beside Glenna. The blonde cupped Glenna's face in her hands and reclaimed her lips.

The slow sensual kiss ignited an unfamiliar fire deep inside Glenna as she slowly ran the tips of her fingers along Dorothy's milky white shoulders. As Dorothy continued to kiss her slowly, almost worshiping her mouth with her tongue, Glenna's fingers gently explored the younger woman's skin. Her fingertips tingled as she felt her lover's skin respond to her touch.

Glenna had never before made love so slowly. In some strange fashion she seemed to have a burning need to make each touch last for an eternity. Perhaps the truth was simply that Glenna had never made love before. She didn't allow her mind to contemplate this new discovery; she simply allowed herself to get lost in touching the beautiful woman beside her. She moaned as Dorothy's lips left her own. She shivered as Dorothy began to slowly trace every inch of her body as well.

Neither woman spoke as they continued to trace the outline of the other's body. Glenna's heart pounded in her chest as her arousal grew with each passing moment. Her breathing became ragged as Dorothy cupped her firm full breasts. Emerald orbs held her in a steady gaze as Dorothy brushed her nipples with her thumbs.

Glenna felt almost virginal as her fingertips moved over the curve of Dorothy's hips. There was a strange shyness that accompanied her movements as her fingers glided along her young lover's body. Her wetness caressed her thighs and still she had no desire to rush the moment. She felt the heat radiating from Dorothy's body as she moved closer to her.

Dorothy slowly traced the swell of her breast with her tongue. Glenna gasped loudly as her body trembled. She didn't rush her lover as she circled her nipple with an agonizing slowness. Instead Glenna slid her hands along the soft silky skin of the blonde's body. She bit down on her bottom lip as Dorothy captured her nipple in the warmth of her mouth.

Glenna pulled her lover closer as her body arched with a burning desire. "Dorothy," she whimpered softly as the blonde suckled her breast eagerly. Glenna felt her lover's desire caressing her skin as their bodies melted together. She clung to her lover tightly as Dorothy teased her nipple with her teeth and her tongue. "Dorothy," she moaned once again as she pressed her thigh into the blonde's wetness.

Dorothy's head fell back as she captured Glenna's thigh between her quivering legs. Glenna felt her lover's thigh slip between her own trembling legs. They stared deeply into one another's eyes as they began to sway their hips in a sensual rhythm. Glenna clasped Dorothy's hips as the blonde wrapped arms tightly around the brunette's body.

They ground slowly against each other as their eyes remained locked in an intense gaze. Their nipples pressed together and they began to thrust harder. They rocked wildly as they clung to each other. "Perfect," Glenna said with a soft sincerity as she felt the climax building inside of her. All she was aware of was the feel of her lover's body meeting her own as they swayed in unison. The moment was truly perfect as they screamed out in unison, the waves of passion crashing down upon their exhausted bodies.

They were covered in a sheen of sweat as they held one another tightly. Glenna reached down and pulled the blanket up over their sated bodies. They snuggled closer, each lost in the simple pleasure of holding the other woman. Glenna could feel sleep creeping up on her. She fought off her weariness as best she could. She never wanted the moment to end. The brunette felt as if her heart had burst open as she lost herself in the pleasure of Dorothy's body.

Finally the need for rest overwhelmed her and she held onto Dorothy even tighter, knowing that she might never be able feel this moment of bliss again. She had broken her promise and was unable to regret the transgression. She prayed that Helga would forgive her, knowing that there was a far more important promise that she would give her life to keep. She vowed silently to keep Dorothy safe.

THE END

WHAT EVER HAPPENED TO?

PART ONE

"What ever happened to what's-her-name?" Holly inquired, trying to sound casual.

"I don't know. What's her name?" Selma asked as she sipped her soda.

"You know, that really tall girl who use to sit behind you in chemistry," Holly continued as she tried to look as if the girl's name had escaped her.

"Oh, you mean Whitney," the darker woman smiled devilishly. "I wouldn't think that you'd have forgotten her name."

"What are you implying?" The blonde scoffed in response.

"Please! You would practically drool every time you saw her," Selma teased. "You and every guy in school."

"I did not," Holly protested as she tossed a rolled up napkin at her old friend.

"You did," Selma laughed. "It was embarrassing. I swear I

don't know why it took you so long to figure out that you were gay." Selma smirked.

Holly snorted indignantly at her old friend. "I forgot what a pain in the ass you are." She wagged her finger as she glared at the other woman.

"Play nice or I won't tell you about Whitney," Selma said dryly as she wiggled her eyebrows.

"So you know then," Holly pried. "Is she coming to the reunion? Not that I care."

"Uh huh," Selma sighed as she stuck her tongue in her cheek. "Then why did you ask?"

"Just trying to catch up on what's happened with everyone," Holly lied.

"She didn't hang around with us," Selma pointed out. "What makes you think that I'd know anything?"

"Because you know everything about everybody," Holly smirked. "You always did. What was it Joan use to call you?" She thought for a moment. "Five-O." She laughed at the memory.

"Yeah well, that was fifteen years ago," Selma winced slightly. "My God, fifteen years. I can't believe it."

"I know," Holly agreed. "I'm glad I came back for this one. I still can't believe they're tearing down the old high school."

"Well at least it got everyone to come back," Selma stated happily. "The school is really run down. The heating is shot and the foundation is shaky. I tell you, every time I'd have to teach a class in there I was afraid the building was going to collapse."

"I still can't believe you're a teacher," Holly laughed as she ran her fingers through her short blonde hair.

"Why not?" Selma protested.

"I don't know. Maybe because I was the one who held your hair back the first time you got sick from drinking," Holly explained. "Or that we got busted for smoking in the girls' bathroom. Or the time you broke into the guys' locker room."

"Stop," Selma squealed. "Hey, I have a reputation to maintain here. I wouldn't want my deep dark secrets getting out. I'm a respected member of the community now, complete with a husband and kids."

"A real pillar of the community," Holly laughed in amazement. "Let's see how much can I tarnish your reputation once I get you start on a few kamikazes."

"Ah, none for me," Selma mumbled as she shifted uncomfortably.

"Uh huh," Holly said carefully as she wondered if her suspicions were correct. "Quit drinking?"

"Well . . . yeah . . . kind of," Selma confessed shyly.

Holly smiled. She knew her friend didn't have a substance abuse problem. And while she respected a person's choice not to drink, she suspected that there was another reason. "So for how long?" Holly prodded. "Nine months?" she added with a twinkle in her green eyes.

"How did you know?" Selma beamed.

"Lucky guess," Holly explained. "You just look . . . oh I don't know. Another baby." She sighed happily as she clutched her chest.

"We are thrilled," Selma confessed. "But you can't tell anyone."

"Rats," Holly pouted.

"It's too soon," Selma explained seriously. "You never know."

"I understand," Holly said softly as she clutched her old friend's hand. "It's going to be hard, knowing this and not being able to tell anyone. I live to gossip."

"Some things never change," Selma concurred.

"So how's life in the big city?" Selma inquired. "You seemed to take the break up with Sherri pretty hard."

"It was a mess," Holly sighed disgustedly. "Deep down I think I knew she was running around. Of course, I never suspected it was with a guy. I felt as if my whole world had collapsed around me. I'm better now. I've even started dating again."

"I was really worried about you," Selma stated sincerely.

"It still hurts," Holly admitted. "But I'm better off without her. I can see that now. Of course those first few months, I was a mess. I just threw myself into my work. The up side is that I got a promotion."

"Alright," Selma said with a smile.

"I'm the head of my department now," Holly smirked, knowing it had really frosted Sherri's cookies when she heard.

"I can't believe the little blonde who sat next to me in kindergarten and ate paste is a big corporate executive," Selma taunted her. Holly buried her face in her hands and moaned. "Don't worry, sweetie. You keep my secret and I won't tell a soul about your dietary peculiarities. But if anyone pats my stomach at the reunion . . ."

"I promise. Not a word," Holly blurted out as she jerked up her head. "So who's going to be there tomorrow?"

"Well, since I'm on the committee I can tell you that everyone from our old gang will be there," Selma answered proudly.

"Everyone?" Holly grimaced.

"What?" Selma asked in confusion.

"Selma, not everyone is as understanding as you are," Holly explained. "A lot of people I thought were my friends haven't spoken to me since I came out. Bobby even sent me hate mail for awhile."

"He's a dufus," Selma snarled. "The guy thought you were going to get married when you were fourteen." Holly started to frown. "Hey, don't worry about it. If anyone has a problem with you, they can just kiss my Mexican ass. I'm serious. I know what's it like. I was the only kid whose parents spoke Spanish. You were the first one to be my friend and not care. So if they don't like it, they can just . . ."

"Eat paste?" Holly suggested playfully.

"Damn right," Selma confirmed. "Speaking of close-minded knot heads, are you going to see your parents while you're in town?"

"No," Holly shivered at the thought. "I still remember my mother wailing that 'if only I hadn't gone away to college' or that they shouldn't have allowed me to play sports."

"I still think you were adopted," Selma moaned. "There's no way that those are your real parents."

"New subject please," Holly said as her body tensed. "I will not have them spoil my vacation."

"Alright, so do you want to know who else is coming to the reunion?" Selma taunted her. Holly's brow crinkled slightly as she wondered just where this conversation was heading. "Whitney," Selma drew out the name as she smiled wickedly.

"Really?" Holly smiled. "Oh my. I had such a crush on her," Holly finally admitted.

"I know," Selma responded in a cocky tone. "I knew then. I was just waiting for you to buy a clue."

"I don't like that look in your eyes," Holly cautioned her. "It was fifteen years ago and she never knew I existed. Plus, she's probably straighter than you are."

"Well, I'll tell you what I know if you buy me dessert," Selma tormented her.

"Waitress," Holly called out.

Holly impatiently tapped her fingers on the table as her old friend read the dessert menu twice before selecting a slice of double chocolate layer cake with a scoop of ice cream. Holly ordered another coffee. "Spill it," Holly demanded after the waitress departed.

"Okay. Don't get your jammies in a bunch," Selma groaned as she rolled her eyes. "She's a lawyer."

The waitress chose that moment to return with their orders. "Oh, this looks so good," Selma cooed as she began to dig in. Holly looked on in horror. "What?" Selma asked between mouthfuls. "I'm eating for two." Holly just looked at her in disbelief. "Cravings?" Selma added hopefully.

"Do you know how many hours I would have to spend at the gym after eating something like that?" Holly said as she shook her head in disbelief.

"You have my sympathy," Selma smirked.

"Okay, now that your sweet tooth is being satisfied . . . ," Holly urged her on, ". . . tell me about the tall, dark, blue-eyed wonder I used to fantasize about as a teenager."

"She's a lawyer," Selma repeated.

"You said that," Holly fumed.

"She works for the public defender's office in Boston," Selma expanded. "So you two live in the same city," Selma noted.

"Really?" Holly responded brightly. Her smile quickly vanished. "That still doesn't mean anything."

"She does volunteer work for LAMBDA," Selma smirked confidently.

"Okay, a legal non-profit group that works to fight hate crimes," Holly noted. "But you do work for them as well," Holly pointed out.

"She also volunteers for BAGLY," Selma added confidently.

"The Boston Alliance for Gay and Lesbian Youth," Holly smiled brightly. "Wow, that's incredible. I feel like a slug."

"Well, don't put yourself down," Selma interjected. "We do what we can. Now the important thing to remember is that . . . Whitney is a big lesbian. Try to focus here."

"Okay. . . okay," Holly laughed. "Still, she's probably in a relationship."

"You are such a kill joy," Selma groaned. "She's attending the reunion alone."

"Really?" Holly perked up. "Interesting."

"She's also staying in the same hotel that you are," Selma added in a singsong voice.

"Well, that's not surprising," Holly argued. "That's where the reunion's being held."

"So when you see her, are you going to worship her from a far?" Selma inquired. "Or take a chance and jump her bones?" She added eagerly.

"There's something wrong with you," Holly narrowed her eyes. "Selma, why are you so excited about this? The woman didn't know my name fifteen years ago. What makes you think she'd be interested in me now?"

"I'm just a hopeless romantic," Selma offered. Holly had the nagging feeling that there was something Selma wasn't telling her.

The two continued to chat until it was time for Selma to leave. Holly decided to take a walk around her hometown. The cool crisp autumn air surrounded her as she walked. Not much had changed over the years. Not really surprising. It was a small town that had always resisted change. That was one of the reasons that Holly needed to leave. She found herself standing on the corner of her old street, debating if she should at least try to talk to her parents.

She shivered at the thought of having yet another fight with them. Tomorrow was going to be hard enough with people treating her differently. She pulled her coat tightly around her body before taking one last look down the familiar street. She turned away and began the walk back to her hotel.

PART TWO

The tall brunette stumbled into the lobby of the hotel. It was quaint to say the least and the perfect addition to downtown Hawthorne, the small New England town where she had grown up. As she drove around, she realized that not much had changed during her absence. There were still no convenience stores or a McDonalds within a twenty-mile radius. People didn't work there unless they owned the local diner or hardware store. They commuted by car or train into the next city. It was a good place to settle down if you lacked a pulse.

So why did she bother coming back? A part of her still missed the quiet little community where you knew your neighbors. She missed her parents and regretted that she didn't visit more often. But then again, her mother and stepfather were always traveling. She was happy that they actually were enjoying their retirement.

Now the town was tearing down the old high school and, as a fundraiser, throwing a reunion for all of the alumni. The money would be used for programs and equipment at the new high school. There were even a few surviving members from the class of 1917 that would be in attendance. Whitney sighed, thinking that she would probably be hanging out with her parents during most of the festivities.

She had been a shy awkward teenager and never made any

really close friends except for Kenny. And he had been gone for almost ten years now. She made a note that she should visit his parents. He wasn't the first friend she lost to AIDS, but he had been the closest to her heart. She smiled at the memory of him. Two gay kids locked in a small town. Everyone thought they were a couple. They did look great together at the prom.

"Reservation for Ward, " she offered to the desk clerk who punched her name into the computer.

"Yes, we have you in Room 103, " the young man confirmed as he smiled brightly at her. "Queen size bed, non-smoking. I just need a credit card. "

She slid over her Visa and waited for everything to be processed. "The bellhop will take your luggage and show you up to your room. Enjoy your reunion, " the young man continued brightly as she placed her credit card back into her wallet. "And if you need anything . . . , " he added.

"I'll let you know, " she responded dryly, not missing his lame attempt at flirting with her.

Once she was in her room, she called her parents. After agreeing to meet them for dinner, Whitney checked her watch, noting that she had just enough time to catch a nap. Then she could take a nice relaxing shower and go see her folks. What could be better than a nice visit and a home-cooked meal?

Whitney smiled as she stretched out on the bed. "Not a very exciting evening," she smiled brighter. To the tired lawyer, the thought of a couple of days with nothing to do but relax and enjoy some time with her family sounded like heaven. Of course, she could always look up that little blonde from chemistry class.

Whitney's blue eyes fluttered shut. She couldn't believe that she had asked Selma about her. She tried to seem casual about her inquiry, but it must have been obvious. She and Holly hadn't hung around together. A crowd of people had forever surrounded the energetic little blonde. If Selma suspected Whitney's true motives, she didn't let on.

Selma was good that way. Whitney was surprised that the outgoing Hispanic girl was still living in Hawthorne and teaching at the local high school. "She must be great at keeping those kids in line," Whitney chuckled. Selma was thrilled when Whitney told her who she was. *'She even remembered me. I didn't think anyone would know who I am. '* She'd been more than willing to fill her in on what was happening with Holly.

That had surprised Whitney. Selma was always the one person who had the dirt on everything, yet she wasn't a gossip. Whitney found it strange that she would just blurt out what Holly had been up to. She knew she was probably just imagining things, but she could have sworn that Selma was . . . *'Nah, don't be silly. Holly is probably married with a ton of kids. '*

Well, not married. Selma did mention that. But she didn't say she was gay. Whitney had blushed during the entire conversation with Selma. She didn't know what made her ask about Holly. Being sentimental was one thing, but checking up on the girl you first fantasized about when you touched yourself was just odd.

Though those were some really hot fantasies. Whitney smirked as she drifted off to sleep. After her nap, she finished dressing and blow-drying her hair. As the last of the dampness dissipated from her long raven tresses, she cursed herself for not just cutting it off. "One of these days," she groused.

Whitney double-checked her coat pockets to insure that she had her wallet and card key to her room before shutting the door. Just as she started down the hallway, the elevator opened up. "Perfect," she smiled at her good fortune. Her smile vanished as her mouth hung open. Stepping off the elevator was the most adorable blonde. She quickly snapped her mouth shut and donned a cool expression, hoping to hide her ogling.

She smiled brightly at the smaller woman as she stepped into the elevator. Their bodies brushed slightly as they passed each other. Whitney trembled from the contact. Her blue eyes fluttered shut for an instant as the sweet scent of jasmine and vanilla invaded her senses. She opened her eyes to watch as the blonde's well-defined backside made it's way down the hallway. "Perfect, " she repeated as she watched her carefully.

Whitney's brow suddenly furrowed as she noticed something decidedly familiar to the woman's gait. Her eyes widened as the elevator doors began to close, eclipsing her view. "Holly?" She stammered in surprise. She could see the blonde turning towards the elevator just as the doors closed. Whitney blushed furiously as she realized what had just happened. "Oh great," Whitney slapped her forehead. "I didn't recognize her face, but her ass I know. " Whitney started to bang her head lightly on the wall of the elevator as it made its descent. "Way to go, Whitney," she berated herself.

PART THREE

Holly sat in the bar off the lobby of the hotel, surrounded by her friends laughing and chatting about the old days. Yet her mind wasn't focused on the festivities. It was focused on the tall brunette she'd passed in the hallway earlier that evening. She didn't think it was possible but Whitney had grown even more attractive with the passing years. She'd been sitting alone in her room scanning through the program for tomorrow night's events when Joan called her. On the spur of the moment, Joan had managed to corral as many of the old gang as possible for an impromptu meeting.

Holly was hesitant at first, not wanting to spend time with those individuals who had shut her out years before. Joan rambled off the names of the people who'd be there. None of the people in attendance were among those who had treated her badly. Holly eagerly agreed to join them.

Holly sipped her drink as she continued telling her tale. "So Principal Skinner burst in, catching Joan, Selma, and I standing there in the middle of the boys' locker room. I wanted to die. "

"I wanted to see what Freddy was hiding under his towel," Joan laughed.

"Had I only known," Freddy winked.

"Please! You turned four shades of red when you saw us," Holly interjected. "Where was I? Oh yeah, Joan and I were trying to hide behind what's-his-name, Kenny, the linebacker on the team. But not Selma. "

"Don't rush the story. Get back to Kenny dropping his towel," Joan encouraged as the rest of the group snickered.

"Oh my, even I have to admit that boy was blessed," Holly

fanned herself. "When we tried to hide behind him, his towel dropped. He was so flustered."

"I didn't mind," Joan confessed. "He had the tightest ass I'd ever seen. That's when Selma stepped up."

"She handed him his towel like nothing had happened," Holly explained. "And started rambling off this spiel to Skinner about doing research for the school paper. She was so convincing I almost bought it."

The crowd erupted in laughter. "What happened? Did he believe her?" Julie, Freddie's wife, asked eagerly.

"He might have . . . but he knew that none of us were on the school paper," Holly rolled her emerald eyes in amusement. "We were suspended for three days. My parents were so mortified that they grounded me for an entire month."

"That I remember," Freddie stated grimly. "Good thing they were clueless about half the stunts you and Selma pulled."

"My parents were thrilled," Joan added. "Up until that point, I think they thought I was some kind of shrinking violet."

"Oh yeah, that sounds like you, sweetie," Jake, Joan's husband, chuckled as he winked at her playfully.

"You? A shrinking violet?" Holly snorted. "I had to stop you from grabbing Kenny's ass." This comment brought on another round of laughter as Joan blushed. "Whatever happened to Kenny, the tight-bunned linebacker?"

"I don't know," Joan admitted.

"He Uhm . . . passed away," Freddie informed them sadly.

There was a collective gasp. "How?" someone asked. "When?" someone else inquired.

"A few years back," Freddie blinked shyly as he related the information. "We grew up next door to one another. We weren't close but our folks were. AIDS," he added solemnly.

"AIDS?" Trisha said blankly. "So young. Damn proof that it's not a gay issue."

"He was," Freddie countered simply. "He was gay."

"Come on," Rex, another member of the group, argued. "The guy was going out with Whitney Ward. She was the most beautiful girl in school."

Holly groaned at the statement, partially from the stupidity of it and partially in agreement with Rex's observation of Whitney's attributes. "I thought I was the most beautiful girl in school?" Trisha, Rex's high school sweetheart, teased him.

"Present company excluded of course," Rex blurted out quickly.

"Nice save, buddy," Holly, teased him. The divorced father of two grimaced in embarrassment. "So I shouldn't tell you that I saw her today?" Holly taunted him. She watched in delight as her former male classmates looked at her eagerly. "And let me tell you, she grew up *nice*." She smiled warmly at the memory of Whitney smiling at her. It was almost flirtatious. She'd felt a pleasant jolt run through her body as they accidentally brushed against one another. As she was walking towards her room, she could have sworn she heard Whitney say her name. She shook her head, thinking it was just her overactive imagination.

"She's here?" Rex inquired eagerly, bringing Holly back to the present. "Well, that doesn't do much for you married guys but as for Holly and me . . . " He winked at her playfully. "Who am I kidding?" He sighed. "I was never in her league. Plus she probably has a gigantic husband. Kenny certainly scared us off for all those years."

"I feel so special all of a sudden," Trisha growled.

"I'm just kidding," Rex apologized sincerely. "You were and still are the most beautiful girl in town."

"Aah," the group teased with a collective sigh. Holly looked over at Joan and nodded. They both wondered if the two might get back together now that they were both single.

"Well, now that Rex has graciously bowed out of the running, it's safe to tell you that Whitney's gay," Freddie informed them, adding a knowing smirk towards Holly.

"How do you know?" Joan asked curiously.

"Because Kenny lived on one side of my house and Whitney lived on the other side," Freddie informed them with a shrug.

"Freddie used to peep at her," Rex added smugly.

"You pervert," Holly chastised him. "Tell me everything."

"I never actually saw her," Freddie confessed shyly.

"You little liar," Rex said as he smacked him in the back of the head.

"What was I supposed to say?" Freddie whined.   "Sorry guys, but she caught me trying once and was smart enough to close the blinds after that."

"I'm so glad we have girls," Julie sighed heavily.

"I'm not. I don't trust that little Romeo next door," Freddie gritted his teeth.

"He's five, dear," Julie said as she patted his arm reassuringly.

"Sure, now," Freddie stammered in frustration.

The crew laughed heartily as they teased Freddie. "Hold on, guys. I'm with Freddie on this one," Rex interrupted. "My girls are getting close to their teens. I'm terrified. What if they bring home someone like me?" He squeaked out fearfully. "Wait," he said as he reached inside his jacket pocket and retrieved his wallet.

"Yes!" Holly squealed. "Pictures! Come on the rest of you." She waved her fingers in encouragement. "I just know you can't wait to set off my biological clock."

"Well, if you insist," Joan beamed as she reached into her purse. The others frantically did the same, eager to show off their children.

PART FOUR

Whitney entered the hotel lobby. She enjoyed her time with her parents. During her visit she managed to convince herself that she hadn't made an ass out of herself when she saw Holly earlier.   She looked so different with her shorter hair and confident stride.

Still feeling wide-awake from the pot of coffee she'd consumed at her mother's, she decided to have a nightcap. As she stepped into the bar, she was greeted by the sound of laughter. She quickly found the source. The bar was empty with the exception of a group of people hovering around the far end.

Her mouth went dry as she spotted a very familiar set of emerald eyes staring back at her.   She thought about turning around and heading up to her room. But then Holly flashed her a friendly smile. *'A nightcap,'* she thought to herself. *'And perhaps a bucket of ice,'* she added as her eyes drifted over Holly's well-toned body.

Still feeling slightly shy, Whitney seated herself at the bar away from the crowd. She ordered a glass of white zinfandel and sipped it silently while she stole glances at the group off to her right. She felt alone. She recognized most of their faces. But with the exception of Freddie, she really didn't know any of them. A pang struck her as she suddenly missed Kenny. *'Perhaps coming back wasn't such a good idea.'* She sighed deeply.

She was also feeling like a voyeur, watching Holly's smile out of the corner of her eye. Freddie kept whispering to her. She kept pushing him away and blushing. *'Well, that answers that, doesn't it?'* Whitney kicked herself mentally for even looking at the blonde. *'Still, it doesn't make sense,'* she contemplated. *'Freddie is happily married. In fact, his wife is standing next to him. Julie doesn't seem bothered by his actions. Maybe they're into that kind of thing? Yuck!'* She grimaced at the unpleasant image that popped into her mind. *'Still, my radar went off the scale when I saw her earlier. I wonder?'* Whitney pondered the possibilities, some in very interesting detail.

A tap on her shoulder roused her from her thoughts just as they were getting interesting. She blushed as she turned to find Freddie standing next to her. "Hi, Whitney," the dark-haired mild-mannered man addressed her.

"Hello, Freddie," she responded warmly. "Good to see you again."

"Glad to see you could make it," he continued. "Been to the old neighborhood yet?"

"Oh yeah," she nodded in response. "I've just come from having dinner with my parents."

"How are Mr. And Mrs. Staverson?" Freddie inquired.

"I can't believe that you're a grown man and still call them that," she teased.

"Habit," Freddie smiled. "I just couldn't see myself calling them . . . you know, I don't think I know your parents' first names."

"Mom and Dad," she said flatly. "Sorry, I couldn't resist."
"Why don't you join us?" He suggested.
"I . . . Uhm . . . ," she stammered as her heart raced. "I wouldn't want to intrude," she finally managed to squeak out.
"Nonsense," he encouraged her. "It's a reunion. Come on."
Still feeling apprehensive, she nodded in agreement and followed him over. She managed to exchange hellos with everyone without making a fool of herself. She knew Joan who'd been close to Holly and Selma. She noticed that Selma was missing. She also noticed that Bobby Ransfort, who had been Holly's steady all through high school, was among the missing. There were a few other faces missing as well. Whitney wondered about that. They all had been a pretty tight group back in the old days.
"Where's Selma?" She finally inquired. "I wouldn't think that she'd miss out on this get together."
"She wasn't up for it." Joan pouted. "She seemed kind of tired when I talked to her earlier. I hope she's alright," she added.
"She seemed fine at lunch today," Holly volunteered quickly. "I mean . . . " Whitney noticed the blonde's discomfort. ". . .She's just been real busy with classes and organizing the reunion."
Whitney looked at Holly curiously as she thought, *'You're lucky I don't have you on the witness stand. You're a terrible liar. '* Whitney smiled as the small blonde tucked her hair behind her ear in a nervous manner. "You know guys . . . , " Holly said suddenly in a thoughtful tone, ". . . I can't help but notice a few gaps in our little group."
Whitney noticed as everyone, even the spouses of her old classmates, began to avert their eyes and shift uncomfortably. "I see," Holly said dryly. "Thank you, Joanie. I appreciate this." The blonde's eyes became slightly misty as her voice lowered.
"Ah fuck 'em," Joan announced boldly, startling the bartender in the process. "Those idiots were never any fun."
"That's my shrinking violet," Joan's husband said proudly as

he kissed his wife on the cheek.

"Well, they weren't," Joan reasserted. "We love you, Holly."

The others toasted in agreement. Whitney smiled at the sight, still not fully understanding just what was happening. But if it made Holly smile like that then it was most definitely a good thing. "Thanks guys." Holly blushed as she spoke. "Sorry, Whitney." Holly smiled over at her. "It's just that some of my old friends turned out not to be my friends," she explained with a hint of sadness.

"Well, now that's out in the open," Joan declared, "there is something we all have been waiting years to tell you, Holly."

"Uh huh?" Holly responded tentatively.

"We never liked Bobby," Joan announced boldly.

Whitney watched in amusement as Holly simply blinked in amazement. "Personally, I hated the guy," Freddie said.

"Never understood what you saw in him," Trisha added. "I mean, he was practically stalking you from the time you guys were in diapers."

"Honestly, the guy was a jerk," Rex tossed in.

"Now you tell me," Holly said sarcastically. "Back in high school Selma was the only one to tell me."

"Well, that was Selma," Joan pointed out. "She's the only one who could have gotten away with it. Of course, none of us thought you would last that long with him. Who knew you'd date him for both junior and senior years?"

"I didn't know what I wanted back then," Holly explained. Whitney couldn't help notice that the comment was directed towards her. "So who did he end up marrying?" Holly added.

"Colleen," Joan informed her with a smile.

"I knew it," Holly laughed. "She was always all over him like white on rice. I hope they're very happy together." She chuckled.

Joan shot her a look of disbelief. "It's true," Holly defended herself. "I don't want him. I never really did. And if they're happy, it keeps him away from me. Enough of this," Holly stated firmly. "I really don't want to talk about him. It's bad enough he'll be here tomorrow. The guy is not stable."

Whitney's senses went on full alert upon hearing this statement. "So what's everyone up to these days?" She inquired in order to change the subject. Thankfully the others picked up on her cue. They continued to chat until the bartender announced that it was closing time. Everyone moaned and complained, with the exception of Trisha and Rex who were locked in a deep conversation.

The rest of them shuffled back into the lobby, some leaving the hotel and the others making their way to the elevator. Whitney chose to linger behind so she could walk with Holly. They joined the others in the crowded elevator. Their arms and thighs brushed against one another. Whitney was thankful to discover that they would be the last stop and they would be alone for at least two floors. Well, thankful and silently nervous.

"So if you don't mind me asking . . . ," Whitney began carefully once they were alone. She almost forgot what she was going to say when she looked into Holly's eyes. " . . . what happened with Bobby?" she finally managed to say.

"Well, let's see," Holly stepped slightly closer. Whitney's heart pounded against her chest. "First, I broke up with him right before I left for college. He smashed my car windshield. My mother asked what I did to upset him."

"Excuse me?" Whitney flared.

"I know. I never expected that," Holly responded. "My dad told me I was better off without him. Then Bobby tried to win me back. I refused and went off to college. Bobby kept showing up there. Finally I told him I was gay. He didn't take it very well. He never tried to hurt me but I ended up calling campus security and having him barred from the campus. He told my parents about me."

"Nice guy," Whitney groaned.

"They didn't take it well either," Holly explained. "By the time I graduated, we weren't speaking. Still don't. Of course, for years Bobby sent me nasty letters."

"Charming," Whitney muttered as the elevator doors opened. "I'm sorry about your parents," she offered sincerely as they made their way down the corridor.

"How about your parents?" Holly inquired tentatively.

Whitney smiled at the question. "They weren't surprised in the least. My real dad is gay so it wasn't foreign territory. My coming out really helped Kenny with his parents." Whitney felt another tug on her heartstrings as she stopped in front of her door.

"I heard," Holly whispered softly. "Freddie told us. I'm sorry."

Holly touched her arm gently. Whitney felt the sadness rush out of her as the smaller woman caressed her arm. "Thank you," Whitney whispered in response. They lingered outside her door as Whitney tried to think of something to say. She didn't want to say goodnight to Holly just yet.

"We're neighbors," Holly said lightly, her hand still resting on Whitney's forearm. "I'm in the next room," she explained as she motioned with her head.

"Well then." Whitney licked her lips as she drank in the sight of Holly's exposed neck. "I should walk you home then. It is rather late." Whitney's body practically hummed from their nearness. "Or if you want . . . to come in for a while," Whitney suggested.

"Yes," Holly answered softly.

PART FOUR

Holly smiled as Whitney fumbled to open the door. She'd been attracted to this woman back when she was a girl. The attraction she felt this evening was overwhelming in comparison. They entered the hotel room. After some idle chatter, they found themselves sitting on the bed, having removed their shoes.

Holly was beyond nervous and her palms were beginning to sweat. She tried hard to fight off the feeling of desire. But all she could think about was how much she wanted to kiss this woman. "Whitney?" She began tentatively.

"Hmm?" The brunette responded as she stretched out beside her.

Holly inhaled sharply as she looked down at this beautiful woman clad in a simple pair of blue jeans and a white T-shirt. "I was wondering if there was someone waiting for you back in the city?" She finally gathered up enough courage to ask.

"No," Whitney answered with a knowing smile. "I've been single for a couple of years now. And you?"

"My last relationship ended over seven months ago," Holly offered eagerly. "I have a confession to make," Holly began as she stared at Whitney's full lips. At that moment Whitney's tongue darted out, wetting her lips. "I . . . uhm." She sighed as she slipped down next to Whitney. "I had a huge crush on you in high school."

"Really?" Whitney smiled as her fingers began a tantalizing trail along Holly's arm. "Wow." She laughed.

"What?" Holly encouraged her as she placed her hand on Whitney's hip. Her fingers began stroking the material under her hand.

"It's just that I had a big crush on you as well," Whitney confessed with a blush.

Holly's body heat rose as Whitney leaned closer to her. Holly's body leaned in as well. After all these years, she wouldn't deny this woman. Their faces were a breath apart as their legs wrapped around one another. Holly's nipples hardened as they brushed against Whitney's body. Their lips met shyly.

The shyness quickly vanished as Holly wrapped her fingers in Whitney's long silky hair. Pulling her closer, Holly parted the taller woman's lips with her tongue as her body pressed urgently into Whitney's. She moaned as their tongues danced together. Holly needed to feel more of Whitney's body. She ran her hands down the strong back. She found herself tugging Whitney's shirt out of her jeans.

Surprised by her own boldness, she slipped her hands up under the cotton material. Her fingers felt the warm exposed body. She rolled Whitney onto her back and pressed her thigh into the taller woman's center. Whitney moaned beneath her as she rubbed herself into her body. Holly could feel her wetness growing as she pulled Whitney's shirt up further.

Annoyed that the shirt wouldn't travel any further, she broke the sensual kiss. Staring down at the woman beneath her, she rocked her hips against her as she removed her shirt and then her bra. She gasped at the sight of Whitney's half-naked body. Lowering her head, her tongue began to trace the curve of Whitney's full breast. She continued her exploration as she felt her own top being pulled up. Her hips increased their rhythm as she licked the valley between Whitney's breasts.

She whimpered as Whitney pushed her away slightly. Knowing hands removed her top and bra as Holly pressed herself into Whitney's body. She groaned as Whitney captured her nipples between her fingers and pinched and rolled them. One hand slid down her firm abdomen and unbuttoned her pants. Holly was aflame with desire as she allowed Whitney to pull her pants and underwear down to her thighs.

"God, you are so wet," Whitney moaned from beneath her as Holly pressed her center against her stomach. Holly ground against Whitney's firm body as she once again lowered her mouth to her breast. This time she captured Whitney's erect nipple in her mouth. "I want you," Holly murmured against her skin as she felt Whitney's fingers tease her slick folds.

Whitney's body arched beneath her as Holly suckled her greedily, moving from one breast to the other and then back again. Whitney's thumb began to stroke her throbbing clit, Holly's body arched in response. Her hips thrust as she leaned over her lover. Whitney's face reflected her desire as Holly unzipped her jeans. Whitney continued to tease her swollen nub as Holly lowered her pants and underwear. Holly could smell her desire filling her.

Holly's fingers dipped into Whitney's wetness. Their bodies rocked in unison as Holly ran her fingers along Whitney's swollen lips. "We need to slow down or I'm going to explode right now," she panted. Whitney nodded in agreement as they both took a moment to catch their breath. "I've never been so turned on in my life," Whitney confessed to her with a slight whimper as Holly lowered herself.

Lying side by side, they kissed gently as their hands cupped and teased each other's breasts. Holly raised herself slightly and kissed Whitney's long graceful neck. Her tongue circled her ear. She heard her lover moan as she nibbled on her earlobe. Then she continued to kiss her jaw as her hands moved, caressing her ribs and down to the curve of her hip. Holly whimpered as she felt Whitney's tongue flicker across her nipple, circling it as Holly cupped her backside.

Holly arched as Whitney began to suckle her nipple. Running her fingers back up Whitney's long body, she cupped her breast and began to tease the sweet rose-colored bud with her fingers. She could feel the tender panting against her skin as they continued to tease one another. Holly's body was on fire as they both began to rock against each other.

They broke away slightly. Holly lowered herself once again as their lips met in a searing kiss. Tongues danced as they fought for control, while exploring the warmth of one another's mouth. They were gasping as the kiss ended, staring deeply into each other's eyes. Holly knew what they both wanted, but the need was too great. Quickly they shed the remainder of their clothing.

Their naked bodies quickly reunited. Once again lying side by side, locked in a passionate kiss, they pressed their firm thighs into one another's center. Bodies rocked together as hands explored. The need to breathe overwhelmed them. Holly eagerly opened herself as Whitney's fingers dipped into her wetness. Her own hand was mirroring Whitney's actions. They moaned in unison at the wetness they discovered.

Both women melted together as they entered each other's center. Their thumbs circled clits as their fingers plunged in and out. Clinging to each other, their bodies were covered in a sheen of sweat, as their pace grew steadily wilder. Holly's thighs trembled as her body tightened around Whitney's fingers. Urged on by Whitney's body joining hers, she suckled Whitney's neck, nipping and licking.

Holly's head fell back as her body arched. They climaxed in unison; calling out so loudly they must have woke everyone else in the hotel. They clung to each other tightly as the waves of passion flowed. As the waves ebbed, they extricated themselves from each other. "Wow," Whitney gasped. Holly chuckled in response, not capable of speaking yet. "Do you know that you just made a dream come true?"

Holly leaned over and kissed her gently. "Tell me about your other dreams," she said. Whitney's eyes darkened with desire as she kissed Holly deeply before rolling her onto her back. "Well . . . ," Whitney purred deeply as she straddled her. Holly could feel her pulse soar as she pulled Whitney's body onto her own.

PART FIVE

The following evening the two women were smiling as they entered the reunion together. "I knew it," Selma patted herself on the back. She looked over and found Trisha and Rex on the dance floor. "Damn, I'm good." She smirked as she waved Holly over. As the couple approached, Selma could see that they were glowing. After a brief round of chitchat, Whitney excused herself to get some drinks. Selma declined.

"So?" Selma nudged the small blonde after Whitney was at a safe distance. Holly just blinked at her innocently. "Don't even try it," Selma warned her. "I saw what you did to her neck."

"Oops," Holly blushed. "Selma, she's incredible."

"Uh huh," Selma clapped gleefully.

"Not just that," Holly swatted her. "We did talk last night and this morning."

"Among other things," Selma added slyly. "And?"

"And we seem to really hit it off," Holly added. "We're going to go out when we get back to the city. And we're driving back together."

"I'm happy," Selma squealed.

"You set this up, didn't you?" Holly accused her. "Whitney told me that her room was moved just before she drove down here."

"So what if I did?" Selma smirked in a cocky manner. "She asked about you."

"What?" Holly smiled.

"She asked about you when she called," Selma informed her.

"I knew you had a thing for her back in high school. Hey, you might not have hit it off. I just leveled the playing field. Just a little."

"A little?" Holly laughed.

"Yes, just a little," Selma argued. "The rest was up to the two of you. It still is."

"I'm a little nervous," Holly grimaced slightly. "She wants me to meet her parents."

"That's understandable," Selma responded. "And not in a moving-to-fast kind of way. They'll be here and you two are definitely here together."

"Thank you," Holly sighed in relief. "You responsible for that as well?" she asked, pointing to Trisha and Rex on the dance floor.

"Maybe," Selma shrugged just as Whitney returned.

"What are the two of you grinning about?" Whitney inquired, absently rubbing the hickey on her neck. Selma shrugged innocently before making her escape. Whitney was a tall woman who looked like she could hurt her.

"She was the one who moved your room reservation," Holly explained.

"I always liked her," Whitney smiled brightly down at Holly.

"Me too," Holly agreed as she wrapped her arm around Whitney's waist.

THE END

RING IN THE OLD,
RING IN THE NEW

Danielle looked around the gala. It was elegant enough without being pretentious. She brushed her auburn hair out of her eyes, cursing herself for not taking the time to get a hair cut. It wasn't long by any means; it was just shaggy and unruly. The holiday season just seemed to come out nowhere. For the first time in years, Danielle found herself unprepared. Like everyone around the country, the events of the fall had thrown her for a loop. Before she knew it, Christmas had arrived. Now it had passed. Perhaps it was because she was single this year. It wasn't a new development; she and Sheryl had split up last winter after the holidays. It just seemed strange this year to be alone after spending the past four years together.

She wasn't lonely or upset by the breakup. They both knew it had been coming. Despite their efforts to make it work, they both finally needed to admit that they didn't belong together. They had fallen into a familiar trap, confusing passion with a relationship. Far too late they realized that they would have made really good friends; they just weren't meant to be a couple.

Of course that didn't mean that it hurt any less when Sheryl announced that she'd met someone else. So now here she stood surrounded by happy couples. She suddenly regretted her choice of attending the party. Well, it was this or sit at home in her flannel Tigger jammies, eating a pizza while trying to find something to watch on television. She had to admit that she did look good, clad in a black beaded dress that accented her figure.

However she did have one motivation for attending the large party. Leigh McCormick had mentioned that she was thinking of going. Of course she didn't sound positive that she wanted to make the drive all the way into the city. Danielle felt a strange sense of disappointment when Leigh left things up in the air about whether or not she would be attending. Danielle suspected that there was a personal reason for Leigh's reluctance, but she didn't want to pry.

Danielle drifted towards one of the buffet tables as she watched happy couples twirling around the dance floor. She sighed and smiled slightly, deciding it was time to get something to eat. She pondered her decision, as she carefully studied the array of food. One good thing about working for such a large company was that they threw great holiday parties. This year McPherson Inc. opted for New Year's Eve. They were trying to be politically correct by not having a Christmas party.

"So many choices," a deep sultry voice drifted softly from behind her. Danielle could feel her stomach clench as the voice drifted through her body. Danielle couldn't understand why her palms were sweating. She swallowed hard as she turned to find the owner of the rich voice that had sent her libido racing. There had been something distinctively familiar about the voice that made the hair on the back of her neck stand on end. Her arms broke out in goose bumps. Her green eyes grew wide in delight as she drank in the vision of beauty standing before. "Oh yeah," she blew out before she could stop herself.

She blushed as she realized what she had just done. Clearing her throat, she feigned a cough. "I mean yes," she said firmly as she tried to cover up her blunder. She caught the amused look twinkling in the tall raven-haired beauty's sparkling blue eyes. As her mind raced trying to think of something clever to say, the tall woman reached across her and snatched a plump strawberry from the fruit tray.

"See anything you like?" The woman teased her before taking a small bite of the fruit.

"I Uhm . . . uhm . . . ," Danielle stammered uncontrollably. "You . . . uhm . . ." She finally blew out an exasperated breath and shook her head as she tried to comprehend the events unfolding before her. "Who are you?" She finally managed to blurt out.

The woman flashed her a brilliant smile. "Leigh McCormick," she announced as she wiggled her eyebrows playfully with a slight giggle. Danielle's eyes widened with delight. She and this woman had been exchanging emails, telephone calls, and memos for over two years. Although they had never met each other, a friendship had blossomed.

They were both in the accounting department of the company but in different cities. The first time they spoke, Danielle could feel the other woman's voice resonating through her body. "I thought you weren't coming," Danielle beamed as she accepted the hand that Leigh offered.

"I wasn't but I'd already made my reservation," Leigh explained with some hesitation. "I can't believe that we're finally meeting each other," Leigh added with delight.

As the taller woman finally released her hand, Danielle felt a strange sense of loss. "How did you know it was me?" Danielle asked as they stepped away from the buffet table, allowing other guests to get something to eat. Leigh blushed slightly as she tossed the rest of the berry she had teased Danielle with into a trash barrel. "Well . . . , " Leigh began slowly as she pretended to wipe her hands. "OOh, boy." She finally blew out an exasperated breath. "I hope you won't be offended."

Danielle's over-active curiosity kicked in. Leigh looked so nervous that Danielle couldn't resist teasing her just a little. "Did you know it was me or are you in the habit of picking up strange women at parties?" Danielle said, sensing what was really behind her discomfort. During all of their correspondences they had revealed very little of their personal lives. Oh, they'd talked about their interests; they both mentioned that they were relationships and what not. Danielle had even told her when hers had ended. Yet the references to their significant others had always remained gender neutral. Based on that alone, Danielle had long suspected that they had a lot in common.

"Oh, so you're strange?" Leigh teased her in return. "Good to know."

Danielle smiled at Leigh's playfulness while she drank in the sight of the tall woman, clad in a red dress that stopped just above her knees. Leigh's legs seemed to go on forever. Danielle mentally shook off her lustful thoughts as she reminded herself that Leigh was taken. Although over the past year, Leigh didn't seem very happy about her relationship. *'Let it go,'* she mentally chastised herself.

"So, are you going to tell me how you knew it was me?" Danielle inquired as they drifted away from the crowd. They managed to snag a couple glasses of champagne as they walked.

Danielle couldn't understand how but they ended up standing outside on one of the balconies. Danielle watched as Leigh sipped her champagne nervously. "Come on. Tell me," Danielle urged as she admired the view of her friend bathed in the light of the moon. "If you don't, I'll just have to torture you until you do," she added with a cocky glare.

"Hmm," Leigh smiled seductively. "Now that could be fun," she added in a husky tone.

Danielle's stomach clenched as her nipples hardened. There was something so seductive about this woman's voice. It had been the first thing that had attracted Danielle. Now that she was standing face to face with her, she found herself overwhelmed by Leigh's physical beauty. Danielle's chest heaved slightly; she noticed Leigh's blue eyes drifting to her cleavage.

"Okay," Leigh said finally as her gaze returned to Danielle's eyes. "Please don't be offended," she repeated. "But I asked someone who the attractive red head was. Imagine my surprise when I discovered that it was you."

"Why would I be offended?" Danielle said, trying to fight back her excitement. *'She thinks I'm attractive!'* she thought gleefully. "But won't your other half have a problem with it?"

"We split up," Leigh responded with a shrug. "We've been on again off again for most of the year. She moved out last March. We made the mistake of getting back together just before

316

the holidays. That's why I was so up and down on whether or not I would be coming to the party tonight."

"I'm sorry," Danielle said sincerely as she touched Leigh's arm gently.

"Don't be," Leigh reassured her. "By the time Christmas rolled around, we both admitted it was a mistake. It was just, you know, the holidays and we got sentimental. Next thing we knew we were dating again. I had booked a room here at the hotel for the two of us so we could come to the party and not worry about the drive." Leigh's eyes dimmed slightly before catching Danielle's gaze once again. They seemed to come alive once again. "So I take it by your reaction that you're ..."

"Family, gay, a big old dyke," Danielle filled in for her. "God yes." Danielle laughed as she spoke.

"That's a relief," Leigh said before taking another sip of champagne. "I was worried. We seemed to have become friends. At least I think so."

"So do I," Danielle confirmed eagerly.

"It would have been awful if one of us turned out to be a big old homophobe," Leigh concluded.

"To say the least," Danielle agreed.

They stared at each other, unaware of the chill from the winter evening. "I can't believe it's you," Danielle finally said, becoming lost in Leigh's eyes.

"I know," Leigh, replied quietly, the smile never leaving her face. "After all this time, it's nice to put a name with the face. Or is that the other way around?" Leigh jested.

"And such a nice face," Danielle said absently, her body responding to the look Leigh was casting in her direction.

"Yes," Leigh agreed as she stepped slightly closer to Danielle.

Danielle was trying to rationalize the way her body was reacting. Her heart was pounding as she felt the heat emanating from both of them. It was the end of December in New England; she was standing outside in the middle of the night in a short dress and felt hot. She knew that her libido had taken over. She was fighting to control her desire and failing miserably. Her lower anatomy was pulsating in rhythm with her heart.

"Maybe we should go inside?" Leigh suggested, her tone lacking conviction as the two stepped closer to one another. "Rejoin the party? Get warm?"

"I'm not cold," Danielle confessed as she felt Leigh's hand on her arm. She stared into fiery blue orbs as they inched even closer to one another while stepping into the dark corner of the balcony away from prying eyes.

"Neither am I," Leigh purred as Danielle leaned back against the brick wall.

She could hear the count down begin from inside as Leigh's inviting form lingered dangerously close to her. She briefly wondered just how long they'd been standing out there in the cold simply gazing into one another's eyes. From inside voices counted down, "Ten . . ." Danielle placed her hands on Leigh's hips. "Nine . . ." Leigh sighed as she leaned into Danielle's body. "Eight . . ." Danielle swallowed hard, her mouth suddenly feeling dry as she felt their hardened nipples brush together. "Seven . . ." Danielle moaned as Leigh's thigh pressed against her center. "Six . . ." Danielle parted her thighs, inviting Leigh to press more of herself into Danielle aching body. "Five . . . " Leigh's arms encircled Danielle's waist. "Four . . . " Danielle wrapped her arms around Leigh's body, pulling her even closer. "Three . . ." Danielle slipped her thigh between the warmth of Leigh's legs. "Two . . . " Their bodies seemed to melt together as their faces neared each other. "One . . ." Danielle could feel Leigh's breath on her skin. "Happy New Year!" was shouted from inside as their lips met.

Instantly they found themselves locked in a smoldering kiss. Danielle swooned from the fiery intensity as their tongues battled for control. Their hips swayed together in a sensual rhythm. Danielle's hands roamed - clasping Leigh's firm backside, groping her lover, guiding her to thrust harder. Danielle moved to meet her lover's urgent pace. She sucked Leigh's tongue as her wetness coated the taller woman's pantyhose.

They moaned into each other's mouth as Leigh's hands slipped up under the hem of Danielle's dress. Never before had Danielle been so happy that she had chosen to wear stockings instead of pantyhose. They broke apart, gasping for air, their eyes still locked in a passionate haze. Danielle's mind was screaming for her to slow down. Leigh's fingers teased the garters holding up her stockings and stroked her bare thighs.

Moaning deeply, Danielle let her head fall back slightly. Silencing the inner voice that was telling her to slow down, she felt Leigh skillfully unsnap the clasps of her garter belt. Firm strong hands cupped and massaged her backside through her silken panties. Danielle guided one of the thin straps of Leigh's dress down her shoulder.

Their bodies gyrated against each other wildly as Leigh's fingers pressed firmly into Danielle's backside. Danielle was mesmerized as she lowered part of Leigh's dress, revealing a red lacy bra. Danielle could see nipples straining against the material. Leigh groaned deeply as Danielle cupped one of her breasts, teasing the aching nipple with the palm of her hand.

Their mouths reclaimed each other and they found themselves once again locked in a fiery kiss. Off in the distance, Danielle could hear noise from the party. Feeling that they were quite alone, she pushed aside the material of Leigh's bra. As their tongues danced together, Danielle captured Leigh's nipple between two fingers, pinching and teasing the swollen bud. One of Leigh's hands moved between them. Danielle panted as she broke the kiss. Leigh's palm cupped her mound as fingers teased the damp silk materiel of her undergarment.

Danielle's eyes focused on the rose-colored bud trapped between her fingers. Licking lips gone dry with desire, she lowered her head. Her tongue sought out the taste of Leigh's flesh, circling her full breast slowly, enjoying the taste of her lover and then slowly circling her nipple as she felt Leigh touch her through the silk of her panties.

Leigh clasped her tighter as Danielle captured her nipple in her mouth, sucking it as her lover arched against her. She parted her thighs, eager to feel more. Danielle teased Leigh's nipple with her teeth and her tongue. The scene was almost surreal as they tried to stifle their moans of pleasure while they rocked together in the darkness.

Releasing Leigh's breast from her mouth, she found herself locked in another passionate kiss. Danielle whimpered as the kiss ended. Leigh began kiss her jaw then her very sensitive neck. Her mouth descended lower. Danielle felt a jolt of excitement run through her as Leigh lowered herself down her body. Her hands caressed all of her as she moved. Danielle's body quivered as she looked down to see Leigh kneeling before her.

She whimpered when Leigh tasted the inside of her thigh. Danielle opened herself further as her lover kissed the sensitive flesh again and again. Danielle ran her fingers through the long raven tresses as Leigh buried her face in her passion. Slowly, Leigh's fingers brushed aside the material of her panties. Danielle fought to keep her eyes from closing as she watched her lover. Leigh was gliding her fingers along her swollen nether lips, seemingly mesmerized by Danielle's wetness.

Danielle couldn't believe what was happening as Leigh tasted her. Her tongue and mouth drank in her passion. Up until tonight, this woman had only been a friendly voice on the telephone. Now she was kneeling before her, feasting upon her. Silently, Danielle urged her on as she pressed against the back of Leigh's head. Leigh eagerly accepted her invitation as she entered her center. Danielle thrust wildly as Leigh sucked her throbbing clit.

Not wanting to alert the other party guests to their activities, Danielle bit down on her bottom lip to keep from screaming. Leigh's fingers plunged in and out of her as she teased her nub with her mouth. The feel of Leigh's fingers and mouth and her own underwear quickly drove Danielle over the edge. The intense spasm ripped through her body as she clenched her jaw to keep from crying out.

Still kneeling, Leigh held Danielle tightly as the waves of pleasure continued to pulsate through her body. As her breathing returned to normal, she felt Leigh's fingers leave her. She whimpered as the brunette dragged herself back up to a standing position. Danielle quickly pulled Leigh in for a kiss. The taste of champagne and strawberries mixed with her own passion ignited her desire once again.

Danielle pushed Leigh's thighs apart with her knee. Her hands roamed along Leigh's long body, pulling the material of her dress up. Leigh broke the kiss as she moaned deeply. Encouraged by the primal sounds emanating from her lover, Danielle swiftly lowered Leigh's pantyhose and underwear. She dipped her fingers into the wetness awaiting her.

Her thumb stroked Leigh's clit as her eyes drifted to her exposed breasts. With delight, she watched as Leigh began to caress her own breast, teasing the nipples just as Danielle had. The red head entered Leigh with two digits as her free hand cupped her backside. Danielle plunged in and out of her lover's wetness as Leigh thrust against her hand. Danielle loved the feel of their bodies meeting as her thumb stroked Leigh's clit. Danielle took her lover higher as her pace intensified. Capturing Leigh's lips in a passionate kiss, she felt her lover tremble. Leigh screamed into her mouth as she climaxed, clinging to the smaller woman.

"Hold me," Leigh panted in her ear. Danielle smiled as they wrapped themselves up in each other's arms. She held Leigh tightly as the aftershocks trembled through her long body. Finally, Leigh pulled away from her slightly, brushing Danielle's bangs out of her face. "Happy New Year," she whispered before placing a tender kiss on Danielle's lips.

"Happy New Year," Danielle responded merrily as she brushed her fingers along Leigh's jaw.

Suddenly they both found themselves laughing as they took in their disheveled state. "That was the craziest and nicest thing I've ever done," Leigh confessed as they adjusted their clothing.

"I know," Danielle agreed, smiling as she refastened her stockings. "I mean it was great. But we just met. And what if someone had walked out here?"

Leigh chuckled as they stepped back into the party, which had dwindled considerably. Danielle briefly panicked, wondering what would happen now? She knew what she wanted to happen. She wanted more. She wanted Leigh to take her to her room and make love until neither of them could move. "Danielle?" Leigh began in a soft shy tone. "Would you like to go upstairs with me? I could order some more champagne,"

Leigh offered hopefully. "I mean, we could talk or . . ."

Danielle silenced her with a lingering kiss. Stepping back, she smiled sweetly up at her lover. "Order the champagne and some strawberries and we don't have to talk. Except for telling each other what we want." Danielle's voice dripped with desire. "I'm not usually this forward, but I really want to continue what we've started. Only this time with a lot more privacy."

Leigh took her by the hand and flashed her a knowing smile. "I really like the way 2002 has begun," she said sincerely as she led Danielle out of the ballroom.

THE END

COFFEE BREAK

PART ONE

Monica made her way to the back of the coffeehouse. She sat and took in the deserted surroundings and smiled happily. No one was around. She could just relax, enjoy her coffee, and do the crossword puzzle in The Boston Globe. No one was going to run up screaming the all too familiar *'Mommy!'*. No one would ask her what she was reading and could they watch Blues Clues or The Rugrats.   *'Ah, the sweet bliss of silence'* she thought merrily.

A sudden pang struck her; she instantly missed the noise and her son. Jon-Michael was the light of her life and she truly missed him. But she also needed the stimulus of the adult world. For the next seventy-two hours she would be on her own for the first time in months. The inquisitive five-year-old was a ball of fire. Of course, there was little hope that she and Thom would produce a quiet child.

Thom finally had some time off and could take their son for the weekend. It wasn't Thom's fault he hadn't been able to spend more time with Jon-Michael. Thom was a firefighter and EMT. Monica couldn't help but support her ex-husband's choice to assist with the rescue and cleanup efforts in New York. In fact, she was damn proud of him. She knew that Jon-Michael missed his time with his father, but she explained that he was doing something very brave and noble.

The little boy tried very hard to understand. But it was hard for him. He simply missed his daddy. When Monica and Thom were married, their schedules had been difficult enough. Divorcing made it damn near impossible for each of them to spend as much time with their son as they would like.

Thom and Monica had been married for seven wonderful years. There was only one little problem in their relationship. She was in the closet. Thom had been her best friend and when she finally came to terms with her sexuality, he supported her. Well, not at first. In the beginning he did freak out. But after they'd talked and fought, things calmed down. Now two years later they were still friends and raising their son together, just from separate apartments.

As a cable installer who was also trained in DSL installation, she was in high demand. Everyone wanted two hundred channels and to get online as quickly as possible. As the demand grew, so did her hours. Somehow she and Thom and their parents balanced their lives. Everyone did his or her best to ensure that Jon-Michael's happiness didn't suffer.

And now Monica could relax for the entire weekend. She just needed to stop worrying about Jon-Michael. She opened up the newspaper and took a sip of her coffee. She pulled out a pen as she quickly read her horoscope. *'Opportunities to make new friends may result in a new romantic connection.'* "I wish," she muttered as she folded the paper. Licking her lips eagerly, she began the crossword puzzle.

Brushing her long black hair off her shoulders, she quickly began to fill in the blanks. She was cruising through the puzzle when a shadow was cast over her. "Excuse me?" A sweet voice inquired.

Despite the sweetness of the tone, Monica stiffened from the interruption. "Would you mind if I borrowed part of your newspaper?" The voice continued. Monica pinched her nose as her blue eyes fluttered shut. She took a cleansing breath before she exploded. *'Relax, Monica. She just wants something to read.*

Everyone borrows the paper in these shops. She's not going to make paper airplanes out of it or try to flush it down the toilet.' Monica kicked herself out of mommy mode and opened her eyes.

Monica looked up and found herself mesmerized by the brightest green, no wait, blue err. . . blue green eyes she had ever seen. She grinned like an idiot when she discovered that those eyes were a part of the sweetest looking blonde. "Help yourself," she stammered out, trying to sound seductive. She failed as her normally low voice squeaked. *'Smooth,'* she mentally kicked herself.

"Thank you," the blonde smiled in response. *'Thank you! All is not lost.'* Monica sighed in relief.

As the blonde began to flip through the paper, Monica allowed herself to look at the full package. The blonde was petite but possessed a powerful build. Absently Monica licked her lips as she took in her ruffled short blonde locks, the curve of her neck, and her well-defined backside.

As the stranger turned Monica found herself greeted with a full view of the younger woman's cleavage. *'Hello!'* her mind screamed like an adolescent boy. "Oh," the blonde sighed. Embarrassed, she snapped her eyes up. She blew another sigh of relief when she realized the blonde was looking at her crossword puzzle and had failed to notice her ogling her breasts. "Was this what you were looking for?" Monica inquired as she tapped her pen against the puzzle.

"Yeah," the blonde shyly confessed. "I'm addicted to those things."

"Me too," Monica smiled, hoping that she sounded as charming as she thought.

"The Globe sells out so quickly," the stranger continued. "I don't really care for the one in The Herald. Silly me. I forgot to buy a paper on my way into work this morning."

"It's a rare treat I actually get to do these," Monica said, hoping to keep this beautiful woman talking longer. "My son usually interrupts," Monica, added since she liked to get that information out right away. Some women were uncomfortable that Monica had a child and kept a good relationship with her ex-husband.

"Your son?" The blonde stammered slightly. "How old is he?" She recovered quickly.

"Five," Monica answered, recognizing the wide-eyed look in those pretty eyes. It was the old Ooops-my-gaydar-must-be-broken look. "Would you like to join me?" Monica offered quickly before the stranger could bolt for the door. "I'm kind of stuck on a couple answers."

"Sure," the blonde smiled nervously as she sat down next to the tall brunette. "I'm Candice, by the way," she introduced herself before taking a sip of her coffee.

"Monica," the brunette responded as she slid the crossword puzzle over.

"Where's your son?" Candice inquired pleasantly.

"Jon-Michael is spending the weekend with his father," Monica answered, noticing the green hospital scrubs underneath Candice's wool coat. "You work at the hospital?" She inquired, pointing towards her attire.

"Yes," Candice smiled brightly. "I'm a phlebotomist. No vampire jokes," Candice cautioned her.

Monica could only smile in response. "Timmy and Lassie," Candice said softly.

"Excuse me?" Monica shook her head in confusion.

"Fifty seven across," Candice pointed towards the crossword puzzle. "TV twosome. Timmy and Lassie."

Monica's crystal blue eyes widened in excitement. "You're right," she chuckled. "I get it now. Kids and their dogs. So let me see, twenty across, Movie Duo, is . . . "

"Dorothy and Toto," Candice supplied.

"Hey, you're good at this," Monica beamed as she touched Candice's forearm gently. She smiled from the warmth of the woman's body and the fact that Candice didn't move away from her touch. She simply smiled back at her. "Okay then, thirty eight across, A Broadway team, would be Annie and Sandy. Well, with those I'm almost finished. I can't remember the last time that happened. Jon-Michael's quite a handful."

"You're divorced?" Candice inquired carefully.

"Yes," Monica responded, giving Candice's arm a gentle

squeeze, hoping that she'd get the message. "For about two years now. Thom and I actually get along pretty well. All things considered."

"That's nice," Candice answered with sincerity. "So what are you going to do besides the crossword puzzle? You know, with your free time?"

"I don't know," Monica answered honestly.   "It's been awhile since I had a whole weekend to myself. Normally I have to work. I'm a cable installer. We get problems from customers constantly on the weekends."

"Cable?" The blonde's eyes lit up.

"Now, no hitting me up for free channels," Monica teased her. "My newspaper is one thing. But for cable theft you need to at least buy me dinner first."

Monica held her breath, hoping that she hadn't overstepped her bounds or misread Candice's intentions. She relaxed as she saw the slight blush emerge on Candice's cheeks. Candice nervously ran her fingers through her hair. "Monica, are you flirting with me?" She asked as her eyes darkened.

"As a matter of fact, I am," Monica replied honestly. "I hope I haven't offended you."

"God no," Candice laughed lightly. *'What a great laugh,'* Monica thought. "I'm not offended. In fact I'm relieved. When you said something about your son . . ."

"Jon-Michael," Monica stated firmly, making it clear how much her son means to her. "I know, my son, an ex-husband, big breeder, yada yada yada. It happens." Monica shrugged. "Big dyke who was clueless," Monica explained further.

"Sorry," Candice apologized. "I know I shouldn't jump to conclusions. But these days it's so hard to tell. I was also afraid that you had a partner."

"Nope," Monica encouraged her, hoping that the blonde would ask her out before the turn of the century. Frankly it had been so long since she'd been on a date or even met a woman she was interested in that she was afraid she was going to end up being one of those crazy women with four hundred cats.

"Would you like to go out to dinner?" Candice asked

nervously as she bit on her bottom lip.

"Yes," Monica blurted out a little too quickly. Instantly she dropped her face in her hands to hide the blush that she was certain now covered her entire body. "Sorry," she muttered.

"Hey," Candice reassured her as she began to pat her back gently. The touch instantly caused Monica's nipples to harden. "It's nice to know that you're as nervous as I am."

"Thank you," Monica choked out as she finally raised her head. She found herself locked in an intense gaze. *'How am I going to get through an entire meal with her?'*

"There's just one thing," Candice began hesitantly. "I can't this weekend."

"Oh?" Monica's heart dropped at the thought of not spending more time with this woman right away.

"I'm on double shifts," Candice explained quickly. "What about dancing tonight?"

"Dancing?" Monica responded brightly.

"I get off work at eleven. I could meet you at The Galaxy," Candice suggested.

"Sounds great," Monica agreed quickly.

"Speaking of work." Candice grimaced. "I need to get back. My coffee break is almost over."

Monica thought about that for a moment. "Don't they have a ton of coffee shops at the hospital?" She inquired.

"Yeah," Candice smiled. "I was out looking for a paper when I saw . . . never mind." She blushed as she stood.

"When you saw what?" Monica urged her on.

"You," Candice reluctantly confessed, once again chewing on her bottom lip.

"Oh, so now you're stalking me," Monica teased the blushing blonde.

"I guess you'll find out tonight," Candice countered. It was now Monica's turn to blush.

PART TWO

After Candice left, Monica couldn't concentrate on her beloved crossword puzzle. She tossed it and her coffee in the trash. She had a date tonight. And that meant one thing - she needed to go shopping. Somehow she didn't think the ragged blue jeans she wore to 'Mommy and Me' would cut it. The rest of the day, Monica was a nervous wreck. She finally found an outfit that wasn't too dressy but looked good on her.

Once she returned to her apartment, she tried on her outfit several times just to make certain that it looked okay. Thom called to let her know that Jon-Michael wasn't feeling well. Nothing serious he reassured her, just a slight temperature. She told him that she would have her cell phone with her all night if Jon-Michael got worse. This, of course, led to her having to disclose that she was going out on a date.

Thom proceeded to tease her endlessly. When Thom had finally accepted her lifestyle, he became a little too accepting. In fact he was always trying to set her up. "See, I told you that I could find a woman on my own," she retaliated. "Perhaps I should start looking for one for you, buddy boy?"

"No thanks. Between you and my Mother . . .," he laughed. "Have fun tonight. And don't do anything I wouldn't do."

"Thanks. That should leave the field wide open," she snorted happily. "Keep me updated on Jon-Michael."

"I will," he promised.

Later that night she found herself sitting at the bar nursing a Drunken Monkey. *'I'm glad I had the good sense to take a nap today,'* she complimented herself as she smoothed out the crease in her black jeans. Normally at this hour Monica was fast asleep. The sound of the techno music beat steadily as she looked around the crowded nightclub once again.

She was nervous about seeing Candice. She'd been thinking about the blonde all day long. Her thoughts were far from pure since she was more than a little attracted to blonde. Of course, she knew that she would go home with her that night if Candice gave the slightest indication that she was interested. This wasn't Monica's usual style. In fact, Monica didn't have a style. But there was something about the blonde that set her senses on fire.

She straightened as she noticed the object of her desires approaching her. The sight of Candice dressed in a short PVC mini-skirt and an emerald silk tank top made her body ache with desire. Absently she licked her lips as she took in the curve of smaller woman's breasts. Her eyes drifted down and drank in the sight of her firm thighs. A part of her felt like a complete floozy while another part of her was too turned on to care.

"Hi," Candice greeted her brightly.

"Hi," she responded in turn, her knees trembling slightly.

"I hope you weren't waiting long," Candice offered.

"No," Monica lied. She had shown up early, unable to wait any longer. She was glad that she'd arrived first; she wouldn't have missed seeing the sight of the beautiful woman walking into the nightclub. Monica wasn't the only one who had noticed her. More than a few pairs of eyes had turned to watch as Candice strode confidently across the room. "You look incredible," she said before she could stop herself.

"Thanks," Candice responded with a slight blush. "So do you," she added in a dreamy tone.

"Would you like a drink?" Monica offered, knowing that she needed to cool down.

"Great," Candice answered. "What are you drinking?"

"A Drunken Monkey," Monica confessed as she crinkled her nose. "It's good, just a bit much for me."

Candice took a sip of Monica's cocktail. "Hmm. That is good." Candice licked the Irish Cream from her lips. "But I think I need something a little less rich. Hard Cider is fine."

Monica ordered a Savannah for Candice and a bottle of spring water for herself. She was almost tempted to pour the water down her jeans. As she turned to hand Candice the cider, she caught the blonde checking her out. Her blue eyes twinkled with amusement; she was relieved to know she wasn't the only one feeling this way. "Here you go," she said gleefully as she handed the drink to the smaller woman.

"Thanks," Candice said as she averted her eyes. Their fingers brushed as Monica handed her the bottle. Both women's breathing seemed to increase slightly.

"Interesting outfit," Monica said, giving her another excuse to ogle Candice's body.

"I'm Uhm . . . went shopping on my dinner break," Candice admitted. "Somehow my scrubs didn't seem appropriate for the occasion. The only place open was Hootin' Nannies. It's a little risqué."

"I know the place. It's in Harvard Square," Monica commented. "Granted I don't get there much, but they have some really nice stuff."

"Well, I'm glad you like the outfit," Candice sighed with relief. "It was this or one of those school girl outfits."

"Hmm," Monica pouted.

"Maybe for our second date," Candice teased. "So do you like what you do? For a living?" Candice added quickly.

"Yes, I do," Monica confirmed. "I get outdoors and I meet a lot of people. How about you? Do you like working with blood?"

"Yes," Candice responded proudly. "I always worry that my work will lead to bad news, especially in this day and age. And no one's thrilled to see my needles or me. But the work I do is important."

"I agree," Monica answered. "I have to admit I just hate having blood drawn. But I still donate every two months."

Monica watched as Candice made a mental note regarding the information she had just given her. "I donate as well. The hospital always has a drive going." Monica digested that information. *'So we're both healthy enough to give blood. That means we can really enjoy ourselves. Good to know.'* They continued to chat as they sipped their drinks. Monica noticed that they both were revealing little details that confirmed that if they wanted to they wouldn't need to practice safe sex. It was hard to slip into a conversation, but somehow they managed.

PART THREE

As the conversation progressed they also talked about

themselves and Monica's son. Casual brushes against one another served to further fuel Monica's growing desire. "Would you like to dance?" Candice asked her. She simply nodded in response, unable to look anywhere but at the blonde. Monica's legs were shaking as she took Candice's hand and walked out onto the dance floor.

Their bodies instantly melted together as they began to sway to the music. Monica's pulse raced as her hands slid down Candice's back. The feel of the smaller woman was making her heart pound and her lower anatomy throb. Monica moaned as Candice's thigh pressed against her center. In response her hands drifted down, capturing Candice's hips.

They continued to sway in rhythm as their hands began to caress one another. Monica was ready to explode simply from feeling Candice's body pressed against her own. Candice's lips gently kissed the valley between her breasts. Monica's head fell back slightly as she stifled the scream that threatened to escape.

Candice continued to kiss her exposed flesh as Monica ground her hips into the smaller woman's body. Lowering her head, she found herself locked in a fiery gaze. Unable to stop herself, she did what she'd been dreaming about since the first moment she laid eyes on this woman.

Their lips met and instantly began to ignite the passion within them. Lips parted as tongues darted out, each tasting the warmth of the other's mouth. As their tongues danced together, Monica's hands slipped down Candice's back, enjoying the feel of the blonde's body.

Candice moaned deeply as Monica cupped her firm backside. Squeezing and massaging the material of the skirt roughly, she sucked on Candice's tongue. Candice wrapped her fingers in long black hair, tugging gently as their kiss deepened. Someone bumped into the overheated couple. They halted their movements and stared deeply into each other's eyes.

Candice reached up and her mouth began an assault on Monica's neck. The blonde began to suck the pulse point causing Monica to gasp in pleasure. Monica tore away from Candice slightly. Taking her by the hand, she led the younger woman off the dance floor. Pulling Candice away from the crowd into a dark corner, she pressed her against the wall.

Candice pulled Monica's taller form tightly against her own and quickly reclaimed her lips. Monica could feel Candice's fingers feeling their way to her breasts. As the blonde pinched and teased her nipples, Monica's hands drifted down Candice's firm body. One hand clasped the blonde's ass firmly while the other drifted up her firm thigh.

Monica could hardly believe that she was acting this way in public. But she didn't care. She needed to know if Candice was as turned on as she was. Her fingers teased as they slipped up under the hot PVC material. Candice broke away from their kiss, panting wildly. Her eyes blazed with desire. Lowering her head, she began to suckle on one of Monica's nipples through her shirt.

Monica groaned as she felt the lace material of a garter belt. She pressed her body into Candice's, her hips beginning to sway. Candice matched her rhythm as Monica's fingers moved further up her skirt. As Monica's touch neared Candice's panties, the blonde began to suckle her breast harder.

Monica cupped Candice's mound and moaned as she discovered that the blonde was just as excited as she was. The feel of Candice's wetness inflamed her need. Unable to control herself, she slipped her fingers under the lacy material. Her fingers were coated with Candice's passion.

Candice broke away from her breast with a growl. Her eyes opened only slightly as her head fell back against the wall. "Please," the blonde pleaded as Monica's fingers dipped in a little further. Her thumb began to circle Candice's throbbing clit. "Tell me," Monica encouraged her as she pressed her body into her. "Fuck me," Candice gasped out.

It was all Monica needed to hear. She pressed her lips against Candice's as she slipped two fingers deep inside the blonde's slick center. Candice wrapped her body around Monica's as the brunette explored her mouth. Her fingers plunged in and out of the smaller woman. She could feel Candice's thighs trembling as her thumb continued to tease her clit. The walls closing around Monica's fingers told her that her lover was nearing the edge.

"Ladies," a harsh masculine voice said from behind her. *'Oh no.'* Monica cringed as Candice's eyes flew open.

Monica instantly halted her movements. This was bad. She didn't need to turn around to know that security was standing behind her while she had her hand up Candice's skirt. The Galaxy was a pretty relaxed place unless, of course, you broke the law. And in the great old prudish Commonwealth actually having sex in the club was illegal.

"Sorry," Monica winced as she reluctantly removed her hand from the warmth of Candice's sex.

Seemingly satisfied, the security man walked away. "How embarrassing was that?" Monica choked out.

"I can't believe we were doing that," Candice blushed. "You should have seen his face. That guy was ticked off."

"Probably just jealous," Monica snickered as she fought the urge to bring her fingers up to her mouth.

"Monica . . . ," Candice began slowly as she readjusted her skirt, ". . . I don't normally behave like this and I like you and would like to get to know you better. But at this moment . . . I really want to take you back to my place and let you do anything you want to me."

"Yes," Monica said firmly as she pressed her lips against Candice's. The kiss quickly ignited and the two found themselves groping one another. Monica reluctantly broke away as she heard a throat being cleared behind her. "Let's go," she whispered in Candice's ear.

The two quickly rearranged their clothing and bolted towards the coat check. Once outside, they quickly hailed a taxi.

PART FOUR

As soon as they gave the driver the address, they melted into one another's arms. "I don't think I've ever been this turned on in my life," Monica groaned as Candice's mouth licked and nibbled across her neck. She moaned as the blonde sucked on her neck. "You are a vampire," she teased as she ran her hands up under Candice's skirt. Her heart pounded against her chest as Candice unbuttoned her jeans and then slowly lowered the zipper.

Just as Candice's fingers were working their way across her stomach, the driver announced that they had reached their destination. Both women growled in frustration. Monica started to refasten her pants as Candice paid the driver. "Don't bother," the blonde whispered hotly in her ear.

Monica whimpered slightly as she allowed Candice to lead her out of the taxi. They rushed into the building and up the staircase. Monica almost tripped over her loose pants. Candice threw open her door and pulled Monica inside. Monica's need was growing out of control as the door closed behind her. Without warning, the small blonde pressed her up against the door.

Monica's thighs instantly parted as she pressed the smaller woman into her body, running her fingers through blonde locks as her shirt was pulled up her body. She raised her arms and allowed the garment to be removed completely. She pulled Candice's coat off as the smaller woman unfastened and removed her bra.

Candice's tongue circled one nipple then the other and back again. It was if the blonde couldn't decide which one she wanted to play with first. Monica's head fell back as her hands tugged on the soft silk top, pulling it up as Candice suckled her nipple. She ran her nails down the blonde's back. Candice teased one nipple with her teeth and tongue while her fingers gently rolled and pinched the other.

Monica unfastened Candice's bra and slid her eager hands against her firm round breasts. Her palms grazed across taut nipples, provoking a wild groan from her lover. Candice's mouth and tongue began to work their way down Monica's body. Candice paused briefly to remove her top and bra that Monica had pushed up. "So beautiful," Monica whispered dreamily. Candice blushed slightly as her mouth returned to Monica's skin.

She tingled from the feel of Candice's knowing tongue working its way down her body. Candice's nipples brushed across Monica's abdomen as the blonde lowered herself. Monica fought to keep her eyes open. She needed to see Candice kneeling before her. Green eyes twinkled up at her as the blonde pulled her jeans down her legs.

Monica fought to remain standing as the rest of her clothing was removed. Gentle hands felt her body along the way. Monica opened herself as Candice kissed and taste the inside of her trembling thighs. She almost exploded as Candice's nipples brushed against her legs.

She trembled as Candice's warm breath blew through her damp curls. The blonde parted her even further as her tongue ran along her swollen lips. Monica ran her fingers through Candice's hair, fighting the need to press her lover into her wetness. Monica's head fell back as Candice's tongue stroked her throbbing clit. Licking and tasting her, the blonde's tongue teased her. Monica's hips thrust forward as Candice's tongue entered her.

Monica pressed Candice to take her deeper as a thumb teased her clit while Candice's tongue pleasured her. Monica's hips rocked, pushing her passion against her eager tongue. She whimpered slightly as Candice moved her attention up. Her body jerked forward as Candice began to suckle her clit, teasing it with her teeth and tongue. Monica's hips rocked uncontrollably. She screamed out in pleasure as she felt two fingers press against her slick center.

Candice entered her as she cried out. Looking down, her passion only grew at the sight of Candice looking up at her as she feasted upon her wetness. "Oh God, yeees!" She cried out as her lover's fingers plunged in and out of her. The sensual rhythm grew as Monica thrust harder, needing to feel her lover taking her higher. Monica tried to steady her breathing, tried to make it last longer. Her efforts were wasted as her lover's pace grew. Candice's fingers and mouth worked together. Monica screamed out as she climaxed against her lover's face.

Monica's body continued to ride out the waves of passion as Candice's fingers stilled, her mouth drinking up every ounce that Monica had to offer. Once Monica's tremors stilled, Candice slipped her fingers out gently. Monica watched as her lover licked her fingers clean. Candice began to kiss her way up the brunette's body.

Monica drew her into a warm embrace and kissed her deeply. Their tongues began a renewed battle as Monica spun the blonde around gently. Pressing her body into Candice's, her hands felt their way. Candice whimpered as Monica's hand slipped back under her skirt. This time there were no interruptions as her fingers blazed a trail to her wetness.

Monica needed to feel her. She pulled her lover's underwear down and slipped her fingers into the wetness that was awaiting her. Monica teased Candice's clit, stroking it as Candice's body arched against her own. Her thumb began to tease as she pressed two fingers against Candice's center. "Yes," Candice whimpered. Monica entered her. Once again Candice wrapped her body around her. Monica thrust against the smaller woman as her fingers slid in and out of her wetness. Monica could feel Candice nearing the edge as her rhythm grew.

Candice bucked against her wildly as her body began to tremble. She screamed out her name as she exploded against her. Monica held onto her lover as the young woman trembled in her arms. "That was . . . incredible," Candice choked out. Monica smiled and kissed her gently. The sound of her cell phone disturbed the moment.

Monica quickly searched through her discarded clothing. She watched as Candice wandered off; she returned clad in a bathrobe as Monica was ending the call with her ex-husband. "Is everything alright?" Candice inquired nervously.

"Yeah," Monica smiled. "That was just Thom letting me know that Jon-Michael's fever has broken."

"Thank goodness," Candice responded sincerely.

The two women stood there in an awkward silence. "Monica, would you like to . . . spend the night?" Candice inquired shyly.

"Yes," the brunette smiled in response. "But only if you lose that bathrobe," she teased. "I'm feeling a little underdressed." She pointed out her nakedness.

Candice smiled sweetly and opened the robe. Slowly she dropped it to the floor, revealing that she had removed her skirt and footwear but still had on the garters, stockings and lace panties.

"Oh my," Monica managed to utter. Candice simply held out her hand and led her to the bedroom.

THE END

DINNER WITH THE FAMILY
(COFFEE BREAK - PART TWO)

PART ONE

Candice checked her appearance for the fifth time in the bedroom mirror. The small blonde's palms were sweating and her knees were trembling slightly. "Why am I so nervous?" She asked her reflection. "It is just dinner." But it wasn't just dinner. It was dinner at Monica's house with her son, her ex-husband, her former in-laws, and her own parents. It wasn't the way that Candice wanted to meet everyone. But they were all getting together to see Jon-Michael in his kindergarten play and then everyone was going back to Monica's for dinner.

Thom's opinion meant a great deal to Candice's new lover, and her son Jon-Michael was the light of her life. "Nope, I'm not feeling the pressure," Candice choked out. She knew that she was falling for the raven-haired woman and she needed to make a good impression on Monica's family. Originally, meeting Monica's entire clan in one fell swoop seemed like a good idea. Now Candice was fighting off a major panic attack.

To add to the mix, the new lovers really hadn't been offered a great deal of time together because of their schedules. Everything about Monica made Candice smile - her looks, the way her mind worked, and her sense of humor. If Monica's son didn't like her, she knew that could mean the end of their budding relationship. Another thing about the impending evening that troubled Candice was whether or not she should stick her toothbrush in her purse.

She didn't want to assume anything. Yet they hadn't really been able to have as many sleepovers as they would like. Candice blushed slightly at the thought of how well their sexual chemistry meshed. "I don't know how I'm going to keep my hands off her," she whimpered slightly at the prospect of having to return to her empty apartment.

Much to her surprise and delight she'd ended up in bed with the beautiful cable installer the night they met. It could have easily turned into a one-night stand. But they both felt the underlying emotions that went beyond the bedroom chemistry. Candice blushed all the way up to her blonde roots. "Heck, we barely made it into the bedroom," she laughed as she recalled how they started to make love in the crowded nightclub. They'd barely made it inside of Candice's apartment.

That weekend had been incredible; Candice had barely dragged herself out of bed the following morning for work. Then she'd rushed back to her lover. After the weekend, Monica's son returned home from spending time with his father. Candice rarely saw Monica and then the time together was spent getting to know one another. And that was a good thing. Candice really loved spending time with Monica. Unfortunately it wasn't as intimate as Candice hoped for. It was like some cruel joke that she had found someone whose passions ran as deeply as her own, and now they really couldn't spend time enjoying it. They had managed to share a few wonderful encounters since they'd started dating as well as some other really nice encounters that unfortunately ended far too soon. "That woman can set my heart racing just by looking at me," Candice sighed happily.

Candice smoothed out her dress once again. It was a simple

black number with beads. "I hope this isn't too dressy or sexy?" She panicked slightly. "Okay, just get a grip and stop stalling," she chastised herself, recalling that it was more or less her idea that she attend the little dinner party. They'd been out on a date when Candice suggested that they get together the following weekend. She had forgotten about Jon-Michael's play; she could have kicked herself for overlooking something so important.

It was then she'd suggested that perhaps, if she attended the performance, it would be a good opportunity for her to finally meet Monica's son. Little did she know that it was to be a full-scale family function. When Monica hesitated, Candice feared that the taller woman didn't share the depth of her feelings. Candice instantly backpedaled and told her lover to forget it. Monica had stopped in the middle of the sidewalk and gently cupped Candice's face in her hands.

'I want you to meet my son,' Monica reassured her. 'I know I've been putting it off.'

'I understand,' Candice said with a heavy sigh. 'It's only been a couple of months and you don't want him getting attached if we don't work out.'

'That's true,' Monica conceded. 'But I think we both know this isn't just a fling for either of us. I mean, it's not for me.' The serious question in her tone tugged at Candice's heartstrings.

'It's not for me either,' Candice said reassuringly as she leaned into Monica's touch.

'It's just that the play isn't going to be just Jon-Michael and I. Thom will be there and his parents and mine as well,' Monica explained. 'And then we're all having dinner back at the apartment.'

'Oh,' Candice said as she swallowed hard. Then something deep inside of her sparked a tiny seed of jealousy. She hated that Thom got to share these precious moments and she was still an outsider. And that's when she suggested attending anyway. Monica seemed to be thrilled that Candice wanted to get to know her family. At that moment in time so was Candice. Perhaps it was the way Monica kissed her deeply right there on the street corner. The intensity of the passionate kiss drove Candice to

forgo their plans for dinner and lead Monica back to her apartment.

Now as Candice grabbed her purse and keys she wasn't as convinced as she had been the previous weekend. The blonde took a cleansing breath before putting on her long woolen coat. "It will be all right. So I'm meeting her entire family," she said bravely as she headed to the apartment door. "It could be worse. We could be meeting my family." She cringed at the thought.

PART TWO

Candice hurried into the dark auditorium, cursing public transportation. The show had just begun and, with the lights dimmed, there was no way she would find Monica in the darkness. She leaned against the back wall as she carefully scanned the crowd. Her heart was beating erratically, thinking that she had screwed up by not arriving on time. Out of the darkness she saw a pair of electrifying blue eyes twinkling at her. The brilliant smile that was flashed in her direction warmed her heart. She knew that she wouldn't be able to join Monica without causing a disturbance. So she waited in the back and tried to follow the group of five-year-old children stumbling through their performance. She watched intently, trying to determine which of the Winter Wonderland goblins was Jon-Michael. She knew the instant she saw those eyes that he was the boisterous snowflake; she'd know that smile anywhere. "My goodness, Monica; your son is adorable," she whispered as her smile grew broader.

The performance lasted about a half hour. Perhaps she was just being biased but Candice was thoroughly convinced that Jon-Michael was the best. The audience clapped and cheered as the children departed the stage, shutting off their camcorders when the last child was gone. Candice's relaxed state quickly vanished as the lights came up and people started shuffling about. She clutched her coat tightly. "I can do this," she encouraged herself in a whispered tone.

Her heart skipped a beat as she saw Monica stand and flash another brilliant smile at her. She watched as her lover moved her way through the crowd. She wanted to sneak a peek at Thom but she couldn't take her eyes off Monica's movements. *'And that is why I'm here,'* she thought blissfully, her gaze still riveted on the tall woman.

"Hi," Monica greeted her with a shy whisper and a gentle touch on her arm.

"Hi," Candice responded in a breathy tone. She started to lose herself in Monica's eyes when the jostling from the departing crowd alerted her to their surroundings. "Sorry I was late. The train was a nightmare."

"I'm glad you're here," Monica reassured her as she gave her arm a gentle squeeze. "Are you sure you're up for this?" she added with concern.

"Yes," Candice responded firmly while internally her mind was screaming *'What the hell were you thinking, meeting them all at once?'* "Jon-Michael was great tonight." She suddenly needed to convey how much she enjoyed the performance.

"He was the . . . ," Monica began to explain.

"The snowflake," Candice stated with a wry smile.

"How did . . .?" Monica questioned her.

"He's beautiful, just like his mother," Candice confessed as she watched her lover's eyes get slightly misty.

"Thank you," Monica responded softly, giving Candice's arm a gentle squeeze. Candice's eyes drifted upward as she noticed the tall dark man standing behind Monica; he was giving both of them a curious look. Candice nodded her head towards him to alert Monica that they had company. Monica turned and hugged the man. Candice's heart dropped slightly as Monica took his hand. "Thom, this is Candice." Monica began the introductions. "Candice, this is Thom."

"Nice to meet you," Candice said in a polite tone. *'Holy Mother . . . He is gorgeous!'* she thought painfully as she noted that they were still holding hands.

"Well, it's good to finally meet you, Candice," Thom said in a cheerful tone. "My wife has told me a lot about you." Monica stared at him oddly for a moment as two elderly couples approached. Candice didn't miss the term, noting that good old Thom may not be as understanding as Monica thought he was.

"There the two of you are," one woman greeted. "Wasn't JM just wonderful!" the woman gushed.

"Mom, this is my friend, Candice," Monica said quickly as she released Thom's hand and placed a gentle hand on Candice's shoulder. "Candice, this is Thom's mother, Eunice, and his dad, Roy. And this is my mother and father, Bill and Dotty." Candice exchanged handshakes with everyone, noticing that they seemed a little uncomfortable with the situation. If Monica hadn't had her hand on her shoulder, Candice would have just bolted then and there.

"Hey, why don't we find the rug rat and get some pictures before heading back to my place," Monica said suddenly.

"Sure," Thom nodded. "I'll ride back with you and Jon-Michael," he added as Candice's heart began to pound in her chest. *'Oh goodie! I get to ride back with all three of them.'* She groaned internally while her fake smile remained plastered firmly on her face.

"Actually Thom, why don't you ride with your folks?" Monica suggested casually.

The grimace on his face told Candice and everyone else standing there just what was going on. They all shifted uncomfortably until Thom spoke. "Fine," he muttered. Monica simply nodded as she led everyone out the side door into the hallway. They located Jon-Michael among the hoards of people. Candice wanted to run; only Monica's hand still resting gently on her shoulder encouraged her to stay.

Once the picture taking began, Candice found that she was standing off to the side. She watched as the family posed for the pictures. She wanted to fade into the background as she silently prayed that she would simply disappear. Once things slowed down and the crowd started to fade, Monica helped her son put his jacket on after removing his little costume. "You did good, little man," she said as she kissed her son on the cheek. She stood and held his hand tightly. "Jon-Michael, I want you to meet someone." She led him over to Candice who was leaning nervously against the wall.

The blonde watched fearfully as the tiny boy and his mother approached her. She couldn't help but notice that the rest of the family was watching closely. "Jon-Michael, this is my friend Candice," Monica stated in a soft proud tone. Candice smiled at the gentle tone of her lover's voice as she scooted down so that she wasn't towering over the five-year-old.

"Hello, Jon-Michael. It's very nice to finally meet you," Candice said brightly.

"You're pretty," the boy gushed as he flashed her a very familiar smile.

"Thank you," she laughed along with the others as she stood. She leaned over and whispered in Monica's ear, "The apple doesn't fall far from the tree."

Monica simply wiggled her eyebrows suggestively as they all headed outside. Candice followed behind everyone, wondering if Thom was going to be a problem this evening. Candice waited as Monica strapped her son into the car seat in the back of her SUV. Monica then walked around and opened the passenger side door for her. Candice caught the stern look she received from Thom in his parent's car.

"You have no idea how much I want to kiss you right now," Monica whispered in her ear as she climbed into the vehicle.

"Back at you," Candice said playfully.

"I'm sorry this is so uncomfortable," Monica apologized as she climbed into the driver's seat.

"This is the first time you've brought someone home to meet them, isn't it?" Candice inquired as she peeked in the rearview mirror and watched Jon-Michael playing with a couple of Matchbox cars.

"No one has ever been special enough before now," Monica reassured her as she patted her thigh.

"Thank you," Candice responded sincerely as she fought the urge to just lean over and kiss her lover.

"I'd like to know what's gotten into Thom," Monica grumbled as she started the car.

'Oh, I think I know what the problem is,' Candice thought grimly as Monica carefully drove to her apartment.

PART THREE

Candice managed to relax during the drive to Monica's apartment. She listened as Jon-Michael and his mother chatted endlessly. She even found herself joining in the conversation. At first she had planned on remaining quiet but the little boy's observations were just too endearing.

As they pulled into the parking lot Candice looked around curiously. "So this is where you live," she noted as she looked around the complex.

"For now," Monica confirmed. "I like it, but I want to have a house with a little yard someday."

Candice smiled at the thought as she unbuckled her seatbelt and stepped out of the car. She could picture Monica running around the backyard with Jon-Michael. "Where is everyone else?" She inquired as she looked around the parking lot.

"Thom probably let them in already," Monica responded absently as she attempted to free Jon-Michael from his car seat.

Candice curled her lip at the comment. *'Of course Thom would have a key. He's Jon-Michael's father,'* she reminded herself.

"I can do it," the boy protested as he tried to assist his mother, making her task all that much more difficult.

"Yes, I know that you're a big boy, but let Mommy do it," Monica pleaded. "There you go, tiger." She sighed as she lifted him out of the car. Jon-Michael raced off, carrying his belongings. "Halt," Monica shouted. Her son stopped in his tracks. "Wait for us, sport. You know better than to just run off."

"Oh my," Candice chuckled. "Is he always this energetic?"

"No, today he's calm," Monica said wearily as she took Candice by the hand and escorted her and her son up to the apartment.

The family was busy chatting when they entered. Candice was thankful that everyone was focused on Jon-Michael and his big day. She offered to help Monica in the kitchen; she had hopes for a quick kiss when no one was looking. Unfortunately,

Dotty decided to join them.

"We just need to heat things up," Monica explained as she and Dotty moved around the kitchen.

Candice's heart sank once again, not knowing where anything was or how to assist. Monica gave her a knowing smile. "Candice, could you get me the sauce pan? It's in the cabinet beside the oven."

"You've never been here before?" Dotty inquired thoughtfully.

"No, ma'am," Candice responded respectfully.

"She's a polite one," Dotty teased. "Call me Dotty."

"Behave, Mom," Monica cautioned her mother.

"Not a chance," Dotty taunted her daughter.

"Now I know where you get it from," Candice muttered to Monica.

Candice assisted as best she could as she listened to mother and daughter bicker back and forth. She couldn't get over how they teased one another. "Everything looks to be about ready," Dotty commented as she opened a bottle of wine. "Monica, why don't you start bringing everything out and call everyone to the table," Dotty said firmly.

"Mom, this is my kitchen," Monica objected.

"Yes, but I want a glass of wine before I go out there and I want to pump your new girlfriend for information," Dotty addressed her flatly.

Candice swallowed hard at the thought of being trapped in the kitchen with Monica's mother. "Oh no you don't Mom," Monica protested.

"Go," Dotty shrugged off her daughter's objections. "Candice, pour us some wine."

Candice nervously started to pour the wine as she looked to Monica for help. "Mom, stop now," Monica pleaded.

"Go before everything gets cold again," Dotty chastised her.

"Go ahead," Candice said weakly. "I'll be fine."

She knew that neither woman was going to give in. If they continued with their stalemate, Candice wouldn't get out of there until next Easter. "Good call," Dotty complimented her as Monica reluctantly began to carry trays of food out of the kitchen.

"Nervous?" Dotty inquired as they both took a sip of wine.

"Yes," Candice responded honestly.

"Good," Dotty chuckled. "Relax. I just wanted to talk to you before the others put you through the ringer."

"Oh good," Candice choked out.

"So what do you do for a living?" Dotty inquired gently.

"I'm a phlebotomist," Candice explained, expecting to see the faraway look she usually got when she told people her profession. When it failed to materialize, she felt a little better.

"I would love to make a vampire joke right about now," Dotty chuckled. "I'm certain that you've heard them all."

"At least twice," Candice confirmed. She could never understand why, when she explained that she drew blood for a living, people always joked about it or winced.

"How did you meet Monica?" Dotty continued with her cross-examination.

"She tried to steal my crossword puzzle," Monica said dryly as she reentered the kitchen.

"Borrow," Candice corrected her. "And we shared the paper," Candice asserted firmly.

"Come on, you two. Everyone is already seated," Monica said firmly.

"Just another minute," Dotty protested.

"Enough, Mom," Monica was firm. "Now, go stop Dad from putting salt on his food."

"He isn't," Dotty fumed as she stormed out of the kitchen. "If I've told him once . . . ," she said, the threat hanging in the air as she left the kitchen.

"Thank you," Candice sighed with relief as Monica wrapped her arms around her.

"I'm so sorry," Monica caressed her back gently. Candice looked up and felt her breath catch slightly. Monica lowered her head as Candice leaned up. They found themselves kissing softly.

"Thank you again," Candice said softly as her fingers traced Monica's full lips.

Monica brushed her lips once again before taking her by the hand and leading her out to the dining room. Candice was seated away from Monica but she was happy to simply sit back and listen to the friendly banter. Thom kept looking at her intently. It was the only uncomfortable part of the dinner. Candice managed to field most of the questions directed towards her with relative ease until Bill asked about her family. It was the last thing Candice wanted to think about at the moment. "Actually I don't see my family anymore," Candice responded slowly, fighting against the sadness that crept over her.

An uncomfortable silence descended on the room. Candice was just about to excuse herself when Jon-Michael decided to have his say. "Are you my Mommy's girlfriend?" He inquired innocently as he played with his mashed potatoes. Everyone just stared at her, waiting for her response. Everyone except Monica who was too busy trying to hide the bright crimson color her face had just turned. Candice blinked once and then twice while staring at the little boy who looked just like his mother.

"Yes," Candice responded carefully. "Are you okay with that?"

"Cool," Jon-Michael shrugged. "Can I have dessert now?" He asked his mother who had buried her face in her hands.

The burst of laughter from the adults suddenly filled the room. Even Thom loosened his tie over his son's attitude. "Yes, sport, you can have dessert now," Monica said as she wiped the tears from her eyes. "Thom, why don't you give me a hand with clearing the dishes?"

Candice looked at her lover curiously. Monica simply winked at her as she and Thom began to clear away the dinner dishes.

"Don't worry," Dotty reassured her with a nod. "He's just being called out to the woodshed."

"I don't understand?"

"Our son's manners have been slightly lacking this evening," Roy explained gently. "It's not you or your gender. It's just that this is new to him . . . and to us," Roy conceded. "Someone who might take his place in the house."

"I'm not trying to . . . ," Candice stated, starting to defend herself.

"We know," Eunice added with a warm smile.

Candice felt the weight being lifted ever so slightly. They knew and they understood, which was more than she would ever get from her own parents. But they also conceded that it was a little awkward. "Well, why don't you just mark your territory?" Monica shouted from the kitchen. Thom's response couldn't be heard. Monica's voice continued to rise as Jon-Michael looked around in confusion. "Now go out there and be nice," Monica continued.

"You can't tell me what to do," Thom shouted in response. "We aren't married anymore."

"That's right. We're not," Monica snapped in response.

The rest of the conversation was carried out in softer tones. Thom finally emerged with a tray filled with slices of cake and a forlorn expression. "Are you in trouble, Daddy?" Jon-Michael inquired innocently.

"Yes, I am," Thom confessed as he flashed an apologetic look over to Candice. "No dessert for Daddy tonight."

"Oh," Jon-Michael shrugged as he accepted his own piece of chocolate cake.

"Word of advice - do not piss her off," Thom addressed Candice. "And the toothpaste should always be squeezed from the bottom."

"Good to know," Candice responded, feeling slightly better as he addressed her in a sincere tone.

As the evening progressed Thom's change in attitude proved to be sincere. He and Candice found themselves sitting on the floor playing with Jon-Michael. "Sorry about earlier," he apologized as his son busied himself with his trucks. "I've been obnoxious all week. You know, I dealt with our divorce a long time ago. But . . ."

"She was your wife," Candice finished for him.

"Yeah," Thom conceded. "I dealt with her being gay. Trust me, I would have been just as impolite if you were a man. I just wasn't ready for the possibility of someone else helping to raise my son. "

"I think you're getting a little ahead of yourself," Candice cautioned him, not entirely convinced that her gender wasn't part of the problem.

"Am I?" He said with a shy smile. "Monica would have never let you meet our son if she wasn't getting serious. " He paused for a moment to ensure that their conversation couldn't be overheard. "If you're not thinking along the same lines, then leave her now. I won't see her or my son hurt."

"I am serious," Candice reassured him.

"Good," he sighed with relief. "Just remember to always squeeze the toothpaste from the bottom. Oh, and the toilet paper must face away from the wall."

"How anal is she?" Candice inquire with a mock gasp.

"You have no idea," Thom cautioned her. "But you'll find out," he teased.

"What are you two up to?" The growl that came from behind them made them both jump in fear. Monica stood over them with her arms crossed in front of her body.

"What did I tell you?" Thom squeaked out.

"Our parents are leaving," Monica said as she offered her hand to Candice and assisted the blonde to her feet. "Jon-Michael, I need you to pick up your toys. Then Daddy is going to put you to bed."

"Okay," Jon-Michael agreed as he stood and brushed off his pants. He motioned for Candice to lower her head and gave her a sloppy kiss on the cheek.

Before the youngster could say anything, his grandparents were hugging and kissing him and they said their goodnights. Candice was still surprised by Jon-Michael's kiss. She exchanged farewells with everyone, receiving a big hug from Dotty. Candice was a little taken aback by this woman's enthusiastic show of emotion. "I like you, Candice," Dotty explained as she released her. "So does everyone else. They just need to get used to the idea."

The grandparents made their departure and Thom took Jon-Michael off to get him ready for bed. "I hope you don't mind Thom sticking around to tuck Jon-Michael in?" Monica inquired. "He'll be on duty for the next three days and won't get a chance to see him."

"No worries," Candice responded calmly. "That must have been a tough schedule when you were married."

"The life of a firefighter," Monica said with a sigh. "Three days on then three days off. Honestly, being apart so much is how we stayed married for so long."

"How long were the two of you married?" Candice inquired.

"Seven years," Monica answered. "Thom was my best friend and I thought that was all you needed to make a relationship work. It did work up to a point, until I finally dealt with my sexuality. I think my mother suspected a long time ago that I was batting for the wrong team. I felt like a first class heel when I left him. It hurt him but eventually he was very cool with it. He even fixed me up with women. That's why his behavior over that last few days really surprised me."

"Dating is one thing," Candice pointed out. "But being in a relationship is different. It can't be easy for him."

Monica simply nodded in understanding as she wrapped her arms around the smaller woman. "You look beautiful tonight," the brunette said softly before placing a gentle kiss on her lips. "I can't believe you did this."

"What's that?" Candice asked as she snuggled against Monica's chest.

"Endured the inquisition," Monica laughed. "I know that meeting my son must have been scary enough, but to face the entire clan must have been terrifying."

Candice smiled against Monica's body, enjoying the feel of her chest rumbling as she laughed. "I think my son has a crush on you," Monica teased as Candice relaxed against Monica. "He's usually a little standoffish with strangers."

"And what does his mother think?" Candice prodded as her hands made gentle circles across Monica's back.

"His mother is a very lucky woman," Monica responded in a tender tone as she kissed the top of Candice's head, "with a sink full of dirty dishes." Monica groaned as she stepped slightly away from Candice, holding her hands tightly.

"I'll help," Candice volunteered, not wanting the evening to come to an end.

As they cleaned up the kitchen Candice noticed that Monica seemed to be lost in thought. Candice was lost in a muddle of confusion herself. Although they were playful while they cleaned the kitchen, there was still that electrifying sexual tension engulfing them. *Do I call for a taxi? Do I stay awhile longer? If I'm here in the morning, will that confuse or upset Jon-Michael? Does she want me to stay?* The nagging questions assaulted her mind in rapid succession.

"What's going on in that pretty blonde head of yours?" Monica purred as she dried her hands with the dishtowel. Candice turned and looked up at the woman who, in a word, looked simply amazing. She swallowed hard as her body reacted in the same fashion it had the first time she'd met Monica. Candice recalled how she had seen Monica through the coffee shop window. She reasoned that she needed to get some coffee and the paper so she went in. She couldn't take her eyes off Monica, knowing that there was something else in the coffee house that she needed as well.

Candice felt her nipples harden as she lost herself in Monica's eyes. "I just . . . Uhm . . ," she cleared her throat, unable to complete her sentence. Candice's mind was focused solely on Monica's body and the heat emanating off the other woman. Candice's eyes fluttered shut as Monica lowered her head.

Candice's body reeled as Monica captured her lips. She felt her lover's tongue brush against her lips, pleading for entrance. Candice parted them, inviting her lover in for exploration, not caring that the woman's child and ex-husband were just down the hall. Candice wrapped her smaller body around her lover's as Monica explored the warmth of her mouth.

The blonde's knees felt weak as the kiss quickly deepened. Without warning Monica pulled away slightly. Candice was trembling; she tried to steady herself as she reached out to hold onto her lover. "You can't just kiss me like that and then walk away," she whimpered. Her stomach clenched as her hands trembled.

"Sorry," Monica responded with a shy smile. "But we're not alone," she added in a disappointed tone as she caressed Candice's cheek.

"I know," Candice conceded with a heavy, sigh as she leaned into Monica's touch.

Which brought back the same nagging question that Candice had been debating earlier. *'Should I stay?'* Monica led her back into the living room and they settled onto the sofa. "It's late," Candice finally said with reluctance as she relaxed into her lover's arms.

"Stay," Monica whispered in her ear.

Candice's body trembled as the brunette's breath tickled her ear. "Are you sure?" She managed to ask as she fought off the urge to wrap her body around Monica's.

"Yes," Monica confirmed while placing a kiss on Candice's neck. "But only if you're ready for this," the brunette added in a cautionary tone. "I know that we've spent the night together before, but never here, and never while my son was around."

Candice turned her gaze to her lover. Her heart melted at the look of pure love she was receiving. "I understand," she whispered as she brushed her lips across Monica's firm jaw. "If I'm here in the morning then I better plan on sticking around. And I do. I'm falling for everything about you, including your wonderful son. I'm not going anywhere."

"Thank you," Monica said while her fingers brushed the back of Candice's hand. "Because you've already won my heart."

"But Monica . . . ," Candice began slowly. "I didn't bring any pajamas," she teased with a saucy grin.

"Oh, that is a shame," Monica said as she leered at her. Then her cocky smirk melted away. "I'll need to loan you a T-shirt or something." Candice simply stared at her in confusion. "Sorry, but there's a very strong possibility that Jon-Michael will barge into our bedroom at the crack of dawn."

"Oh!" Candice exclaimed with a blush.

"Are you still certain you want to stay?" Monica asked in a hesitant tone.

"Yes," Candice said firmly. "This is new to me but I just need to learn the ground rules."

"This is new to me, too," Monica laughed in response.

"We'll get through this together," Candice reassured her as she rested her head against her shoulder.   "I like the way you said that." Candice sighed with contentment.

"Said what?" Monica questioned.

"Our bedroom," Candice confessed as she inhaled her lover's scent.

"You do?"

"Yes," Candice confirmed before recapturing Monica's lips.

"So do I," Monica agreed as she returned her kiss eagerly.

The sound of someone clearing their throat alerted the lovers that they were not alone. They blushed as they turned and found Thom standing in the doorway. He had an amused look on his face. Candice could still see the man's discomfort in his eyes. *'We can do this,'* Candice reassured herself. They stood and said their goodnights to Thom who didn't seem eager to leave the two of them alone.

PART FOUR

Monica groaned with relief when Thom finally departed. Candice simply smiled from behind the taller woman.   She wrapped her arms around her lover's slender waist and pressed her body against her. "You smell good," she whispered against the silk of Monica's blouse.   Candice's hands drifted to her lover's hips. She heard her lover moan, as she pressed closer to her. Candice's hands caressed Monica's hips as they began to sway slightly.

Monica captured Candice's wandering hands and wrapped them around her body, holding them tightly against her stomach. The two lovers simply stood there, enjoying the warmth of one another's body. "This is bliss," Candice whispered as she leaned against Monica. Her lover sighed in agreement.

Monica turned slightly to face Candice.   The two women

began kissing gently. With each meeting of their lips, their kisses grew more insistent. Hands began to roam, feeling every inch of the other's body. Candice clung to her lover as her knee pressed against Monica's center. She felt Monica's hands drifting up under the hem of her dress. Candice moaned into her lover's mouth as their tongues engaged in a sensual duel.

Candice's body needed to feel her lover; she needed to pleasure her. The blonde started to unbutton Monica's slacks and lower them down her lover's body. Monica's hands clasped her shoulder in an effort to halt her movements. Candice looked up in confusion. The smoky haze in Monica's eyes sent a jolt directly to her center. "Baby," Monica said in a breathy tone, "we need to go to the bedroom."

Candice nodded in understanding as she lifted herself back up. "Lead on," she said as she took Monica's hands in her own. Monica led her down the narrow hallway; pausing for a moment, she pressed her finger to her lips as she slowly opened one of the doors. Candice watched in sheer wonderment as her lover adjusted the covers over her sleeping child. Candice couldn't stop the smile that emerged.

Everything about that moment was sheer perfection. Never in her life had Candice been so convinced that this was where she needed to be. The thought of entering or disrupting Monica's family had terrified her to the core. Not anymore. Now she welcomed the chance to become apart of this. "I'm the luckiest woman in the world," she confessed quietly as Monica approached her and took her in her arms.

"No, that would be me," Monica said in an equally soft tone.

With one last look back at the sleeping boy, they left his bedroom, closing the door quietly behind them. Monica led Candice further down the hallway. The blonde was relieved that there was some distance between the bedrooms. As they entered Monica's bedroom, Candice could feel her body reacting to the presence of her lover behind her.

Candice's thighs tingled slightly as she heard the door close. Monica wrapped long arms around her body, filling her with a sense of warmth and desire. "I want to make love to you," Monica said, her voice caressing Candice's ear. Candice's mouth went dry as her body hummed with renewed desire.

Her breathing grew ragged as Monica kissed the nape of her neck. She reached back and wrapped her fingers in Monica's long raven tresses. Candice moaned as her eyes fluttered shut. Her lover's mouth and tongue were leaving a fiery trail along her neck as one of Monica's hands cupped Candice's breast.

Monica's body pressed against her, the heat almost overwhelming, as Monica lowered the zipper of her dress. The blonde quivered in expectation. Monica was murmuring soft words against her skin. Candice wanted to turn around and wrap Monica in her arms and make her feel what she was feeling, yet she was helpless to release herself from her lover's embrace. With every touch Candice felt herself sinking further under Monica's spell.

Monica circled Candice's body and cupped her face in her hands. "You have no idea what you do to me, do you?" Monica purred as she slowly guided her lover to the queen-size bed. Candice couldn't speak; she could only follow her lover. "You drive me to the point of complete and utter distraction," Monica continued as she slowly slipped Candice's dress off her shoulders.

"I do that?" Candice said absently as her lover kissed her shoulder, working her way over to her neck. Candice whimpered once again as Monica feasted upon her neck. She tilted her head back, allowing Monica greater access to her milky white skin.

Candice felt herself being lowered onto the bed as her dress slipped further down her body. Monica's body settled next to her own as their lips met once again. Candice began to unbutton the tiny buttons on Monica's blouse as the brunette pushed Candice's dress lower. The blonde's body was burning as they slowly undressed one another, stealing kisses along the way. There was something about the moment that demanded that the lovers take things slowly. "I love you," Candice confessed as her lover removed her bra. Brilliant blue eyes smiled back at her. "I love you too," came the breathy response. Soon their mouths reunited as they continued to undress each other.

Lying side by side as their tongues wrapped around one

another, their hands explored gently, leaving shivers in their wake. Candice trapped Monica's erect nipple between her fingers and rolled it gently as her lover's tongue explored her mouth. Candice moaned deeply as she felt Monica's wetness pressed against her. "You are so beautiful," Candice murmured as she wrapped her body around Monica's.

They kissed deeply again as they began to rock against each other, each teasing the other's aching breasts. Candice's blood was burning as she felt Monica's wetness caress her own. They whimpered as their hands moved in unison to seek out the other's passion. Candice lost herself in the sights and sounds of their lovemaking.

She could feel Monica's clit throbbing against her thumb as she teased it. Monica's fingers dipped into Candice's desire, caressing the slick folds tenderly. The musky aroma of her lover's need assaulted Candice's senses. The blonde plunged her tongue deeper into her lover's mouth as her fingers plunged into Monica's center.

Candice arched in turn as Monica entered her. The lovers rocked against each other slowly as their fingers moved in unison. The sweet waves rolled over them as they continued their steady rhythm. A sheen of sweat covered their bodies as the sweet climax trembled through both women.

Monica rolled Candice onto her back and began to kiss her way down the blonde's body. Candice moaned in pleasure as she felt her lover's mouth working its way down. She groaned as Monica's mouth reversed direction and tasted its way back up Candice's body. The blonde was about to protest when Monica began to feast upon her breasts.

Monica teased one nipple with her teeth and her tongue while her long fingers taunted the other. Their intense passions surged as Monica suckled her harder, moving from one breast to the other and then back again. Candice panted heavily while she pressed her lover's head against her, urging her on. "Oh God," Candice panted as she wrapped her legs tightly around Monica's long body.

The blonde rocked wildly against her lover's firm abdomen

as her breasts were devoured. Monica lifted her head and pressed her body into Candice's. The blonde's head fell back as her lover's fingers pressed against the opening of her center. "Yes," Candice pleaded as she continued to rock against Monica, urging her fingers to enter her.

Monica kissed Candice deeply as she entered her. Candice clung tightly to Monica's broad shoulders as she rocked against her lover's hand. The walls of her center tightened around her lover's fingers as she screamed into the warmth of her mouth. Monica kept pleasuring her as she rolled the taller woman onto her back.   Candice straddled her lover's body as she rocked wildly, offering all of herself to the woman lying beneath her.

She clasped her lover's wrist firmly and held it steady as she climaxed once again. She felt Monica's fingers wiggling inside of her. Candice lifted her body up while maintaining her hold on Monica's wrist. She lifted Monica's hand up to the brunette's mouth. As she watched her lover taste her fingers, Candice lowered her body and nestled between those incredibly long legs.

She drank in the musky scent of her lover. Her mouth watered slightly as her need to taste and pleasure the darker woman pulsated throughout her entire being. "Candice," Monica said with a pleading tone as the blonde kissed the inside of her thighs.

Candice lowered her mouth to her lover's aching center. She wanted to take all that Monica had to offer and give her every part of herself. She slipped her arms under Monica and lifted her wetness to her mouth. Greedily she drank in Monica's sweet nectar. She suckled Monica's clit in her mouth as her lover's mound rocked against her. Candice moaned in ecstasy as she buried herself deeper inside her lover.

She could feel Monica's body rising higher off the bed. She moved quickly so she could hold her steady with one arm as her tongue plunged into Monica's center. Candice felt the walls of Monica's core tightening around her tongue as she dipped in and out. Monica's thighs tightened around her head as she drank in more of her nectar. Monica's screams of pleasure filled the room as she exploded against Candice. The blonde's tongue slipped out of its warm nest and licked her lover's swollen lips. Soon she found herself suckling Monica's clit in her mouth again as she entered her with two fingers. She felt her lover explode once again as she begged her to stop.

Candice sighed contently as she rested her head on Monica's still trembling stomach. "Come here," Monica purred. Candice kissed her way up Monica's long body. She knew by the gleam in her lover's crystal blue eyes that the night was just beginning. Monica drew the smaller woman in for a fiery kiss as she rolled her onto her back. Candice gave herself over to her lover's touch willingly.

Soon Candice found herself on her stomach. Monica's breasts pressed against her back as she kissed her way down Candice's body. Candice trembled, thinking that Monica seemed insistent on tasting every inch of her. She felt her hips being raised as Monica nestled herself behind her. Candice parted her thighs, offering herself up to her lover. She was not disappointed as she felt Monica's mouth on her firm backside.

Monica moved further down until she was drinking in Candice's passion. Candice's body swayed in pleasure as her lover feasted upon her. Candice screamed into the pillow her face was pressed against as she felt Monica's fingers join her mouth. The blonde's hips rocked back, allowing her lover to take her deeper and harder. The explosion ripped through her body as she fell over the edge. Exhausted and sated, she collapsed on the bed. She felt herself being pulled into a warm embrace.

Contentedly the lovers basked in the warm loving feeling of simply holding one another. They didn't' move until they had to put on some clothing. Monica gave Candice a T-shirt that was far too large for her. They climbed under the covers and held each other as they drifted off to sleep.

PART FIVE

The nagging feeling that someone was staring at her awakened the tired blonde. Her emerald eyes blinked open to find Jon-Michael looking at her with a silly grin. "Good morning," she managed to say. She shifted uncomfortably, realizing that her head was resting on her lover's chest. At that moment she was very grateful that Monica had the foresight to insist that they put on some clothing.

"Did you and Mommy have a sleep over?" Jon-Michael inquired innocently.

Candice felt her lover laughing beneath her. "Yes, we did," Candice said as she fought against her own laughter.

"Cool," Jon-Michael smiled. "When's breakfast?"

Candice once again choked back laughter as Monica raised her body. "This kid is always thinking about his stomach," Candice retorted as she snatched up the youngster and began to tickle him. Jon-Michael squealed with delight until Candice halted her assault. She looked over at her lover who was smiling happily at the scene. "So when is breakfast?" Candice inquired eagerly.

"Good morning," Monica smiled at her.

"Good morning," Candice responded, fighting the urge to kiss her lover.

They continued to stare into each other's eyes. "Mom?" Jon-Michael chimed in. "When's breakfast?" He repeated.

"I just need to get some clothes on then I'll cook for both of you," Monica yawned.

"Why don't I take us all out?" Candice suggested. "We can go to the Pancake House."

"Yeah," Jon-Michael screamed.

"I don't know," Monica hesitated. "And take it down a notch, little man."

"Come on, Monica," Candice continued. "You cooked all day yesterday."

"Please, Mom," Jon-Michael pleaded.

"Please?" Candice taunted her as she batted her eyes. She squealed as she felt her lover caress her thigh.

"Okay," Monica conceded as Jon-Michael bounced up and down happily. "Go get washed up and shut the door behind yourself."

The rambunctious youngster scampered off, closing the bedroom door behind him. "Good morning," Monica repeated as she kissed Candice.

The blonde smiled as she eagerly returned the kiss. "We better get cleaned up ourselves," she suggested. "I'm going to need some sweatpants or something." She grimaced.

"You don't have to take us out," Monica said.

"I want to," Candice reassured her.

"I'm going to need to teach him how to knock or get a lock for that door," Monica said thoughtfully as they climbed out of bed.

"No locks," Candice responded. "What if he needs one of us during the night?" Candice swayed slightly when she realized what she had said.

Monica chuckled lightly as Candice settled her nerves. "You okay?" The brunette inquired.

"I will be," Candice reassured her as she wrapped her arms around her lover.

"You think so?" Monica teased. "A five-year-old at a restaurant." She laughed. "Now you're in for some fun."

"Can't wait," Candice replied seriously, knowing that she was where she belonged.

THE END

STRIKE A POSE

PART ONE

Rebecca looked thoughtfully out the window of her south-end apartment. The sun was just beginning to set, casting a golden haze over the city. She sighed deeply as she mentally kicked herself for watching for a woman who wasn't going to appear. "She'll be here," she grumbled. "And even if she doesn't show up, what do I care?" She did care and she hated herself for it.

Still she watched the busy street below and waited for some sign of the woman who had developed a strange hold over her. "Ugh!" She screamed in frustration. "What am I doing? She's not even late yet."

"I have to be the biggest weenie on the planet," she admonished herself as she brushed her short brown locks off her furrowed brow. She then wiped now sweaty palms on her khaki shorts. She couldn't help herself. Tess was coming.

Tess, the model she had hired to sit for her, came every Thursday at 6:30. Rebecca had hired the raven-haired beauty against her better judgment. Tess wasn't what she'd been looking for. But she took one look into those amazing blue eyes and all her common sense went right out the window. She could always hire a different model later. She had to capture this statuesque beauty on canvas.

Unfortunately for Rebecca it wasn't all she wanted. She didn't understand what was wrong with her. Over the years she had painted dozens of beautiful women and her libido never interfered before. There was something about Tess that got to her. Of course she probably shouldn't have asked Tess to pose in the nude. But nudes were her specialty. Rebecca could just kick herself for her lack of control. This had never happened to her before. There was just something about Tess.

Tess had an amazing body and normally that wouldn't be a problem for Rebecca. Something about Tess got under her skin. After their sessions together, Rebecca couldn't wait for the model to leave so she could ease her tension. As she touched herself she pictured what it would be like to touch the raven-haired woman.

A knock on her apartment door brought the young artist out of her musings. Glancing quickly at her watch she found that it was almost 6:30. Her heart began to race as she jumped down from her perch. She started to race towards the door stopped herself so she could steady her breathing. She centered herself and tried to appear normal. Feeling somewhat confident and a little less like a total weenie, she opened the door.

Rebecca felt her heart skip a beat as she was greeted by the vision standing in her doorway. Mustering all her inner strength she smiled up at the woman who stood a good half-foot taller than her. "Hey there," she uttered quickly, hoping that she sound nonchalant.

"Hi, Rebecca," Tess greeted her with a brilliant smile as she stepped into Rebecca's small apartment.

"Everything's set up," Rebecca offered as she closed the front door.

Tess nodded as she stepped into the area that Rebecca used as her studio. While she stepped behind the screen to disrobe, Rebecca felt her mouth go dry as she ran a shaky hand through her hair. Feeling a need to redirect her attention, Rebecca went over to her easel and nervously checked her brushes and paints.

Rebecca finally managed to steady herself just as Tess stepped out clad only in a short red silk robe. "Where do you want me?" Tess asked in her deep sensual voice.

Rebecca chuckled slightly to herself as she thought, *'Oh, if you only knew.'*

"Over there, same as last time," Rebecca instructed her, smiling at her inner thoughts.

"You have a beautiful smile," Tess commented unexpectedly as she disrobed and lounged on the brass bed.

Rebecca felt the blush creeping across her features. She cleared her throat as she watched the object of her affection toss her long black hair back. "Thank you," Rebecca finally managed to say. Shaking her head slightly she cleared the erotic thoughts from her mind. The artist took over as she drank in the view before her.

"You can relax for a little while. The sun's still up," Rebecca explained as she mentally made notes on the scene before her. She had chosen to have Tess pose on her bed underneath the old floor to ceiling window that she convinced her landlord to keep in. She lifted the cloth covering the painting and looked at it. She sighed as she realized that it was almost complete. There was just something missing. She couldn't quite place it . . . but there was definitely something missing.

PART TWO

Rebecca had spent most of the past couple of hours filling in the small details. The work was almost complete except for one element that eluded her. Working on the minor details allowed her thoughts to wander. The moonlight cascading down highlighted Tess' jet-black hair and chiseled features and caused Rebecca's heart to race as she felt her stomach tightening.

"You can relax for a moment," Rebecca said absently. Tess flashed a bright smile at her as she stretched out, loosing her muscles. Rebecca's dark eyes widened at the sight. As she watched the model raised her arms above her head, giving Rebecca a view of the other woman's perfect breasts. *'If I wasn't already gay, I would certainly convert after seeing this,'* she thought as she quickly averted her gaze.

"How's it going?" Tess questioned her.

"Almost finished," Rebecca answered, turning her attention back to the painting.

"Oh," Tess responded with a slight grimace.

"What is it?" Rebecca asked in an effort to make conversation.

"I'll miss sitting for you, that's all," Tess answered with a hint of sadness.

"I'll be happy to recommend you to some other artists," Rebecca replied, knowing that she too was regretting the eventuality. Unfortunately it would probably be tonight.

"That's not what I meant," Tess muttered softly.

Rebecca looked up quickly to see Tess staring out of the window. She could see the model's reflection in the glass and found herself troubled by the dark look on her face. Tess lifted her head slightly, her eyes moving upward. Rebecca followed the path of those beautiful blue eyes. Across the night sky she saw what had captured Tess' attention. The shooting star blazed brightly just before fading into the twilight.

Before she could stop herself she made a wish. *'You, I wish for you, Tess.'* Shaking her head quickly she kicked herself for the frivolous thought. "Fool," she admonished herself. She should have wished for something more important, like world peace.

Tess glanced over at her quickly, a troubled look clearly written on her face. "Not you," Rebecca explained quickly as she flashed a nervous smile. "Me," Rebecca tried to clarify. There was something in the way Tess was looking at her that stopped her.

Grabbing her brush she went to work quickly. "Don't move," Rebecca instructed Tess as she tried to capture the look she was receiving. Rebecca could see it in Tess' eyes, her skin burned from the other woman's gaze. The look she was receiving was pure desire. Her hands took on a mind of their own as she worked, her attention divided between the canvas and the beautiful woman sitting before her.

Unaware of how much time had passed, she kept working

until she knew she had reached that moment . . . nothing more could be done. The work was finished. As she gazed upon it fully for the first time, she gasped as she realized what had always been there. The painting was erotic. There was no other way to describe it. "It's finished," she stammered as her entire being craved the object she had just created.

Finally she managed to look over at the sullen model. Tess hung her head slightly. Rebecca felt a slight chill run through her as the model refused to look up. "I guess that's it, Tess," Rebecca finally managed to say.

"What was it before?" Tess asked solemnly.

"What?"

"Before, when you called yourself a fool," Tess muttered. "What were you talking about?"

"Oh, that," Rebecca responded casually, trying not to let the other woman know what she was feeling. "It's silly."

"Tell me."

"Well, I saw a shooting star . . . ," Rebecca began slowly as she tried to choose her words carefully. She didn't want to lie but she certainly wasn't prepared to tell Tess the honest truth. " . . . I made a wish. It just kind of slipped out and it was, well, silly."

"Oh," Tess smiled slightly, finally looking up at the artist. "I did the same thing."

"Really?"

"Yeah." Tess chuckled slightly. "So we're done then?"

"Yes," Rebecca answered. "Would you like to see it?"

PART THREE

Rebecca's breathing ceased momentarily as she watched Tess' beautiful form rise up off the bed. Tess seemed to float across the room. Her nipples grazed Rebecca's arm as she stepped past her. Rebecca inhaled sharply as her eyes fluttered shut. "Oh my," Tess breathed out.

Slowly, her nerves on edge, Rebecca opened her eyes and turned towards the model. She hadn't stopped to think when she gave Tess the chance to look at her work. Tess was seeing for the first time how Rebecca saw her. Rebecca swallowed hard, unable to read the other woman's expression.

"It's so passionate," Tess finally said with bright smile.

Rebecca blew out a breath as she relaxed. "For a minute there I was afraid that you'd be offended." Rebecca said.

"Not at all," Tess said quietly as she turned towards Rebecca.

Before she realized what was happening, she felt two perfect lips press against her own. She didn't stop to think. Allowing her body and desire to take over, she returned the taller woman's kiss. Running her fingers through the long raven hair that she had been dreaming about, she pulled Tess in. Someone moaned but neither was certain who it was. Rebecca could feel the gentle tickling of Tess' tongue.

Without hesitation she parted her lips and granted Tess entrance. The kiss deepened as their bodies pressed together. Rebecca felt Tess' thigh pressing between her legs. As she opened herself up for the model she could feel Tess' wetness kiss her own bare thigh.

Their bodies melted together as Tess began to unbutton Rebecca's blouse. Feeling the need to breathe, Rebecca pulled away slightly as long certain fingers freed her from her bra. "This is what I wished for," Tess whispered hotly in the artist's ear. Rebecca's head was spinning as she felt her clothes being removed. Her hips moved in rhythm against Tess' body.

Rebecca's body began to tremble as Tess kissed her neck. Trailing delicate nips down the artist's throat, she worked her way steadily to Rebecca's cleavage. Rebecca squeaked incoherently as her mind to tried to process the sensations and wondered just when she had become topless.

"Wait . . . ," she gasped. Her body seemed to be driving on pure lust.

Tess lifted her head quickly and gave Rebecca a fearful look. "I . . . thought . . . ," Tess stammered.

"Yes . . . ," Rebecca managed to pronounce, " . . . just . . . weak . . . . afraid . . . of . . . falling . . ."

"Was that a sentence?" Tess teased with a bright smile.

Tess gasped as she felt Rebecca's small hand cupping one of her breasts. "Bed," Rebecca said firmly. Tess bit her lip and led the artist by the hand over to the waiting bed. Tess lowered the artist. Rebecca could feel Tess' eyes on her as she in turn allowed herself to drink in the taller woman's beauty. Tess' fingers began to trace every inch of Rebecca's flesh.

Rebecca bit her lip as her breathing became ragged. Long black hair hung down to gently tickle her as Tess lowered her head and captured a nipple with her tongue. As Tess teased the already erect nipple, Rebecca's hips shot up to press against Tess' nakedness.

Rebecca's back arched as Tess continued to tease her by sucking her nipple while strong hands removed her shorts. Clad only in her panties, the artist ran her hands along the back of the woman resting on top of her.

Rebecca began to grind her hips against the woman with urgency. Tess lifted her head and blue eyes captured hers. "Don't you want to take this slow?" Tess asked her as fingers felt their way down Rebecca's stomach. Rebecca stared at her in shock as she shook her head in a negative manner. "Good," Tess chuckled as she slipped her fingers under the waistband of Rebecca's underwear.

"Later," Rebecca suggested as she mimicked Tess' actions. As her fingers slid along silky folds, she was pleased to find that the model was just as wet as she was. Her body ached for more as Tess' thumb teased her clit. Each woman opened herself up further to the other.

They both groaned as they entered one another. Fingers gently felt the other's passion growing, building a steady rhythm as they pressed against each other tightly. They kissed deeply as their bodies rocked wildly. Rebecca could feel herself losing control as her body began to shudder. Her head thrown back, she cried out as Tess increased her pace. Unable to focus on pleasing the model, she allowed the dark-haired woman to take over.

She tried to breathe as she felt Tess kissing her way down her body, teasing every inch of her exposed flesh with her teeth and tongue. Rebecca's hips lifted off the mattress as her eyes shut. She found herself screaming out once again. Tess slowed her movements as Rebecca tried to regain her ability to speak.

As she felt her breathing begin to steady, she could feel her underwear being removed.

Tess kissed her way back up the artist's firm legs. Rebecca could feel Tess opening her thighs and was too weak to protest. A warm breath blowing gently across her curls sent a spasm through her being. Her body arched as Tess' tongue tasted her. "You're trying to kill me," Rebecca managed to gasp out as Tess took her deeper. Her tongue licked and teased, tasting all of her passion.

Tess began to stroke her already sensitive clit. Rebecca felt her world spinning and a strange buzzing in her ears as Tess feasted upon her wetness. Her body was covered in sweat as Tess took her harder and deeper. Rebecca found herself climaxing quickly this time, her body arching as Tess continued to pleasure her. Rebecca collapsed upon the bed. Finally she pulled away from Tess. "You are trying to kill me," Rebecca choked out.

"Never," Tess answered honestly as she climbed up next to the exhausted artist and pulled her into a tender embrace. As they held one another, Rebecca felt like she was a part of Tess.

After a few moments Tess kissed the top of Rebecca's head. "So what did you wish for?" she asked quietly.

"Give me a glass of water and a moment to breathe and I'll show you," Rebecca volunteered brightly.

THE END

QUEEN OF HEARTS

PART ONE

Regina was beyond angry as she approached the downtown apartment house. Pete had called her in the middle of the night to ask her to schlep all the way down there to pick him up. She was once again questioning what the heck she was doing with this jerk. Pete wasn't a bad guy and her mother liked him but he was forever pulling stunts like this. Truthfully, she had been ready to end things for a long time.

It wasn't anything he did it was her. Regina was trying to figure out just how to tell him without actually saying *'It's not you, it's me'*. It sounded like a cliché but it was the truth. She cared for Pete but she had feelings that, no matter how hard she tried, she could not exorcise from her spirit. Of course, Pete wasn't helping his cause any by calling up drunk, asking her to drag herself downtown in the middle of the night.

She had worked late and was looking forward to having the apartment to herself for a change. Pete was playing poker with the boys. Running her fingers through her short blonde hair, she grumbled, angrier with herself than with Pete. Aggravated, she pushed the buzzer and was buzzed in.

Stomping up the staircase, she kicked herself the one-hundredth time for settling for the first guy she felt comfortable with. She knocked on the apartment door and was greeted by someone who was most definitely not one of the boys. The woman stood several inches above her five foot four inch frame. "Hi, Pam," Regina smiled at the woman, her demeanor suddenly brightening.

Regina had always liked Pam. In fact, she had a crush on the taller woman. Like the rest of the guys at the poker game, Pam worked with Pete down at Comtrel. They were all computer geeks but sweet just the same. Regina had noticed Pam from the first moment she laid eyes on her. Not only was she the sole woman in the department, she was also drop dead gorgeous.

Granted, most people with a pulse ended up with a crush on Pam but Regina was uncomfortable with it. She had been down this road before and it never ended well. On top of that, she was in a relationship. Pete mistook Regina's reaction to Pam as jealousy even though she had been quite honest about some of her past experiences.

Regina swallowed hard as she found herself trapped in an intense blue gaze. "Oh Pete," Pam called out in a deep tone that Regina was captivated by. Regina stepped in shyly as she stole an appreciative glance at the beautiful woman before her. She ducked her head to hide the blush that was now creeping across her face.

Movement within the living room caught her eye, jolting her back to where she was. She recognized everyone in the small group of Pete's buddies from work. For some reason they were stepping away from Pete who was looking down at the floor. As Regina approached her soon-to-be ex-boyfriend, she felt like Moses parting the Red Sea. She couldn't help but notice that everyone stepped aside as she approached him and not one of them would look her in the eye.

"Jeez, how much money could he have lost?" She teased, finally realizing why she had been summoned downtown in the middle of the night. No one answered as Pete continued to stare at the floor.

"My paycheck," Pete finally muttered.

"Okay, so you're an idiot," Regina laughed as she quietly noted that it was high time to get out of this so-called relationship. She had other reasons as well, but for the most part it came down to the simple fact that she was unhappy with Pete.

"That's not all he lost," Bob, Pete's best friend, offered quickly.

Regina watched as everyone looked everywhere but at her. Pete continued his fascination with the carpeting. "Out with it," Regina demanded with a heavy sigh. "How much do I owe and to whom?"

Regina began to feel uncomfortable as she was greeted by an eerie silence. "Pam," Bob offered weakly. "I guess you owe Pam."

"No, she doesn't," the taller woman blurted out. "Look, he was drinking. I didn't think he was serious; none of us thought he was serious. We just accepted his bet to shut him up."

"It's true," Bob confirmed as the others nodded their heads.

Regina could tell that they were sincere but there was definitely something amiss. "Pete, how much?" She inquired carefully.

"It wasn't money," Pete stammered in embarrassment.

"Well, just what did you bet?" Regina inquired as she noticed everyone in the room slowly inched towards the front door. The group included Dave, which was odd since it was his apartment. Continued silence met with more inching towards the doorway. Granted, she was upset when she arrived but she had never given anyone in the room any reason to be afraid of her. *'Whatever Pete lost in the game must be a big deal. Yet no one seems in a hurry to collect.'* She eyed the nervous crowd carefully and then turned her attention back to Pete, catching his glance in Pam's direction. "Pete, just tell me what it is," Regina encouraged him. "Besides, Pam seems to be willing to let you off the hook."

"That's right, Pete," Pam asserted. "I told you that when I won the pot."

"There, you see," Regina smiled as she relaxed slightly. "Okay Pete, get your stuff together and we'll get going."

"Okay," Pete looked up, still not meeting Regina's gaze. Everyone seemed to relax now that she had let Pete off the hook.

Regina found herself chuckling at Pete's dilemma. "Well, whatever it was must have been a lulu," Regina addressed Pam and Bob who were the only people close to her. Regina felt the mood become tense once again. Everyone shuffled and looked around the apartment. "Guys, what did Pete put into the pot?" There was no response as the tension intensified.

Finally, Bob and Pam inched slightly closer to Regina. She could see that both of them looked very uncomfortable. "Trust me, Regina. No one took him seriously but, after he lost, he called you before we could stop him," Bob tried to explain. "Look, he's drunk."

"What did you bet?" Regina demanded in an incredulous tone.

"You," Pete finally confessed, meeting her eyes for the first time.

PART TWO

There was a mad dash for the doorway as everyone tried to leave with the exception of Regina and the soon-to-be-dead Pete. "Everyone freeze!" Regina yelled angrily. The group of card players stopped dead in their tracks. "Let me see if I understand this correctly," she stated, her green eyes blazing brightly. "You pack of lowlifes bet on who would win *ME?*"

They all stammered, stuttered, and otherwise protested the accusation. Regina looked around and she knew that, although they weren't the most honorable group, the rats were telling the truth. Pete had gotten drunk, run out of money, and used her as a poker bet, thinking he had a winning hand. "Enough!" She finally bellowed over their protests of innocence. No one in the room could fathom the depth of anger and relief she was experiencing.

Slipping the car keys off her key ring, she tossed them at

Pete. "The car is yours. Have one of your friends drive you over to the apartment to pick up your things," she said coldly before offering him a single digit salute. "You," she addressed Pam who was running a shaky hand through her long raven hair. "Could you give me a lift?"

"Huh?" Pam responded in a shocked tone while looking like a deer caught in headlights.

"The car belongs to dumb ass," Regina scowled. "I need a ride, besides you did win me." Regina snorted at her predicament.

"Regina?" Pete squeaked.

"Don't talk to me," Regina snapped. "You put me up as a stake in a card game. It's over." Regina glared at Pete, as he just stood there dumbfounded, his jaw hanging down. Pam grabbed her keys and wallet while still looking a little frightened of the tiny blonde. Once outside Pam turned to her with a fearful gaze.

"Look Reggie . . . I . . . ," Pam began uneasily.

"I know," Regina responded in exasperation. "I could tell that you guys were being straight with me in there. No pun intended."

"Ha ha," Pam responded dryly, relaxing a little. "So, where to?"

"I have no idea," Regina answered sadly. "I just know that I don't want to go back to my apartment tonight."

"Look, why don't you crash at my place for the night?" Pam offered. "It's small but you can have the couch."

"Thanks, Pam," Regina smiled slightly with relief.

They made their way across town to Beacon Hill, neither of them speaking until after they were inside Pam's studio apartment. "Not much, but it's home," Pam announced as she tossed her keys onto the already cluttered coffee table.

"Thanks," Regina said softly.

"I'll get some sheets for the sofa," Pam offered.

"I can't believe that he bet me in a poker game," Regina reflected in disgust. "If I didn't want out before, I sure as hell do now."

"Maybe I should get us some wine?" Pam suggested as she

ducked into the kitchenette to allow Regina some degree of privacy.

Pam returned with a large bottle of white zinfandel and two glasses. Regina had taken off her shoes and settled down on the sofa. "I hope this okay," Pam said. "You look like you could use it. I know I can. I wasn't drinking earlier but after watching that scene . . . sorry."

"Why are you apologizing?" Regina laughed lightly as Pam handed her a glass of wine. "Truth is, it's been coming for some time now. I just can't believe he would do something so slimy."

"He was drinking a lot and he's not use to it," Pam tossed in as she sat next to Regina and poured herself a glass of wine. "You know, when the words came out of his mouth, none of us could believe what he had said."

PART THREE

Pam was starting to relax. The events of the evening had certainly thrown her for a loop. She was shocked when Pete offered up Regina as a wager. Even though she was appalled by the offer, a part of her was a little giddy at the thought. Pam had always had a crush on the petite blonde. In fact, she had been more than a little surprised to learn that Regina was Pete's girlfriend. Her gaydar had been on full alert the first time she spotted her at the company Christmas party more than two years ago.

Now this woman, who had been the featured player in more than one of her late night fantasies, was sitting in her apartment sipping wine. "I'm sorry about what happened tonight," Pam offered sincerely.

"Like I said, it's been coming," Regina reasserted. "Pete's a good guy and, in all honesty, this is the first time he's done anything this cruel. Should I ask what he was holding?"

"A full house," Pam said. "Jacks and tens."

"That's a good hand," Regina mused as she sipped her wine. "What did you have?"

"The same," Pam smiled slightly. "Only my hand was queens and kings. I tried to warn him not to bet something he wasn't willing to loose." Pam felt herself tensing up, afraid that she had suddenly revealed too much.

"I guess I wasn't worth holding onto," Regina muttered bitterly.

"No," Pam protested. "He's an idiot."

Regina smiled up at Pam, feeling a familiar jolt run through her. Pam felt it as well, and not for the first time either. "I'm sorry I didn't . . . ," Pam stammered, tearing her eyes away from the intense gaze directed at her.

"Why?" Regina questioned as she reached out and started to gently rub Pam's forearm.

"Nothing," Pam lied as she focused on her libido in check.

"You want to hear something funny?" Regina offered in an effort to keep the conversation going. "I never planned on living with him."

"What?" Pam asked curiously.

"He was in between apartments," Regina explained. "He asked if he could crash at my place for a couple of days until he got settled. He just never left."

"You're kidding?" Pam laughed at the situation.

"No," Regina laughed at herself. "The sad part was that I was about to break up with him right before he moved in."

"Wow," Pam said as she began to ponder what Regina had said. A part of her silently wished that perhaps, now that she was single, Regina would consider her.

"Yeah," Regina sighed as she snuck another look at the woman sitting next to her. "I started seeing him when I was on the rebound. I was seeing someone for a few months, but I knew that she wasn't as serious as I was. Plus, I could never tell my family about her."

Pam sputtered as she almost spit her wine across the room. "Excuse me?" Pam choked out as she stared at Regina with disbelief.

"You seem surprised," Regina chuckled, not knowing why she had chosen to reveal something she hadn't shared with anyone.

"Not really," Pam lied. "I just assumed that, well . . . you know, you have a boyfriend. . ."

"Uh huh," Regina responded, feeling more than a little warmth from sitting so close to Pam. "I had a few experiences with women, some mild flirtations in high school and more experimentation in college. I thought Shelia was something special, but in the end I guess I wasn't special to her."

"Another idiot," Pam said sincerely as she tried to process her newfound knowledge. "Wait a minute. I'm beginning to think that you've slept with more women than I have," Pam teased, hoping to hide her increasing curiosity.

PART FOUR

Regina was enjoying the way the evening was turning out. She had dumped Pete and now she was trying to let Pam know that she was definitely interested in women. It was something she fought for a long time but, at this moment with Pam, the battle was most definitely lost. Regina knew Pam was gay since she was far from being in the closet. She'd had many a fantasy about this tall dark haired beauty.

They sat, each lost in their own thoughts, unaware that they were flowing in the same direction. They turned to one another at the same moment and found themselves locked in an intense gaze. Before either realized it, their lips met. The first kiss was shy but full of promise. Regina wanted to pinch herself, not quite certain that it had happened at all. She drank in Pam's beauty and found herself drawn in again.

The second kiss ignited the passion within. It quickly deepened. Regina felt overwhelmed from the heat, her senses reaching the breaking point. Before she could think, her tongue brushed Pam's lower lip. Her body throbbed as Pam opened her mouth, granting her entrance. Regina began a gentle exploration of Pam's mouth. A soft moan greeted her as her hand wandered up and gently cupped Pam's breast.

They broke away gasping for air. Pam shivered as Regina's

fingers continued their exploration. Her nipple hardened from Regina's touch. "Don't," Pam gasped and Regina halted her movements. She looked up with concern, fearful that she had gone too far. "I just want to know . . ." Pam gasped, her features flushed with passion, " . . . this isn't about getting even with him."

"NO," Regina vowed sternly. "I've thought about you, more than I should have. You're beautiful, smart, sexy . . . ."

Her words were cut off as Pam's lips met hers and began a passionate kiss. "Good," Pam whispered huskily as she allowed her hands to roam across Regina's back. Inspired by the sensual kiss, Regina's hands slipped under Pam's t-shirt. She needed to feel this woman. The kiss ended as they both yielded to the need for breath. "You thought about me?" Pam inquired as her fingers gently traced Regina's jaw line. Her own passion increased as she felt Regina shudder lightly from her touch.

"Yes," Regina moaned, her body trembling from Pam's touch. She was drawn back to Pam's lips and began kissing her eagerly. She pushed Pam back onto the sofa as her lips wandered from Pam's lips to her jaw line and down to her throat. Shaking from the intensity, she looked up and found herself lost in a haze of crystal blue. "I belong to you," she offered huskily. "You won me."

"I . . . ," Pam began but she suddenly lost the ability to speak coherently. The woman she had been fantasizing about had just offered herself to her.

"You won me," Regina asserted. "Make me yours."

PART FIVE

The offer was too much for Pam to refuse. Sitting up, she lifted Regina so that she straddled her lap. She kissed Regina once again, this time in a possessive manner. Gently biting Regina's lower lip, Pam's hands fondled Regina's breasts. She could feel the smaller woman's nipples becoming erect. Her fingers slowly undid the buttons of Regina's blouse. Regina moaned as she pressed herself harder into Pam's body.

Their hips began to grind together in a sensual rhythm as Pam tugged the now unbuttoned blouse from Regina's body. She kissed and tasted Regina's neck and shoulders as her fingers unhooked the clasp of Regina's bra. Pam tossed the offending garment across the room. "Pam . . . please . . . ," Regina begged.

Pausing for a brief moment, Pam slid Regina off her lap and stood. Holding her hand out to Regina, she silently requested her to follow. Regina took Pam's hand tightly and followed her the few steps over to the corner where the big brass bed was located. Pam licked her lips, trembling slightly at the thought that she was going to do exactly what Regina had asked her to do.

Regina stepped into Pam's embrace and held her tightly. "Is this what you want?" Pam asked gently.

"Yes," Regina asserted. "This might be the only time we're together. Tomorrow we'll probably blame it on the wine or whatever. For tonight I belong to you."

Pam allowed her hands to roam freely over Regina's exposed breasts. Inspired by the goose bumps she felt beneath her touch, she began to explore further. Lowering her hands, she toyed with the waistband of Regina's blue jeans. Her eyes never broke contact with the blonde standing half naked before her. Pam unbuttoned the jeans and lowered the zipper before kneeling in front of Regina. Kissing her stomach, her tongue tasted Regina's skin as she began to lower the jeans.

Regina tilted her head back. Her senses were in overdrive as she kicked off her shoes. Pam disrobed Regina, tossing the garments across the room. Her fingers tenderly slipped between the smaller woman's lower lips. Her head spun as she felt the wetness and took in the scent of Regina's passion. She looked up to see Regina's head tilted back, her eyes closed.

Pam stood, her fingers caressing Regina's exposed body. "Undress me," she requested. Regina groaned upon hearing Pam's request. Opening her eyes, she saw her own desire reflected in Pam's eyes. She ran her fingers through the thick hair and pulled Pam's head down. She kissed the woman with all the intensity she possessed. She heard a moan escape from the taller woman.

Regina tugged at the t-shirt Pam was wearing and began to

pull it up. Pam broke away from the kiss and raised her arms so Regina could remove the shirt.   Regina licked her lips as she drank in the sight of Pam reaching behind herself to remove her bra.   She allowed herself a moment to gaze upon Pam's half naked body.   Without realizing it, Regina's hands began an exploration of Pam's breasts.

Pam ran her fingers through Regina's short blonde tresses and guided her towards a breast.   Regina eagerly accepted the offer as her tongue snaked out to taste the beautiful nipple. They moaned in unison as Regina began to suckle Pam's breast. Their bodies pressed together as hands touched the other freely.

Pam stepped back slightly and started to unbutton her jeans. Regina simply watched as the taller woman removed the rest of her clothing. "So beautiful," Regina whispered hungrily.

"Yes, you are," Pam said as Regina blushed.   Taking the smaller woman's hand once again, Pam sat down on the bed. Pam placed her hands on the smaller woman's shoulders and guided her to kneel before her.   Regina knelt willingly between Pam's thighs and ran her fingers along the inside of them.

Pam shivered slightly as she leaned back on her palms. Regina lowered herself further so she could inhale the sweet scent of Pam's passion.   Her tongue reached out to taste Pam's inner thighs, kissing them sweetly as Pam ran fingers through her hair. Unable to resist any longer, Regina tasted her.

Pam gasped as Regina slowly increased the rhythm. Looking down she felt her heart stop as she saw the woman of her dreams nestled sweetly between her legs. She opened herself up further as by moving closer to the edge of the bed and Regina's mouth. Regina's tongue teased her opening and finally entered her. Pam groaned as Regina took her with her tongue. Regina slowed as she moved her attention to Pam's now throbbing clit.

Regina began to suckle Pam's clit with enthusiasm as Pam gripped the bedding and the back of Regina's head tightly. "Oh God . . . yes . . . Oh my . . . ," Pam cried out. Regina entered Pam with her fingers as she continued to love her with her tongue. Feeling the crest overcome her, Pam let go, screaming out to every deity she could think of. Her body trembled as Regina continued to pleasure her. Pam collapsed back on the bed as she came once again. She was amazed that the smaller woman showed no signs of stopping. Pam pulled away, begging for mercy. "Hold on . . . I can't breath," she gasped.

Still kneeling before Pam, Regina just smiled up at her. "Come here," Pam requested as she held her arms open. Regina crawled in next to her and snuggled up against her. Pam kissed her tenderly as she rolled the smaller woman over onto her back. Looking down at her, Pam thought she had never seen anything so beautiful.

"I belong to you," Regina reminded her. "Don't you want to collect your winnings?" She wiggled her eyebrows suggestively.

"Oh yeah," Pam purred as her hand slowly felt it's way down Regina's abdomen. Her fingers dipped into Regina's wetness. Teasing at first, she ran one finger along the slick folds then she lowered her head and captured Regina's breast in her mouth. Pam teased Regina's nipple with her tongue and her teeth as her fingers entered the beauty lying beneath her.

Pam pressed against Regina as the smaller woman's body arched. Pam's thumb began to tease Regina's throbbing clit as they rocked together wildly. "Take me!" Regina begged. Pam slowed her movements slightly. Regina looked up, seeing a wicked gleam in the brunette's blue eyes. Pam slid her fingers from Regina's wetness and tasted her fingers. Regina watched as Pam licked her fingers clean. "You're stopping?" She asked in an exasperated growl.

Pam chuckled wickedly. "Not a chance." Her words sent deep shivers through both of them. "Roll over," she said. Regina gasped then simply nodded and turned over onto her stomach, raising her backside up. Pam slowly ran her hands over Regina's bare back until she was rubbing the smaller woman's well-defined backside. Regina found herself spreading her legs as Pam pressed her body against her.

Regina's body responded by pushing into the taller woman. Feeling the wetness pressing against her, she began to rub herself into the woman on top of her. Breasts pressed against her back as fingers began to explore her wetness. Regina opened herself up further, silently requesting Pam to enter her. "You belong to me," Pam repeated as she entered her new lover, gliding in and out with an increasing rhythm as her thumb once again circled Regina's throbbing clit. "Yes," Regina moaned as Pam began to ride her.

The pair seemed to melt into each other as their bodies continued to ride the waves of their passion. "Fuck . . . ," Pam growled as she stroked Regina in a quickened pace. "Oh . . God . . you feel so good . . . ."

She could feel her lover reaching the brink. She began to ride the smaller woman's backside wildly as she neared ecstasy. They screamed out wildly as they climaxed together. Collapsing onto the bed, they found themselves unable to move.

Finally Pam managed to roll off the smaller woman and Regina curled up in her arms. Exhausted, they held onto each other, neither wanting to think past that moment. Their breathing steadied as they clung to each other. Neither was certain who touched who first but once again they found themselves kissing and touching. Sleep eluded them that evening and well into the following day as they allowed themselves to finally live out their fantasies.

PART SIX

Regina looked around the house once more.

"The owner is pleased with your offer. It's just up to the bank now," Samantha said to her.

"I don't think we'll have any problems." Regina had felt confident after talking to the loan officer this morning.

"I think the two of you will really like the neighborhood," Samantha offered. "My partner and I live a few blocks away."

"Really?" Regina smiled at the thought.

"I met her when she was house shopping," Samantha smiled at the memory. "So how did the two of you meet?"

"I won her in a card game," came the sultry response from behind the two women.

They turned to find Pam grinning from the doorway. "Excuse me?" Samantha asked in a curious tone. Regina blushed at the memory.

"It's a long story," Regina chuckled. "Our start was unusual to say the least and it wasn't smooth sailing in the beginning."

"Queens over jacks," Pam teased lightly. "Works every time. That was the bank," Pam explained as she waved her cell phone. "They said yes."

Regina rushed over and hugged her lover of the past four years. "Queens over jacks," she whispered in Pam's ear.

THE END

DEUCES ARE WILD
(QUEEN OF HEARTS - PART TWO)

PART ONE

Pam shifted in her sleep, as something happened to disrupt it. Something very nice was happening. "Baby," a voice purred softly in her ear. "Pam sweetie." She felt a warm tongue dip into her ear. Pam's passion stirred as her lover's naked body pressed against her own. The persistent yapping coming from downstairs clued the sleepy programmer in to the true nature of the morning's seduction.

"I'm not walking the dog," Pam grunted as she pulled Regina closer to her.

"Please," the little blonde begged as she began to nibble on a sensitive earlobe.

Pam ran her hands down Regina's naked back, enjoying the feel of her lover's skin tingling beneath her touch. "No way," she grunted as she cupped Regina's firm backside. She squirmed in pleasure as she heard the soft moan escape from her lover. Knowing fingers captured one of her nipples and began to roll it playfully. Pam's bright blue eyes flew open as she gasped in pleasure. "You don't play fair," she panted as Regina continued to suckle her neck.

"Baby, it's cold outside," Regina whimpered as her fingers

continued to tease Pam's aching nipple. Regina was driving Pam to the brink of insanity. All Pam wanted at that moment was to ravish the blonde until she screamed out her name.

"You wanted to get a puppy," Pam protested as she pressed her thigh against Regina's center. "God, you are so wet," she choked out.

"You can have your way with me," Regina taunted her as her hips began to ride Pam's thigh. "After you take Aloysius for his walk," Regina insisted as she pulled away from Pam's body. "And you wanted to get a puppy too," the feisty blonde reminded her as she wagged her finger at Pam.

"His name is Full House," Pam protested as she rolled out of bed.

"You are not naming him that," Regina groused as she rolled over and wrapped herself up in the bed covers.

"Why not?" Pam whined as she pulled on a pair of sweatpants. "It's sweet and romantic." Pam pouted as she continued to throw on warm clothing.

"No, it's not," Regina chuckled. "I know you won me in a poker game. But I really don't want the rest of the world to know it. It's a little embarrassing. Now get moving before your son piddles all over the kitchen floor."

"Well, we are not calling him Aloysius. The other dogs will pick on him," Pam grunted as she left their bedroom. Despite the familiar argument Pam was smiling. She knew that Regina would probably be sound asleep when she returned. "Paybacks." She chuckled merrily to herself.

As Pam entered their kitchen, the sight of the new puppy dancing happily in his little area of the kitchen greeted her. They'd gated him in, knowing that if they let him loose before he was properly trained there was going to be some disgusting stains gracing their new home.

"Hey, sweetie," she cooed as she watched the little golden puppy hop up and down. He was nothing but ears and feet. Pam unhooked his gate. The puppy instantly jumped on her, licking every part of her face the little guy could reach. "Look! Your papers are dry," she said proudly as she hooked the leash on his collar. "You are such a good boy," she said warmly as she scratched behind his ears.

　　She grabbed her coat and some plastic bags and other items that she would need to properly clean up after the little guy. The cold February morning chilled the tall brunette to the bone. She smiled as she allowed the puppy to lead her through the neighborhood. It was hard to believe that she was living in the suburbs with her partner. The way the two women had begun their relationship was unorthodox to say the least.

PART TWO

　　It had all started with a friendly game of cards with the guys from work. Pam never suspected that it would lead to her falling hopelessly in love. She'd had a crush on the small blonde for a long time, but Regina was the girlfriend of one her co-workers. And not just any co-worker - Pete was one of Pam's male co-workers. The entire situation made Regina completely off limits. Pam almost fell out of her chair that night when a drunken Pete offered Regina as a stake in the poker game.

　　She thought that Pete was a complete jackass for even suggesting such a thing. In fact she told him as much in less than ladylike language. But he was persistent about making the wager. "Never bet anything you aren't willing to loose," Pam muttered in remembrance as she continued to walk the puppy. "You certainly lost big time that night, Pete." *Even though she and the others finally accepted Pete's wager, no one had planned on collecting. Of course when Regina found out, she kicked Pete's sorry ass to the curb right then and there.*

　　Regina went home with Pam that night. They shared a night of incredible passion that was followed by an awkward morning after. The persistent beeping of her alarm clock woke Pam. She felt the warmth emanating from the naked body lying on top of her and smiled as she kissed the top of Regina's head. She was still smiling as a pair of emerald eyes fluttered open. Pam's smile quickly vanished when she caught the look of uncertainty that flashed across Regina's face.

　　Regina climbed out of bed quickly and began to dress.

Pam's heart broke as her offer to make coffee was politely refused. Regina called for a taxi and was gone. Pam felt miserable even though she'd suspected that this would happen. Regina had said the night before that they would probably just blame it on the wine. Pam almost called in sick to work, but she knew that would just cause more talk. She had to face the guys. Mostly importantly, she had to face Pete.

By mid-afternoon Pam was regretting her decision to show up for work. Pete was blocking the doorway of her cubicle as he begged her to help him get Regina back. She felt incredibly guilty knowing that she'd slept with his girlfriend. She was also very angry with the hung over programmer.

"Come on, Pam. Help me out," Pete whined.

"Why should I?" Pam snarled as she tried to ignore the willowy man who leaned over her in the narrow cubicle. "God, didn't you shower this morning?" she said, noting the offensive odor and the fact that he was still wearing the same clothes from the previous evening.

"No, I sat up all night waiting for Regina to come to her senses," Pete explained quickly. "I assume she crashed at your place."

"Yes," Pam hissed as she tugged on the collar of her turtleneck. It was a little warm for the outfit, but the last thing she needed was for everyone to see the large purple mark Regina had left on her neck. "Pete, she kicked you out. Why were you there?"

"Come on. It's a misunderstanding," Pete babbled on.

"A misunderstanding?" Pam spat out. "You used her as a bet in a poker game and lost. Besides, I don't think she was happy with your relationship before that."

"Oh, things were fine," Pete scoffed. "What did she say?" he asked in a quieter tone.

"Go away," Pam hissed as she stood. Rising to her full height, she stood toe to toe with the little weasel. "I'm not going to help you. If you want her back then you need to talk to her."

"You're right," Pete finally conceded. "Wish me luck."

"I can't," Pam bitterly confessed. Pete blinked at her in

surprise before finally leaving her cubicle.

It was true. She couldn't wish Pete luck when she was battling her own emotions. She had felt something more than passion the night before. If Pete and Regina reunited than she would never know if Regina had shared her feelings. The day was quickly becoming a Monday morning in Hell. Pam stared at her computer screen debating on whether to leave early or simply bang her head on her desk until she lost consciousness. It was a tough choice; both sounded really appealing at the moment.

"Pam?" Dave called from the entrance to her cubicle.

"Hey there," she greeted him warily. "I emailed those specs over to Syntax."

"Thanks," Dave said softly, his eyes drifting around her tiny workspace. "Uhm . . . some game last night. You certainly cleaned up."

"Yeah," Pam groaned, wishing she had never agreed to go to the Sunday night game. "I was a real winner."

"Yeah." Dave chuckled slightly. "Look, I'll try to keep Pete away from you. I noticed him running back here every five seconds. I'm trying to keep him away from the boss as well. The guy is a mess."

"No kidding," Pam agreed with a slight sneer.

"Well, he really screwed up last night," Dave continued. "She's not going to take him back, is she?" He asked hesitantly.

"Should she?" Pam barked in response.

"Honestly, no," Dave said quietly. "If he had just kept his mouth shut and not told her maybe she wouldn't have dumped him in front of everyone."

"So you think his only mistake was telling her?" Pam gasped in horror.

"No," Dave responded honestly as he stepped slightly closer to Pam. "Remember me?"

"Yeah." Pam smiled. "You called him an asshole." Her smile vanished as she recalled some of the other comments made at Regina's expense. "Not everyone shared your sentiments."

"I know," Dave began slowly. The guy looked around nervously. "This whole mess is going to create some problems. Half the department was there and the other half has already

heard the story in various versions. I'm the head of our division and I've got one programmer who's a basket case and another I'm worried might be on her way."

"What are you talking about?" She inquired fearfully, once again tugging on the collar of her sweater.

"Awfully warm for a turtleneck," Dave said with a slight cringe. Pam blushed as she turned away. "Pam, look; I don't care. In fact I'm not really surprised. I just want to know when to duck when all of this hit's the fan," he explained quickly.

"It won't," Pam lied. "I'm not about to tell him. Wait! Why aren't you surprised?"

"I'm not blind," Dave shrugged. "I've gone out a few times with Pete for beers after work. Let's just say that I had a feeling they weren't as happy as he led everyone to believe they were. And I suspected some time ago that maybe Regina isn't as straight as Pete would like to think she is."

"You're a bright guy," Pam said with a light laugh. "That must be why you get the big bucks."

"Right," he choked out in amusement. "Like I said, just let me know when to duck."

"Based on the way Regina ran out of my apartment this morning, I don't think it's going to be a problem," Pam admitted sadly.

"I'm sorry to hear that," Dave responded in a sincere tone.

The rumors and gossip persisted all week. The mood in their small department became increasingly tense. Pam endured some good-natured ribbing to which she outwardly didn't respond. On the inside it hurt her deeply. Dave was the only one who seemed to understand. Pete, on the other hand, was a mess. Dave finally had to pull him into his office and tell him to get his act together over the weekend.

That Friday night Pam went out for a drink with Dave. "Have you heard from her?" He finally asked her after a couple of rounds.

"Nope," Pam responded sadly.

"Well, don't take it to heart," Dave said, trying to console her. "Pete's been giving her a hard time. He keeps going back to the apartment like he still lives there."

"Idiot," Pam sneered.

"Maybe she just needs some time to finish dealing with him," Dave offered hopefully.

"And maybe she just needed a roll in the hay," Pam suggested painfully. "It's for the best. If I started dating her, it would send Pete over the edge." She tried to sound nonchalant about the entire situation even though her heart was breaking.

"You don't know that," Dave surmised. "Have you tried to call her?" He inquired thoughtfully.

"No," Pam answered in surprise. Dave just stared at her with a challenging look. "What would I say? Hey, thanks for letting me collect my winnings?"

"Pam," he chastised her. "Call her. You'll never know what she's thinking or feeling until you ask her."

"No," Pam said, shrugging off his advice. "If she wants to see me then she'll call me."

"Don't let your pride get in the way," Dave cautioned her.

"Now how did you get to be so wise in matters of the heart?" Pam asked him with a sense of genuine curiosity.

"I'm not wise," Dave offered solemnly. "Let's just say I have my pride but I lost the girl."

"Ouch," Pam winced.

"Think about it," Dave urged her. "The worst that could happen is that your fears are right and you still feel like hell. "

"You're not cheering me up," Pam groused as she played with the ice in her drink. "Let's talk about something else."

They ended up chatting for a couple of hours. Pam nursed her last drink the entire time. Finally she called it a night and went home. She couldn't get her mind off what Dave had said. She sat alone in her studio apartment, holding the telephone and nervously listening to the unanswered ringing. She was just about to hang up when she heard a breathy "Hello." It was repeated when Pam failed to respond.

"Hi, it's Pam," she finally blurted out.

"Hi," Regina responded softly.

For long lingering moments neither of them spoke. It was the sound of shouting in the background that snapped Pam out of *her funk. "Is that Pete?" She blurted out.*

"Yes," Regina groaned in disgust. "I've changed the locks but he was causing such a scene outside my door I had to let him in before one of the neighbors called the cops."

Pam rolled her eyes in distress as she listened to Pete whining in the background. "Do you want me to come over there and bitch slap him?" She finally offered.

"Don't tempt me," Regina laughed lightly. "Pam, I really want to talk to you about everything. But right now I need to deal with wonder boy. Could we get together this weekend for coffee or something?"

"Yes," Pam responded hopefully.

Regina promised to call over the weekend and make plans. Pam sat by the telephone eagerly awaiting the call that finally came late on Saturday. They got together and enjoyed a quiet afternoon. They met for coffee and ended up going for a long walk around the city. They talked about a lot of things including Pete and what Regina was going to do about him.

Pam was still confused after they parted at the end of the day. She and the blonde still hadn't talked about the night they spent together. Pam was left wondering what, if anything, it had meant to Regina. She was just about to call Regina the following day when Regina called her.

The two women got together again and had fun. They ended up spending the entire day together. Pam finally suggested that they go out for dinner and a movie. Regina eagerly accepted. They exchanged gentle touches but nothing that couldn't be explained away as a friendly gesture. By the end of the evening, Pam felt more confused than ever.

They were standing outside Regina's apartment building, each seemingly reluctant to say goodnight. Looking back on everything Pam should have realized that Regina was just as confused as she was. But at that moment she was completely clueless. "I'm sorry," Regina finally said as they stood outside with the cold night air chilling them to the bone.

"About?" Pam asked her anxiously.

"The other morning," Regina explained quietly. "I

panicked. Everything happened so fast."

"I know," Pam agreed as she braced herself for the let's-just-be-friend's speech.

Pam found herself staring into Regina's eyes. Despite the coldness of the January evening, Pam's body temperature was quickly rising. "I . . . Uhm . . . don't want to add any more confusion to your life," Pam began slowly. "But I really want to kiss you right now." Before Pam had a chance to regret her words, Regina's lips were pressed against her own.

Pam's body went into overdrive as she felt Regina's tongue brush her bottom lip. She parted her lips, inviting Regina in as she pulled the blonde's body closer to her own. Their tongues wrapped around each other as their hands began to roam freely. Pam's knee slipped between Regina's firm thighs as she backed the smaller woman against the wall of the building.

Regina moaned into her mouth as Pam's hips thrust against her. The passion ignited within her was too much for Pam to control. Her inner voice was cautioning her to slow down and not rush things with Regina once again. As they broke away from the kiss gasping for air, she felt Regina's body moving in rhythm with her own. "I want you," Regina panted heavily as she clung tightly to Pam's body.

Pam responded by increasing her movements against Regina's body as she cupped the back of her head, preventing her from striking the cold hard wall behind her. "Not here," Regina groaned as Pam thrust against her harder. Regina let out a whimper as she continued to respond to Pam's body. "Yes," Regina hissed as her thighs tightened around Pam's leg.

"Come for me, baby," Pam urged her on as she gyrated against her.

Pam could feel her lover trembling against her. She held the little blonde tightly as she felt the waves of passion pulse through her. "You are incredible," Regina murmured against her neck.

"I can't help myself," Pam confessed as she continued to hold onto her lover. "There's something about the way you kiss me that drives me insane."

"I need you," Regina said softly as she began to kiss Pam's

neck eagerly. "Take me home," the blonde insisted.

Pam was certain her heart would explode when she heard the desire in Regina's voice. She couldn't speak; she simply took Regina by the hand and led her away from her building. Pam understood that there was a definite possibility that Pete would make an appearance there. She didn't want to deal with any of that; she simply wanted to make love to Regina over and over again.

PART THREE

Back in the here and now Pam fought the cold morning air, lost in her thoughts. She arrived back at the house to find Regina cocooned in the warmth of a down comforter. She'd drifted back off to sleep. A pair of very icy hands clutching her backside disrupted Regina's peaceful slumber. The blonde shrieked when she felt the cold appendages. "I can't believe you did that, " she scolded her chuckling lover. "Your hands are freezing," she continued as she wrapped the bedding around her naked body.

"It's cold outside," Pam pointed out as she began to strip off her clothing. "You'd be proud of our boy. His papers were dry."

"Really?" Regina responded, happy with the news and her unobstructed view of her lover's backside. "We really need to agree on a name for him," Regina continued thoughtfully as she watched Pam.

"Any suggestions?" Pam asked her as she started to pull her hair back.

"Oh yeah," Regina answered as she licked her suddenly dry lips. She had already been in a frisky mood that morning and seeing Pam standing there naked certainly fueled her desires.

"What?" Pam inquired innocently as she turned towards Regina. The blonde knew that she was leering but she couldn't help herself. "Oh no. I know that look," Pam cautioned her.

"Come back to bed," Regina offered huskily, not understanding why her lover was resisting.

"Have you looked at the clock?" Pam inquired regretfully.

Regina blinked in confusion as she turned towards the clock. "Crap." She pouted. "Why were you gone so long?"

"I got lost in thought," Pam responded absently.

"What were you thinking about?" Regina inquired as she lowered the sheets to reveal her naked breasts. She heard her lover whimper softly.

"You," Pam purred as she turned towards her lover.

"Good answer," Regina responded softly as she took Pam by the hand and pulled her towards the bed. "Kiss me?" Regina pleaded softly, knowing that her lover would rarely refuse her.

"We don't have time," Pam protested weakly as she pulled the sheets further down Regina's body.

Regina could feel Pam's breath on her face as she captured her lips. As Regina pulled Pam closer, she could feel her lover's excitement coating her naked thigh. Regina moaned as she deepened the kiss. Their bodies melted together as they stretched out on the bed. Regina parted her thighs, inviting Pam in. After all these years it still amazed her how quickly her lover could fuel her passion. Just one look from those baby blues could melt Regina's heart and set her body on fire.

Regina felt Pam's fingers pressing against her center. "Yes," she hissed as she wrapped her legs around Pam's body.

"Tell me," Pam teased as her fingers slipped into Regina's opening slightly and then stilled their movement.

"Don't tease me," Regina choked out as she began to tease one of Pam's already hardened nipples with her fingers.

"Tell me," Pam repeated as she began to kiss Regina's neck. "Tell me what you want," Pam insisted.

Regina groaned as she felt Pam's wetness pressing against her. "You know what I want," Regina moaned. "I want you to take me. I want you to show me how much you love me." She felt Pam's breathing become ragged as she entered her. Regina's body arched as her lover's fingers plunged in and out of her. Their bodies rocked together wildly as Pam began to tease Regina's throbbing clit with her thumb.

The beeping of the alarm clock interrupted their lovemaking. "Don't stop," Regina implored her.

"Not until you beg me to," Pam reassured her as she brought her closer to the edge.

Regina wrapped her legs tighter around Pam's body. Her senses were reeling as Pam took her higher. The blonde bit down on her lip as she looked up, watching Pam pleasure her and seeing the tension in her lover's chest and neck as her hand glided in and out of Regina's wetness. Regina loved to watch Pam when she made love to her. The sweat glistened as it ran down her firm body.

Regina arched her body in an effort to melt into Pam's, knowing that Pam was nearing the edge herself. There was no mistaking the way the muscles in her throat were tightening or the hazy look clouding her baby blues. Regina tried to steady herself in hopes that they would climax in unison. Their bodies shuddered and arched against one another as they screamed out in ecstasy.

Clutching each other tightly, they collapsed onto the mattress. Pam released a throaty chuckle. "You are such a bad influence on me," the brunette whispered as Regina planted gentle kisses on her neck.

"You're just figuring that out now?" Regina teased her as they rose from the bed. "Sorry you didn't take Pete up on his offer for double or nothing?" Regina continued to tease as Pam simply rolled her eyes. "Come on. I'll use the shower in the guest room. You can use ours," Regina graciously offered.

****

Later that day Regina was busy setting up the flowers at St. Joseph's Church. Watching her staff working carefully, she smiled at the results. "It is going to be a beautiful wedding," her assistant, Caroline, said as she approached her.

"Looks good," Regina confirmed as she began to walk back down the aisle, rechecking each and every floral arrangement carefully.

Regina put on her best smile as the mother of the bride raced towards her frantically. "You are a miracle worker, Regina," the tall heavyset woman gushed.

"Thank you, Mrs. Clemens." Regina accepted the compliment with a sense of relief. Mrs. Clemens had proven herself to be the typical mother of the bride. She listened as her daughter carefully told Regina what she wanted and then she instructed the florist to do something completely different. It wasn't a new experience for Regina; the trick was to find a happy medium that both the bride and her mother would fall in love with. Regina was thankful that this time the mother of the groom didn't put her two cents in as well.

Regina gathered her staff and they all climbed into the two vans she used for deliveries and headed back to the shop. The tiny floral shop she had started six years ago was a flurry of activity. Regina shook her head, knowing that she was doing well. When she'd first started out, it was just her doing all the work. She couldn't afford to hire anyone to help even for a few hours a week. When she was involved with good old Pete, he never offered to help.

Another one of the many differences between the life she lived then and the life she was living now. Pam insisted on helping her out every chance she got. Now that both of their careers were doing well, they could relax a little and enjoy their lives together. Now all they had to do was come up with a name for the puppy.

"Have the two of you come up a name for the dog yet?" Caroline inquired as Regina scanned the orders for the day.

"Nope," Regina chuckled slightly. "Pam is insistent on using a poker hand for him. Make sure we get the extra shipment of roses confirmed for Valentine's Day."

"Why poker?" Caroline inquired with curiosity.

"Long story," Regina smirked. She always hated explaining to people how she and Pam ended up together.

"So how long have the two of you been together?" Caroline continued as the tiny redhead followed Regina closely. Caroline was a good assistant but there were times when she seemed a little too interested in Regina's personal life.

"Just over five years," Regina responded brightly. She noticed the small frown Caroline was trying to hide. She made a mental note to sit Caroline down soon and have a little chat with her. Regina wasn't certain if it was she or her partner that Caroline had a thing for, but it was time to make it clear that neither she nor Pam liked to share.

"So how did you two meet?" Caroline persisted as they continued to work.

"I met her at a Christmas party her company had," Regina explained dryly, hoping that Caroline would drop the subject and refocus her attention on work.

"Oh, so you were friends with someone she worked with?" Caroline continued with interest.

"No," Regina sighed, feeling her earlier good spirits vanishing quickly. "I was involved with someone she works with."

Caroline perked up when Regina revealed that piece of information. "Caroline, let's focus on the flowers and not my marriage," Regina asserted firmly. She felt slightly guilty when Caroline's frowned reemerged. Then again, as much as she liked the energetic young woman, she wasn't born yesterday. Caroline wasn't just making casual conversation. She was up to something.

Just when it seemed that Regina could leave for the day and let her staff take over for the rest of the evening, another unpleasant event occurred. Pete walked in. Every once and awhile Pete would have a revelation and decide that he and Regina really did belong together.

"I swear he's worse than a rash," Regina groaned as she ran her fingers tensely through her short blonde hair. "Why are you here?" Regina barked out as she crossed the shop and grabbed him by the arm. Forcibly she led her ex-boyfriend out the door. "What is wrong with you?" Regina spat out.

"Regina, we need to talk about this," Pete offered in a pleasant voice.

"We split up over five years ago," Regina asserted as she waved her arms frantically. "I don't want to see you anymore. Pam is going to go ballistic if she finds you here. Pete, she's your boss now."

Regina knew that Pete's visits usually coincided with some upset at work. He never forgave Pam for their breakup, and when she was promoted to a position directly above him, it only added grist to the mill. Regina was at her wit's end. All she wanted to do was go home and argue with Pam over what to name the puppy and then make love to her all night long. How many different ways can you tell someone that you don't love him or her? That you never did?

"This is ridiculous," Pete protested. "I made one mistake so you decide to turn gay? When are you going to wake up and realize that we belong together? She couldn't possibly make you happy."

"Will you listen for once?" Regina said slowly as she tried to rein in her temper. "We were over long before that stupid poker game. I love her and she loves me. I didn't just decide to turn gay. I am gay. I was gay before I met you and I was never happy when we were together. My only regret in all of this is that you and Pam were friends once and that ended the moment I got together with her."

Pete just stared at her coldly. Regina could see Caroline watching with interest from the window. "I have a business to run; I want you to leave," Regina fumed at Pete. He just stood there staring at her in disbelief. It had been like this between them from the moment he caught her and Pam together. It was their first Valentine's Day together. It had been wonderful until they made the mistake of going back to Regina's apartment.

Regina flushed slightly at the memory of Pam making love to her. Their passion was never a quiet encounter. On more than one occasion when they traveled, they received complaints from other guests. Good old Pete must had been lurking outside the door. He burst in, breaking the lock, and found the last thing he could have expected. The two of them were naked with Regina bent over in front of Pam. The scene that followed was nasty with Pete and Pam almost coming to blows.

Regina and Pete continued to stare at one another, neither willing to give the other what they wanted. Then Regina felt the hairs on the back of her neck stand up. "Pete, you need to go now," Regina suggested in a panicked tone. She didn't need to turn around to know that Pam was approaching.

"Well, if it isn't dumb ass," Pam said from behind Regina.

The blonde cringed, knowing that the contest was about to begin.

"This doesn't concern you," Pete said in a cold voice.

"Sure it does," Pam sneered as she took her place at Regina's side. "Tell me something, Sparky. Is it that she's with someone else or that I'm a woman?"

Something inside of Regina snapped. Five years of watching the two of them whip out the measuring stick was more than she could stand. She hated the tug of war that she had been trapped in. "Enough!" She finally barked out. "You two finish your pissing contest. I'm out of here." She took one last look at the two of them before marching down the street in a huff. Pete looked shocked which was his normal response whenever someone told him off. Pam looked embarrassed and her shoulders slumped, knowing that she and the puppy would probably be sharing a bed that night.

PART FOUR

Regina found herself sitting at a bar nursing a gin and tonic. She wasn't surprised when Caroline planted herself in the stool next to her. "Want to talk about it?" The redhead offered eagerly. *'Well, that answers that question,'* Regina thought wryly as she fiddled with the peanuts in the bowl in front of her.

"No," Regina responded absently.

"Who was the guy?" Caroline persisted after a moment.

"My ex-boyfriend," Regina answered with a heavy sigh.

"Huh?" Caroline choked out. "You were straight?"

"Briefly," Regina chuckled, suddenly finding the entire situation amusing. "It didn't take."

"So how did you and Pam end up together?" Caroline continued as Regina felt the hairs on her neck stand up once again. She smiled, knowing what was coming.

"I won her in a card game," a sultry voice drawled.

Regina found herself laughing lightly despite her sullen mood. "That you did, darling," Regina confirmed as Caroline's jaw dropped. "Caroline, if you don't mind?" Regina said as she nodded her head towards the doorway.

"Are you sure?" The redhead inquired as she placed a comforting hand on Regina's arm.

Regina didn't miss Pam arching her eyebrow as she glared down at Caroline's hand with an icy stare. "Yes," Regina reassured her assistant. Caroline reluctantly released her arm and departed.

"Can I sit down?" Pam asked her carefully.

"Yeah," Regina sighed deeply. Her body tingled as her lover took the stool next to her.

They sat in an awkward silence. Pam ordered a drink and leaned on her elbow, waiting for Regina to say something. "I'm not angry with you," Regina finally said. "I'm just tired of going through this every few months."

"I know," Pam agreed softly. "It's that time of year again. Every year at this time Pete shows up on your doorstep and asks you to come back to him. I try not to let it get to me but I guess deep down I'm afraid that one of these days you'll wake up and think that I was a mistake."

Regina turned to her lover with a stunned expression. "How could you think that?" Regina blurted out. "I love you."

"I know," Pam conceded. "Still, sometimes I'm afraid. Everything between us is so good. Maybe things are a little to good at times. I see the way other people look at you. And I see that little assistant of yours following you around like a lost puppy dog."

"Excuse me?" Regina said as she blinked in surprise. "Are you blind? Don't you see the way people look at you? Pam, you look like you just jumped off the pages of some swimsuit ad."

"Right," Pam scoffed.

"It's true," Regina reaffirmed as she gently clasped her lover's hand. "What really has you worried? It can't be Caroline; she's just some kid with a crush. Is it that I was with a man before you? I've explained that a thousand times. I got burned by other women and freaked out."

Pam just sat there sipping her cocktail. "After all of these years how can you doubt my feelings for you?" Regina said quietly. "I knew from the first time you kissed me that you were the one. I know I did my fair share of freaking out early on but that was a long time ago. Do you remember what I said to you the first time we made love?"

"This might be the only time we're together?" Pam said with uncertainty.

"Not that," Regina chided her. "I told you to make me yours. And you did. I've belonged to you since that night. Keeping that in mind, I just don't appreciate it when you and Pete make me feel like I'm a possession or nothing more than a prize to be won or lost. All joking aside, I feel that you and I would have ended up together regardless of how that silly card game turned out."

"You really think so?" Pam offered hopefully.

"Yes, I really do," Regina reassured her. "I belong to you. Just like you belong mind, body and soul to me. Now go home and take care of Aloysius before the little guy explodes."

"We are not naming him that," Pam chastised her vehemently.

"We'll see," Regina responded coyly.

Pam stood up and waited for Regina to join her. "Aren't you coming?" She inquired hesitantly. Regina smiled up at her. "I need a little more time. I'll see you at home," she said confidently. Pam seemed a little surprised but kissed her gently on the cheek and left for their home. Regina rolled her eyes at the surprised looks she was receiving from the other patrons. "Get over it," she muttered. "Now I need to plan something special for tonight. I think both of us need this."

Regina sat at the bar formulating her plan. They'd had a great night last night and this morning was certainly a nice way to wake up. But Pam was right. Every year her old flame would show up and try to disrupt their happiness. This year they were going to start off the Valentine's Day celebration a little early and make it the first time they could really celebrate their love for one another.

PART FIVE

Pam was sitting on the kitchen floor as the puppy crawled all over her. "Simon? Frank? Skippy?" She rambled on, trying to see if the puppy would respond to any of the names.

"Skippy?" Regina laughed from the entryway.

"Just trying out a few names," Pam explained quickly as she rose to her feet. "Hi," she said shyly as she brushed the dog hair off of her slacks.

"Hi," Regina said with a warm smile.

"Do you want me to start dinner?" Pam offered.

"No," Regina shook her head as she spoke. "I'm not really hungry. I'm going upstairs. Could you come up in about ten minutes and gave me a hand with something?"

"What would that be?" Pam asked. Her curiosity was thoroughly peeked.

"You'll see," Regina purred in response.

Pam moved to follow her but Regina placed a firm yet gentle palm on her chest. "Give me a few minutes," she instructed her lover. Regina reached up and placed a gentle kiss on Pam's lips. The taller woman could only nod in response. She watched Regina's hips sway as she walked out of the room. "What are you up to, my love?" Pam said aloud as she placed her fingers against her lips, the warmth from Regina's kiss still lingering upon them.

Pam could hear Regina moving about above her as she settled the puppy down for the night. She quickly glanced at her watch. "Close enough," she surmised as she raced out of the room and up the staircase. Her heart lurched when she found the bedroom door shut tightly. She noticed a plastic bag hanging from the doorknob. She removed the bag from the knob and found a pink Post-It firmly attached the outside. "Put this on and then come back," she read aloud.

Pam arched her dark eyebrows in curiosity as she peeked inside the bag. "Are you kidding?" She choked out as she looked at the skimpy material inside. Pulling the item out of the bag she inspected it carefully. It was a black lacy thong with a matching bra. "This is awfully small," she called out. When no response seemed to be forthcoming, she accepted her fate and marched off to the guest bathroom to change into the tiny undergarments.

A cool draft greeted her overexposed body as Pam stepped back out into the hallway. She approached the bedroom door once again and opened it slowly. The snide comment about her wardrobe died on her lips once she stepped inside their bedroom. Candles had been lit all around the room, illuminating it softly. On the floor was a blanket. Resting comfortably on the blanket was Regina clad in an emerald green silk camisole and matching tap pants.

"Reggie," Pam squeaked out as Regina beckoned her to come closer with her finger.

Pam's mouth was watering as she followed Regina's command. She knelt down on the blanket and leaned closer to her lover. "Not so fast, hot stuff," Regina taunted her. "There's something I want you to do first."

"Anything," Pam responded in a breathy tone.

Regina smiled slyly as she leaned back and pulled something out from under her firm body. "I want you to teach me how to play cards," Regina stated firmly as she placed a deck of cards between them.

"Excuse me?" Pam stammered.

"Teach me," Regina repeated. "You're so proud of that winning hand that brought me into your life. I want a chance to win you. So what do you say, stud muffin? Are you willing to bet your heart?"

"You've already captured my heart," Pam reassured her as she stretched out before her lover on the opposite side of the blanket. "Besides, you should never bet anything that you're not willing to lose," Pam carefully reminded Regina.

"Hmm," Regina purred as she drank in her lover's long body lying only inches away. The blonde sat up slightly with a mischievous gleam in her emerald orbs. "Well, I have something that I am most willing to part with," she suggested as her fingers tugged on the strap of her lingerie. "So what's it going to be? You want to play?"

"Yes," Pam managed to say as she swallowed hard. "Just so I understand, what exactly are we playing for?" Her voice cracked as she spoke. Pam could feel the warmth spreading throughout her entire being.

"The winner gets whatever the winner wants," Regina said in a husky tone that left no room for misinterpretation. "For the entire evening."

Pam's heart nearly leapt out of her chest as she heard the words and saw the evil glint in her lover's eyes. The only question in Pam's mind at that point was whether or not she wanted to win or lose. "Are you ready?" Regina challenged her.

"Oh yeah," Pam readily agreed. "Uhm . . . just one question. Is everything going to ride on one hand or do you want a few practice runs first?"

"It's all or nothing, so to speak," Regina continued to tease Pam, fanning the flames of the taller woman's desire. "Five card draw, nothing is wild. That's for frat boys and old ladies."

"I thought you didn't know how to play this game?" Pam accused her.

"I lied," Regina said with a confident smirk.

Pam blushed deeply as she found herself staring at her lover's ample cleavage. She picked up the deck and started to shuffle the cards slowly. She sat up slightly as she took her time with the cards. Regina watched the slow certain movement of Pam's fingers. She could feel her breathing become ragged as her nipples suddenly pressed against the silk material of her camisole.

Pam placed the deck between them once again as her eyes locked in a fiery gaze with Regina's. The blonde felt her body tremble slightly as her lover held her in the intense stare. "How do you still do that?" Regina said softly as she reached for the cards and carefully cut the deck.

"It's what you do to me," Pam explained as she watched her lover cut the deck.

Pam dealt five cards to both of them, her eyes never losing her lover's gaze. They retrieved their cards, both studying them carefully. Sneaking glances at each other, they both tried to maintain their look of utter confidence. Pam's palms were sweating when Regina discarded only one card. The brunette blinked for the first time as she dealt Regina a new card.

Regina continued to smile confidently as Pam discarded the maximum of three cards. Both shuffled their cards and studied them intently. Neither woman was entirely certain as to why that was. This was an all or nothing hand. There was no bluffing; no more bets to be placed everything rested upon the luck of the draw. Regina smiled, knowing it didn't really matter. They had won each other's hearts years ago. Tonight was about celebrating their love.

"Show me what you've got," Regina finally commanded. Her heart fluttered as she saw Pam's eyes darken with desire. Her face dropped slightly as she watched Pam lay each card down on the blanket slowly. "Three of a kind, Jacks," Regina congratulated her.

The blonde sat there blinking with a complete look of innocence. "Do I win?" Pam taunted her boldly. Regina smiled sweetly as she laid each of her cards down slowly. "Like you always say, sweetheart. Queens over Jacks - a winner every time."

"A full house?" Pam choked out. "A Queen high full house. That's the same hand that brought us together," she said absently. "The exact same hand I was holding that night."

"I guess it is kismet," Regina said with a bold smile.

"Did you do this?" Pam inquired as she kept staring down at Regina's cards.

"You shuffled the deck," Regina reminded her. "You dealt the cards. It's fate. You belong to me."

"Yes, I do," Pam responded happily as she looked up. The look in her lover's eyes caused her breath to catch in her throat.

Pam crawled across the blanket and kissed her lover's lips tenderly. "You won me," she whispered as Regina ran her fingers through her thick black hair. "I belong to you," she reasserted as she once again captured her lover's eager lips. "Make me yours," she pleaded in the same voice Regina had used on their first night together.

Pam was still bent over her lover as Regina cupped her breasts. Regina sighed as her lover moaned. "I want you,"

Regina said as she raised her body slightly, running her fingertips along her lover's back as she moved behind her. Pam lifted her backside and parted her legs slightly. Regina pressed against her lover as she began to kiss her way down Pam's body.

Regina was urged on by Pam's murmurs of pleasure. The blonde tasted Pam's skin, slowly working her way down the back of her sinewy body and pausing briefly to unclasp the black lacy bra. Regina moaned as she felt the silk material of her outfit clinging to her body as she pressed herself deeper into Pam.

The brunette was gasping as Regina's fingertips teased her. She could feel the bra being lowered down her body. The lacy material teased her already sensitive skin. As Regina's mound pressed into her backside, the blonde wrapped her arms around Pam's body. Regina's palms grazed her aching nipples, causing them to become fully erect.

Pam moaned as she continued to support herself on her hands and knees. Regina teased her nipples harder. The brunette's hips swayed, begging for more. The feel of silk caressing her body was driving her wild with desire. Regina's hands moved down her body slowly, savoring each curve and dip. Pam whimpered as she felt Regina cup her backside.

Regina's senses were fully attuned to the intensity of Pam's desires. She kneaded the firm flesh beneath her hands. Her mouth watered as Pam parted her legs even further. Running her fingers along the elastic of the tiny thong elicited another deep moan from her partner.

Regina stood behind her lover who whimpered from the loss of contact. She removed her clothes and dropped them so that they landed in front of Pam. Regina smiled devilishly as she returned to her position behind her lover. Once again she kissed her way down Pam's body, enjoying the new sensation of their exposed flesh meeting.

As Regina once again reached Pam's quivering backside, she ran her fingers down along the seams of the thong. "Are you trying to kill me?" Pam pleaded.

"Can you hold on, baby?" Regina asked as her fingers became coated with Pam's desire.

"No," Pam panted. "I need you. I've been thinking about you all day."

The brunette groaned as her lover's fingers dipped into her wetness. Pam's hips swayed more urgently as Regina's fingers caressed her lower lips in a slow torturous exploration. As Regina continued to feel her, the blonde pressed her mound into thrusting backside. "Yes," Pam growled as she rocked into Regina. Pam released a strangled moan as she felt the thong being tugged down.

Regina steadied Pam's hips so she could lower the thong down her legs. She kissed her way down Pam's body as she removed the tiny undergarment. Regina kissed her way back up her lover's body, dipping her tongue into her wetness. Pam cried out in pleasure as she opened herself up further, giving her lover greater access.

All of the negative energy from earlier in the day and from the past five years melted away as Regina tasted her. The blonde's tongue entered her center. Regina's mouth showed her how much she loved her. Regina's tongue retreated from her center and moved slowly up her firm cheeks. Regina dipped and tasted every inch of her eagerly.

Pam felt her lover straddling her backside. "This is how you loved me that night," Regina panted as she pressed her wetness into Pam. "I loved you then and I love you more each day," she groaned as she held onto Pam's swaying hips. Their passion built as their bodies rocked together wildly. Pam grunted and moaned as Regina rode against her.

Regina's fingers entered her lover. Pam arched in response as her body gyrated faster while her lover plunged in and out of her. She was begging for more as Regina took her deeper and harder. Their bodies were covered in a sheen of sweat as they began to tremble. They called out each other's names and praised any higher power they could think of.

Pam's heart was racing as she clutched the blanket; her head snapped back as they climaxed in unison. Their bodies continued to move together in a passionate rhythm as they collapsed onto the blanket. Pam was still panting heavily as Regina nestled on top of her, slowly removing her fingers from her center. She trembled as Regina brushed her hair from her face and kissed her cheek. "I love you," Regina repeated over and over again as they lay there.

"The night's not over yet," Pam reminded her exhausted partner.

"I know," Regina whispered hotly into her ear.

Pam whimpered slightly as Regina lifted herself off her body. Pam rolled over to find her lover standing above her. From her position on the floor, the brunette could feel her lover's desire radiating down upon her. Without thinking about anything but Regina's pleasure, Pam moved so that she was now kneeling before her lover.

"I love you," Pam whispered into Regina's damp curls as her lover guided her gently to her. Pam's tongue dipped inside the silky folds and began to feast hungrily upon her passion. Regina clutched the back of Pam's head as her hips thrust into her hungry mouth. Pam suckled Regina's throbbing clit as her fingers entered her. Plunging in and out of her lover, she teased her clit with her teeth and her tongue.

Regina cried out as Pam held her steady. The brunette loved the feeling of her lover exploding against her. She wouldn't need to wait long. Regina's body shook uncontrollably as she fell over the edge. Pam held her lover tightly and guided her back down onto the blanket. She held the smaller woman close as the waves of passion filtered through her body.

They remained curled up on the blanket, waiting for their hearts to stop racing and their breathing to return to normal. "I just want you to know that we're not finished yet," Regina gasped.

"I know," Pam purred in expectation. "I wouldn't dream of welching on a bet," Pam reassured her, knowing that once her lover's breathing returned to normal she was going to be happily paying off her obligation until the sun was peeking out across the horizon.

THE END

MISS LARILIA'S LESSON

PART ONE

LATE AUGUST 1883

Nellie leaned against the counter and looked thoughtfully out the window of her father's mercantile. She was daydreaming again, something her parents were constantly scolding her for. She couldn't help herself. She tried to pay attention to what was happening around her. It might help if something exciting would happen. Nothing ever did. One day progressed into the next without causing the slightest ripple in her life.

She worked from one day to the next behind the counter at the mercantile. It was her duty until the day when she married Freddie. He was nice enough and she had known him since they were children. Growing up in a small town in South Dakota, the town seemed to grow as they did. Still it was in the middle of nowhere. It wasn't a surprise when Freddie asked for her hand or when her father gave his consent willingly.

Freddie's family owned the largest farm in the area and her family owned the mercantile and restaurant/boarding house. Despite her mother's objections that it be called a hotel, it would always be known as the Winslow Boarding House. The only change was when someone rented a room. Nellie would find herself prying stories out of the traveling strangers. Of course, her parents chastised her constantly. They finally resorted to banishing her to the store so she wouldn't bother their guests.

She sighed in boredom as she continued to stare out the window. It was late on a Friday afternoon. Soon she would be allowed some time to herself. Tomorrow was Saturday and that meant she would be needed in the kitchen at the restaurant. Then Sunday the entire family would dress in their finest clothes and attend church. She found herself frowning, thinking about what would happen on Sunday afternoon. Freddie would naturally want to go for a buggy ride and picnic.

Her green eyes rolled in despair. She liked the tall dark-haired man well enough. But he would naturally want them to touch. She wished that she felt some spark when they kissed and touched one another. Instead she simply felt something was lacking. She had read stories about how a girl's heart would race and her head swoon from the touch of her lover's lips. "Perhaps after we're married," she muttered to herself, not truly believing her words.

Of course she and Freddie hadn't consummated their relationship. But they did feel one another underneath their clothing. Freddie seemed to enjoy this activity immensely. She didn't have the heart to tell him that his fumbling simply bored her. She noticed that the stagecoach had arrived. The sight always filled her with a sense of excitement. Perhaps something would come in the mail or a new visitor would arrive to brighten her existence - a tall dark stranger that would capture her heart. Normally there wasn't any mail for her since she didn't know anyone outside of Cedar Grove. And the only strangers were creepy older men who only seemed to exhibit a distasteful interest in the young strawberry blonde. It saddened her each time she realized that Freddie was the only option in life. Well, the new schoolteacher was due to arrive soon. That would be interesting. Perhaps she would be someone close to her age; someone she could talk to.

Nellie didn't have any friends; all of the girls her own age had already married. It wouldn't be proper for them to spend time with her. Not that she found any of the girls in her little town the slightest bit interesting. Still it would be pleasant to have someone to talk to. She watched with interest to see if anyone exited the stagecoach. She felt her heart skip a beat as she spied the tallest woman she had ever seen step down into the dirt street. "She's beautiful," she whispered as she drank in the tall raven-haired beauty.

Nellie's stomach clenched as the tall woman turned. A pair of piercing blue eyes stared at her. Nellie couldn't understand the sudden flutters filling her stomach. "That couldn't be the new school teacher," she whispered in disbelief. The stranger smiled slightly before turning and speaking to the driver. Nellie's mouth hung open as she continued to watch every move the mysterious woman made.

Once the woman had disappeared into the restaurant, Nellie released a tense breath. Absently she wiped her hand across her mouth. She was shocked when she discovered that she was drooling. "Huh?" She blurted out in surprise. She shook her head in an effort to clear her obviously muddled mind. Nellie hiked up the hem of her skirt and spun on her heels. The tiny woman rushed around in a flurry. She locked the front door and totaled the receipts for the day.

She had to go through the cash and the ledger several times before everything balanced. It frustrated her. Normally she was very good with numbers but her mind kept drifting to the mysterious woman. Her palms kept sweating. Despite her efforts to convince herself that it was the late summer heat, she knew it wasn't the truth.

Finally the books were balanced, the shades drawn, and the sign turned around. She put the money and ledger into the safe and departed the store. She double-checked the locks before she rushed quickly across the wooden sidewalks towards her home.

Nellie rushed through the deserted foyer and quickly glanced into the dining room that served as the restaurant. Her mother was busy laying out tablecloths in hopes that there would be some business that evening. Nellie stepped out of the room quickly before her mother could notice her. "Nellie," the tiny woman called out vehemently.

Nellie cringed and stomped her foot slightly before stepping into the dining room. "Hello Mother," she responded flatly.

"Gave me a hand setting up," her mother instructed her sternly.

"Yes, Mother," Nellie, grumbled as she crossed the dining room and entered the kitchen. She knew that there would be few patrons dining this evening. There was Doc Hansen unless he received a dinner invitation from another one of the townsfolk. Rev. Farley would be there unless, of course, he also received an invitation as well. Then there were the three men who were taking up lodging for the week. Nellie couldn't recall their names - only that one was a salesman, the other two were with the railroad, and they all had bad manners. The only other people coming into town for the evening were the men who would bypass their little establishment in favor of the saloon that was on the opposite end of the street.

Nellie didn't mind helping her mother. Since her two older brothers and her sister had married and moved on, she was the only help that wasn't hired. "Hello, Nellie," Jack, the handyman, greeted her.

"Hey, Jack," Nellie waved to him as she moved through the kitchen to retrieve the linens and flatware that would be needed to service the few patrons. She paused for a moment to look into the pot resting on the stove.

"Get out of there," a stern voice scolded her.

Nellie blushed as she turned to see Melinda, the cook, glaring at her. The portly older woman who was Jack's wife wagged her finger at Nellie. The strawberry blonde shrugged as she replaced the lid on the simmering pot. "Where's Pa?" She asked nonchalantly.

"New guest checked in," Melinda explained as she shooed Nellie away from the stove. "The new school teacher will be staying here."

"I saw her. She doesn't look like a school teacher," Nellie said as she gathered her things.

"You're not to bother the guests," Melinda cautioned her as Nellie exited back into the dining room.

Nellie was lost in thoughts of the beautiful new schoolteacher as she assisted her mother. Fortunately the older woman seemed content in prattling on about Nellie's wedding and Freddie's endless virtues.   The only thing about her upcoming nuptials that pleased Nellie was that they were more than a year away.

They finished their preparations and Nellie was excused to wash up for dinner. She retreated to her room on the second floor. The family's quarters were located on the opposite side of the building, keeping them securely away from the paying guests. She joined her parents in the family's private dining room.

Her father offered the prayer and they ate in silence. Talking was not permitted during the meal. It was something that bothered the normally chatty young woman. Her parents would send her off to her room after the evening meal and then they would talk quietly. Nellie would be left alone with her thoughts and the few books she was allowed to read.

The following morning Nellie dressed in a hurry. She told herself that she simply wanted to assist her mother and Melinda. Secretly she was aching to meet the new schoolteacher.

"Now what would you be doing down here so early?" Melinda teased the inquisitive young woman.

"I just wanted to help," Nellie protested adamantly.

"Fine," Melinda handed her a tray of food. "You want to meet her so much, you can serve her breakfast."

"Thank you," Nellie giggled as she eagerly accepted the tray. She almost tripped as she rushed into the dining room. Nellie could feel the tray trembling as she approached the dark-haired woman. She thought the woman looked even more beautiful close up. Yesterday her hair had been tied up in a tight bun. Today it hung down her back in a tight braid.

"Good morning," Nellie managed to squeak out as she placed her breakfast before her.

"Good morning," came the deep rich reply accompanied with a brilliant smile.

"I'm Nellie Winslow," she introduced herself as she held the now empty tray in front of her. She couldn't for the life of her understand why she felt so nervous.

"I didn't realize that Mr. And Mrs. Winslow had children," the beautiful stranger said in a pleasant voice.

"I'm the youngest," Nellie explained as she looked around quickly to ensure that her parents weren't lurking nearby. "My two brothers and my sister are married and have moved away."

"Oh," the woman said as she pursed her lips thoughtfully. "I'm Miss Larilia, the new schoolteacher."

"A pleasure to meet you, ma'am," Nellie said as she stared into crystal blue eyes.

"Will you be one of my new students?" Miss Larilia inquired sweetly.

Nellie groaned at the all too familiar assumption. "No," Nellie explained. "I finished my schooling quite some time ago."

"Oh?" Miss Larilia said with surprise.

"In fact, I'm to be married a year from next fall," Nellie continued to explain.

"Really?" Miss Larilia's stunned expression was written clearly across her chiseled features.

Nellie rolled her sea green eyes in amusement. "That's when I turn twenty one," Nellie explained in exasperation. It was a common occurrence. If the truth was told, her youthful appearance was one of the things that had successfully assisted her in delaying her impending marriage.

"My apologies," Miss Larilia said with a light laugh. "You just look so young."

"It is quite all right," Nellie said as she smiled shyly. "It happens all the time, Miss Larilia."

"Please call me Vivian," the schoolteacher offered in a friendly tone. "Since you're not that much younger than myself."

"Nellie," her mother called out sternly from the doorway of the kitchen.

"I have to go," Nellie apologized quickly as she cringed. "It was nice meeting you," she said quietly. Her heart stopped as a firm yet gentle hand touched one of her own.

"I enjoyed meeting you as well, Nellie." Vivian's eyes seemed to sparkle as she spoke.

Nellie stood there enjoying the woman's touch. The sound

of her mother clearing her throat from behind her snapped her out of trance. "Sorry, I'm not supposed to bother the guests," Nellie added with a slight grimace.

"It was no bother," Vivian said softly as she gave Nellie's hand a light squeeze before releasing it. "Perhaps later today you could show me around town? Mr. Coughlin offered but I would prefer someone closer to my own age."

"That old letch," Nellie said with a disgusted groan. "He's always shopping for a new wife," she added with a snort, knowing that the aging bachelor would try to court the beautiful woman. "I'd be happy to show you the town. I won't be free until after lunchtime though."

"Just come by my room when you're free," Vivian offered.

Nellie finally pried herself away from Vivian to face the scolding that she would surely get from her mother.

PART TWO

Nellie spent the remainder of her day hurrying, trying to finish all her chores so she could meet up with Vivian. It was well after two in the afternoon when she thought she was finally free to enjoy the day with her new friend. Unfortunately Freddie decided to surprise her with a visit. She tried to get rid of her eager fiancée but her mother insisted that she spend time with him.

They sat in the family sitting room under the watchful eye of her father. Nellie was thankful that her parents insisted that the couple not be allowed alone together with exception of their Sunday afternoon picnics. They cautioned her constantly about not rushing anything before her wedding night. She didn't have the heart to tell them that she really didn't enjoy Freddie's attention. She dreaded their picnics, as Freddie's advances grew bolder.

They spent a long boring afternoon visiting. The entire time Nellie made every attempt to cut their visit short. Freddie seemed determined to stay as long as possible.   Nellie was forced to endure dinner with her intended as well. The day had vanished. Finally Freddie had departed and she was then forced to endure a lengthy lecture from her Mother regarding her rude behavior towards him.

After realizing the only way to free herself from her mother was to apologize and promise to do better, she did exactly that. She quickly rushed off and searched the lodger's registry to find out what room Vivian was in.

As she approached Vivian's room, she felt a wave of nervousness wash over her. Meekly she knocked on the door. Her breath escaped her when Vivian opened the door and greeted her with a bright smile. "Hello," Vivian purred softly. "I was beginning to think you were going to stand me up," the schoolteacher teased her.

"I'm sorry. I couldn't get away," Nellie blurted out quickly. "The sun is still up. If you would like, I can still show you around. There really isn't that much to see."

"I would like that," Vivian responded in a sweet tone. "Come in while I get my wrap."

Shyly Nellie stepped into the modest room. She looked around quickly, not surprised by the sparse amount of luggage. After all, schoolteachers weren't paid very much. The town allotted them a small salary and paid for her lodgings. As Nellie glanced at the tall woman she felt suddenly small. Granted she had never been a tall girl, but Vivian was very tall.

They spent the rest of their day together, walking down the main street of the small town. Nellie prattled on about the town and some of the folks. She introduced Vivian to everyone they encountered. She and Vivian chatted politely. The only time Nellie felt uncomfortable was when Vivian inquired about Freddie.

Nellie tried her best to talk about the man she was to marry. Somehow she just didn't feel comfortable talking about him with Vivian. Nellie couldn't quite put her finger on what it was that bothered her about it.

After they finished their walk, the sun was just about to set. The two women exchanged their goodbyes in the foyer. Nellie felt strange at the thought of leaving this woman's company. She felt suddenly lonely when she retired for the evening.

PART THREE

Months had passed since Miss Larilia's arrival. Nellie's days seemed just a little brighter. She enjoyed spending time with the woman and they would often talk in the schoolteacher's room.   Her parents objected at first until Vivian politely explained that it was a comfort to have someone her own age to talk to.

From the window at the mercantile Nellie would watch Vivian gather the children together at the start of every day. Then, even if she were with a customer, she would watch at the end of the school day to see Vivian leave the tiny schoolhouse that was nestled just across the road.

The only gray spots in her days were her Sunday afternoon picnics. She gathered the courage to explain to Freddie that she didn't think that her parents would approve. Reluctantly he finally agreed. Their picnics went from uncomfortable groping sessions to uncomfortable talks. Freddie did try using his large puppy dog eyes to sway her. Nellie did allow a few kisses and the occasional touch.

One Saturday afternoon Freddie called on her. She was talking with Vivian in the foyer when Freddie entered. She didn't miss the appreciative gaze Freddie cast in the schoolteacher's direction. She also noticed Vivian's apparent discomfort when she introduced her fiancée. The normally friendly brunette seemed cold. Vivian excused herself quickly and left them alone.

Nellie escorted Freddie into the dining room. They shared a cup of coffee while her mother kept a watchful eye on the young couple. Throughout the entire visit Nellie could only think about Vivian; she'd seemed so sad when she left them. Freddie, of course, extended his visit.

After dinner Freddie was still there. Vivian stepped out onto the porch just as Freddie was leaning in to kiss Nellie. The young blonde was embarrassed and felt slightly guilty as she pushed Freddie away. "I'm sorry," Vivian said in a quiet sad tone.

"Miss Larilia?" Nellie's mother beamed as she stepped out on the porch. "Have you met Nellie's young man, Frederick Cartwright?"

"Yes," Vivian said in a polite tone. Nellie could see the sadness clouding her normally bright blue eyes. "Excuse me," Vivian offered as she quickly retreated inside.

"She's a bit of a strange one," Freddie muttered in bewilderment.

"Don't say that," Nellie snarled. "She's very nice."

Freddie was stunned at her outburst. She said a curt good evening to him before retreating inside. As she climbed the staircase she knew where she was heading. She knocked on the door. Vivian looked so weary when she opened it that Nellie couldn't stop herself from reaching out to cup Vivian's cheek.

Her body tingled as Vivian leaned into her touch. Then she felt suddenly cold as Vivian pulled away. "Are you all right?" Nellie asked fearfully.

"I'm fine," Vivian said softly.

"Are you certain?" Nellie said as she reached out for Vivian once again.

"Yes, I'm just tired," Vivian responded as she pulled away. They stood there just looking at each other. Nellie's breathing became ragged as she leaned in slightly; she could see that Vivian was breathing heavily as well. She seemed to be drawn to the tall woman. Her senses were suddenly alive as she stepped even closer.

Vivian's eyes fluttered shut as Nellie leaned into her body. She could feel Vivian's hand caressing her shoulder. Nellie could smell the scent of lavender on Vivian's skin, as she pressed closer. Suddenly Vivian stepped away. The movement was so sudden that Nellie found herself swaying. "Good night," Vivian said quickly.

Taken aback by Vivian's sudden rejection, Nellie could only blink in response as she stepped away. Nellie was confused and uncertain about what was happening. "Good night," she mumbled absently as she stumbled back, her eyes unable to focus on anything. She finally steadied herself just as Vivian's door softly clicked shut.

The days that followed were uncomfortable for Nellie. She couldn't seem to get Vivian out of her thoughts. Even prior to the night of Freddie's visit, she had become increasingly aware that Vivian was her constant focus. Now her only question was what she going to do about it. Whatever it was.

PART FOUR

It was a Sunday afternoon and Nellie was driving her father's buggy. For the first time in weeks she felt good about her afternoon picnic. After Freddie had met Vivian his touching grew more insistent. Nellie had finally come up with a solution that made her very happy. She informed Freddie that he could just forget about their weekly picnic until he learned better manners. So instead of spending her free afternoon fighting off Freddie's advances, she was spending the day with Vivian.

Vivian had been increasingly distant. Nellie wasn't certain that her idea would work but she had to try. It was late the other evening when she'd snuck out of her room and made her way quietly to Vivian's. The schoolteacher was still half asleep when she opened the door, her blue eyes widening in surprise when she discovered Nellie standing there wrapped in her robe. "I'm sorry to wake you," Nellie apologized quickly before Vivian had a chance to speak. "I need to ask you a favor and don't want my parents to know about it," she continued boldly.

"Nellie, is everything all right?" Vivian asked, her voice thick with concern.

"Yes and no," Nellie pushed forward. "I know this is going to sound silly but I need you to go on a picnic with me Sunday."

"Excuse me?" Vivian asked in confusion.

"I need time away from Freddie and I told him that I couldn't see him on Sunday after services because I had plans with you," Nellie blurted out excitedly.

Vivian just gave her an odd look before speaking. "Do you ever take a moment to breath when you speak?" Vivian asked in dismay.

"Please say yes," Nellie pleaded as she stepped slightly closer to Vivian.

"Do I have a choice?" Vivian asked as a small smile emerged.

Nellie stepped even closer as she pouted slightly. "Please," she repeated.

"Yes," Vivian conceded, as her smile grew brighter.

It was at that moment that Nellie realized how much she had missed that smile. "Thank you," she gushed as she hugged Vivian. Vivian stumbled back slightly. Strong arms held her tightly in an effort to hold the joyful blonde up. Instinctively Nellie tightened her hold on Vivian's body. The strangest things happened at that moment. Nellie's breasts ached as her nipples hardened. Her body tingled from the warmth of Vivian's body pressed against her own. She felt Vivian pull her closer. The schoolteacher's hands roamed down her back. She could feel Vivian's breath on her neck. Nellie felt Vivian's lips brush against her skin.

Nellie moaned deeply as she pressed her body closer to Vivian's. Then she whimpered softly as Vivian pulled away. The tall schoolteacher didn't meet her gaze as she stepped further back. "It's late," Vivian, said in a soft voice.

"I'll see you on Sunday," Nellie said hopefully as she stepped back into the hall. "Thank you," she added quickly before retreating back to her room.

Now it was Sunday and Nellie kept the horses on a steady pace to the secluded grove. She felt slightly giddy at the thought of finally being alone with Vivian. The schoolteacher remained strangely quiet. Nellie was quiet in turn, allowing Vivian to enjoy her thoughts and the countryside. Nellie found the perfect spot. The grove was empty and would remain that way. The trees and flowers that surrounded them were beautiful.

Nellie unhitched the horses and allowed them to roam free and graze. She knew that the team wouldn't stray very far. Vivian walked around, seeming to enjoy the beautiful view. Nellie laid out the blanket and proceeded to unpack the simple basket of food she'd brought along. She smiled at how she had hovered over Melinda as she prepared the meal. She had never done that with Freddie.

"It is very beautiful and peaceful here," Vivian commented as she approached the blanket. Nellie looked up at Vivian, her dark hair hanging down her back braided tightly. The way the sunlight shone from behind her seemed to illuminate her. The simple blue dress brought out the color of Vivian's eyes. "Yes, it is," Nellie, agreed as she drank in Vivian's beauty. She wasn't fooling herself; she knew that this was the person she wanted to be with.

Vivian smiled shyly as she lowered herself down onto the blanket. "Do you know what you're doing?" Vivian asked her coyly.

"No," Nellie answered honestly.

"Do you know why you're doing this?" Vivian inquired, her eyes twinkling slightly.

"Yes," Nellie answered in a ragged breath, suddenly feeling nervous as she felt the energy flowing between them.

"So what's for lunch?" Vivian inquired lightly.

Nellie smiled and breathed out a sigh of relief. She laid out their lunch, feeling thankful that Vivian didn't continue their conversation. Instead they fell into friendly banter as they ate their lunch. "So why did you want to spend your free afternoon with me instead of the young Mr. Cartwright?" Vivian asked as they repacked the basket.

"I enjoy spending time with you," Nellie answered with sincerity. "And Freddie has been pressuring me to be more intimate."

"What do you mean pressuring you?" Vivian asked hotly, her face tense as she spoke.

"It seems all he wants to do is kiss and . . . you know," Nellie turned away slightly.

"Do you and he . . .?" Vivian's voice trailed off.

Nellie turned back to her. Her heart almost broke at the sad look on Vivian's face. "We touch one another. We never go too far since we aren't married yet."

"No, not yet," Vivian said solemnly. "Do you love him?"

"No," Nellie responded flatly.

"Then why are you marrying him?" Vivian asked in dismay.

"Because it's what I'm expected to do," Nellie felt like crying as she made the confession.

"I understand," Vivian hung her head in dismay.

"Perhaps I'll grow to love him or start to feel something when he touches me," Nellie reasoned, knowing in her heart that she had felt more by simply hugging Vivian. "Maybe I'm just doing it wrong. I mean he's the only one I've ever kissed before."

Vivian chuckled at her rationalization. Nellie smiled in response as the two women settled themselves against a large tree that Nellie had laid the blanket in front of. Nellie felt a strange but comfortable sensation course through her body as their shoulders touched. She smiled as they both leaned into the touch. Somehow she knew what she wanted to happen. And she was clueless as to how to bring it about.

Nellie folded her hands nervously in her lap as Vivian picked at the blades of grass surrounding their blanket. Nellie stole a glance over at the schoolteacher who seemed preoccupied with a long blade of grass she had plucked out of the ground. She watched as long fingers twirled it. Nellie's mouth became suddenly dry as her green eyes focused on those fingers.

Nellie was fighting off the strange desire to feel those fingers touching her. She didn't understand these thoughts and she didn't want to. But they remained, humming through her already confused mind. Her eyes drifted slightly upwards to Vivian's ample bosom. She watched in fascination as the brunette's chest heaved slightly as she took in a breath.

Nellie wrapped her own fingers together even tighter, fearful that she might give in to the temptation to touch Vivian. Her knuckles turned white from the tight grip. All the while her eyes remained firmly focused on Vivian's breathing. It wasn't the first time she had spied another woman's bosom but it was the first time she'd been unable to look away. She noticed the pattern of Vivian's breathing increase slightly.

Nellie pressed her thighs together tightly in an effort to fight off the sudden throbbing she was experiencing. Still she remained helpless to look away from Vivian's bosom. She found herself pondering what Vivian's undergarments looked like. Again this wasn't a new experience for the young shop girl. It was the first time that she allowed herself to linger upon thoughts that she'd been told were unnatural.

But this time she somehow sensed that it was all right for her to explore these foreign thoughts. A slight tickling sensation brushed across her arm. She blinked in confusion. She reluctantly moved her gaze down to her arm to discover that Vivian was slowly trailing the blade of grass across the exposed skin on her forearm. She smiled as the tickling continued. The blade of grass wisped across her arm and down to her tightly clenched hands.

Nellie's body trembled as Vivian leaned in closer. She felt Vivian's breath caress her cheek. She tightened her hands, fighting off her unexplainable urges. Vivian's breath moved down her face and she could feel Vivian nuzzling her hair. She couldn't look at Vivian as she felt her breath gently tickle her ear.

Nellie's focus remained on her hands that were still planted firmly in her lap. "You're going to break your fingers if you keep squeezing them that tightly," Vivian whispered hotly in her ear. The sound of Vivian's voice and the feel of her hot breath sent a sudden jolt through Nellie's already tense body. Nellie's eyes snapped shut as she tried to fight off unfamiliar sensations.

Nellie shifted nervously as she felt the blade of grass tickle her tightly clenched hands. "Relax, Nellie," Vivian whispered. "I won't do anything to hurt you," she added in a soft sincere tone as she continued to tickle Nellie's hands.

Nellie felt herself relax slightly as her senses continued to pulsate uncontrollably. She felt the delightful sensation of Vivian's lips brushing her neck. Nellie's lips parted as she began to breathe heavily. She tilted her head back, unknowingly granting Vivian greater access to her neck. Insistent lips began nibbling along her creamy white skin.

Nellie unclasped her hands. With her eyes still closed, she trailed one hand up along Vivian's arm. As Vivian's mouth continued its exploration, Nellie's hand continued its path upwards. Nellie clutched Vivian's firm shoulder as the brunette started planting gentle kisses along her jaw. Nellie moaned as Vivian's lips moved closer to her own.

Nellie felt Vivian's body pressing against her own. Nellie's hand clasped the back of Vivian's head and she opened her eyes as she drew Vivian closer. Their lips met shyly. Nellie felt the warmth of Vivian's full lips spread through her body. The kiss felt so right and so very good. She wanted nothing more than to keep kissing Vivian.

Vivian's tongue brushed against her lips. She melted into the touch as she parted her lips, granting the schoolteacher entrance into the warmth of her mouth. Her own tongue greeted Vivian's and wrapped around it. Nellie's passion stirred as the kiss continued to deepen. She moaned as one of Vivian's strong hands cupped her breast.

Her body arched in response. She seemed to be pressing her breast deeper into the palm of Vivian's hand. She needed to feel more of this woman's touch. Their tongues continued to dance together sensually. Nellie was fighting the need to breathe. She simply wanted to lose herself in this woman's kisses.

Nellie's lips tingled as their kiss finally ended. Fueled by her desires, Nellie pulled Vivian back in for another kiss. Vivian kissed her quickly and pulled away. "Please," Nellie pleaded as she stared into Vivian's brilliant blue eyes. Vivian's hand continued to caress her breast. "I've never felt anything like this before," Nellie groaned softly as Vivian lowered her down onto the blanket.

"You can't . . . we can't let anyone know about this," Vivian cautioned her as she lay down beside her.

"I know," Nellie agreed sadly as she started to loosen Vivian's hair from it's tight braid. She wanted to see it flowing down her shoulders. She had loved seeing it that way when she'd awoken Vivian the other night.

Vivian smiled at her as Nellie ran her fingers through her sable-colored hair. "It's so beautiful," Nellie commented absently. Vivian in turn ran her fingers through Nellie's long strawberry blonde hair.

"Yours reminds me of sunshine," Vivian whispered softly.

Vivian sighed contentedly as her fingers moved to Nellie's face. Her thumb grazed gently across Nellie's lips. Nellie kissed Vivian's fingers as they brushed her lips. "I can't believe that I'm here with you. That you kissed me," Vivian said in a gentle tone just above a whisper.

"I've wanted to kiss you for the longest time," Nellie confessed as she allowed her hand to drift down Vivian's chiseled features. "I didn't understand it. I just needed to feel you," Nellie continued with uncertainty. "I want to kiss you again."

Vivian responded by capturing Nellie's lips with her own. A surge of desire pulsated throughout Nellie's entire being. Vivian cupped her breast once again. Nellie moaned with pleasure as she wrapped her arms around Vivian's body, drawing her closer to her. Her body arched in response as Vivian caressed her breast.

Nellie ran her hands down Vivian's long back. She began to unbutton the schoolteacher's dress. She needed to feel more of this woman. She needed to see her. The tiny buttons seemed to go on forever as Nellie's fingers skillfully undid each one. She felt Vivian's hand moving across her chest. The buttons of her best Sunday dress located in the front were being slowly freed.

Nellie had finally undone the last button on Vivian's dress. Now she was pulling Vivian's dress down her broad shoulders. Vivian had opened the front of Nellie's dress and was now kissing her way down her neck. The closeness of their bodies hampered Nellie's efforts to further undress the object of her desire.

Nellie whimpered as she felt Vivian pull away from her. Vivian smiled as she sat up and began to unbutton the sleeves of her dress. Nellie smiled in return as she sat up slightly and shrugged her dress jacket off. She tossed it off to the side. Nellie sat there clad in her skirt and chemise. Vivian gave her a knowing smile as she stood, allowing her dress to fall to the ground.

Nellie's heart pounded against her chest as her eyes drifted down Vivian's seemingly endless legs. Vivian knelt down beside

Nellie. Nellie was once again locked in a passionate kiss. She could feel Vivian unfasten her skirt and lower it down her body.

Nellie ran her fingers through Vivian's hair as the brunette began to kiss her way down her body. Vivian ran her hands along Nellie's skin as she removed her skirt. Nellie was lying blissfully on the blanket as Vivian removed their footwear. Vivian lay down beside her, leaning on her elbow to look down at Nellie. They were dressed only in their undergarments and yet somehow Nellie felt overdressed.

"Are you a virgin?" Vivian inquired in a careful tone.

"Yes," Nellie answered honestly.

"And so you will stay," Vivian reassured her.

"But . . . ," Nellie began to protest.

Vivian pressed her fingers to Nellie's lips to silence her. "I can still pleasure you without taking your innocence," Vivian explained in a husky tone.

"And if I want to give myself to you?" Nellie protested eagerly.

"You're to be married," Vivian said with a hint of disappointment.

"I don't want him," Nellie choked out. "I want you."

"How can you know?" Vivian asked her in disbelief.

"He never made me feel the way you do," Nellie asserted as she pulled Vivian in for a lingering kiss.

Nellie kissed Vivian deeply, hoping to convey all of the emotions and desires she felt. Their bodies melted together as Vivian untied the lacing of Nellie's chemise.

Vivian's fingers burned her skin as she touched her gently. Nellie thought she was going to explode when she felt Vivian's palm brush against her nipple. Nellie's body seemed to take on a life of its own as her hips thrust into Vivian's firm body. She felt a dampness gather in her bloomers as her hips began to rock rhythmically against Vivian. She plunged her tongue deeper into Vivian's mouth as she began to loosen the ties on her chemise.

Vivian gasped as she pulled away from the kiss. Their hips ground together wildly as Nellie pulled open Vivian's chemise. She moaned as she was greeted by the vision of Vivian's beautiful breasts. She felt her own chemise being removed as their bodies continued to rock together. Nellie reached up to feel Vivian's bosom, touching her shyly at first until she felt Vivian's nipples harden from her touch.

Vivian was panting heavily as she lowered herself down to Nellie. The blonde shop girl trembled as she felt Vivian's mouth taste her skin. Nellie gripped her tightly, feeling her naked back as Vivian kissed the valley between her breasts. Nellie parted her thighs and wrapped her legs around Vivian's body.

She continued to thrust against the taller woman as her hands roamed down Vivian's back. She paused for a moment as she reached the waistband of Vivian's bloomers. Vivian's tongue circled one of her breasts, teasing her. Nellie slipped her hands into Vivian's undergarment, feeling the firm flesh eagerly as Vivian captured her aching nipple in her mouth.

Vivian teased her nipple with her tongue and her teeth while Nellie clutched her backside firmly. Nellie's body couldn't stop grinding against Vivian's. As the schoolteacher's mouth pleasured her breast, Nellie felt an overwhelming passion consuming her. Vivian teased her other nipple, pinching it between her fingers. "Vivian," Nellie gasped as her hips began to grind against Vivian's body at a furious pace.

Nellie's head spun; she was certain that she was going to pass out as Vivian moved her mouth from one breast to the other and then back again. Nellie whimpered in disappointment as Vivian's mouth moved away from her breasts. Her body arched as the brunette began kissing her way down Nellie's body.

The sensations of gentle kisses, licks, and Vivian's soft hair touching her body were incredible. Nellie never wanted this feeling to end as Vivian blazed a fiery trail down her torso. Nellie felt her passion coating the insides of her thighs as Vivian lowered her bloomers. The brunette kissed her legs as she removed the last of Nellie's clothing. Instead of feeling exposed, the blonde felt suddenly free.

Vivian kissed and tasted her way back up Nellie's firm legs and thighs. Nellie gasped in pleasure as she felt Vivian's breath blowing through her blonde curls. She opened herself wider as Vivian settled her body between her legs. Nellie draped her legs over Vivian's shoulders as the brunette lifted her backside, cupping her cheeks firmly as she kissed the inside of Nellie's thighs.

Nellie could feel Vivian shifting and then parting her now swollen nether lips. Nellie looked down to see her lover looking back up at her with fierce blue eyes. The look of passion made Nellie quiver. Nellie released a strangled cry as Vivian's tongue flickered across her throbbing button. Vivian moaned with pleasure as her tongue tasted Nellie slowly.

Nellie never realized that doing this to another woman would feel so incredible. She watched as Vivian drank in her passion. Nellie's body rocked against Vivian's eager mouth as the brunette's teeth grazed across her button. Vivian steadied Nellie's gyrating body with one arm across her firm abdomen as she suckled her harder. "Sweet Jesus," Nellie cried out as she tried to press herself deeper into Vivian's touch.

Nellie clutched the blanket with one hand as she pinched one of her nipples with her other. She could feel her thighs shaking uncontrollably as Vivian's mouth and tongue quickened their pace. Nellie's head fell back as her entire body exploded. Vivian continued to pleasure her. Nellie was certain that her heart was about to burst as she cried out for more.

Nellie collapsed in a quivering heap, her body covered in sheen of sweat. Vivian licked the inside of her thighs clean before gathering Nellie up in her arms. "I never knew," Nellie panted as Vivian held her tightly. "I never knew you could do that or that it would feel so wonderful," she finally managed to choke out as Vivian planted tender kisses across her brow.

Nellie buried her face in Vivian's naked chest. The smell of her skin and the sight of her nipples were far too tempting for the little blonde. Nellie dipped her head and captured one of Vivian's nipples in her mouth. She began to suckle it furiously, enjoying the taste of Vivian's skin.

Nellie circled the rose-colored bud with her tongue as her hand drifted down Vivian's firm body. She felt Vivian shift as she lowered her lover down. Nellie's hand drifted underneath the material of Vivian's bloomers. Her excitement grew as her finger touched Vivian's damp curls.

Releasing Vivian's breast from her mouth, she stared deeply

into her lover's eyes. "Teach me," Nellie said in an insistent voice as she cupped Vivian's mound. The brunette gasped with pleasure. Nellie reached down and gripped Vivian's bloomers. The blonde began to remove Vivian's undergarment quickly. She needed to see the entire woman who had stolen her heart.

She tossed the last of Vivian's clothing over her shoulder as she stared at her lover's black triangle. The sight was so inviting it made Nellie's mouth water. With a gentle hand Vivian reached out to her and guided one of Nellie's hands to her. Nellie watched with fascination as Vivian gently took two of her fingers and guided them to her wetness. "Do you feel what you do to me?" Vivian asked her in a breathy tone.

"Yes," Nellie choked out as Vivian guided her fingers across her wetness. Nellie's desire grew as Vivian's wetness coated her fingers. Vivian guided her gently showing Nellie how she wanted to be touched.

Nellie could only watch in amazement. Vivian opened her legs wider as she placed Nellie's fingers against the opening of her womanhood. "But?" Nellie inquired in confusion.

"I'm not a virgin bride," Vivian answered her with a reassuring tone. The revelation filled Nellie with a strange mix of disappointment and desire. Vivian's hand guided her fingers inside of her. She moaned as she entered her lover, feeling her walls capture her fingers.

Vivian slowly moved Nellie's wrist so that her fingers plunged slowly in and out of her center. Then her lover gently guided her thumb so that it would brush against her throbbing button as Nellie thrust in and out of her warmth. Vivian released her hand, allowing Nellie to make love to her. Nellie loved the feel of Vivian's body as her hand began to quicken its pace.

Vivian cupped her backside and gently lifted Nellie. The blonde straddled her lover's quivering body as Vivian reached down and began to stroke Nellie's button. Their hands moved in unison as their passion grew. "Please," Nellie gasped. She knew what she was pleading for as she took her lover harder.

"Nellie, I can't," Vivian panted as her body trembled.

"I belong to you," Nellie insisted as she felt herself nearing the edge. "I don't want it to be him," she choked out on the verge of tears.

Nellie lowered her body so their naked forms could melt together. Instinctively she knew that they were both nearing the edge. "Please," she repeated urgently. "I'm yours. Take me," she implored her lover.

"Nellie, I love you so much," Vivian whimpered as her fingers were suddenly pressed against Nellie's opening.

"I love you, Vivian. I need you," Nellie responded honestly as she opened herself to her lover. Their bodies rocked together wildly as Nellie felt her lover enter her. She winced at the sudden jolt of pain. Vivian seemed to be trying to slow down their erotic rhythm. Nellie was too far gone to slow down. Her body arched as she thrust deeper into Vivian.

Nellie still felt the rush of desire despite the pain she was experiencing. She rode against Vivian's hand furiously. Everything felt so good as the sweat rolled down their naked bodies. Nellie looked down at her lover thinking that she had never seen anything so beautiful as Vivian's face caught in the throws of passion.

Nellie felt Vivian's body explode in pleasure beneath her. Quickly she followed her lover into ecstasy. They collapsed together as their hands continued to pleasure one another. Vivian captured her in a fiery kiss as she rolled Nellie onto her side. They plunged in and out of each other as they screamed into the warmth of the kiss.

Finally they clutched each other tightly as their hands stilled. They clung to one another as the waves of passion continued to rush through them. Sated, Nellie rested her head against Vivian's chest. Their breathing finally calmed as they gently caressed each other.

The cool air flowing across their exposed bodies alerted the lovers to the lateness of the hour. "We need to get going," Vivian said, the regret ringing clearly in her tone.

"I don't want this to end," Nellie whimpered as she reluctantly released her lover.

"I don't know what we can do about this," Vivian sighed

heavily as she turned away from Nellie.

They sat in an uncomfortable silence. "Is there somewhere we can wash up?" Vivian inquired in a somber tone.

"There's a creek just past those trees," Nellie responded as she began to gather up her clothing.

She couldn't look at Vivian, knowing that it would only cause her more pain. She heard Vivian gather up her belongings as well. Nellie led her to the creek where they washed quickly, unable to look each other in the eye. They dressed and picked up the remnants of their picnic, each checking carefully to ensure that there were no signs of their tryst. Nellie hitched the team and they climbed into the buggy.

She fought back the tears and steadied herself. "Can I come to your room tonight?" She asked in a slow fearful voice.

"I don't think we should," Vivian responded, her voice cracking slightly as she spoke.

Nellie turned to her lover, knowing that she was fighting with her feelings. Nellie reached over and took her by the hand, lifting the larger hand to her lips and placing a gentle kiss on her fingers. She could still smell her scent lingering on them. "I do love you," Vivian confessed as she leaned in and kissed Nellie's cheek tenderly.

"That's a start," Nellie responded with a smile as she laid both their hands in her lap.

Nellie signaled the team and started to drive off, keeping a tight hold on Vivian's hand. "Come to my room tonight," Vivian said softly as she laid her head on Nellie's shoulder. Nellie smiled, knowing that they were about to begin a very dangerous journey. She also knew that she couldn't stay away from Vivian. She needed her as much as she needed air to breathe.

THE END

Mavis Applewater

STOLEN MOMENTS
(MISS LARILIA'S LESSON - PART TWO)

PART ONE

Vivian waited in her room at the boarding house, knowing that she would come to her. Nellie was like a force of nature. A fire burned deep within the young girl and it drew Vivian in. At first the quiet schoolteacher was certain that she would be able to resist the young blonde's charms. After all, Nellie was to be married. Now the thought of another person touching the girl repulsed Vivian. They had made love and nothing would ever be the same between the two of them.

Vivian knew without question that she should be the one to end their relationship. Yet she was unable to resist. She had been burned by Nellie's fire and now she wished to drown in it. She was pacing the floorboards of her tiny room, knowing that she was one who had given in to the temptation of Nellie's body. She was the one who had nuzzled the young girl's neck. She was the one who started touching the blonde in an inappropriate manner. And she was the one who had taken Nellie's virtue. Now she was waiting for the woman that she was in love with because she had invited her to her room that evening.

"We could go to jail or be hung for what we have done," Vivian said quietly in the darkness. This wasn't a new fear in her life, but now she had endangered an innocent girl who was about to be married. "I must turn her away if she comes to me tonight," she vowed as she stared out onto the darkened streets of Cedar Grove. "I am going to miss this town and her," she choked out just as a shy rapping invaded her solitude.

Vivian fought against the tears as she kept her back to the door. "I can't let her in," she reasoned, knowing that she was causing her lover pain. She held her spot at the window firmly as the shy knocking grew steadily more insistent. "Vivian?" A hushed whisper sounded and the schoolteacher's resolve and good intentions melted away. She ignored the inner voice telling her to stop and threw open the door.

Nellie was trembling as she stepped quietly into the room. Vivian's heart was pounding as she closed the door quietly behind them. "You were planning on turning me away?" Nellie said quietly in confusion.

"Yes," Vivian confessed as she turned away from the sight of her lover had her robe wrapped tightly around her tiny body. "Do you know how dangerous this love is?" Vivian's voice caught slightly as she stared down at the floor. "There are people, some of them are your friends and neighbors, who will think that lynching would be too good for us if we are caught."

"I know, Vivian," Nellie responded firmly. Vivian heard the floorboards creak as her lover stepped closer to her.

"Do you?" Vivian persisted as she felt the warmth of her lover's body standing dangerously close to her.

Vivian trembled as Nellie's fingertips lightly caressed her arm. "I know that I love you," Nellie said in a voice barely above a whisper. "I know that the only obstacle that could keep me away from you would be my death." Nellie wrapped her arms around Vivian's trembling body from behind. The tall schoolteacher was helpless to resist her young lover. Her body leaned into the touch and Vivian was lost in the warmth emanating from behind her.

"I love you," Vivian said in a meek tone, knowing that she would do anything her lover asked of her. Her blue eyes fluttered shut as Nellie's hands made comforting circles across her abdomen. Vivian's head fell back slightly as Nellie's caresses grew bolder. The schoolteacher's nipples hardened as her thighs began to quiver.

Nellie's hands drifted up Vivian's body and gently cupped her breasts as she nuzzled her face into Vivian's back. The tall schoolteacher's back arched as her lover's palms grazed her aching nipples. Vivian released a strangled whimper as Nellie's palms began to trace her nipples in a circular pattern. "I need to feel you," Nellie said softly, her hot breath seeping through the material of Vivian's nightgown.

"Nellie," Vivian panted in response. Her mind was clouded by Nellie's touch as she struggled to tell her lover what she wanted. "Nellie," she repeated, trying to form the words of passion that were pulsating through her body.

"Yes, my love," was the breathy response as tiny fingers began to roll and pinch her aching nipples.

"Aah," Vivian cried out as Nellie's fingers and hands increased their exploration. Vivian clasped her hand over her mouth, praying that none of the other guests had heard her cries of pleasure. Her back arched as she pressed her breasts harder into her lover's hands.

One of Nellie's hands drifted in a slow tantalizing path along Vivian's body while the other continued to tease her breast. Vivian felt her lover's hand on her hip as Nellie began to gather up the soft material of her sleeping gown. "I need to see your beauty," Nellie pleaded hotly against the nape of her neck. Vivian's breathing grew ragged as she felt Nellie's lips brush the back of her neck.

Vivian stepped out of her lover's embrace and turned to her. She found herself lost in a smoky green haze as she pulled up her sleeping gown. Slowly the schoolteacher removed her clothing and tossed it across the room. "You as well, my love," Vivian instructed her young lover in a husky tone that was filled with desire. Her lips trembled with sweet anticipation as she watched her lover's robe fall to the floor. "Everything," she implored the young blonde. "Our clothing must not gather the fragrance of our passion," Vivian cautioned Nellie tenderly. The blonde nodded in understanding as she quickly shed her clothing.

"I love you," Vivian whispered in wonderment as she drank

in the glorious slight of her young lover's firm naked body standing before her. She held out her hand, beckoning her lover to join her. Nellie reached out and clasped her hand tightly. Vivian had every intention of leading the beautiful blonde over to her tiny bed. It appeared that Nellie had other desires to satisfy first as she sank to her knees. Vivian inhaled sharply as she looked down at the emerald orbs twinkling up at her.

Nellie's warm breath caressed the dark curls as Vivian's legs opened, inviting her lover in. Vivian stroked Nellie's golden locks as she guided her towards her passion. Nellie clasped Vivian's hips tightly as she placed gentle kisses along her abdomen. Vivian whimpered in response as Nellie's tongue dipped playfully into her navel. Vivian bit down on her lower lip as she fought against the urge to press her lover deep inside her passion. Instead she enjoyed the feel of Nellie's soft silky hair.

Nellie continued to stare deeply into Vivian's eyes as her mouth drifted lowered, further fueling the brunette's longing desire. Vivian's thighs parted even further as her lover clasped her firm backside with one hand and parted her nether lips with the other. "Taste me," Vivian encouraged her in a soft tone. "Taste the passion you have created simply with your smile." Nellie never broke the intensity of her gaze as her tongue dipped into Vivian's wetness.

Vivian's breathing caught as her lover's tongue slid along her slick folds. Nellie murmured with delight as she drank in Vivian's essence. The need to breathe was subdued as Vivian's clit pulsated. Her passion flowed as Nellie buried her face deeper into her cleft. The feel of Nellie's tongue slowly licking away every drop of wetness was driving the schoolteacher insane. Her breath rushed out in a throaty gasp as Nellie captured her throbbing button in her mouth and began to suckle it greedily.

Vivian's hips swayed as she pressed Nellie harder against her. The blonde seemed to understand her urgency and suckled her nub harder as she pressed two fingers against Vivian's center. Vivian's mind was spinning as her lover devoured her clit while her fingers entered her center. "Yes, Nellie," she pleaded helplessly as her hips thrust forward. Nellie's fingers plunged in and out of the warmth of her center.   She felt Nellie's teeth grazing her button as she pressed tightly on the back of the blonde's head, driving her deeper inside of her.

"Sweet Jesus," Vivian choked out as she felt her thighs trembling against her lover's face.   Nellie's hands and mouth began moving in a frantic rhythm as Vivian clung to her.   The schoolteacher's breathing was labored as she neared the edge of pure bliss.   Vivian's hips rocked wildly as her passion exploded.   Her knees felt weak as her body convulsed against her lover.

Nellie's fingers stilled and remained deep inside of her.   Vivian gazed down upon the soft golden hair nestled between her thighs.   Her lover was humming happily as she continued to taste the schoolteacher's wetness.   Vivian smiled down upon her eager lover.   "Nellie," she said, beckoning her lover who was insistent upon continuing her exploration.   Vivian could still feel the passion pulsating through her body as she stepped slightly away from Nellie's touch.   Her lover grumbled in disappointment as she reluctantly slid her fingers out of the warmth of Vivian's center.   "I need to hold you," Vivian implored her as Nellie rested her head on the brunette's quivering stomach.

Nellie stood and wrapped her arms around Vivian's naked body.   The schoolteacher wrapped her arms around Nellie's warm body and kissed her golden crown tenderly.   "We do not have much time," Vivian explained.   "And I need to pleasure you.   I need to feel your body responding to my touch."   Nellie raised her head and Vivian watched her emerald eyes dancing merrily.   "Is it any wonder that you have stolen my heart?" Vivian confessed as she caressed her lover's cheek.

Nellie turned away shyly.   Vivian captured the blonde's face gently and turned her towards her gaze.   "Why so shy all of sudden?" Vivian teased Nellie brightly.

"I don't know what it is you see in me," Nellie confessed with a blush.   Vivian stared back at the younger woman in confusion.   "You are so beautiful," Nellie continued as she leaned into Vivian's body.

"Is it possible that you are completely unaware of just how captivating you are?" Vivian said in soft wonderment.   Nellie's eyes once again drifted away shyly.   "If my words have failed to convince you then perhaps I should show you just how deeply I care," Vivian asserted as she brushed her lips along Nellie's cherubic features.

Nellie moaned softly as Vivian's lips continued to caress her milky white skin. Vivian could feel Nellie's firm body trembling against her own. "Lay down on the bed," she whispered huskily into her lover's ear. Nellie clasped Vivian's hips tightly, her breath caressing the brunette's skin. "Lay on your stomach," Vivian continued firmly. Nellie gasped in response. Vivian felt her lover's wetness pressing against her thigh as Nellie placed a tender kiss in the valley between her breasts.

Vivian's smile grew brighter as Nellie stepped away from her and reclined on her bed. The schoolteacher's clit began to throb in a steady rhythm as she watched her lover roll over onto her stomach. As Vivian crossed the small distance, her eyes never left the sight of Nellie's firm young body lying across her bed, bathed in the soft glow of the moonlight streaming through the window. Vivian climbed up onto the bed, allowing her long dark tresses to brush across her lover's skin. Nellie moaned with pleasure as Vivian's hair tickled her sensitive flesh.

Vivian straddled her lover's body and brushed her long strawberry blonde hair away from the nape of her neck. Vivian lowered her mouth to her lover's neck as she pressed her wetness into the blonde's firm backside. "Can you feel what you do to me?" Vivian said huskily as her warm breath teased the nape of Nellie's neck.

"Yes," Nellie responded weakly as her hips rose slightly to greet Vivian's dark wet curls.

Vivian kissed her way down her lover's body, her mouth and tongue drinking in every delightful inch of Nellie's quivering form. Vivian brushed her aching nipples across Nellie's firm back. Her eager young lover rolled her hips harder against Vivian's passion. Vivian moaned deeply as she licked the length of Nellie's spine. "Please," Nellie pleaded as Vivian began to worship her backside with her hands and mouth.

Vivian ran her hands slowly up and down the length of Nellie's body as the blonde raised herself up on her hands and knees. "Yes, that's it, my love," Vivian encouraged the young blonde before she traced her tongue along Nellie's firm round cheeks. She could hear Nellie's breathing becoming increasingly ragged.

Vivian knelt behind her lover and smiled at the sight of Nellie freely offering herself to her. "So full of love and passion," Vivian said in sheer amazement as she clasped her lover's hips firmly. Nellie moaned as she parted her thighs wider. Vivian sighed deeply as the scent of her lover's arousal invaded her senses. The schoolteacher straddled her lover's hips just as they thrust backward.

Vivian's hips thrust forward to greet her lover's urgent need. The brunette pressed her desire against Nellie. The blonde gasped as she pressed her hips harder against Vivian's wetness. "I need to taste you again," Nellie pleaded. "Please, Vivian, let me taste you." The schoolteacher responded by grinding her hips harder against Nellie's body.

"Not yet, my love," Vivian said softly. "First I need to feel you explode against me." Vivian's body thrust harder as Nellie rocked in a wild rhythm, meeting her every move. She watched in lustful amazement as Nellie's head jerked back, her eyes filled with a wild abandonment. Vivian could feel her own climax growing near as she reached around her lover's body.

Her heart pounded faster as her lover's overflowing desire coated her fingers. Vivian hissed as she dipped her fingers into her lover's wetness. Nellie released a strangled whimper as Vivian entered her center. Their bodies continued to grind together wildly as Vivian felt the walls of Nellie's center grip her fingers tightly. Vivian's control slipped as she ground her throbbing clit frantically against Nellie's body. She began to plunge in and out of the blonde's wetness as the bed creaked from their frantic pace.

Nellie buried her face in the down pillow as she screamed in ecstasy. Vivian felt Nellie's body trembling as she exploded against the schoolteacher's body. Vivian bit down on her bottom lip so she could stifle her own screams of pleasure. She was still thrusting against Nellie as their bodies arched and collapsed against the bed.

Nellie was still crying out into Vivian's pillow as the

brunette continued to ride her body, driving them both over the edge once again. Vivian's movements stilled as she allowed the aftermath of the pleasure to seep through their exhausted bodies. She brushed Nellie's hair aside to reveal the blonde's flushed features. Vivian kissed her sweat-stained brow gently as Nellie smiled up at her.

Once their breathing had calmed, Vivian finally had enough energy to reluctantly roll her body off of Nellie's. The blonde reached out to her and Vivian captured the small hands in her own. "The moon is fading, my love," she said with soft regret as she began to kiss each one of Nellie's delicate digits. It broke the schoolteacher's heart as her lover's smile vanished. "I need . . ," Nellie started to protest.

Vivian cut off Nellie's pleas as she pulled her lover in for a long sensual kiss. "We need to get cleaned up and you need to return to your own room," Vivian instructed Nellie firmly. She felt a pang in her heart as her lover simply nodded sadly in response. Vivian's body felt cold as Nellie climbed out of her bed.

"Will it always be like this?" Nellie inquired sadly as she poured water from the pitcher into the basin.

Vivian opened her mouth to speak but the words failed to come. She had no answer to offer. Soon Nellie would marry and they would never be allowed to enjoy even these few stolen moments of pleasure. She watched as Nellie's body stiffened before she began to wash up. A tear ran down Vivian's cheek as she watched her lover wipe away all traces of their passion.

As Nellie dressed, Vivian washed her own body before redressing in her night clothing. Both women remained silent as they embraced one another tenderly. After a brief kiss Nellie stepped out of Vivian's room, leaving the schoolteacher alone with her thoughts. Vivian pressed her fingers to her own lips; they still tingled from Nellie's touch.

PART TWO

Nellie hurried downstairs in hopes that she would see Vivian before she left for the schoolhouse. The energetic blonde's heart was pounding at the thought of seeing her lover even for a few brief moments. She still found it hard to believe that just a few short hours ago she was making love to the beautiful schoolteacher. In one day her life had changed completely.

She hurried into the dining room with a tray of food. Her mother seemed surprised at her eagerness to help out. Nellie was happy that her mother was pleased. She had been rather cold towards Nellie when she discovered that the blonde had shunned her intended to enjoy a picnic with Vivian instead. Nellie blushed slightly when she saw the sparkling blue orbs watching her carefully from across the room. She chuckled slightly as she served the other guests, saving Vivian's table for last in order to steal a few lingering moments with her lover. If Nellie's mother had any idea what had transpired between her and the schoolteacher yesterday afternoon, she was quite certain that she would be locked in her room until her wedding day.

"Good morning, Miss Larilia," Nellie greeted her lover brightly as she placed her breakfast on the table.

"Good morning, Nellie," Vivian purred in response. The deep timber of her lover's voice made the blonde's knees tremble in expectation. "Steady," Vivian cautioned her in a low tone.

"You have no idea what you do to me," Nellie whispered softly so that only Vivian could hear her words. "Tonight?" Nellie inquired hopefully as she heard her mother's stern voice calling her.

"Yes," Vivian responded in a rich tone that once again caused Nellie's heart to beat a little faster. Nellie stared deeply into Vivian's crystal-blue eyes; aware of the promise they held. Their fingers brushed slightly, causing Nellie's body to become covered with goose bumps. Nellie smiled slyly before gathering up her tray and answering her mother's frantic call.

"I swear, girl, I don't understand what goes on in that head of yours," her mother chastised her as they entered the kitchen. "Didn't you hear me calling you?"

"Yes, mother," Nellie, responded dryly.

"Why are you always bothering poor Miss Larilia?" her mother asked, continuing her tirade.

"We are friends," Nellie snapped quickly, instantly regretting the tone she had taken.

"Excuse me, young lady?" Her mother glared down at her. " I want you to leave that schoolteacher alone. You shouldn't be spending your time with a spinster. Thankfully this nonsense will cease once you are married."

Nellie's heart sank at those words. She couldn't marry Freddie or anyone else. She belonged to the raven-haired beauty sitting in the dining room; the same woman her mother had just instructed her to stay away from. She knew from the tone her mother used that there was no room for debate. For now she would need to settle on sneaking out of her room at night. "Mother, Vivian and I are friends," Nellie explained in a quiet obedient tone.

"Since when do you call her by her first name?" her mother inquired suspiciously.

"We are friends," Nellie reasserted in a gentle tone. "She is only a few years older than myself and the other girls my age are already married. Please, Mother. I don't have anyone to talk to."

"You can talk to me or your father." Her mother sniffed in disdain. "Or Frederick. After all, the two of you are to be married."

Nellie's mind raced quickly. "Mother, how can I talk about the lace for my dress or flowers for the wedding with Freddie? It would bore him to tears," Nellie explained dryly as she rolled her eyes.

"True," her mother conceded. "So come to me. I am your mother." Nellie opened her mouth to protest but her mother held up a firm hand to silence her. "I don't want you spending time with *that* woman. I never trust a woman her age that isn't married. I could understand if she was unattractive," her mother continued thoughtfully. "But a woman who looks like that and is without a husband . . . Trust me, there is something that she is hiding."

Nellie could see the wheels of her mother's overly curious mind spinning. She wanted to scream that she was what Vivian was hiding, that she was madly in love with the raven-haired school teacher and that there was no way on God's green earth she was going to marry Freddie or any other man. But since she did love her mother and didn't want to be the cause of her dropping dead from a major heart attack, she bit her tongue. "I need to get over to the mercantile," Nellie grumbled before storming upstairs. "If she is going to treat me like a child then fine, I will act like one," she fumed as she slammed every door in her path behind her.

PART THREE

Vivian made her way over to the mercantile. The afternoon sun was beating down as she crossed the dirt streets. She paused for a moment and gazed up at the bright sun, allowing its warmth to caress her chiseled features. It was apparent that Indian summer was upon them. Her students had been restless all day.

She couldn't blame the youngsters. She too had wanted to run off and enjoy the unseasonably warm weather. Her crystal blue eyes drifted towards her goal. The mercantile was only a few feet away and inside was the woman who had captured her heart. She found herself smiling as she resumed her journey.

How nice it would have been to spend the day with Nellie. They could have enjoyed a simple picnic at their special spot. They could have run around barefoot while stealing kisses. It would have been ideal if they lived in a perfect world where she could just bask in the sunshine that poured from her new love. A slight frown clouded her face briefly. Once she caught a glimpse of golden hair shining from inside the mercantile, she found herself smiling again.

Vivian blushed as she stepped inside the shop that could cater to every need from clothing to feed for livestock. Her blush grew deeper; the only thing in the mercantile that she needed was standing behind the counter.

Emerald eyes cast a warm knowing glance her way as she closed the door behind her. Nellie's gaze darkened as she followed Vivian's movements. The schoolteacher knew that her lover was telling her that she needed her as well. Vivian's smile broadened in response before she shyly looked away, afraid that she was going to melt into a pool of desire right there in the town store. She could hear Nellie softly chuckle as she returned her attention to the woman she had been attending to before Vivian made her entrance. Vivian pretended to browse around the store as Nellie finished with her customers.

It was the first of the month and many of the local hands had just been paid; it made for a busy day for the young shop girl. As Vivian browsed through the various sundries, she would stiffen as some of the gentlemen became a little brazen with Nellie. Her heart dropped each time Nellie politely reminded the gentlemen that she was spoken for.

Finally the last of the customers shuffled out of the store and Vivian found herself racing to the counter. They were painfully aware of the large window at the front of the shop; they were in full view of anyone passing by. "Last night was amazing," Nellie said softly as she blushed deeply. Vivian took another quick glimpse around to ensure that they were quite alone. Feeling safe, she brushed her fingertips along the back of her lover's hand.

Nellie gasped as her eyes fluttered shut. The ringing of the bell announced that their bliss was over for the moment. Vivian quickly withdrew her hand, instantly missing the feel of her lover's skin. She looked up at the clock, knowing that Nellie would be stuck in the mercantile for a few more hours. "Thank you for your help, Miss Winslow," Vivian said softly as she walked to the door, almost running into Nellie's mother. "Excuse me, Mrs. Winslow," she apologized as the woman brushed past her. Vivian turned to find her lover watching her. *'Tonight,'* she mouthed. Nellie's smile told her everything she needed to know.

Later that evening Vivian paced the floor of her tiny room just as she had done the previous night. The moon once again was shining brightly into her little room. This evening Vivian wasn't pacing from fear but from the anxious desire that was filling every fiber of her being. She hadn't seen Nellie at dinner that evening and she began to fear the worse. Mrs. Winslow had become suddenly curt with Vivian, adding another weight to her already fearful mind.

Still, the thought that Nellie would soon be in her arms overrode all of her fears. "You are the flame and I am a helpless moth unable to escape your spell," she said softly as she stared up at the almost full moon. The shy rap on her door made her heart beat just a little faster.

She licked her lips in anticipation as she tightened the ties of the dressing gown covering her naked body. She calmed her erratic breathing as she crossed the room and opened the door. Vivian found her heart's desire standing on the other side. She quickly stepped aside and allowed her younger lover to enter the darken room. Vivian closed the door and turned to her lover. The golden-haired lass' smile melted her heart and her smoldering eyes sent a shiver through her body.

Vivian's knees went weak and she found herself leaning against the door, gripping the knob tightly in order to support herself. "I love it when you wear your hair down," Nellie said in a sultry tone as she approached Vivian's trembling form. Nellie seemed mesmerized as she began to run her fingers through Vivian's long black hair.

As Nellie's fingers drifted slowly through her silken locks, Vivian knew that she had made the right choice when she carefully penned the letter to the Fulton School earlier that evening. She would mail the letter tomorrow and pray that the school would have a position for her. She knew that she had to leave Cedar Grove with or without Nellie. For tonight she existed only for the young woman whose fingers were gently massaging her scalp.

"I've been on the verge of screaming from not being able to spend more time with you today," Nellie confessed as her fingers drifted down the front of Vivian's bosom. The brunette trembled as her lover gently cupped her firm full breasts. "My mother is being impossible. She wants me to stay away from you."

"Do you think she suspects anything?" Vivian choked out as Nellie's hands slowly caressed her aching nipples through the thin material of her dressing gown.

"No," Nellie said as she shook her head. "If it wasn't for the existence of myself and my three siblings, I would swear that my mother knew nothing when it comes to matters of intimacy, "

Nellie explained wryly. "Are you naked under your robe?" Nellie inquired in a mischievous tone.

"Yes," Vivian responded with a strangled hiss.

"It is amazing how I can feel your desire without touching you," Nellie murmured as she began to nibble on Vivian's sensitive neck.

Vivian reached between their overheated bodies and loosened the belt of her robe. As Nellie continued to trail her tongue along her neck, the brunette opened her robe to reveal her body to her lover. Nellie gasped with pleasure as Vivian dropped it to the floor. "Take your clothes off, my love," Vivian instructed her in a quiet yet commanding tone.

Nellie stepped away from her slightly, the bravado clearly written across her face. "I think you just enjoy seeing me naked," Nellie teased the grinning brunette. Vivian's face felt flush as she watched Nellie removing her clothing. Unable to contain her desire, one of the schoolteacher's hands began to drift down her body in a slow determined path. She watched the rise and fall of Nellie's bosom become erratic as she pinched and teased one of her own nipples.

Vivian watched with some degree of amusement as her lover halted her movements. The blonde's mouth dropped open and her eyes became fixated on Vivian's wandering hand. A wave of confidence filled the brunette as her hand drifted lower. "Undress for me, my love," Vivian encouraged her stunned lover as her fingers began to caress the damp curls.

Nellie nodded mutely as she continued to stare; Vivian's fingers were now dipping into her wetness. As Vivian gently stroked the swollen nub she watched as her lover's eyes glazed over with a brazen look of passion. Vivian parted her thighs, giving her lover a better view of her glistening fingers. She smiled slyly as she raised her fingers from her wetness; her lover's eyes were firmly fixated on her long fingers as she painted one of her nipples with her own passion.

Nellie growled deeply as she began to remove her clothing with lightening speed. Vivian gazed upon the rapidly approaching form of her lover, taking in the swell of her breasts and the soft supple curve of her hips. Before Vivian could realize what was happening, the blonde captured both of her wrists and raised her arms above her head. Nellie placed a searing kiss on her hungry lips. The blonde growled fiercely as she bit down on Vivian's lower lip.

Vivian was moaning loudly as Nellie's passion pressed urgently against her thigh. She pressed her thigh against Nellie's overflowing wetness. She could feel her lover's desire pouring out over her skin as their hips rocked in a wild sensual rhythm. Nellie's tongue circled her nipple, licking away every drop of Vivian's essence.

The brunette tried to free her hands as her lover captured her erect nipple in the warmth of her mouth. Vivian's hips thrust forward as they drove one another closer to the edge of ecstasy. "I belong to you," Nellie panted against her skin. The feel of her lover's warm breath and the sensual tone of her voice sent a jolt through Vivian's body. "Take me," Nellie pleaded as she released her hold on Vivian's wrists.

Vivian's hands moved quickly down Nellie's quivering body. With one hand she guided Nellie to continue suckling her breast while the other slipped between their sweat-covered bodies. The feel of her lover's desire only further fueled her raging passion. She found Nellie's swollen hood and began to stroke it rapidly. Nellie's teeth nipped at a rose colored nipple while Vivian's fingers continued to stroke her nub wildly. Nellie's body arched against her as her head fell back. The blonde's thigh trembled and then closed quickly, trapping Vivian's hand between them.

Vivian bent her neck and captured Nellie's lips in a fiery kiss. Her tongue grazed Nellie's teeth as it plunged deeply into the warmth of the blonde's mouth, stifling her screams of passion. She felt their bosoms pressing against one another as her lover's body exploded against her own. She continued to savor the taste of her lover's mouth as she felt Nellie's body heaving.

She finally tore her mouth away from Nellie's sweet lips when the need to breathe overwhelmed her. Nellie started to slip out of her grasp and Vivian quickly captured the quivering woman in her arms. She caressed Nellie's back tenderly as the smaller woman clung tightly to her. She nuzzled Nellie's soft golden hair and found herself becoming lost in the faint scent of strawberries. She murmured softly as her closed her eyes and relaxed into the feel of her lover's embrace.

Vivian felt her lover's breathing slowly even out. She opened her eyes to find Nellie's sweet cherub face looking up at her. She simply smiled in response, unable to speak as she became overwhelmed by her lover's smile. She kissed Nellie's brow tenderly before leading her to the bed. Vivian reclined onto the lumpy mattress and pulled her lover to her.

Their bodies melted together as they quickly reclaimed one another's lips. Vivian felt Nellie's fingers drifting along her body in slow shy movements that were causing her body to tremble. As their lips finally released their fiery hold on one another, Vivian reached out and traced Nellie's lips with her fingertips. She couldn't help staring at the beautiful young woman who was lying atop her
. Vivian had so much to tell her young lover, so many questions that she needed answers to, but now was not the time. Now was for continuing Nellie's education in the ways of passion. In a careful guiding tone, she explained to the blonde exactly what she wanted her to do.

"Won't I smother you?" Nellie questioned her in disbelief.

"No, my love," Vivian responded with a little chuckle. "If you become too heavy, we can lie side by side."

"And we can taste one another?" Nellie continued.

"Yes," Vivian reassured her. "If you want to?"

"Yes," Nellie responded eagerly. She quickly shifted her body so that her passion was within Vivian's reach. Vivian parted her thighs as her lover straddled her face. She could feel Nellie's warm breath teasing her wet curls as she clasped her lover's firm backside and brought her wetness down to greet her watering mouth.

She felt her lover's soft golden hair caressing her thighs as Nellie dipped her tongue into her wetness. Vivian moaned in pleasure as her lover's tongue slid along her slick folds. She lowered Nellie to her mouth and began to drink in the blonde's passion. She suckled her throbbing button in her mouth as she felt Nellie's tongue enter her center. Vivian moaned into Nellie's wetness as they pleasured one another.

Vivian fought to maintain her focus as she suckled Nellie's nub harder. She fought against her own pleasure as Nellie's tongue plunged in and out of her. Soon both women were rocking against one another's mouths as the passion welled up from deep inside of them. Vivian felt her body rising as Nellie's thighs trembled against her cheeks. She was groaning into Nellie's overflowing desire as she suckled her harder while the blonde's fingers replaced her tongue.

Vivian plunged two fingers deep inside her lover's womanhood and felt the walls capture her fingers. Nellie's tongue was now flickering across Vivian's nub. The brunette's fingers and mouth moved in rhythm as she felt her lover's thighs closing. Vivian's shoulders moved to prevent her lover from trapping her hand. She felt her lover's teeth nip playfully at her button and soon they were both screaming into one another's wetness while their bodies bucked wildly.

They clung tightly to each other as they exploded in unison. Vivian's head fell back and she began to lick the inside of Nellie's still trembling thighs. Nellie was panting as Vivian rolled her lover onto her back and quickly buried herself between her lover's thighs. She began to feast upon her lover eagerly, sending over the blonde once again into the throws of ecstasy.

Vivian gathered her lover up in her arms and held her tightly. She would allow Nellie to catch her breath before she needed to send her away. *'Someday,'* she silently vowed as she held Nellie tightly.

PART FOUR

Nellie was ready to pitch a fit. Actually, if Reverend Farley hadn't been standing in the mercantile, she would have thrown a full-fledged tantrum that would have made a two-year-old envious. First her mother had forbidden her from serving Vivian. Then she informed Nellie that she was to accompany Freddie on a buggy ride after church services on Sunday. Apparently the two had been talking and neither was pleased with Nellie's distance.

The decision had been made and Nellie had no reasonable recourse. She and Vivian had been lovers for almost three months and her bliss was about to come to an end. As if being told what to do by her mother wasn't enough of a thorn in her side, the stagecoach delivered the mail that afternoon. It brought with it a letter that made Nellie's blood boil.

The letter was for Vivian and it was from the Fulton School in Massachusetts. Despite her valiant efforts to find out what was in the letter, she couldn't see through the envelope. Passersby must have thought she had lost her mind as she stood in the front window holding the envelope up to the sun.

She scolded herself for her childish behavior and tried to convince herself that the letter meant nothing, but she knew it wasn't good news. Vivian was a schoolteacher and the letter was from a school that was thousands of miles away. She heard the afternoon school bell chiming, announcing the end of school for the day. She smiled at Reverend Farley who seemed to be doddering more than usual that day.

Nellie did her best to smile; all the while her heart was racing and her anger grew. As Vivian stepped into the shop, she received an icy glare from her lover. Vivian returned a quizzical look. Nellie's jaw clenched tightly as she tried to hurry the Reverend out of the shop. Nellie was certain that her head was going to explode by the time the Reverend left.

Vivian approached the counter slowly. Before the schoolteacher could speak, Nellie slammed the letter on the counter. "You're leaving?" She spat out in an accusing tone. Vivian blinked in surprise. "When were you going to tell me?" Nellie demanded bitterly.

"I can't stay in Cedar Grove," Vivian started to explain. *'It's true!'* Nellie's thought as she fought the tears that were welling up in her eyes. "You don't understand," Vivian said softly as she reached out to caress her cheek. Nellie jerked away from her touch. "I want you to come with me," Vivian choked out. "If we stay here, you'll be married and . . ."

"Yes," Nellie responded brightly. She fought the urge to

leap over the counter and wrap her arms around her lover.

"I don't even know if I have the position yet," Vivian said wearily.

"Open it," Nellie demanded as she shoved the envelope into Vivian's hands.

Vivian's hands trembled as she tore open the envelope. She nodded in the affirmative without smiling. Nellie released a heavy sigh. "When do we leave?" Nellie asked urgently.

"If we are to beat the weather, we will need to go soon," Vivian said in a heavy tone. "I start in the fall. I told them that my niece would be joining me."

"We will need to sneak out of town somehow," Nellie said thoughtfully as her mind started to formulate a plan.

"Do you understand what this means?" Vivian asked her cautiously. "You will be giving up everything. Can you do that? Walk away from your family and your home?"

"I wouldn't be giving up everything," Nellie said firmly. "To me, you are everything. So you better start thinking of a good plan that will get us to the east coast."

"With you by my side, I can do anything," Vivian responded with a brilliant smile.

Nellie's heart filled with joy as she lost herself in her lover's smile. She knew that her life had finally begun and somehow she and Vivian would be together.

THE END

Nellie's Quest
(Miss. Larilia's Lesson Part Three)

Early September 1884

Nellie snuggled closer to the small campfire she had managed to start in the darken woods. She blew into her clenched fists in a futile effort to warm her tiny hands. "I can do this," she muttered as she shivered from the cold night air. "I'll be with her soon." She reasoned as she shivered even harder. This time her body wasn't responding to the cold but from the sudden jolt of fear that trickled through her.

"She must be in Massachusetts by now," the blonde grumbled nervously as her mind conjured up the image of her tall dark lover whom she hadn't seen in almost two months. If only Nellie's mother hadn't interfered than she would be nestled in her lover's arms that night instead of freezing in front of the pitiful excuse for a campfire.

In her minds eye she pictured her own naked body sprawled across Vivian's bed on the last night they spent together. It was in the wee hours just before the dawn kissed the sky. Their nights together grew longer with each visit; even though both women were well of aware of the danger of being caught. Each of them had become trapped in the spell that their lover had woven.

Vivian was naked lying on her side facing her young blonde lover. Nellie could still recall the hushed whispers as they went over their plan one last time. If she shut her eyes tight enough she could still feel Vivian's blunt fingernails as they slowly traced the supple curve of Nellie's body. "Soon my love," Vivian vowed in a husky tone that never failed to make Nellie quiver with need. "Soon," the schoolteacher repeated before Nellie slipped from her bed and room before their bliss was revealed to prying eyes.

Nellie began her day feeling confident that their plan was set and soon they would begin their new life together. Vivian would leave town the next morning in full view of the townsfolk and Nellie would slip away a few nights later.

Each of them knew that it might take up to a fortnight before Nellie could make her escape. They hated being separated for even such a short time. Yet, the both of them understood that it was the only way that no one would suspect that Nellie ran off to be with Vivian. If Nellie vanished the same night as Vivian some one in the dingy burg of Cedar Grove might actually put things together.

Vivian was reluctant to accept the plan at first. She was weary of her young lover traveling alone at night especially since the girl out never traveled as far as the next town. Nellie quieted her fears, reminding her that she had mapped out a route off the beat and path and would disguise herself as a man. The blonde could still feel her lover's concern that last night as each of them pretended to enjoy the going away party the townspeople had thrown for Vivian at the restaurant Nellie's parents owned,

For the shop girl the party had been an exercise in torture. She wasn't allowed to speak to Vivian since her mother had forbidden it months ago. Freddie clung by her side and whenever someone spoke to her all they wanted to know were details of her upcoming nuptials. Thankfully Freddie and her mother were more than willing to supply the details of the one event Nellie had silently vowed never to attend.

The only bright spot during the hideous party were the secret glances she and Vivian stole. That night after everyone had gone home and Nellie was convinced her parents had retired for the evening she snuck out of her room just as she had almost every night for the past year. Fate turned on her with a cruel blow when she discovered her mother standing in the hallway of the family quarters demanding to know where she was sneaking off.

Nellie never knew if her mother believed her quickly blurted out excuse of needing to relieve herself or not. Mrs. Winslow seemed to be far to focus on Nellie's manners and attitude regarding her wedding. To Nellie's credit she bit her tongue and allowed her mother to spew out her lengthy lecture. Dejected Nellie returned to her room knowing that her mother would not be settling down for the night and she would be unable to sneak over to the boarder's rooms and crawl into Vivian's awaiting embrace.

Nellie's mother detained her in the kitchen the following morning robbing her of the chance to wish her lover a safe journey. Nellie managed to swallow her pain knowing that Vivian was only taking the stagecoach as far as Rumford and then she would wait for her lover to join her at the Rumford Inn. The brunette promised to place a lit candle or lantern in the window so Nellie would know which room she was in and could sneak in under the cover of darkness.

Rumford did not offer much except that it was a busy crossroads where people came and went on the new railroad so quickly no one really took notice of strangers. From there they could catch the first train heading East and be half way across the country before anyone realize which way Nellie had headed.

It was a simple plan with one fatal flaw, Mrs. Winslow. Nellie had one suitcase packed for her journey, which she had hidden under her bed. Her mother must have suspected something was going on with her troublesome daughter because the day before Nellie was to make her escape her mother searched her room. Her Mother was so enraged that she locked her youngest child in her room vowing only to release her on the day of her wedding.

Nellie had hoped that her father would come to her rescue but this seemed to be the one and only time he agreed with his overbearing wife. Nellie didn't let the set back break her spirit, since thankfully she had hidden the men's clothing, a revolver and money she had liberated from her father's mercantile beneath a floorboard in her room. She didn't feel any guilt or remorse about taking the items or the money.

The money she had skimmed from the till was the exact amount of the dowry he father had promised to pay the Cartwright family. After working in the family business for free since she could walk Nellie felt that she was far more entitled to the cash than Freddie's family. Her only problem was just how she was going to escape from her bedroom located on the third floor of the boarding house and away from the guest's rooms. She could only ponder what the wagging tongues of the town's busy bodies were saying about her sudden disappearance.

Only her parents, Jack, Melinda and Freddie knew that she was locked up in her bedroom. What none of them knew was that she was spending her time alone to construct a rope from her clothing and spare sheets. Making a binding that would be strong enough to support her was a painstaking task that took much to long.

Almost two months later just a week shy of her wedding day she had finally completed her task. On a moonless night she shimmied down the rope dressed in men's clothing. After she dropped a few feet to the ground below she spied Melinda watching her from the kitchen window. Her heart seized with fear until the cook simply winked and waved at her before drawing the curtains.

Nellie quietly scurried to the stable. She packed her meager belongings in a saddlebag and took her one of her favorite horses and galloped off into the night towards Rumford. She never glanced back as she left the only home she had ever known.

The following night she slipped into Rumford unnoticed by

the few strangers that were wandering the dirt covered Main Street at the late hour. She knew that it was too much to hope that she would find a light burning in a window. Yet, she held onto a sliver of hope that Vivian had waited for her.

She circled the Inn three times tears filling her emerald orbs as she turned each corner looking in vain for a light in one of the windows. She sniffed as she wiped her nose on the sleeve of her dark cotton shirt. She held firm in the belief that Vivian had waited as long as she could before she had to start heading east. Nellie reassured herself that she knew where Vivian was heading and once the petite blonde caught up with her lover they would be together forever.

She threw the saddlebag containing her money and clothing over her shoulder. She slid the revolver into the waistband of her pants and walked the horse over to the stable. She woke up the caretaker. The sleepy man gaped at her as they came to an agreement regarding a fair price for her horse. She knew that man must have thought she was crazy dressed the way she was. Still he gave her money took the horse and gave her directions to the train station.

Nellie lurked in the shadows until the following morning when she could buy a ticket and board the first train heading east. She pulled the Stetson down over her face as she took her place on the wooden bench on the train. She held her saddlebag close as she carefully stayed as far away from the other passengers as possible.

She tapped the saddlebag nervously as she waited for the train to leave the station. She gasped as she peeked out the window and spied her father and Freddie standing on the platform talking to one of the baggage handlers. "Please," she blew out in a hushed tone as her heart pounded violently. She scrunched down in her seat when she saw her father looking in her direction. Thankfully the train whistle blew and the large black iron beast jerked into motion.

Nellie's palms were sweating as she silently willed the train to hurry along. She was uncertain if either Freddie or her father had seen her. She also couldn't be certain that no one in Rumford had noticed her and would share the information with her father and former beau. She would have to get off at the next stop and change direction in an effort to throw them off track. She hated adding more time to her journey, yet she knew that she had to be careful. If either of them found her they would drag her kicking and screaming back to Cedar Grove and the wedding chapel.

She couldn't sleep on the way to the next stop in Horse Creek. Nellie grumbled thinking that she was finally on her way and still wouldn't be across the county line by the end of the day.

In Horse Creek she lucked into getting the last seat on a stagecoach, which was heading towards Cheyenne. She bought her ticket on the Deadwood Stage praying that the infamous stage wouldn't be robbed as it had so many times in the past. The journey was arduous to say the least. Normally Nellie would have been completely enthralled by the adventure she was embarking on. Knowing that the love of her life may have moved on and forgotten her was plaguing her every thought.

The journey took her to Bear Springs, Chugwater, Chug Springs, Eagle's Nest, Fort Laramie, Rawhide Buttes, Hat Creek, Cheyenne Crossing and finally up to Deadwood. With each passing mile Nellie felt confident that her family was not going to track her down.

By the time the small blonde finally arrived in Cheyenne County, Nebraska every muscle in her body ached. Thankfully she had finally arrived in a place where the Union Pacific Railroad stopped and she could start heading east. She tossed her precious saddlebag over her shoulder and sought out the general store.

She purchased a tablet of writing paper and composed a letter that could never express everything she needed to say. Those words would remain silent until she was face to face with the one who still held her heart. The words she did choose were careful and precise, knowing that her letter could very likely fall into the wrong hands.

Dear Aunt Vivian,

I hope you had a safe journey. I apologize for not

*meeting you at the station.   Mother took a turn for the worse.
There is no need to worry; I will explain everything upon my
arrival in Massachusetts.*

Your loving niece,
Cornelia

She used her given name and Vivian's last name just as they
had planned to do once the arrived at Fulton. She said a silently
prayer as she sealed the letter in an envelope and paid the clerk.
'Please understand' Her silent prayer continued as she walked
out of the store and crossed the street to the small boarding
house.

For the first time Nellie took a long hot bath and relaxed in a
real bed. Sleep eluded her that night as she anxiously waited the
morning. Before the sun had risen she was dressed in a simple
cotton dress and hurrying down to the railway station. Her hands
were trembling as she purchased her ticket and prepared to once
again embark on her journey that would hopefully end when she
was safely wrapped in her lover's arms.

Along the journey Nellie tried to enjoy her adventure. She
was careful whom she chose to speak to. Her normally friendly
nature in the past would lead her to chat on endlessly but she
wasn't back home in the safe confines of Cedar Grove any longer
and wisely opted to be more selective.

When she would find some one to share a conversation with
she stuck with the story she and Vivian had contrived. She was
Cornelia and she was on her way to live with her only relative her
Aunt who was a schoolteacher. She didn't miss the looks of pity
the other passengers would cast upon her when she told them of
her plans. *'If you only knew that I'm not off to lead the mundane
life of spinster but finding my way to the embrace of the most
amazing woman who ever walked the face of the earth,'* She
would often think smugly.

She never spoke with gentlemen who were traveling without their families. Yet, they still sought out the young blonde. She almost came to blows on more than one occasion thankfully the nice men who worked on the train always intervened on her behalf.

The journey was very long and boring to say the least. Nellie had only her memories of Vivian to keep her company throughout most of the trip. Until they reached Colorado when she met the Fuller family. The Fullers were a lovely couple traveling with their two-year-old son. They were traveling all the way to Maine to visit Mrs. Fuller's Mother.

Nellie eagerly offered to assist them with the care of their rambunctious child. "Did you enjoy growing up in Nebraska?" Mrs. Fuller inquired midway through their journey as her son Joshua slept in her lap.

"Oh yes," Nellie lied having told everyone that she was from Nebraska. "I am looking forward to seeing my Aunt Vivian, she is a very special person. I still can not believe that a train can take you all the way across the country."

"The one good thing to come out of the war," Mr. Fuller said with a heavy sigh. "The tracks were finally connected. You've never been back East?"

"No sir," Nellie exclaimed eager to finally see her new home and her lover.

"Boston should be interesting for you," he chuckled. "I bet you'll be missing all that open space and quiet."

"I guess I'll find out," Nellie laughed. "I can't wait."

"We lived in Boston for a few years after the war," Mrs. Fuller explained. "All that noise and people was just too much for us. We joined a wagon train heading west, when we reach Colorado we just knew it was where we belonged. I hope you find that someday."

"I know I will," Nellie reassured the older woman knowing that she had already found what she was seeking and it couldn't be found on any map. "I just hope that I can find a way to earn my keep," she added in a troubled tone. "I hear that there are a lot of factories that are always hiring."

"You'd do best to steer away from that life," Mr. Fuller

cautioned her in a protective tone. "It will make you old before your time. Surely your Aunt most knows of some respectable establishments."

"Aunt Vivian is very wise when it comes to these matters," Nellie reassured him as she said a silent prayer that Vivian would still welcome her after all of this time.

Fuller's had taken the young girl under their wing warding off any and all prospective suitor's until the train finally chugged into Boston. "Be careful," Mrs. Fuller cautioned her as she hugged the small blonde.

"I will and enjoy your visit with your mother," Nellie smiled as she ruffled the squirming Joshua's dark hair.

"Don't forget you can take a train to Andover," Mr. Fuller informed her. "Just ask at the station they run pretty regular. But if you have to stay over night don't forget about Mrs. Beasley's Boarding House you just need to hop onto the Back Bay Trolley."

"I have the directions you gave me," she reassured the kind man as she gathered up her saddlebag and with a wave to her new friends departed the train.

The first thing Nellie noticed was all of the people hurrying about and the noise of the city. The hustle and bustle was a far cry from her quiet existence back in Cedar Grove. She looked around as people bumped into her without so much as a backward glance. She clung tightly to her saddlebag keeping the pocket close to her bosom as she tried to push her way through the crowd and to the ticket window.

"Good Day," she greeted the tired looking man with the neatly pressed black suit who was behind the bars at the ticket counter.

"Good Day to you Miss," he greeted her with a very odd accent.

"I need a one way ticket to Andover," she politely explained.

"Next one leaves at seven fifteen tomorrow morning," he explained.

"That will be fine," Nellie agreed.

"That will be seventy five cents," he informed her.

She blinked in surprise at the large sum as she pushed a bill under the window. He moved quickly preparing her ticket. "Thar' you go," he said as he slid the ticket and her change through the slot. "It will be departing from that track right over thar'."

She nodded as she looked over to where the man was pointing his gnarled finger. "I need to get to this address," she continued holding up the slip of paper Mr. Fuller had written Mrs. Beasley's address on.

"Yup," he said. "Just step outside the station the trolley for the Back Bay should be passing soon. Get off at the hospital it's about a block up the street across from the hospital.

She thanked the man and headed out of the busy station. The flurry of activity on the street took the young shop girl by surprise. She jumped when she heard the clanging of a bell. Her emerald eyes widen with amazement when she spied the large open wagon with people seated on benches. On the top of the strange carriage the words *Back Bay* were boldly printed. She raced over and much to her surprise managed to catch the trolley. She paid the fare and took the only open seat available.

The horse drawn trolley chugged and swayed down the bustling streets of the city. Nellie was so caught up with watching she almost missed her stop. She got off at the large hospital. She checked the slip of paper and looked up and down the busy street. "Everything is so big here," she gasped in wonderment as she headed up the street. She got lost and wandered around the block for almost an hour until she finally stopped and asked for directions.

Her feet were swollen and her legs aching when she finally found the Charles Street address. She had wished that she were still dressed as a man knowing that her feet would be far more comfortable during her trek. She knocked on the front door of the brick building and waited for someone to respond.

A plump white haired woman answered the door. The woman stared down at the little blonde curiously as Nellie tried to regain her wits. "Mrs. Beasley?" She politely inquired.

"Yes," the woman greeted her cautiously.

"I was given your address by Mr. Adam Fuller and his wife," Nellie courteously explained. "They said that you might be able to provide me with lodgings for the evening."

"Oh my how are Adam and Lucy?" The woman gushed as she stepped aside-allowing Nellie to enter her home. "Come in child."

"They are well," Nellie answered as she gratefully stepped inside the foyer. "I met them on the train."

"Off to visit Lucy's Mama I suppose," Mrs. Beasley chuckled as she led Nellie further into the well kept home. "Their little one must be adorable. I was so happy to hear that after all these years they had finally been blessed. And shame on them for not stopping by. They did the right thing sending you here, with all the shady places in this city not to mention the foreigners," Mrs. Beasley rattled on as Nellie quirked her eyebrows at the woman's comments. "Now how long will you be staying?   Are you looking for work I can give you a reference?"

"I only need a room for this evening," Nellie chuckled at the woman's excitement. "I am traveling up to Andover in the morning to join my Aunt. She is a teacher at the Fulton School. I will be looking for employment once I join her."

"Stay away from those factories," Mrs. Beasley cautioned her. "If you stay out of the North you should be fine. Fulton now that is a fine place. Here you are. It isn't much but should do you for the night. The bath is down the hall."

Nellie's eyes lit up at the sight of a comfortable bed and the mention of a bath. "Do you need to get in touch with your Aunt?" Mrs. Beasley inquired. "She must be worried."

"Yes, but how?" Nellie asked in confusion. Mr. Fuller had explained that Andover was at least twenty-one miles outside of Boston.

"Ring the school," Mrs. Beasley explained in a curious tone. "Ring?" Nellie asked as she set her saddlebag down.

"Yes," Mrs. Beasley explained in a slow careful tone. "I know that the school has a telephone."

"A telephone?" Nellie blurted out like a small child. "I'm sorry. I've heard of them of course I just never seen one."

"My goodness child where in the god forsaken wilderness have you been living?" Mrs. Beasley gasped in a horrified tone as she led Nellie back downstairs and to the back parlor.

"Nebraska," Nellie lied in a dry tone.

"I just love my telephone," Mrs. Beasley chattered on as she led the girl over to a small wooden box that had a black cone sprouting out from the center and a crank on the side. "I still don't understand why everyone hasn't gotten one," she continued as she picked up an earpiece and pressed it closely to her ear while she turned the crank vigorously.

The plump woman pulled over a stool and plopped her large frame down. "Clara? Yes it is me who else?" The woman laughed as she shouted into the cone. "Fine, you know it still aches every time it rains."

Nellie shuffled nervously as she listened to Mrs. Beasley prattle on and on about her various aliments and what the neighbors were doing. She blew out a sigh of relief when Mrs. Beasley finally got to the part about needing to place a call to the Fulton School. "Yes in Andover," Mrs. Beasley groused. "One of my guests needs to let her Aunt know that she has arrived safely. What is your Aunt's name dear?"

"Vivian Larilia," Nellie quickly supplied.

"Vivian Larilia," Mrs. Beasley repeated into the strange contraption. "Tell her it is from her niece . . . "

"Cornelia," Nellie quickly supplied.

"Cornelia," Mrs. Beasley shouted. "No Cornelia. Cornelia!" The woman shouted once again. "Just tell her it is her niece. For pity sake how many relatives do you think she has traveling in from Nebraska? This is going to take a little while they will ring back," Mrs. Beasley explained as she hung up the telephone.

"Simply amazing," Nellie said as she stared at the wooden box.

"Well we need to get you fed while we wait for your Aunt to call," Mrs. Beasley explained.

Nellie nodded in agreement and returned upstairs to freshen up and retrieve the money so she could pay Mrs. Beasley for the room and the telephone call. After a light supper a strange ringing filled the small home. Nellie was startled as Mrs. Beasley rushed to the back parlor. Nellie dutifully followed the plump woman.

After Mrs. Beasley exchanged some pleasantries with the operator she handed Nellie the earpiece. "Just talk into here," she instructed the girl before walking away. It didn't escape the blonde's notice that Mrs. Beasley didn't travel very far.

"Hello?" Nellie said with a nervous excitement. "Hello?" She repeated when she didn't hear anything in response.

"Nellie?" Came the echoing response.

"Aunt Vivian is that you?" She answered the voice that sounded like it was coming from the bottom of a well.

"Yes," came the cold response that still sounded like an echo. "Where are you?"

"Boston," Nellie blurted out excitedly. "I will be arriving in Andover in the morning."

"Why?" The echo coldly inquired.

"Excuse me?" Nellie choked as she felt her knees buckle.

"Go home," Vivian's voice echoed.

"I am," Nellie fumed.

"Go home," Vivian repeated.

Nellie's throat closed as she felt the tears welling up. "If you can't meet my train I understand," she dryly explained fighting against the pain as Mrs. Beasley looked on. "I will see you tomorrow."

She held her breath as she waited for Vivian to say something. All she heard was a faint clicking sound then a stranger's voice informing her that the other party had hung up. "No, I don't have any other calls," Nellie managed to choke out as she responded to the operator's inquiry. "Thank you," she added before she hung up.

"Thank you Mrs. Beasley," she said as she managed to conjure up a convincing smile. "That was simply amazing," she added as she motioned towards the telephone. "The folks back in Nebraska will never believe it."

"Welcome to the big city, Mrs. Beasley laughed.

"I think I need to take a bath and get some sleep," Nellie explained with a slight yawn. "After my trip I really need to clean out more than a few cob webs."

"I can only imagine," Mrs. Beasley smiled. "Good night

Cornelia."

Nellie wasn't lying about needing a bath, but she knew in her heart she wouldn't be able to sleep that night. *'Why would Vivian send me away?'* She silently sobbed as she tried to understand what had changed her lover's feelings in such a short time? Despite the comfortable bed she tossed and turned all night as Vivian's painful words replayed in her mind.

Somehow the small blonde managed to drag her tired body out of bed. She cleaned up, dressed and gathered her meager belongings. She joined Mrs. Beasley and some of the other boarders for a simple breakfast. Mrs. Beasley made some very unnerving inquiries during the meal. Nellie answered politely never revealing what had transpired between her and Vivian during their brief conversation.

Nellie's jaw clenched tighter each time Mrs. Beasley asked if she was certain that she should take the train that morning. *'Apparently the operator listens and shares what she hears,'* Nellie mentally fumed at the way Mrs. Beasley had invaded her privacy. The blonde managed to contain her anger as she thanked Mrs. Beasley and departed for the train station.

Once again she boarded the trolley and traveled the bustling streets of Boston. She would have enjoyed the brief trolley ride if only her heart wasn't breaking. She held firm to her resolve that she and Vivian were meant to be together and once the schoolteacher saw her, everything would be all right.

By the time the train rolled into the station at Andover Nellie was not only sick to her stomach but she had almost chewed a hole in the inside of her mouth. Basically the small blonde had worked herself into such a frenzy she was ready to explode. *'Please be waiting for me,'* she thought fearfully as she hurried towards the exit on the train.

Her eyes drifted up and down the wooden platform searching desperately for any sign of her tall dark lover as the conductor helped step down onto the platform. *'Please Baby!'* She screamed silently as she searched the crowd for some small glimmer of hope.

Nellie's heart was breaking as she watched the crowd thinning and still no sign of her lover. "Fine," the tiny blonde huffed as she clutched her saddlebag and stormed through the train station.   "If she thinks I'm just going hop on a train and pretend nothing happened she has a nothing thing coming," Nellie continue to ramble under her breath as she looked up and down the city street. Andover was a pretty picture with tree lined streets and neatly trimmed lawns.   It wasn't the bustling metropolis Boston was but it was certainly more progressive than the dirt streets she had left behind.   "I didn't climb out my bedroom window, steal a horse, travel across the country, end up smelling like a horse that had been rode hard and put away wet just be sent back like some child," her tirade was reaching full force when she suddenly stopped and looked up and down the street.

She had no idea, which way she should start walking. She fought against the urge to simply collapse onto the sidewalk and burst into tears. Instead she swallowed a few deep breaths and calmed down. She needed to make a decision. Bursting into the school and confronting Vivian would only get the brunette dismissed and not help Nellie win her hand.

"First things first I need to find a place to live," she reasoned out loud as she began to stroll down the street. "Then I need to find a job."

She began to wander aimlessly through the town looking around for a boarding house that would be suitable. Her travels took her further away from the main streets.   Once again with aching feet and a crushed spirit. She dropped her saddlebag and leaned on a white picket fence. The house just beyond the fence was quaint little house that brought a smile to her lips. "Now that is kind of house I would love to share with Vivian," she said softly as a tall gray haired gentleman emerged from the front door. "Great now the owner is going to run me off. Another new experience."

"Good day," the man warmly greeted her with a smile and a tip of his hat. "Are you interested?"

"I beg your pardon?" Nellie choked out as the angry that was welling up inside of her tinted her cherub cheeks with blotches of red.

"The house?" He quickly amended his statement. "I don't recognize you and I thought perhaps you were here to see the house. Will your husband be arriving soon?"

"No I'm not . . .," Nellie's words drifted off as she met his gaze. "The house is for sale?"

"Yes," he explained in a curious manner. "Miss Gulch retired from Fulton and moved to Philadelphia to be with her sister. I had hoped that the new teacher would be interested. I thought that with her niece joining her it would better suit her needs rather than the dormitory. Sadly she said she could only afford to rent it and Miss Gulch prefers to simply sell it."

"Yes," Nellie breathlessly exclaimed as he stepped slightly away from her. "My apologies," she laughed as she glanced over at the quaint little house. She hooked her arm in his and guided the unsuspecting fellow back into the yard. "Aunt Vivian told me about this place. Vivian Larilia," she added as he gave her a questioning look. She was relieved as she saw the man visibly relax as they stepped up onto the wrap around porch and entered the house. "I am Cornelia and you are?"

"Forgive my manners Miss Larilia," he said as he removed his felt hat. "Sven Gustafson. A pleasure to make your acquaintance."

"The pleasure is all mine," Nellie offered in a charming tone. "Now down to business. How much is Miss Gulch seeking for this charming little abode."

"One thousand," he said with a brilliant smile.

"One thousand?" Nellie pondered knowing that with the money she had skimmed from her father she could easily afford the house. Yet spending all of those years working at the mercantile she had learned a great deal. The men who came and went would talk freely and Nellie learned much more about construction than a girl really should. Men had the silly notion that women either couldn't understand them when they talked about tools and building, that or they were completely unaware of the fact that sound traveled. "That would be a fair price if the roof wasn't in such poor condition. And of course despite the fresh coat of paint I see that many of the fixtures and doors need to be replaced," Another benefit of her up bringing at the family boarding house. Following Jack and her father around when she was bored gave her a lesson in the up keep of their home.

"Come now Mr. Gustafson," she chastised him. "I know you are a reasonable man and wouldn't dream of taking advantage of two women who are new to your community."

"I wouldn't dream of it," he conceded seeming to understand that this was not going to be the easy sale he had assumed it would be.

After a lengthy negotiation and a trip to Mr. Gustafson's office and a trip to the records office Nellie was the proud owner of the tiny little house. The small blonde was elated and terrified. She got the house at very good price, which still left her with a substantial amount of money. Still the house needed the repairs she had used as a bargaining chip against the eager realtor. Add in the taxes, furnishing her new empty home, the yearly up keep and her day to day living expenses Nellie could easily find herself in a very deep hole in a relatively short period of time.

She went directly to the bank once she had the deed in her hands. She opened an account in her name. She deposit most of the rest of her money for safe keeping after Mr. Gustafson almost fell over when she paid him the full price for the house in cash. She wasn't concerned about Mr. Gustafson but there was always the chance that he might mention it to someone else who might think that the blonde would make an easy mark.

The next stop was the general store where she picked up a few supplies to get her through the next few days. She also picked up all of the local gossip. She knew that she would since after years of lurking behind the counter at her families store she learned it was the spot where most of the town would meet. The most important piece of information she acquired was that the Fulton School was just up the hill from her new home.

Vivian was just a short walk away from her front door. The only question she possessed was how to get Vivian to not only agree to knock on her front door but move into their new home. It could be difficult since Nellie was quite certain Vivian wasn't speaking to her. She brushed aside all thoughts of her present quandary as she proceeded to the lumber mill and ordered the materials she needed to repair the roof and fixtures.

She was exhausted by the time she entered Miss Grace's shop to pick out some material to make some new clothing. The dress she was wearing was more than a little dilapidated. Once inside the shop she furrowed her brow. The crease in her forehead grew deeper as she looked around having trouble finding what she needed.

She had heard that Lillian Grace was a very talented dressmaker from the women buzzing around the general store. She also heard that most of the women only shopped there when they had no choice. Looking around the shop and seeing the owner who was far too busy with stitching to assist her she now understood why the women in town didn't frequent the woman's shop.

"This is all wrong," Nellie blew out as she looked around.

"I beg your pardon," the bird like woman who was stitching asked as she looked up from her project.

"My apologies," Nellie offered as she turned towards the irate looking woman. "But the shop is set up all wrong. You've made it difficult for your patrons to find what they need," Nellie explained as she moved some of the fabrics around and formed a small neat display on the table. "I can see that you are very talented," Nellie added as she brushed her fingers along the garment that was neatly folded on the stunned woman's lap. "You should let your potential customers see your work. A window display like the shops in Boston would be nice, plus around the shop as well," Nellie continued. "And the small sundries should be on the counter not behind it. And I've overstepped my bounds," Nellie winced once she realized what she had just said.

"Who are you?" The woman asked with a shy smile.

"Nellie," she offered as she held out her hand. She decided to drop her formal name before she was stuck with it forever. "My aunt and I just moved into town. She's a teacher at Fulton."

"I am Lillian Grace," the woman offered as she firmly shook Nellie's hand. "Are you a teacher as well?"

"No," Nellie laughed. "In fact I will be seeking employment. I just don't know what skills I have to offer."

"I'd say you have a talent," Lillian laughed. "I wish I could hire you but as you can see business isn't very good."

"It could be," Nellie theorized. "The problem is that you are an artist not a salesgirl. You need someone to handle the business and the customers. You already have a firm reputation but trying to run the shop takes away from your creations. I am willing to wager that if you hire the right person you would be the premiere dressmaker in the county."

"Sounds like I should hire you," Lillian responded thoughtfully.

"Well I do have the experience," Nellie explained as she brightened at the idea. "I grew up behind the counter at my father's mercantile. I know more about selling than girl needs to."

"I wish I could afford to hire," Lillian said with disappointment. "So far everything you've told me would bring in twice the business I already have. But it still wouldn't be enough to pay you a decent wage."

Nellie thought about what the woman had just said. "What if I worked on commission?" Nellie volunteered. "You would only have to pay me a little bit of what I sell. That way I could fix up the shop and you would have time to make your wonderful creations."

"I'd be a fool not to say yes," Lillian readily agreed. "If you half as good at selling to my clients as you are with me then I'll rich. When can you start?"

Nellie accepted the offer and headed back to her new home with a bolt of cloth and an order for a new dress both at a large discount, plus Lillian threw in the name of a good handyman who could fix up Nellie's new little home.

Nellie felt good when she finally returned to her new home. She put away her few purchases and looked around her empty home. "I need to get some furniture," she noted as she curled up her lip.

"Among other things," the familiar sultry voice echoed from behind her.

Nellie's heart leapt as she spun around to find Vivian leaning in the front doorway. "Vivian," she gasped as she stared at the woman who had filled her every thought since the day they had met. Nellie could feel the electricity flowing between them as each of them stood there staring at the other. "Did you get my letter?" Nellie asked in a hushed tone.

Her heart was breaking as Vivian's eyes drifted to the floor and the schoolteacher closed the door as she stepped into the foyer. "Yesterday, just before you called," Vivian, explained in a dejected tone.

"Stupid," Nellie admonished herself as she slapped her forehead. "I should have wired you. I didn't even think that my letter was probably traveling on the same train that I was. But Vivian if you got my letter then why did you tell me to go away?"

"I promised myself I wouldn't see you," Vivian muttered as she continued to gaze down at the floor.

"Why?" Nellie pleaded.

Vivian gaze shot up and Nellie stepped back from the fiery gaze burning into her body. "Because I do not keep company with married women," Vivian hissed in anger.

"What are you talking about?" Nellie screamed as she stared at the tall schoolteacher with utter disbelief.

She could see the pain clearly written across Vivian's chiseled features. "I waited and waited until I had to leave Rumford," Vivian choked out as tears filled her eyes. "Then when I arrived the Reverend sent me a copy of the Cedar Grove newspaper so I could still know what is going on back there."

"I still don't understand," Nellie pleaded as she took a shy step towards her lover.

"You wedding announcement was in there," Vivian sobbed as she buried her face in her hands.

"Vivian," Nellie called out to the sobbing woman as she closed the distance between them. Vivian jerked away. "Vivian listen to me I didn't marry him. How could I marry him when it is you who holds the key to my heart?"

Vivian met her gaze as Nellie's hands rested on the taller woman's hips. The blonde now understood why Vivian told her to leave. She sat in her hotel room for weeks lighting a candle to signal a lover who never came. She arrived only to read that Nellie was to be married. Vivian had assumed that the blonde had changed her mind and given up on the love that they shared. "Not long after you left my mother found my suitcase," Nellie explained as she brushed the tears from Vivian's face. "After she confirmed that Freddie and I weren't eloping she locked me in my room. I was only allowed out to bathe. I even ate my meals in that room. No one saw me except for my mother and the occasional visit from Freddie. I climbed out the window and stole a horse the first chance I got. Unfortunately the first chance I got was two months too late."

"She locked you up?" Vivian gasped as she wrapped her arms around the smaller woman.

"Yes," Nellie confirmed as she sank into her lover's embrace. "I couldn't take the train from Rumford after I spotted my father and Freddie at the station. I took the stagecoach and picked up the rail in Nebraska. Which is where I am from in case anyone asks."

Vivian tilted the blonde's head up with her fingers. Nellie melted into the searing kiss her lover placed on her lips. Nellie moaned as her lover's tongue parted her lips and began to explore the warmth of her mouth. Unable to breath and feeling her knees buckle the blonde forced herself to end the kiss. "How missed that," She panted as she brushed her tingling lips with the tips of her fingers.

"I love you," Vivian choked out as she nestled the nape of the blonde's neck.

"And I love you my darling," Nellie said with deep sigh as she took a slight step back and took her lover by the hand. "Now tell me what you think of our new home?"

"I love this house," Vivian said with a smile. "I had wanted to rent it for us even when I thought you had abandon me. How did you convince them to rent it?"

"I didn't," Nellie boldly explained as she picked up the comforter and pillows she had purchased that day.

"I don't understand?" Vivian stammered as Nellie reclaimed her hand and guided her up the staircase.

"I bought it," Nellie explained as the reached the top step.

"How?" Vivian asked in bewilderment as they fumbled through the dark hallway.

"The day you received the letter from Fulton I began taking money from the store," Nellie continued as she felt her lover stop.

"You stole from your father?" Vivian asked in disbelief.

"Yes," Nellie confessed as she turned to face her lover in the darkness. "And no, I only took what would have been my dowry. If I could marry you then the money would have been yours. Plus my family never paid me for the work I did. I understand that they raised me, fed me and clothed me but still I worked everyday since the time I could walk. The money is ours."

"I don't know," Vivian mumbled. "I suppose there is nothing we can do about it now."

"And my father got to keep the dowry money," Nellie reasoned. "I understand that on some level what I did was wrong. Yet, I also feel that you should be the one to get my dowry. The only problem is deciding who gets what bedroom?"

"You wish to sleep in separate rooms?" Vivian laughed as Nellie guided her into one of the empty bedrooms.

"Never," Nellie vowed as she released her lover's hand a spread the comforter out onto the floor. "I only want the outside world to think we have separate bedrooms. We wouldn't want to stir up any trouble now would we Auntie Vivian?"

"Promise never to call me that when we are alone," Vivian grimaced as she closed the small distance between them and captured Nellie's face in her hands.

"I promise," Nellie whispered as she felt Vivian's breath caressing her face.

With one kiss Nellie could feel the fire burning deep inside of her as she undid the ribbon that held her lover's hair captive. "Do you have any more surprises for me?" Vivian murmured as they sank down onto the comforter.

"I got a good price for the house," Nellie groaned as she felt her lover kissing her neck as the brunette's hands began to unfasten the buttons of her dress. "I opened a bank account, I added your name to the account, and I got a job, ordered lumber to fix up the house and hired a handyman to do the work."

Vivian halted her movements and stared down at her lover. "Good Lord Nellie you've only been in town a few hours," Vivian offered in admiration.

"I still have one task left to complete," Nellie explained as she ran her fingers along the front of her lover's white ruffled blouse.

Despite the darkness she could still see her lover's brilliant smile. Nellie's mind and body reeled as she realized this was the first time they could make love without fear of being discovered. Vivian captured her hands and slowly ran her tongue along the palms. Nellie whimpered softly as she felt her lover's body melting into her own.

Nellie laid back as her lover slowly undressed her. The brunette's hands caressed her skin as it was revealed to her smoky gaze. Nellie could feel her skin erupting as Vivian's touch glided along her naked flesh. "I missed you," Vivian whispered as she caressed the inside of the blonde's thigh.

"I love you so much Vivian," Nellie professed as she began to slowly remove her lover's clothing. "Nothing was going to keep us apart."

She could feel Vivian's fingers drifting along the supple curve of her body as Nellie removed the last of her lover's clothing. Each of them slowly ran their fingers slowly along the other's naked body savoring the feel of their lover's skin reacting to their touch. Nellie heard her lover inhale sharply as the blonde's fingers lightly brushed across her nipples. Nellie smiled as she felt the bud hardening from her touch.

Nellie's leaned into her lover's touch as she felt her lover massaging her scalp and tickling her neck. Nellie licked her lips and smiled mischievously as she felt their thighs brush against one another. Their kisses were filled with hunger as their bodies melded together. Nellie could feel Vivian's need painting her skin, as they pressed closer together.

They wrapped their legs around each other and their desire met and slowly their bodies swayed gently. Her lover cupped her backside and guided the small blonde hips to meet her sensual rhythm. As they reclined side by side their bodies became one.

Mavis Applewater

Nellie could feel the passion seeping from her body as moved her body in perfect rhythm with her lover. The months of separation fueled on their desire as they rode against one another. Nellie's body shuddered as she felt Vivian's hands caressing her bottom, and up along her back as their kisses grew deeper.

Nellie felt her body taking control as she rocked harder against Vivian's thigh. The blonde broke away from the kiss and pressed her nipple against her lover's eager lips. The feel of Vivian suckling her breast drove the blonde deeper into the abyss as she clung to her lover filling her hands with the brunette's long silky tresses.

Vivian's teeth teased her nipple as Nellie cried out with pleasure. Her lover was now beneath her. Nellie's body trembled as they filled one another. She could feel her lover inside of her as her own fingers explored the brunette's wetness.

Making love to Vivian was the one thing in Nellie's life that still amazed her. It was the way they moved in perfect rhythm each seeming to know just what the other wanted. No words were spoken as they glided in and out of one another. For the first time they allowed the cries to fill the night air as they plummeted over the edge of ecstasy.

"Oh my love," Nellie panted as Vivian's fingers continued to explore her womanhood. Nellie rode against her lover's touch as she filled her hands with her lover's breasts. Her hips rocked harder as she caressed her lover. She loved the feel of Vivian's body wriggling beneath her as she cried out her lover's name.

She didn't allow her body to still as she squirmed out of her lover's embraced and began to kiss her way down the brunette's long inviting body. She tasted her lover's skin slowly before suckling her like a newborn. Vivian was pleading for release as Nellie teased her slowly. She licked away the sweat that was beading up between the valley of Vivian's breasts before tasting her way down the gasping woman's body.

She licked and tasted every inch of her lover's skin until she was nestled between her thighs and drinking in the musky aroma of Vivian's desire. The brunette raised her hips offering up the sweet nectar. Nellie couldn't refuse she wished to drown in her lover's passion. She dipped her tongue into her lover's wetness

478

and drank in her passion.

She held Vivian's body steady by cupping her firm backside. She captured her throbbing nub in her mouth and suckled it eagerly. She became lost in the nectar of her lover's passion as Vivian cried out. She took her lover deeper as the brunette's body thrust against her touch. Not until her lover begged her to stop did she release the woman and kiss her way back up her body.

Vivian wrapped her arms around her lover's body drawing her in for a lingering kiss. Nellie was certain that her heart would explode as she felt her lover's hands exploring her body. Soon the blonde's hands were mirroring her lover's actions. They clung to one another, gazing deeply into each other's eyes as they slowly stroked the other's throbbing nub.

Nellie felt as if they had become one person as their hearts beat in unison and their bodies trembled against the other's knowing touch. Nellie knew at that moment that the words she had told her lover the first night they had made love were true. Only death could keep her out of this woman's embrace. The rush of emotions tore through her body as her passion caressed Vivian's touch. Her lover smiled at her as she leaned over and kissed her tenderly. "We need our rest my love," Vivian informed her with a smile as she wrapped the comforter around the both of them.

"I know we both have to work tomorrow," Nellie yawned as the miles she had traveled to arrive at this moment finally caught up with her. "And we are going shopping."

"I hate shopping," Vivian grumbled.

"And hate sleeping on the floor," Nellie teased as she rested her head on her lover's chest.

"Nellie," Vivian whispered as she ran her fingers through Nellie's long blonde hair.

"Hmm?" Nellie murmured as she listened to the steady beating of Vivian's heart.

"Welcome home."

The End

Mavis Applewater

Bedlam

Part One

Amanda was lying on her bed staring at the ceiling, pondering. Just how did she end up a patient in a mental institution? Her life had been so normal. She was married to a great guy. She had a good job. Data entry wasn't the most exciting thing to do for eight hours a day but it was reliable. Matt, her poor husband, drove a cab. They had been struggling to save up enough money so they could buy a house and start a family, something she thought the both of them had wanted. Now she wasn't sure about anything except that she had to get out of Pinewood as soon as possible.

She blew out an exasperated sigh as Jackie, another inmate, entered her room. "Hey Blondie," the lanky brunette greeted her as she flopped down onto Amanda's bed. She had grown fond of Jackie and her wit since she had been locked up. Strange thing was, most of her fellow inmates at times seemed more normal than the staff. "What'cha up to?" Jackie inquired as she stretched out her long legs.

"Just thinking," Amanda responded softly.

"Must be easier since you've started pocketing your meds," Jackie noted thoughtfully.

"It is," Amanda responded brightly as she sat up and stared down at her companion. "Thank you for teaching me how to do that. I just don't understand how I ended up here."

"I don't get it either," Jackie agreed as she folded her hands behind her head. "Once you came out of the fog they had you in, you just seemed far too normal to be here. I know we all have our problems, but you don't belong here. When did it all start?"

"I guess it all started when I won the lottery," Amanda began as Jackie cast a suspicious look at her. "I did." She asserted firmly. "I'm not like Fred who thinks he is Howard Hughes. I hit Mega Millions for over twenty million dollars. Funny thing is, I never played before. Grace was buying a ticket and told me I should give it a try. What the hell, I thought, it's only a dollar. I won, and now I'm rich and locked up in the nut house. No offense."

"None taken," Jackie, the former financial analyst, laughed. "Trust me, when I was getting my MBA I didn't think it would end up landing me here at the farm." Jackie chuckled again as she used the nickname the patients had for Pinewoods. "Tell me everything, and lets see if we can figure out how you went from lottery winner to the lock ward of one the finest mental healthcare facilities on the East Coast?"

"You sure you want to hear this?" Amanda inquired as she leaned against the wall and looked down at her new friend.

"I was going to go out dancing tonight but since all the doors are locked and there are bars on the windows, I might as well just hang out and listen to your story," Jackie offered with a brilliant smile. Amanda just loved the way Jackie smiled. She brushed away the warm feeling and decided to tell her story. Jackie was, after all, the only person who had been willing to listen to her since she woke up and discovered that she was a patient at Pinewoods.

"Okay, here goes," Amanda began her story. "It all started when Grace, my best friend, and I stopped at the corner market on the way home from work. Grace and I worked together at McMillan & Associates. She's an administrative assistant and I did data entry. She also lives in my building. Since Matt was always working at nights we would hang out at her place and watch the soaps she had taped while we were at the office."

Part Two

Six Months Earlier

Amanda and Grace were standing in line at the tiny little store. "Amanda, why don't you give it a shot?" Grace encouraged her. "They think the jackpot is going to hit eighteen million."

"I've never played before," Amanda confessed sheepishly. "Money's been so tight. I don't understand how Matt can be working all of these extra hours and we have less money." Grace simply snorted in disgust. Amanda had long suspected that Grace didn't care for her husband. "But with the economy being so bad, tips are way down." Amanda rationalized.

"Is that what Matt says?" Grace grumbled. "So are you going to buy a ticket or not?"

"All right," Amanda sighed in agreement. "What the heck, its only a dollar. How do I do this?"

"Just ask for a quick pick," Grace instructed her. "And hurry up so we can find out what happened on Days of Our Lives."

Amanda did as Grace instructed and bought her ticket. Later they sat in Grace's tiny apartment catching up on who was sleeping with whom. Amanda didn't really care for the shows, but she loved Grace's commentary. She loved to call all of the men pigs while she drooled all over them. Amanda thought the men were attractive enough, but certainly not enough to gush over the way her best friend did. "So how long is Matt gone for?" Grace asked as she fast-forwarded through the commercials.

"All week," Amanda quickly offered, wondering why she didn't miss him as much as she thought she should?

"Who did he go fishing with?" Grace asked casually. "Oh my God, this man is gorgeous." Grace swooned as she hit play. "Please take your shirt off?"

"You're incorrigible," Amanda teased her friend.

"I think it sucks that you are sweating spending a dollar on the lottery and Matt takes off for a week of fishing," Grace commented in a snide tone. "Oh yes," Grace purred when the buff, young actor finally removed his shirt. "Crap, another commercial," Grace grumbled. "So who did he go with?"

"His buddy, Bob," Amanda responded offhandedly as she watched the commercials spin by. "Do you think this Mark is going to sleep with Carrie?"

"Bob Ferguson?" Grace asked in a worried tone.

"Yeah," Amanda answered with a shrug, wondering why her friend's face suddenly looked troubled. "Why?"

"No reason," Grace responded distantly. "And no, Mark would never sleep with Carrie. But she is going to try."

After watching hours of attractive men and women trying to bed one another, Amanda went upstairs to her tiny apartment and went to sleep. The following morning she met Grace downstairs and they began their walk to the office. "So are you a multimillionaire?" Amanda teased her friend.

"No," Grace grunted sounding truly disappointed. "I didn't get one number. What about you? Did you hit for anything?"

"I didn't check," Amanda confessed with a shrug.

"What?" Grace screeched. "Do you have the ticket?"

Amanda searched her pockets and handed the ticket to her inpatient friend who proceeded to drag her into the market. Grace stared at the ticket and up at the large colorful sheet that listed winning numbers. "Come on, we are going to be late," Amanda grumbled as she checked her watched. She looked at her friend who was staring up at the board with her jaw hanging open. "What?" She demanded in confusion. "Did I win a free bet or something?"

"Amanda, I don't think you need to worry about being late for work today," Grace stammered.

Part Three

The Present

"So you won?" Jackie asked in amazement. "Wow, and you never played before?"

"No," Amanda confessed. "I always thought it was a waste of money. I won twenty million and some change. I offered to split the ticket with Grace. She refused."

"Now that's a good friend," Jackie noted.

"She really is, or was," Amanda said as her brow crinkled. "In the end, she let me buy her a condo and a new car. It doesn't make sense now, but once things started happening I never heard from her."

"Matt must have been thrilled," Jackie prodded her with a slight grimace.

"He was," Amanda explained in a distant tone. "Well, once he found out. I tried to contact him, but since he was fishing up in Maine, I couldn't reach him. After a few days of staring at the ticket I cashed it in, not wanting to leave it lying around. Since it wasn't what folks considered a really big jackpot, there wasn't a lot of press. But everyone I worked with knew I had won after I quit my job. I thought the money would be safer in the bank instead of having the not-cashed ticket just lying in my sock drawer. I was just busting until I could tell Matt that we were rich."

"You mean you were rich since you cashed the ticket in without him," Jackie corrected her.

"We were rich," Amanda corrected her. "We *are* married. He was upset that I didn't wait for him to get home. But he was two days late coming back and like I said, I didn't feel safe having the ticket just lying around. He calmed down once he quit his job and we bought a new house. It was great. We even finally got to have a honeymoon. We couldn't really afford much when we got married."

"It must have been heaven," Jackie said with another smile that made Amanda's heart skip a beat for some unknown reason.

"It was, except that after we moved I didn't see or hear from my friends," Amanda continued, still bewildered by the way people just suddenly dropped out of her life.

"That's strange," Jackie noted. "You'd think after winning all of that money people would be coming out of the woodwork?"

"That's what I thought," Amanda admitted. "But Matt said I shouldn't worry. So it was just him and me. Then the strangest things started happening."

"Like what?" Jackie encouraged her.

"I started hearing things at night when Matt wasn't around," Amanda began. "I was confused all of the time. It was like I was in some kind of fog. It was just weird stuff like phones ringing and no one on the other end. Then Matt would tell me the phone hadn't rung. When he was out I could swear that I could hear him in the house. Things got stranger and hazier. Matt finally took me to see Dr. Asher. But she didn't seem to be able to help me. In fact things seemed to get worse I rarely knew what day it was."

"Wait. Dr. Joyce Asher?" Jackie interrupted her. "She's your doctor here? I didn't think she had a private practice. Tell me what happened next?"

"Not much to tell," Amanda continued. "I felt like I was in a fog and the next thing I knew I woke up in this room with you staring at me, asking me what I was in for."

"I remember," Jackie chuckled. "I had to explain to you where you were and that you've been here for over two months."

"That totally freaked me out," Amanda admitted. "I just can't understand how this happened. I feel fine now that I'm off my meds. Matt and Dr. Asher tell me I need to be here. None of this makes sense."

Jackie looked up at her with a thoughtful expression. "What do you think?" Amanda finally asked.

"I can't believe that you would ask me for advice after I told you what I'm in here for," Jackie responded with a wry chuckle.

"I still find it hard to believe that you crawled across a boardroom table and tried to strangle your CEO," Amanda laughed heartily.

"He pissed me off." Jackie reasoned. "Don't forget that I also tried to set my assistant on fire."

"I think you made that part up," Amanda teased her new friend as she poked the tall brunette in the ribs.

"Okay, I only threatened to set the little whiner on fire," Jackie admitted her lips curling into a sly smirk. "But enough about me and my much needed break down. Let's focus on you. Here is what we know. You were a happy little blonde with friends until you suddenly found yourself stinking rich. Prior to that, your only worries were financial, which could be said for most people. That, and your husband worked a lot of overtime and had no extra money to show for it."

"Right," Amanda agreed, before a troubling thought occurred to her. "Wait, what are you implying?"

"I'll get to that," Jackie softly promised. "So you win the lottery and up with more money than God, but it is all in your name. Suddenly you start to lose your mind and end up here at the farm. You are so out of it that you don't even know where you are until your doctor goes on vacation for a few weeks and your meds are adjusted."

"What?" Amanda blurted out in surprise.

"It's true. You came out of your haze during Dr. Asher's absence," Jackie informed her. "She came back right about the time the fog had lifted. How did you make Dr. Asher's acquaintance in the first place?"

"Matt knew her," Amanda supplied, suddenly feeling her stomach becoming queasy.

"Matt knew her?" Jackie responded in a sarcastic tone. "Your husband, the former taxi driver, hung out with a lot doctors? Did you ever ask him how he knew her?"

"Well, no," Amanda admitted. "It just never occurred to me to ask. But I was pretty out of it by then."

"Amanda I don't want you to get upset," Jackie began in a careful tone. "Well, anymore than you already are, but do you trust your husband?"

"Of course," Amanda protested despite the uneasy feeling that was creeping over her.

Jackie's face grew sober as she sat up. "I should go," the brunette said as George, one of the other patients, peered into the room. "Paper or plastic?" The rumpled man shouted into the room before wandering off. They were the only words George ever said. It wasn't hard for the small blonde to surmise what sent poor old George over the edge. Jackie, on the other hand, was an enigma. She seemed perfectly fine, except that she tried to strangle her boss. But who hasn't pondered the thought on at least one occasion?

"Don't go," Amanda said in a pleading tone as she reached out and gently caressed Jackie's arm. The warmth of the taller woman's body made her own body heat in response. It always happened whenever she touched the tall, quirky brunette. It made her feel really good and really nervous. *'Maybe I am crazy?'* She wondered as Jackie sat back down on the tiny bed. "Tell me why you think I'm here?" Amanda asked in a pleading tone.

"I would, but I think you'd freak out again," Jackie responded in a solemn tone. "You don't want to end up in restraints again."

"Please," Amanda pleaded as she wrapped her arms around the brunette's waist. Jackie sighed deeply as she returned the hug. "I feel fine, but Dr. Asher says that I'm not ready to go home." She felt Jackie lowering her down onto the bed and her body tingled from the close contact. "Please help me, I don't belong here." Amanda felt her stomach clench as Jackie's body rested on top of hers.

"I am going to get you out of here," Jackie promised with a soft whisper.

Amanda's eyes fluttered shut as she felt Jackie's breath caressing her face. "First, I need to get a look at your file," Jackie explained.

"How are you going to do that?" Amanda asked as she felt Jackie's thigh slipping between her legs. The small blonde suppressed an unexpected moan as her small hands began to absently roam up and down Jackie's back.

"Break in after hours. Greta will help me," Jackie explained calmly as if it was an every day occurrence. "In the meantime call your friend Grace and start asking her about why she was so interested in Matt's fishing trip."

Amanda's body chilled as Jackie raised her body and moved

off of the bed. "I don't have phone privileges," Amanda explained as Jackie held out her hand. Amanda accepted the brunette's hand and allowed her to help her to her feet. Since she had awoken in the hospital, it just seemed completely natural for her to accept the comfort in being physically close to the taller woman.

"Don't you find it strange that you are not allowed to use the phone or have visitors? Since the only thing wrong with you is that you were a little out of it?" Jackie pointed out as they made their way out into the hallway.

"Yes," Amanda agreed. "Since you have those things, and you tried to kill someone."

"Whore," John, who was strapped to a wheelchair, muttered as they passed. John called everyone that, so they simply ignored him. It troubled Amanda that she was becoming so accustomed to the others' strange behavior.

"Until we can figure things out, I think you should act like your meds still have you gorked out," Jackie explained quietly as they entered the occupational theory room. "If Asher figures out you are off your meds there could be trouble."

"But she's my doctor?" Amanda questioned her, as Jackie led them over to one of the tables where the patients would create whatever arts and crafts project the staff threw at them in an effort to keep them busy.

"Just trust me," Jackie grumbled as she pretended to help Amanda into her chair before sitting next to the constantly mumbling Greta. "Think of it this way, the nurse won't expect you to finger-paint if you're napping and you might just get your meals in your own room."

"Okay," Amanda agreed as she looked down at the paints waiting for her to play with. She decided that Jackie might not have a bad idea.

"Greta?" Jackie whispered to the preoccupied woman. "I have a mission for you."

Amanda couldn't hear what they were saying as Elvis and Batman sat down to join them. Amanda let her head fall forward as she pretended to be out of it. Jackie's idea turned out to be a good one, which spared Amanda from painting some silly picture while she tried to hold up her end of a conversation with the King and the Caped Crusader.

Amanda must have nodded off. Jackie poking her playfully in the ribs awoke her. Amanda yawned as she slowly opened her eyes. "O.T. is over," Jackie informed her quietly as she helped her out of her chair. "Have a nice nap?" Jackie whispered as they made their way back to Amanda's room.

"Yes," Amanda confirmed with a yawn as they stepped into the room.

"Keep the door open," Laura, one of the duty nurses, scolded in Jackie's direction.

"What are they afraid of?" Amanda grumbled as she flopped down onto the bed.

"That I will take advantage of you," Jackie informed her flatly as she crawled up onto the bed with Amanda.

"You wish," Amanda, teased as Jackie stretched out next to her. It hadn't taken the little blonde long to figure out that Jackie was gay. It didn't bother her in the slightest; in fact she really enjoyed flirting with the attractive brunette. Of course, that was when she didn't think about it for very long.

"Hmm," Jackie responded with a sly smirk as she closed the distance between them. "Greta is going to help me break into the doctor's office tonight." She whispered.

"I want to go with you," Amanda whispered in response.

"I don't think so," Jackie protested softly.

"Why not?" Amanda argued softly.

"It could be dangerous," Jackie responded. "What you can do for me is give me your friend Grace's telephone number."

Amanda leaned closer and whispered it into Jackie's ear. It wasn't uncommon for the two of them to be seen snuggling. They used the misconception that there was something going on between them as a cover, so they could plot against the staff.

"Break it up," Bruce, one of the doctors, requested politely as he peeked his head into the room.

Amanda rolled over and pretended to be sleepy. "Spoil sport," Jackie grumbled as she climbed up off of the bed. Amanda had already learned that Bruce was one of the nicer people who worked in the locked ward but still she had no idea who she could trust. "He's gone," Jackie, informed her as she knelt beside her bed. "I think we could trust him, but you don't want him telling Asher that you are doing better. Not just yet anyway."

"Thank you," Amanda said softly as she rolled over and looked at her new friend. "Why are you doing this?"

"Doing what?" Jackie asked her in confusion.

"Helping me," Amanda further explained.

"Because you are stinking rich, plus you have a nice ass," Jackie quipped playfully.

"You've been helping me from the moment I woke up," Amanda pointed out. "You didn't know I had any money until today. Besides, I could be making that up or only think I have millions tucked away somewhere."

"Must be your nice ass then," Jackie retorted with a sultry purr that sent a delightful jolt down Amanda's spine. "I'm going to call your friend Grace and see what she knows. I'll meet up with you after lights out."

Part Four

Amanda continued pretending to be thoroughly sedated and went to bed. She tossed and turned as troubling thoughts regarding Matt and Dr. Asher's intentions plagued her. Once she did manage to fall asleep, her dreams seemed to soothe her. Not for the first time she dreamt about Jackie not just Jackie, but getting to know the leggy brunette in an intimate manner. Even though the dreams relaxed her while she slept, she found herself confused and agitated when she woke up. Dreaming about touching another woman wasn't uncommon for her. It was something she had accepted years ago. What troubled her now was that dreaming about Jackie was so constant and led her to believe that perhaps Matt and Dr. Asher were right and she really did need help.

That night, as visions of caressing Jackie's body filled her sleep, she felt a hand gently caressing her shoulder. In her sleep she leaned over and captured Jackie's soft lips. It felt so real that she moaned in her sleep as suckled the brunette's bottom lip. The kiss deepened as their tongues caressed. Amanda's heart was racing as she felt her desire growing.

Amanda's eyes snapped open she felt someone pushing against her shoulders. She was stunned to see she had her arms wrapped around Jackie's neck and shoulders. "Not that I'm complaining but what was that all about?" Jackie panted.

"Sorry, I was asleep," Amanda, stammered as her eyes drifted to the lips she had just been kissing.

"If you kiss that good when you are asleep, you must be amazing when you are awake," Jackie offered softly.

Amanda's body was still reeling from the kiss, and before she could think about what she was doing she pulled Jackie back towards her and reclaimed her lips. Amanda parted Jackie's lips and began to explore the warmth of her mouth. Both of them moaned deeply as she felt Jackie lowering her down onto the bed. Amanda pulled the brunette down on top of her as their tongues wrapped around one another.

"Ahem!" A loud voice startled them.

They quickly broke away from each other and found Bruce glaring at them from the doorway. "What is going on in here?" He demanded in frustration as Amanda tried to calm the rapid beating of her heart and Jackie bolted off of the bed.

"What does it look like?" Jackie challenged him.

"Come on Jackie, you're getting out of here soon," he chastised her.

"You're leaving?" Amanda gasped in horror.

"So they tell me," Jackie confessed shyly.

"What is that?" Bruce demanded gruffly as he pointed to something on the floor that Amanda couldn't see in the darkness.

"Nothing," Jackie blurted out as they both tried to retrieve the object.

"Jackie, what is going on?" Bruce pleaded as she snatched what appeared to be a large file from his grasp.

Amanda looked on as the two them glared at one another. "Bruce, can we trust you?" Amanda finally asked in an effort to end their standoff.

"Of course you can trust me," Bruce vowed in a sincere tone as he kept a watchful gaze on the file that Jackie was clasping tightly to her chest.

"I hope so," Jackie muttered softly as her hold on the file slightly eased. "Why did you come in here in the middle of the night?" Jackie inquired in an accusing tone.

"I heard voices," Bruce wearily explained. "And since I'm pretty certain that Amanda isn't MPD I thought she might have a guest, which is against the rules."

"MPD?" Amanda asked.

"Multiple Personality Disorder," Bruce explained.

"You know, like Wendy down the hall," Jackie supplied.

"I thought her name was Lucy," Amanda said.

"Occasionally," Jackie responded. "And on occasion it's Larry."

"Enough about . . .," he paused for a moment. "What's her name? Do the two of you want to tell me what is going on? If your deep, dark secret is that the two you have the hots for one another then, Duh? Just hold off until you get out of here, or I'm not on duty."

"That's the problem," Jackie snapped as Amanda tried understanding why Bruce was convinced that there was something going on between her and Jackie. "Not the hots part," Jackie quickly explained. "Amanda is never going to get out of here."

"What are you talking about?" Bruce asked in a weary tone.

"Just close the door and listen to what we have to say," Jackie instructed the exhausted physician.

"I don't think so," Bruce sternly protested. "Being alone in a patient's room with the door closed, especially in the middle of the night with two female patients in their pajamas, wouldn't be very good for my career. We can go to my office."

Jackie wasn't thrilled, but since Bruce and Mary, one of the nurses, were the only ones on duty that night, she finally agreed. "Getting paranoid on me Jackie?" Bruce teased her as he sat down behind his desk. "I wish you wouldn't, since I have enough problems dealing with Diane's fear of ice and the CIA."

"Trust me, I'm still the burnt-out executive who had a break down and tried to stab you with a pen," Jackie reassured him as Amanda chuckled.

"What do you think about Amanda?" She asked him directly, ignoring both his and Amanda's teasing.

"She's very nice and I hope the two of you will be very happy together after you get out of here," he offered stressing the last part.

"So you think that someday she will be well enough to leave?" Jackie pushed, as she handed him the file.

"Yes," Bruce concurred as he looked at the file. "Do I want to know how you got your hands on this?"

"No," Jackie said with a cocky smirk.

"Is that my file?" Amanda asked with curiosity.

"Yes," Jackie confirmed. "What is your diagnosis of Amanda's condition?"

"She's not my patient," Bruce argued.

"Fine, just look at her file," Jackie pressed.

"I can't; it would be unethical," Bruce protested.

"Amanda, do you mind if Bruce looks at your file?" Jackie inquired in a sarcastic tone.

"Fine by me," Amanda readily agreed eager to know what was in it.

Bruce seemed hesitant but finally nodded in agreement as he opened the file. "Anything to get the two of you to go back to your own rooms and behave," he grumbled, as he began to flip through her file.

"Does Dr. Asher have her own practice?" Jackie asked in a casual tone.

"No," Bruce grunted as he continued scanning the file. "Why do you . . .?" He voice trailed off as he began to study the file intently. "This can't be right."

Amanda looked over at Jackie who was smiling at her. The blonde felt her stomach flip as she stared deeply into Jackie's crystal blue eyes. Bruce was tearing through her file like a mad man as Amanda was trying to understand why she had kissed the brunette. More importantly, Amanda wanted to know why it felt so good?

"Amanda, please tell me you've stopped taking your meds?"

Bruce asked in a panic. "According to this you only became responsive when a resident changed your meds while Dr. Asher was away."

"I haven't taken anything since I came to and discovered I was here," Amanda confessed shyly.

"Thank God," Bruce said with a sigh of relief.

"I feel a lot better since I've stopped taking them," Amanda offered.

"Why did you stop?" Bruce asked.

"Someone convinced me that I'd feel better if I simply pretended to take them," she offered sheepishly.

"Jackie you may have saved her life," Bruce congratulated the brunette in a grim tone.

"What?" Amanda stammered fearfully as Jackie reached over and clasped her hand. The brunette gave her hand a gentle squeeze. "Bruce, what exactly is wrong with me?"

"According to this, everything," Bruce explained in frustration. "The diagnosis is all over the place. Plus the meds you were on would have kept you behaving like a zombie and could have eventually killed you."

"Why?" Amanda gasped.

"I'd like to know that myself," Bruce blew out.

"Maybe I can help," Jackie brightly offered.

Bruce and Amanda stared at the brunette in wonderment. "First, Amanda won the lottery." The brunette began in a careful tone. Bruce looked at the both of them suspiciously. "Its true. I talked to a friend of hers this afternoon. By the way, Grace didn't just drop out of your life. Every time she tried to see or talk to you, Matt told her you were out or sick. Matt is her husband," she added for Bruce's benefit. "Oh, and she explained the reason she was curious about Matt's fishing trip is because she saw the guy you said he was away with the morning before."

"Wait, if she saw Bobby the morning before, then who was Matt fishing with?" Amanda asked in confusion. Her face turned red as she finally put all of the pieces together. "That bastard!" She spat out bitterly. "He was screwing around."

"Apparently," Jackie confirmed with a slight grimace as

Amanda tightened her grip on the brunette's hand.

"All right, this is all very informative, but it doesn't explain why Dr. Asher had you brought here for care?" Bruce tried to reason. "Wait, your husband's name is Matt? Was he a cabby by an chance?"

"Yes," Amanda growled. "Let me guess, Dr. Asher is dating someone who was a taxi driver until he struck it rich."

"Uhm, yes," Bruce confirmed with a hard swallow.

"How long?" Amanda demanded as she felt the veins in her forehead bulging.

"A year or two," Bruce mumbled quickly. "But still, that doesn't explain going to this much trouble. He could have just left you and still walked away with half of the money."

"Except that Amanda cashed in the ticket alone," Jackie explained. "And if you were smart, you opted for being paid in installments, just a couple of million a year?"

"It made sense for tax purposes," Amanda confirmed with a groan.

"All Matt would have gotten was alimony. The most he could hope for was half," Jackie continued. "But in the scheme of things and if you had a halfway decent lawyer, he probably would have settled for very little. So instead, they gas lighted you and then tossed you in the loony bin, kept you knocked out on drugs so they could have all of the money."

"Nice guy," Bruce choked out. "Okay, first things first, we need to get you declared competent and I need to bust Joyce."

"We need to move quickly or else Amanda's money and those two weasels are going to be long gone," Jackie pointed out. "How long will it take to get Amanda free? I don't know much about these things. The big board was my specialty."

"I need to start right now," Bruce responded eagerly. "Time to wake up the director and see what I can do. In the meantime the two of you need to go to bed and not together."

"Bruce we're not . . .," Jackie tried to explain.

"Let's go," Amanda cut her off as she squeezed her hand tightly.

"Looks like you will be rejoining the world soon," Jackie said as they strolled back towards their rooms. "I'm going to miss you," the brunette confessed in a shy voice.

"You'll be out soon too," Amanda offered brightly as Jackie finally released her hand. Amanda instantly missed the contact.

"I hope," Jackie sighed. "I know I'm better. I just snapped."

"What happened?" Amanda asked, not wanting the night to end. She leaned against the wall hoping that Jackie would stay and talk for a while longer.

Jackie sighed heavily as she appeared to be organizing her thoughts. "I worked so hard. All those years I put in for the company, just crunching numbers and making money meant nothing. The market was down and so were the profits. Mr. Crandall, the CEO, was an aging figurehead who just wouldn't step down. Day after day he berated us about our profit margins. I just couldn't make him understand that there was nothing anyone could do. I blew a gasket and climbed across that long table and throttled the miserable old bastard."

"Didn't anyone try to stop you?" Amanda asked in amazement.

"Not at first," Jackie responded with a light laugh. "I think they wanted me to kill him. Finally one of the other VP's pulled me off of him. I stormed into my office and my assistant Roger starts whining about being over worked. I threatened to set him on fire and he still wouldn't shut up so I smacked him upside the head with the month's-end report. Then I walked over to the copy room and ran my Armani suit through the shredder. Then I strolled back into the boardroom and quit."

"That must have been quite a sight," Amanda laughed as she mentally pictured a very naked Jackie standing in the middle of the boardroom.

"It was great until the cops hauled me off," Jackie chuckled. "I wouldn't have ended up in the lock ward if I hadn't tried to strangle Mr. Crandall."

"But you're better now." Amanda encouraged her.

"I am," Jackie softly admitted. "I realize that I hated what I did for a living, and that my career made me tense and bitter. Cracking up was probably the best thing that happened to me."

They fell into a comfortable silence. "Why did you kiss me?" Jackie broke the silence in an uneasy tone.

"I wanted to," Amanda uneasily confessed. "I'm really confused right now."

"Don't think about it," Jackie said in a comforting tone. "You have enough to deal with right now."

"Yeah, like a divorce, and seeing if I can have my husband and shrink tossed into jail," Amanda groaned.

"Try to get some sleep," Jackie offered as she gave Amanda's shoulder a gentle squeeze.

"I liked it," Amanda confessed as she relaxed into Jackie's touch. "The kiss, I really liked it."

"So did I," Jackie responded with a slight blush. "We can talk about this later, in the meantime we need to get you out of here before Greta starts making sense to you."

"I don't know how to thank you for everything you've done for me," Amanda said as her gaze drifted up and down the leggy brunette's body.

"You don't have to thank me," Jackie's deep voice snapped the blonde out of her overt ogling. "It was nothing, just a little breaking and entering. Greta is really good at it."

"What is Greta in for again?" Amanda asked, suddenly curious about the older woman who was constantly muttering.

"According to her, she was trying to overthrow the government," Jackie supplied, with a bright grin that warmed Amanda's body. "She swears that her plan would have worked if it hadn't rained."

"Okay," Amanda responded with a wide-eyed expression. "Well, when you get sprung, at least let me buy you dinner. And if it's possible, you can be there when I give Matt his walking papers."

"Oh yes, please," Jackie responded enthusiastically.

Part Five

Over the next few days, Amanda, Jackie, and Bruce were very busy making plans to have the blonde released before Dr. Asher or Matt could find out what was happening.

Unfortunately, all of their planning proved not only that Amanda was competent, but Jackie was as well. Which meant she would be leaving before Amanda. They sat on Amanda's bed the night before Jackie was to be released. "I'm going to miss you," Amanda said as Jackie wrapped her arms around the smaller woman.

"You'll be out soon enough," Jackie reassured her. "Once your rat-bastard husband and the good doctor get caught, we will get together for dinner. I can still be there when you tell Matt to take a hike, can't I?"

"Of course," Amanda agreed. "I just wish I could make sense out of all these feelings I have for you."

"No, we agreed that you don't need to think about that right now," Jackie cautioned her. "Once the dust settles, then we can have a nice long talk."

"Talking isn't what I have in mind," Amanda said as she snuggled closer to Jackie.

"Me either," Jackie whispered hotly in the blonde's ear. "But we need to wait until you get your life back. As much as this place has helped me, I don't think I can stick around."

The sound of Bruce clearing his throat made them quickly separate. "Ladies?" The tired looking man greeted them. "Jackie, are you all packed for tomorrow?"

"Yes," Jackie answered him in a sad tone. "Can't we put this off until Amanda is ready?"

"No," Bruce informed them in a hushed tone. "But don't travel too far from the hospital tomorrow morning. Amanda you are having a competency hearing in the morning."

"Really?" Amanda responded brightly.

"Yes, but we have to keep it quiet," Bruce cautioned her. "The cops want to catch your husband and Dr. Asher off guard."

"You pulled it off?" Jackie congratulated him.

"Not yet," Bruce responded in a tired voice.

"Thank you," Amanda said as the man scurried out of the room, but not before cautioning them against any hanky-panky.

"Amanda, you could be out tomorrow," Jackie beamed as she tightened her arms around the small blonde. Amanda couldn't resist pressing her body closer to Jackie's. "I should go back to my room," Jackie said in a labored breath. Amanda held Jackie tighter as she nuzzled the brunette's neck. "Amanda?" Jackie squeaked out, as the blonde was busy inhaling the soft delicate scent of her skin. "Amanda," Jackie protested in a weak tone as Amanda began to place soft kisses on the brunette's neck. "We should wait," Jackie's voice trembled as she spoke.

"Why?" Amanda whispered into the crook of Jackie's neck. Amanda could feel the rapid beating of Jackie's heart, as the brunette seemed to be struggling to breathe. Amanda looked up and was captured in a fiery blue gaze. They moved in unison until their bodies melted together. Soon Amanda found herself lost in the most passionate kiss she had ever experienced. The blonde allowed her tiny hands to roam across Jackie's body as they slipped down onto the mattress.

She covered Jackie's body with her own as the brunette's hands began a gentle exploration. Kissing deeply, they began to caress each other. "I've never felt like this before," Amanda confessed as they both gasped for air.

"Neither have I," Jackie answered as she reached up and captured Amanda's face in her hands.

Amanda felt alive from the loving touch. "We have to stop," Jackie repeated in a weak voice. "If we get caught now it could mess up both of our releases."

"Okay," Amanda reluctantly agreed, as she climbed off of Jackie's body. The brunette took a moment to compose herself before kissing Amanda goodnight and stumbling off to her own room. Amanda tried to still her trembling body as she watched Jackie stumbling out of the room. She blew out an exasperated breath as she tried to calm her quivering body. She clenched her thighs as she fought against the urgent need pulsating between them. "All this from kissing," she blew out in wonderment.

Part Six

Over breakfast Amanda and Jackie formulated a plan. The first thing they did was to enlist Greta's aid. Greta readily agreed, claiming that she lived to cause anarchy. The older woman climbed up on one of the dinning tables and started screaming and throwing things about. Since she was Dr. Asher's patient the good doctor rushed over to calm her down while Bruce collected Amanda and her belongings and rushed her out of the ward and to the courthouse.

Amanda breezed through her hearing since there was nothing wrong with her in the first place. Her only regret was that Jackie wasn't released until after she was taken to the courthouse. When she stepped out of the judge's chambers with Bruce, she was a free woman. A bright smile lit up her face the moment she found Jackie waiting for her.

"It's almost over," Amanda squealed as she jumped into Jackie's arms. "The cops like our idea and told us to go for it."

"They are going to put a wire on her," Bruce explained. "And they helped shut her husband out of her bank account the moment the judge signed the order. What about Asher?"

"I was sprung about twenty minutes ago. Greta was still going full force and she got Batman, Larry, and Marvin to join in. Asher was so flustered by all the flying food and screaming she had no idea that Amanda was gone," Jackie proudly informed them. "Hopefully, she still doesn't know and we can beat her to Matt."

"The police have been keeping an eye on him and said he went out for breakfast and isn't back yet," Amanda said, thankful that once the police and the DA heard what had happened, they jumped in immediately.

"I have to get back to the hospital," Bruce informed them. "The police are going to take the both of you over to Amanda's. I'm glad this all worked out."

"Thank you again," Amanda said and gave the stunned man a hug.

"Go on, you two have a lot to do," Bruce said with a blush.

The police rushed both women over to Amanda's house and instructed them on what to do and what they needed to hear on the wire that Amanda would be wearing. Amanda let herself into the house while Jackie followed closely behind her. The blonde changed into her favorite evening gown, which still hid the tiny microphone the police had taped to her body. Much to her delight, Jackie stretched out across her bed and watched her every movement.

"I don't know what I enjoy more, watching you take all of your clothes off, or seeing you in that dress?" Jackie said with an appreciative sigh.

Amanda blushed as she looked down at the black evening gown. "The police heard that," she informed the brunette with a saucy grin.

"Oops," Jackie grimaced as she rose and crossed the room. She wrapped her arms around Amanda's tiny waist. "Promise me, if it looks like this isn't going to work, or if he gets violent, just give him the money. Your safety is far more important."

"You wouldn't care if I was flat broke?" Amanda inquired as Jackie tightened her hold on her.

"I don't care if we end up living in a cardboard box," Jackie assured her. "So long as we are together. I told you before, I'm in this because you have a nice ass." The brunette cupped and squeezed Amanda's firm backside to emphasize her point.

Amanda released a throaty growl as she laced her fingers through Jackie's long dark hair and guided her down to her. They exchanged soft kisses until they heard the sounds of someone downstairs whistling. "He's here," Amanda gasped as they released their hold on one another.

"I'll be right here waiting for you," Jackie vowed. "Just be careful."

"I will," Amanda, promised, before stepping out of the bedroom.

She walked along the banister and looked down to see her loving husband in his jogging shorts reading the newspaper as he whistled. He was completely unaware of her presence. She almost didn't believe that he had actually done all those horrible things until Dr. Asher let herself in the front door. Amanda remained at the top of the staircase watching them.

"Matt, she's gone," Joyce Asher blurted out.

"What are you talking about, darling?" He asked in confusion as he set the paper down.

"Amanda," she bellowed. "She's gone. There was a disruption in her ward and while I was taking care of it, someone helped her escape."

"Calm down," he sternly instructed her. "We'll just call the police and once they find her, they will lock her up again."

"What if they don't find her?" Asher said frantically.

"So, the checks will still come," he reasoned in cold manner.

"You should have let me give her an overdose," the skinny blonde fumed.

"No," Matt spat out as Amanda's chest tightened. "If she's dead, then the checks stop. If the stupid little bitch had taken all of the money at once then we could have killed her without a problem."

Amanda had heard enough and she hoped that the police had heard everything as well. She started to descend the staircase. They were still bickering as she came closer. Suddenly Matt's head snapped around and he saw her.

"Hello honey, I'm home," she addressed him in an icy tone.

"Amanda?" He choked out before he flashed her his trademark boyish grin. "Why did you run away from the hospital? I've been worried sick about you."

"Of course you have," she snickered. "I didn't run away."

"What?" Asher stammered as her face paled.

"I'm sorry, did you miss that, doctor?" Amanda toyed with both of them. "I've been released."

"No, you couldn't have been," Asher protested as she rolled her eyes in disbelief. "Now, we need to get you back to the hospital."

"Oh, but Dr. Asher, I don't need to go to the hospital since a very nice judge and three of your colleagues agree that I'm quite sane," Amanda carefully explained. "It wasn't hard since I stopped taking the pills you prescribed quite some time ago. In fact, everyone agreed that I was never crazy in the first place. I think your boss wants to talk to you."

"We're screwed," Asher choked out.

"Nonsense," Matt disagreed with a shrug. "Amanda, I'm happy that you are better."

"Shove it, Matt," Amanda spat out in disgust.

"Fine, have it your way," Matt shrugged again before he grabbed her roughly around the throat. "You wanted to be home and now you are," he hissed.

"Matt, let her go," Asher screamed as Jackie came barreling out of the bedroom.

Amanda was struggling to breathe and to free herself from her husband's grip. "Shut up, Joyce," he yelled at his lover. "I'll just keep you doped up here," he informed her in a cold voice. "Better this way. Fewer witnesses."

"Let her go," Amanda heard Jackie growling.

"You?" Asher said in confusion as the police finally poured into the entryway.

"Mr. Farmer, let go of your wife," one of the detectives informed him.

"It is about freaking time," she heard Jackie shouting over the melee.

Before Matt could comply with the instructions Jackie had already grabbed him and pulled him off of Amanda. The room filled with a flurry of activity as Jackie cradled Amanda in her arms. "It's over," Jackie whispered in her ear over and over again as Amanda clung to her.

Part Seven

After Matt and Joyce were arrested and carted away, Amanda endured an endless stream of questions and had to give her statement. Hours later, after everyone was gone, she was still sitting on the staircase clinging to Jackie. "Are you all right?" Jackie asked her carefully.

"I'm free," Amanda said as she blew out a sigh of relief. "I'm sure that this is all going to hit me later, but right now, all I feel is how good it is to be free and how good it feels to have your arms around me."

Amanda took another deep breath before she stood and held out her hand to Jackie. The brunette gave her a curious look before accepting her hand. The blonde smiled as she led Jackie up the staircase. "I thought we were going to have a long talk?" Jackie said cautiously as Amanda led them to the bedroom.

"Later, right now I want to thank you for saving my life," Amanda informed the taller woman as she turned to her and rested her hands on the brunette's hips.

"I think you just want to get fresh with me," Jackie teased as she caressed the smaller woman's shoulders.

"I do," Amanda agreed as her hands slid up the taller woman's side. "I think that I've wanted to get fresh with you from the first moment I woke up in the hospital."

Jackie kissed the blonde once again as she led them over to the large canopy bed. Amanda felt nervous as she began to unbutton the brunette's blouse.   Jackie captured the blonde's trembling hands in her own. "We don't have to," Jackie said gently before she kissed Amanda's trembling fingers.

"Yes we do," Amanda explained as she looked up at her lover. She almost felt like crying as she saw the love reflected in Jackie's eyes. "You have no idea how much I want you. How much I need you."

"If it is half of what I feel, then it is everything," Jackie tried to explain. She released Amanda's trembling hands and gently cupped her face. "Let me make love to you?" Jackie pleaded softly as she guided the still trembling blonde down onto the bed.

Amanda was so overwhelmed with emotion and desire she could only nod in response. Jackie stared deeply into her eyes as she ran her fingers through Amanda's long blonde hair. Amanda released a tiny whimper as she felt Jackie's fingers caress her neck. Jackie kissed her gently as her hands began to explore Amanda's body. Amanda melted into Jackie's touch with a craving to feel the brunette's hands touch her everywhere. The kisses grew deeper as Amanda's hands once again returned to the buttons on her lover's shirt.

Amanda fumbled slightly as she tried to remove her lover's clothing while Jackie continued a slow gentle exploration of her body. Jackie pulled away from her slightly and looked down at the trembling blonde. "We have all night." Jackie reassured her as she removed her shirt and cast it aside.

"I need to feel you," Amanda whimpered as Jackie nodded in understanding and climbed off of the bed.

The brunette propped Amanda up against the headboard and supported her with a large pile of pillows. Amanda tried to reach for her lover only to have her playful advances brushed aside.

Jackie stood beside the bed and slowly removed her clothing. Watching each article of clothing vanish from the beautiful brunette's body was pure torture. Amanda tried to calm her breathing as she watched, fighting against the urge to leap off of the bed and ravish the brunette.

Amanda kicked off her high heels as Jackie crawled up onto the bed. "You are so beautiful," Amanda gasped as her lover moved closer until she was hovering dangerously close to the small blonde. Amanda was surprised to see the blush emerge on her lover's chiseled features. "Didn't you know that?" Amanda questioned her in amazement.

Jackie's eyes shifted in embarrassment as Amanda captured her face in her tiny hands. Amanda felt her heart warm as Jackie leaned into her touch. The brunette's gaze drifted down the blonde's body as she ran the tip of her finger in the same path. Amanda inhaled sharply as she felt Jackie's finger brushing along the edge of the vee-cut top of her gown. Amanda's body began to burn with a needy desire as she felt the material of her gown being brushed aside and Jackie's touch running along the swell of her breast. "Does this hurt?" Jackie asked in a breathy tone as she was gliding her finger over the reddish mark left by the tape that had held the microphone in place.

Amanda looked down at the small blemish. "Not really," Amanda struggled as she fought against the urge to touch the naked woman resting beside her. "I could kiss it and make it better?" Jackie whispered hotly in the blonde's ear. The feel of Jackie's breath and her hair caressing the bare skin of her shoulder invoked a shiver, which ran through the tiny blonde's body.

"It hurts," Amanda lied as she laced her fingers through Jackie's hair and guided her down to her breasts.

Amanda cried out as she felt Jackie's tongue tracing her breast. She tightened her hold on Jackie's head as the brunette began to lick and kiss the bruised flesh. Amanda was whimpering as Jackie's mouth left her skin. "Why did you wear this?" Jackie asked her softly, once again her breath caressing the blonde's skin as she spoke. Amanda quivered, trying to process her lover's words.

"Uhm," she cleared her throat as she fought to respond. "Because Matt gets very distracted when I wear this dress. I thought it might keep him off center if I was wearing this instead of a pair of dirty old sweats.

"Good call," Jackie panted before running the tip of her tongue along the valley between the blonde's breasts.

As Jackie's mouth continued its exploration, one of her hands drifted down the blonde's body and came to rest on her hip. "You're driving me insane," Amanda said as she felt her lover massaging her hip. Jackie released a light laugh against her body.

"Don't knock insanity," Jackie murmured as she began to lower one of the straps of Amanda's gown down her shoulder. "If I hadn't gone over the edge, we might have never met."

"Uh huh," Amanda choked out as she felt the other strap being lowered.

Amanda cried out and her body arched, when she felt her lover's mouth moving up to her overly sensitive neck and then down along her shoulders. Jackie's mouth worshipped her neck and each of her shoulders and back down to the valley of her cleavage. Amanda squirmed beneath her lover as she tried to press her body harder against the brunette's.

She was fighting to control her breathing as she ran her hands up and down Jackie's back. "Turn over baby," Jackie instructed her in a husky tone that Amanda feared was going to kill her. She stifled a whimper as she turned over onto her stomach. She felt her body being guided down from the pillows and she clutched at the bedding as the zipper of her gown was lowered.

She could feel herself burning as Jackie's mouth caressed every inch of newly exposed skin until the zipper was fully opened just above her backside. She released a cry into the comforter as she felt Jackie's tongue running along the elastic waistband of her panties. Her clit was throbbing as she felt her lover's nipples brushing against her skin.

"I love your body," Jackie said softly as she guided the small blonde up into a kneeling position. Amanda trembled uncontrollably from the feel of her lover's naked body pressing against her as her gown was lowered down. Once the fancy dress was pooled around Amanda's waist she felt Jackie's hands begin a slow exploration of her skin. She moaned as Jackie's hands ran up the side of her body and past her ribs until Jackie was feeling the weight of the blonde's breasts.

"So beautiful," Jackie murmured with pleasure before she began to kiss Amanda's neck and shoulders while she cupped the blonde's breasts. Amanda's body arched again in response as Jackie teased her nipples with the palms of her hands and feasted upon her neck and shoulders. "Tell me what you want?" Jackie inquired in a sultry tone. She teased Amanda's nipples with her fingers and their hips began to sway.

Amanda pressed her backside into her lover's body urging her to touch her. "I don't know," Amanda confessed weakly, grinding harder into Jackie's body. "I've never felt like this before," Amanda timidly confessed. She had never been with a woman and feared that she would fail to please her lover. Jackie's touch seemed to quiet the blonde's fears as she rolled her erect nipples between her fingers. Amanda groaned in protest when she felt Jackie's hands leaving her breasts and drifting back down her body.

Amanda was ready to explode as she felt the gown being lowered past her hips and her lover guiding her to lean forward. Amanda reached out and gripped the headboard of the bed tightly in an effort to steady her quivering body as she felt the last of her clothing being removed. "Oh God," the blonde cried out when she felt her lover kissing her way up her legs. Her hips swayed urgently as her clit began to pulsate in a demanding rhythm while Jackie kissed and tasted the back of her knees.

Certain that she was going to die or pass out, Amanda tightened her grip on the headboard as she felt Jackie's hands and mouth moving up along the back of her trembling thighs. Instinctively, the blonde parted her thighs and felt her wetness painting her skin. Her body began to rock wildly when she felt Jackie's tongue licking away each drop of her wetness from the inside of her thighs.

Amanda's entire body arched when she felt her lover's

tongue running along her sex. "Yes," Amanda pleaded as Jackie dipped further into her wetness. Her lover parted her further as she began to feast upon Amanda's desire. The blonde thrust her body against her lover as she begged her for more. She cried out in desperation as she felt Jackie's mouth moving away from her aching nub.

Soon she was once again moaning in pleasure as she felt Jackie's fingers replacing her mouth. Jackie dipped her fingers further into the blonde's wetness and kissed her way along the curves of Amanda's backside. The blonde was ready to collapse as she felt Jackie's thumb brushing against her throbbing clit and her tongue trailing a tantalizing path up along her spine.

She felt Jackie's wetness pressing against her as the brunette's fingers teased the opening of her aching center. She felt Jackie's hot breath in her ear as the brunette entered her. Amanda felt the walls of her center tighten against her lover's fingers as the brunette filled her. Jackie's desire painted the firm flesh of her ass while the brunette stroked her clit and wiggled her fingers inside of her.

She thrust her body against her lover's hand. Jackie slowly began to plunge in and out of her as their bodies moved in a slow sensual rhythm. As Amanda rode against her lover's touch and felt Jackie's body melting against her own, she felt complete for the first time in her life. They thrust harder against one another, each demanding more. Amanda was lost in the feel of her lover's body melting into her own as she gave herself over to Jackie's touch. Amanda's ears were ringing as they bucked against one another wildly. She knew that she was crying out but was completely unaware of what she was saying as her body began to convulse. She climaxed against Jackie's touch as she felt her lover exploding against her.

Amanda had never felt her body explode with such intensity before, and expected that it was all the brunette had to offer. But Jackie continued to plunge in and out of her until they were once again crying out in ecstasy. Amanda found it hard to breathe as they continued to explode against each other until they both collapsed onto the bed.

Amanda's body was still on fire as she straddled her lover's body and kissed her deeply. Soon she was kissing her way down the brunette's body. She savored the taste of her lover's skin as she teased Jackie's nipples between her nimble fingers. Needing to feel more of the beautiful woman squirming beneath her, she parted Jackie's thighs with her knee as she captured one of her nipples in her mouth.

She suckled her lover's nipple eagerly and felt Jackie's thigh pressing against her wetness. She mirrored her lover's actions and soon they were rocking against each other. Amanda sucked her lover harder as her clit brushed urgently against Jackie's. She felt the brunette's body arching against her as she thrust harder. Amanda released Jackie's nipple as her own body arched and her head fell back.

She continued to sway against her lover and looked down at the woman who had captured her heart. The sight of Jackie lost in the throes of ecstasy drove the petite blonde closer to the edge of oblivion. Jackie was clasping her hips tightly as they became one. They climaxed in unison, each trying to cling to the other's body, until they collapsed into one another's warm embrace.

Amanda felt the sweat rolling off of both of their bodies as she rested her head against her lover's chest. She felt the rapid beating of Jackie's heart as the brunette gently ran her fingers up and down Amanda's body. Content to stay where she was Amanda nestled her body even closer to Jackie. She knew that there were a great many things they had to talk about. None of it mattered at the moment, as she felt Jackie guiding them under the covers. Amanda curled up in Jackie's arms. It felt right to be held by Jackie and whatever questions or problems lay ahead of them would just have to wait until morning. Sighing happily, Amanda drifted off to sleep while listening to the steady beating of her lover's heart.

The End

FINAL EXAM

"If I never utter another word of French, my life will be complete," Briar groaned in disgust as she tossed down her textbook. "Okay, what's next?" She asked as she tucked an errant strand of short blonde hair behind one ear. The lock of hair immediately sprung back out into her sea green eyes.

Mina smiled at her roommate as she reached over and re-tucked the lock behind her ear. After four years of college the two shared a comfortable friendship. They had hit it off immediately when they found themselves sharing a room during freshman year. Sharing space with a complete stranger should have been awkward for the two girls, both of whom treasured their privacy. Instead they bonded and quickly became inseparable. "I think we're done," Mina smiled as she to set aside her textbooks. "I can't believe that our last finals are this week." Mina suddenly felt sad at the thought that she and Briar would soon go their separate ways.

"What time is it?" Briar inquired as she tried to stifle a yawn. She flopped down on the twin bed they had chosen to study on.

"Ask me in French," Mina teased as she stretched her arms over her head.

"Bite me," Briar groused bitterly as she tried to kick her

roommate who quickly grasped her foot.

"Okay," Mina teased, her hazel eyes brightening at the thought. "Where?" She added teasingly. Internally she secretly prayed that someday Briar would pick up on her flirting. Much to Mina's disappointment Briar never did, not once in all the years they lived together.

Briar ignored Mina's comment as usual and the red head reluctantly released the blonde's foot from her grasp. Mina had developed a slight crush on Briar right from the start. Still confused about her sexuality, she let it go. When they both finally admitted that they shared an attraction for women, Mina had hoped that something might happen between the two of them. But Briar never seemed interested in Mina that way, even after they both found themselves confessing that their interest in the same sex wasn't just a passing phase or curiosity.

Over the years Mina started flirting with Briar, but the blonde simply laughed it off as a private little joked they shared. Although the two were physically comfortable with one another, Mina yearned for more. Of course, she told herself that she should just tell Briar how she felt. Normally an outgoing person, she simply couldn't work up the courage to tell Briar that she had feelings for her and so she spent four years in silent frustration watching Briar go out with other girls. She dated other women as well but somehow neither of them stayed with anyone for long.

"Have you decided what you're going to do after graduation?" Briar inquired thoughtfully, interrupting Mina's thoughts.

"Not yet," Mina confessed. "It's strange. I've spent four years busting my ass to get my degree. Now I have no idea what I'm going to do with the rest of my life."

"Grad school," Briar gruffly supplied.

"My parents won't go for it," Mina argued weakly. "I've already told you that." It was an old argument between the two.

"I know your dad wants you to go into the family business which you'll hate. Yada yada yada," Briar yammered as she waved her hand dismissively. "You know they just want to get you back home so they can de-gay you."

"I know," Mina groaned. "If they send me one more article about Anne "I'm a Freakin' nut ball" Hecht, I'm going to throw up."

"We could get an apartment together," Briar suggested in a hopeful tone. "My folks just adore you and they're going to help me out while I'm looking for a job."

"Still planning on taking a year off before grad school?" Mina inquired as she allowed her eyes to drink in the sight of Briar lounging casually on her bed.   "You're not going to fall asleep on my bed again, are you?"

"You still haven't told me what time it is," Briar pointed out as she made herself more comfortable.

Mina curled her lips as she watched Briar settling in for the night.   Even though she complained about it constantly, she secretly loved it when Briar slept in her bed.   She loved feeling Briar's body pressed up against her.   Waking up next to Briar was a unique experience that caused her to feel both wonderful and miserable at the same time.   Mornings would find the two of them curled up together.   Mina would always bolt out of bed instantly before her body could betray her.   Her next stop was always a long cold shower.

"So, you still want to live with me?" Mina asked suddenly, trying to take her mind off the sight of the steady rise and fall of Briar's chest.

"Of course I do, you goof," Briar snorted as she tried once again to nudge Mina with her foot.   Mina quickly halted Briar's attempt.   "Stinker," Briar shot back as she pulled her foot away. "You know I never told you this, but every time we had to be apart during the breaks, I really missed you.   God knows why since you're a big pain in the ass."

"Gee thanks, I think," Mina chuckled lightly.

"I was just thinking about your reaction when I got back after last summer's break," Briar said absently.   "What was that all about?"

"I don't know what you're talking about," Mina lied.   She could never forget the sight of Briar when she walked into their room.   Briar had a new hairstyle.   Gone was the long blonde hair that Mina had adored.   Briar's new look was incredible.   Her new short hair made her look so much more like a woman not the impish girl she had first met. Mina took one look at Briar and a stirring began in the pit of her stomach. She couldn't stay in the same room with Briar. She ran out in search of someplace to go where she could find some privacy. She found herself in the communal bathroom pleasuring herself.

"Whatever," Briar dismissed Mina's lie with a groan. "Mina . . . can I ask you something?" She began slowly. "Never mind," she added suddenly.

Mina stared down at Briar in disbelief. "I hate when you do that," Mina grumbled, recalling the thousands of times Briar had started to say something then would stop. Mina would end up dragging it out of her only to discover that Briar wanted to ask her something really lame. "Just ask what you want to ask me," Mina urged as she shoved their textbooks onto the floor and curled up next to Briar.

"It's nothing," Briar said with a nonchalant shrug.

"Come on," Mina encouraged as she nudged her roommate. "Don't make me drag it out of you," she threatened as her fingers dug into Briar's side. Briar squirmed with a giggle.

"Don't," Briar protested as she snuggled up against Mina.

"Tell me," Mina growled in fierce tone as she wiggled her fingers in a threatening manner. "Tell me," she repeated, a confident smirk gracing her full lips.

The smirk quickly vanished as she took in the look of despair on Briar's delicate features. The blonde grew strangely quiet. "Briar?" Silence greeted Mina as Briar snuggled even closer to her. Mina wrapped her arms around her. "Hey, what's going on in that pretty blonde head?"

"Nothing," Briar said softly as she tried to sit up.

Mina quickly drew her back into her arms. Her heart dropped when she saw the sadness clearly written in Briar's normally bright eyes. "Briar?" She repeated as she tucked two fingers under Briar's chin and tilted her face up. They were so close to one another; Mina knew that if she leaned in just a little closer she could capture those soft sweet lips that haunted her dreams on a nightly basis.

Briar wrapped one hand around the back of Mina's head then

suddenly pulled away. "I'm just a little down," she admitted as she sat up and turned her back to Mina. The taller woman sat up and scooted up behind Briar. Wrapping her arms around Briar's firm abdomen, she rested her head on Briar's shoulder.

"What are you so sad about?"

"It's silly," Briar said with a heavy sigh as she placed her hands over Mina's. "I'm going to miss you," she said in a heavy tone.

"That's not silly," Mina reassured her as she hugged her friend a little tighter. She felt guilty as her nipples hardened when her breasts brushed against Briar's back. "I'm going to miss you too," she added as she guiltily enjoyed the pleasure of holding Briar's body.

"I really . . .," " Briar tensed for a moment. "You're my best friend."

Mina's body tensed up as she released her hold on Briar and pulled away slightly. It was the "*f*" word. That was all there was between them, an ugly fact that Mina needed to continually remind herself of. It was the real reason why she was heading back home. "Yeah well, you're my best friend too," Mina's voice trembled as she spoke. "Why else would I put up with your snoring for the past fours years?"

"I don't snore," Briar protested as she spun around and swatted her roommate.

"You do to," Mina countered playfully.

"I do not!" Briar argued as she once again swatted Mina who was trying to defend herself. "As for you . . . you're a big covers hog."

"Well, maybe if you slept in your own bed every once in awhile, I wouldn't have to pull the covers over my head so I can drown out your snoring," Mina laughed as she fended off Briar's hands. "Enough with the hitting, you little brat."

"You wouldn't be making disparaging comments regarding my size, would you?" Briar said as she poked Mina in the ribs. "Huh?" She stressed poked the now smirking Mina once again.

"Okay, that's it, shortie," Mina cautioned her as she grasped both of Briar's wrists firmly.

"Shortie?" Briar flared as she tried to free herself. "Just who are you calling short. . . *whoa!*" Briar squealed as Mina flipped the smaller woman onto her back.

Mina pinned Briar's squirming body beneath her as she held her arms firmly above her head. "Bully," Briar laughed as Mina straddled her hips. "Oh poor baby," Mina teased, fighting to calm her racing heart. Her excitement grew as Briar's body moved against hers. It was a familiar situation for both of them. One of them always broke away from their little wrestling matches before Mina could give into the temptation. Mina felt her body aching with desire as they struggled.

A sudden sense of panic overcame Mina as she realized that they were both dressed simply in boxer shorts and t-shirts. That was fine when they were studying but now Mina was all too aware of her growing excitement as her passion began to pool between her thighs. If she didn't pull away now, Briar would know how her body was reacting.

Mina released her hold on Briar's wrists as she pulled away slightly. She swallowed hard as she gazed down at Briar, drinking in the sight of her hardened nipples pressing against the thin material of her white cotton t-shirt. Her eyes moved up to that beautiful face now flushed from their activities. She smiled at the mess of blonde hair. Reaching down, she gently brushed the hair out Briar's eyes.

Briar's eyes were filled with a deep intensity that drew Mina in. She couldn't think as her breathing became labored. Her body simply reacted as she shifted her position. One of her firm thighs found it's way between Briar's legs. The smoky gaze reflected back at her mesmerized her.

Mina's clit began to throb as she felt wetness caress her thigh. She licked her lips absently as she realized that the passion painting her flesh wasn't her own. Her heart was screaming for her to finally take the chance she had been too afraid to take before. She was paralyzed as her mind finally kicked in. She had been in love with this woman for so long, and now their time was coming to an end. Could she risk everything?

She trembled slightly as she felt Briar's hands gently clasping her hips. Her internal struggle intensified as she mentally debated the consequences. As she felt Briar pulling her closer she decided that thinking was the last thing she needed to do. She smiled as she leaned into Briar's touch.

Mina allowed her body to take control as she followed her heart. She found herself lying almost completely on top of Briar. Their lips were a breath apart as she felt Briar's arms wrap around her waist. She brushed Briar's lips gently. Her heart swelled, as she tasted their sweetness. Instantly she needed to taste them again.

She traced Briar's bottom lip with her tongue as she felt gentle hands roaming across her back. She pressed her lips to Briar's once again. The second kiss quickly deepened as she felt Briar's lips part, inviting her in. She explored the warmth of Briar's mouth, as she was pulled closer to Briar's body.

Their hips began to dance together sensually as she pressed her thigh into Briar's center. She moaned into Briar's mouth as she felt her wetness caressing her bare skin. Briar's hands slipped up under the back of her shirt, her fingertips warming every inch of her. Briar's tongue began to caress hers as she felt a firm thigh slip between her own legs.

The need to breathe overwhelmed them as they broke away from the kiss. Their hips were grinding together as they gasped harshly. Mina pulled away slightly as realized that she was crushing the smaller woman. Supporting herself with her arms she looked down at Briar who was smiling up at her.

The air was filled with their ragged breathing, as their pace grew steadily wilder. The scent of their passion surrounded them as they drove one another closer and closer to the edge. Their bodies trembled in unison as they moved together at a furious pace.

Mina was certain that her heart would explode. Her body arched as they climaxed together. She collapsed against Briar. Her heart was pounding so loudly that she could hear ringing in her ears. Briar panted heavily beneath her. She pulled away slightly and looked down at Briar's smiling face.

Briar reached up and brushed the hair out of Mina's eyes. Mina smiled back brightly as she tilted her head lowering it so she could kiss Briar's swollen lips. "I love you," she whispered before kissing her once again. She felt Briar smiling against her lips. "I've loved you for so long," Mina asserted as she kissed the beautiful woman again and again.

Briar wrapped a hand around the back of Mina's head and drew her in, deepening their kiss. Once again their tongues battled for dominance. Suddenly Briar broke the kiss. Mina pulled away in surprise, feeling suddenly nervous as she looked down at the smiling blonde. Briar placed a reassuring hand against Mina's rapidly beating heart. "You just said the one thing I've been trying to tell you for years," Briar choked out.

"Why didn't you tell me?" Mina questioned her as she fought back the tears that were threatening to overcome her.

"Why didn't you?" Briar laughed lightly.

"I was . . . "

". . . afraid," Briar finished for her, knowingly. "So was I," she confessed as she gently nudged Mina.

Mina chuckled lightly as she shifted so that she was now lying beside Briar. "We've wasted a lot of time," Mina noted as she ran a finger along Briar's jaw line.

"I know," Briar agreed, as her voice deepened. "An oversight which I for one plan on atoning for right now."

Briar's hand began a slow path down the front of Mina's shirt. "And you plan on making up for the past four years tonight?" Mina inquired as she shivered slightly from Briar's touch.

"Yes," Briar responded in a deep rich tone as her hand slipped up under Mina's shirt.

Mina's abdomen tightened in pleasure from Briar's touch. Mina lowered herself onto the bed as Briar climbed on top of her. "I love you," Briar repeated as her hand cupped Mina's breast. Mina inhaled sharply as nimble fingers teased her already sensitive nipple. "I want you," Briar whispered as her other hand lifted Mina's shirt over her breasts.

"I'm yours," Mina moaned as Briar lowered her head and kissed the valley between her breasts.

Briar kissed Mina's sensitive flesh, her lips and tongue blazing a trail across her breast. Mina's eyes fluttered close as Briar captured her nipple in her mouth. Mina ran her fingers through Briar's short blonde hair, pressing her eager mouth closer to her. She arched her back, offering more of herself as Briar tugged gently on her nipple.

Mina enjoyed the slow torture Briar was inflicting on her. Her mouth pleasured one breast while her fingers teased the other. She opened her legs as Briar settled her body between them. Briar ceased her attentions, pulling away slightly. Her hands gripped Mina's t-shirt. Mina raised her arms allowing Briar to remove it from her body. "I've dreamt about doing this," Briar said quietly as she stared blatantly at Mina's breasts.

"Do you like what you see?" Mina teased as she cupped her own breasts.

"Oh yes," Briar moaned as she started to lower her head once again.

Mina reached out and quickly halted her assault. "Ahem," she cleared her throat as she tugged playfully on Briar's shirt. Briar smiled brightly as Mina playfully wiggled her eyebrows. Mina wet her lips as Briar raised her body. Kneeling above Mina, the blonde quickly discarded her own shirt.

"You are so beautiful," Mina said quietly as she drank in the sight of Briar's beautiful body.

"You've seen me naked before," Briar pointed out as she lowered her body once again, resettling between Mina's long legs. "We've been getting changed in front of one another for years," Briar murmured as she placed gentle kisses along Mina's long neck.

"Yeah," Mina gasped, "but back then I had to sneak peeks at you since the thought of us being together was the impossible dream." Mina yelped as Briar nipped her on the neck.

Briar chuckled evilly as she continued to taste her way down Mina's body. Mina's breathing became labored as her boxer shorts were lowered down her legs. She gripped the blanket tightly as Briar began kissing her way up her legs. Briar kissed and tasted the inside of Mina's thighs. Mina opened herself up wider, feeling Briar's hot breath caressing her damp curls.

Mina shuddered as Briar parted her with two fingers before dipping her tongue into her wetness. Her tongue circled Mina's throbbing clit before taking it into her mouth. Mina struggled to hold on as Briar entered her with two fingers. Her thighs began to tremble as Briar quickened her pace. Her fingers and tongue drove Mina closer and closer to the brink. Mina looked down to see a pair sea green eyes twinkling up at her. That was her undoing. Her body arched as the orgasm ripped through her.

She tried to steady her breathing after collapsing on the mattress. She trembled as Briar's fingers left her. She held out her hand to Briar who quickly joined her. Mina gathered her up in her arms. Their bodies covered in a sheen of sweat, the two held onto one another.

Suddenly their bliss was interrupted by a persistent beeping noise. They sprang up in unison. "No," Mina wailed in despair as she shut off the offensive alarm clock.

"Why didn't you tell me how late it was?" Briar questioned as she put her shirt back on.

"I thought we were going to sleep; I didn't know we'd end up making love," Mina explained honestly.

Briar leaned down and kissed her sweetly. Mina's body ignited once again as she tasted herself on her lover's lips. Briar pulled away as Mina tried to wrap her arms around her. "We can't," Briar said breathlessly.

"But . . . ," Mina protested.

"It's our finals, baby," Briar pouted.

Mina nodded in agreement as she started looking for her clothing. "You're right," she grumbled. "Well, I'm glad that we decided to take the same classes this semester, because we'll finish at the same time."

"Did you have something in mind?" Briar inquired hopefully.

"Yes," Mina said confidently as she pulled on her clothing. "I'm going to make love to you. I'm going to take my time and show you everything I've been dreaming about for the past four years." She laughed as she watched Briar turn a delightful shade of red.

"Mina?" Briar asked in a shaky tone. "I don't want to push anything, but what happens after graduation? Are you still . . ."

"No, baby," Mina said confidently. "I'm not going back. I've spent four years running away from my feelings. I'm staying.

No more running for either of us. We belong with each other."

"We'll make this work," Briar said confidently as Mina gathered her up in a warm embrace.

THE END

About the Author

Mavis Applewater was born in Massachusetts in 1962.As a child she was an avid reader and honed her creative side to major in Theatre at Salem State College. While supporting herself waiting for her big break, she became a "resident" and well known bartender at a nightclub in Cambridge, MA.

Mavis has done several commercials and lots of extra work but her creative juices were still flowing so she turned to another one of her hidden talents, writing. This jump started her writing career and culminated with several manuscripts one of them being "The Brass Ring".

Currently Mavis lives with her partner of 11 years; they reside in the North Shore area of Massachusetts.

Order These Great Books Directly From Limitless, Dare 2 Dream Publishing

Title	Price	Note
The Amazon Queen by L M Townsend	20.00	
Define Destiny by J M Dragon	20.00	The one that started it all…
Desert Hawk, revised by Katherine E. Standelll	18.00	Many new scenes
Golden Gate by Erin Jennifer Mar	18.00	
The Brass Ring By Mavis Applewater	18.00	HOT
Haunting Shadows by J M Dragon	18.00	
Spirit Harvest by Trish Shields	15.00	
PWP: Plot? What Plot? by Mavis Applewater	18.00	HOT
Journeys By Anne Azel	18.00	NEW
Memories Kill By S. B. Zarben	20.00	
Up The River, revised By Sam Ruskin	18.00	Many new scenes
	Total	

South Carolina residents add 5% sales tax.
Domestic shipping is $3.50 per book

Visit our website at: http://limitlessd2d.net

Please mail your orders with credit card info, check or money order to:

Limitless, Dare 2 Dream Publishing
100 Pin Oak Ct.
Lexington, SC 29073-7911

Please make checks or money orders payable to: Limitless.

I

Order More Great Books Directly From Limitless, Dare 2 Dream Publishing

Daughters of Artemis by L M Townsend	18.00	
Connecting Hearts By Val Brown and MJ Walker	18.00	
Mysti: Mistress of Dreams **By Sam Ruskin**	18.00	HOT
Family Connections **By Val Brown & MJ Walker**	18.00	Sequel to Connecting Hearts
A Thousand Shades of Feeling **by Carolyn McBride**	18.00	
The Amazon Nation **By Carla Osborne**	18.00	Great for research
Poetry from the Featherbed **By pinfeather**	18.00	If you think you hate poetry you haven't read this
None So Blind, 3rd Edition By LJ Maas	16.00	NEW
A Saving Solace **By DS Bauden**	18.00	NEW
Return of the Warrior By Katherine E. Standell	20.00	Sequel to Desert Hawk
Journey's End **By LJ Maas**	18.00	NEW
	Total	

South Carolina residents add 5% sales tax.
Domestic shipping is $3.50 per book
Please mail your orders with credit card info, check or money order to:
Limitless, Dare 2 Dream Publishing
100 Pin Oak Ct.
Lexington, SC 29073-7911
Please make checks or money orders payable to: Limitless.

Name:	
Address:	
Address:	
City/State/Zip:	
Country:	
Phone:	
Credit Card Type:	
CC Number:	
EXP Date:	
List Items Ordered and Retail Prices:	

List Items Ordered and Retail Prices:

You may also send a money order or check. Please make payments out to: Limitless Corporation.
You may Fax this form to us at: 803-359-2881 or mail it to:
Limitless Corporation
100 Pin Oak Court
Lexington, SC 29073-7911

South Carolina residents add 5% sales tax.
Domestic shipping is $3.50 per book

Visit our website at: http://limitlessd2d.net

Introducing...
Art By Joy

By JoyArgento

Hi, allow me to introduce myself. My name is Joy Argento and I am the artist on all of these pieces. I have been doing artwork since I was a small child. That gives me about 35 years of experience. I majored in art in high school and took a few college art courses. Most of my work is done in either pencil or airbrush mixed with color pencils. I have recently added designing and creating artwork on the computer. Some of the work featured on these pages were created and "painted" on the computer. I am self taught in this as well as in the use of the airbrush.

I have been selling my art for the last 15 years and have had my work featured on trading cards, prints and in magazines. I have sold in galleries and to private collectors from all around the world.

I live in Western New York with my three kids, four cats, one dog and the love of my life. It is definitely a full house. I appreciate you taking the time to check out my artwork. Please feel free to email me with your thoughts or questions. Custom orders are always welcomed too.

Contact me at ArtByJoy@aol.com . I look forward to hearing from you.

Making Love

Towel Cuddling

Motorcycle Women

Joy Argento

Check out her work at
LimitlessD2D or at her website.
Remember: ArtByJoy@aol.com !

Printed in the United States
103687LV00005B/157/A

9 780975 573914